RECIPROCITY

LAWRENCE C. BECKER

RECIPROCITY

ROUTLEDGE & KEGAN PAUL
London and New York

TO *Lewis Thompson*

First published in 1986
by Routledge & Kegan Paul plc

11 New Fetter Lane, London EC4P 4EE

Published in the USA by
Routledge & Kegan Paul Inc.
in association with Methuen Inc.
29 West 35th Street, New York, NY 10001

Set in Linotron Sabon 10 on 12 pt
by Input Typesetting Ltd, London
and printed in Great Britain
by Billings & Sons Ltd, Worcester

Library of Congress Cataloging in Publication Data

Becker, Lawrence C.

Reciprocity.
Includes index.
1. Ethics. 2. Values. 3. Social ethics. I. Title.
BJ1012.B422 1986   179'.9   85–19431
British Library CIP Data also available

ISBN 0–7102–0828–6

Contents

Acknowledgments

This book grew slowly, in the interstices of other projects, out of work I began to do as long ago as 1971. Very little of the early work is recognizable here, however, except in the most general themes and positions. It began as a loosely related set of views on moral theory and the virtues; then evolved into arguments about reciprocity and various nonvoluntary obligations; then finally changed into an examination of reciprocity as a fundamental virtue. As the project became more and more protracted, the list of people who contributed to it also grew. Most of the acknowledgments will be found in Part Three, in the discursive notes to the various chapters. But here I want to mention some very general debts.

In January of 1983 Hollins College granted me a leave of absence in which to finish the book. I was supported financially, during various portions of that leave, by grants from The Rockefeller Foundation, The National Endowment for the Humanities (FC 20029), The Andrew Mellon Foundation, The Center for Advanced Study in the Behavioral Sciences, and the Trustees of Hollins College. Without that extraordinarily generous support, I could not have brought the project to completion. The Center for Advanced Study, in particular, provided not only financial support but a serene and fulfilling place to work. It is a pleasure at last to be able to thank in print all those institutions, and the good people who run them.

I also want to express my thanks, for bibliographic help of major proportions, to Judith Farb, Virginia Johnston and Phyllis Dooley (research assistants during the preliminary stages), Shirley Henn and Thomas Mesner (Reference Librarians at Hollins College), and Margaret Amara and Bruce Harley (librarians at the Center for Advanced Study in the Behavioral Sciences). For typing early drafts of portions of the manuscript, my thanks go to Carolyn Stevens,

ACKNOWLEDGEMENTS

Madaline Spickard, Robin Sitten, Anne-Marie Meyerhoffer, Dorothy Brothers, and Matt Fenner. Deanna Knickerbocker produced beautiful typescripts of several 'final' drafts of the entire manuscript. Robin Sitten (research assistant during the final stages) helped to check citations, and Madaline Spickard helped to read proof.

To all these people and institutions, and to the readers acknowledged in Part Three, my grateful thanks.

LCB

Epigraph . . . 3. A short quotation or pithy sentence placed at the commencement of a work, a chapter, etc. to indicate the leading idea or sentiment; a motto.

O.E.D.

Extended epigraph . . . 1. A story, parable, aphorism or anecdote, longer than an ordinary epigraph, placed at the commencement of a work, a chapter, an argument, etc. to illuminate the leading idea or sentiment; a moral.

A Note about Form

The argument of this book is arranged in three parts, titled respectively Theory, Practice, and Scholium. The core of the argument is
in the first part, but crucial elements of it are tested, expanded,
and reinforced in the second. The third part, as its title suggests,
contains the scholarly apparatus, given here in the form of bibliographic essays on the various chapters. Those essays cite sources,
give references to the relevant literature, and comment on related
philosophical work. They offer the opportunity to consider at
length some matters that would have been unproductively
distracting in the chapters themselves.

What I hope will be a *productive* distraction is the use of
epigraphs throughout the book. Some of these are conventional in
form, but most of them are narratives ranging from several hundred
to several thousand words in length. They are, for lack of a better
term, *extended* epigraphs. Since the point of using them in an
otherwise conventional academic work may be obscure, I should
say a few words about them.

Epigraphs provoke or amuse or provide a sense of proportion.
They give the reader some distance, some sense of scale, some
pointed contrast to what follows. The epigraphs here are meant to
do those things in a way that is productive for the argument of
the book. They are meant to bring vividly to mind the intricate,
subtle, and particular lives within which, and for which, moral
philosophy is done. They are cautionary then, and complicating.
They are intended to raise the eye repeatedly from the line of
argument to the lives through which that line is drawn. But nothing
in the argument formally depends on them. No new evidence is
presented in them, no new distinctions or assumptions or connections are made that cannot be found elsewhere in the book. So in
that sense the epigraphs are dispensable. Readers who find them
irritating may skip over them without losing the thread.

A NOTE ABOUT FORM

Some of the stories in the epigraphs are in the first person. That does not mean, of course, that they are autobiographical, except in the attenuated sense in which every story is imagined out of things its author has remembered, or heard about, or read, or dreamt. In a work of fiction such a disclaimer would no doubt be out of place, but readers of a work of philosophy are entitled to know where its author stands, and should know that I do not stand exactly where any of my narrators does.

In the argument (as opposed to the epigraphs) I have tried throughout to make my views as clear and forthright as possible. I have assumed that readers will need only occasional reminders of the uncertainties in this sort of endeavor, and will not mistake economy of expression for dogmatism. In that connection, it may help to pay attention to the tone of the exchanges between 'Objection' and 'Reply' that occur intermittently throughout the book. Both voices in those exchanges are mine.

LCB

PART 1
THEORY

Introduction to Part 1

This is a book of moral theory about reciprocity. Its destination is the following set of propositions: Reciprocity is a moral virtue. We ought to be disposed, as a matter of moral obligation, to return good in proportion to the good we receive, and to make reparation for the harm we have done. Moreover, reciprocity is a fundamental virtue. Its requirements have presumptive priority over many competing considerations, and that priority makes reciprocity a crucial consideration for a wide variety of important moral problems. Specifically, reciprocity fixes the outline of our nonvoluntary social obligations – the obligations we acquire in the course of social life, but acquire without regard to our invitation, consent, or acceptance. Leading examples include some of our obligations to our families, to future generations, and to obey the law.

The argument offered in support of those propositions is virtue-theoretic. It is not directly about obligations, rights, duties, interests, preferences, values, or social welfare. Instead it is about excellence of character; it proposes part of a substantive theory of the virtues.

Reciprocity has been the subject of ethnographic studies, experiments in social and developmental psychology, hypotheses in social anthropology and political theory, speculations in phenomenology and structuralist anthropology, and even treatment techniques in clinical psychology and psychiatry. It has been less prominent, by name at least, in moral philosophy, but its controlling ideas lie behind much of the moral theory about restitution, retribution, gratitude, fair play, and proportionate justice.

Almost all of the work on reciprocity treats it as a fundamental notion – as something of paramount importance for at least some aspects of human social life. Some of the claims for it are sweeping. It has been held to be a defining, or 'structural' element in the human psyche, giving rise to our most basic social practices and

institutions. It has been held to be a central feature of social transactions, and the determining factor in the development of personal
and political power. Other claims are more modest: that reciprocity
enhances some sorts of relationships but not others; that it plays
an important part in individual social development; that it is the
best strategy for dealing with iterated prisoners' dilemma games;
that it helps to develop the trust necessary for friendship.

Disagreement about these matters can often be traced to different
definitions of reciprocity. For some writers it is a simple tit-for-tat
notion, referring to more or less direct and exact returns 'in kind'.
For others it refers also to elaborately indirect exchanges that are
decidedly not in kind. There is dispute about whether it is an
obligation or an ideal, whether it includes retaliation or is limited
to returns of good for good, whether it underlies or is derived from
the concept of justice, and whether it conflicts with benevolence.
Such diversity makes it difficult to connect all of the work on the
subject.

The argument of this book is not meant to connect all of that
work, though the Scholium does refer to a wide range of it. Rather,
the argument here is meant to explicate and defend, in considerable
detail, a particular conception of reciprocity, to show how a disposition to reciprocate in that way can be justified, and to draw out
some of the implications of those conclusions for concrete moral
issues.

The concept of reciprocity that I shall defend may be summarized
in the following maxims: that we should return good for good, in
proportion to what we receive; that we should resist evil, but not
do evil in return; that we should make reparation for the harm we
do; and that we should be disposed to do those things as a matter
of moral obligation. Reciprocity is a 'deontic' virtue.

Three things about those maxims should be noted in advance.
First, I will argue that we owe a return for all of the good we
receive, not merely for the good we accept. That contention is a
crucial feature of the arguments, and it is one of the surprising
results of taking a virtue-theoretic approach. Second, I will argue
that the obligations of reciprocity come from the justifiability of
being disposed to *make* reciprocation obligatory. Again, the
conclusion is established by way of virtue theory. And third, I will
argue that the sense of obligation here ought to appear to us, at
least in many cases, only in retrospect. This result defeats some

important objections to reciprocity arguments. It is easily available to a virtue-theoretic approach, though not (or at least not obviously) to what are sometimes called act-morality approaches.

The argument begins (Chapter One) with an explication of what I call the 'general' conception of morality. It holds that the moral point of view is the most inclusive one we can manage – the one we use when we say 'All things considered, here is what we should do.' Prudence, self-interest, altruism, social welfare, efficiency, economy, etiquette, and aesthetic considerations are all relevant, then, to moral argument understood in this way. They *must* be relevant, at least in principle, if moral argument is argument about what to do *all* things considered. That sort of argument is defined by a set of aims, limits, standards, and procedures. Constructing a moral theory 'under' the general conception is therefore a rule-governed activity. There are criteria of validity and soundness for its arguments.

Moral theory is then defined (Chapter Two) as the attempt to work out a way of life that can be given a reasoned justification under the general conception of morality. It has an *a priori* part, consisting of whatever can be derived from the constraints of the general conception alone, but it is also based on experience. In particular, its virtue-theoretic arguments appeal to empirical hypotheses about human nature. The outline of an Aristotelian argument for virtue is sketched and defended in Chapter Two.

Chapter Three (Reciprocity) is the core of the book. It explicates and defends at length the notion of reciprocity outlined above. Readers who wish to work quickly through the two preliminary chapters will need to extract from them at least the following ideas. From Chapter One: the concept of a well-defined activity; the general conception of morality; the well-definedness of the general conception. From Chapter Two: virtue theory; grounding a moral judgment; generalizability; the teleological tendency and deontological commitments of morality under the general conception.

Chapter Four (Virtues and Priorities) argues that reciprocity is a fundamental virtue, and explicates briefly a cluster of related ones: generosity, empathy, conviviality, and practical wisdom. Chapter Five (Virtue, Social Structure and Obligation) is meant to show how reciprocity generates obligations, and how it supports conclusions about social practices and institutions. The chapters of Part Two consider some particular institutions in the light of the reciprocity arguments.

I know a man who thinks he lives in debt. Not ordinary debt. (His house is clear, he pays his bills.) And not a miser's debt. He gives to causes and helps his neighbors. He has a worthwhile job.

What I mean is something different. What I mean is gratitude. Even for a thing as small as a meal we make or a joke we tell a flicker of it is in his eyes. Not for me, or for anyone in particular. Just gratitude.

He acts as though he were never, ever, fully entitled to anything. As though good will, and good motives, and conscientiousness on the part of others were never his by right or reason, but always something to admire.

He is grateful to his parents, even though he cares for them in their old age. He is grateful to his employer, and loyal, even though his work is barely noticed. And he is grateful to his country too (the strength of those emotions is embarrassing), even though he's suffered for it.

He is aware of what he does for others. He just thinks that everything he is and has is somehow owed to them. Without them, he would never have been anything. Without them, he would collapse like a house of sticks.

It is, he thinks, a debt that cannot be repaid. He is not, he thinks, an atom – not a solitary, lonely, self-sufficient provider of his own good life. He is mortgaged to the teeth by the love of his friends.

He is a fool.

CHAPTER 1

The General Conception of Morality

Every moral theory is embedded in a conception of the moral point of view, and suffused with ideas about what counts as a moral judgment, a moral reason, a moral justification. To the extent that these ideas are obscure or implausible the theory will be unconvincing; to the extent that they are muddled the theory will flounder. The purpose of this introductory chapter is to outline the concept of moral argument that will be used throughout the book, and to give reasons for thinking that it is a plausible one. I adopt what I call the *general conception* of morality, in which the moral point of view is taken to be the most inclusive one possible – the all-things-considered point of view. Moral argument 'under' the general conception of morality is reasoning in the same plain sense that figuring out what move to make in a chessgame is reasoning; it is *moral* reasoning only in the sense that it is done without any special-purpose restrictions.

Practical Reasoning

Once a game is defined, reasoned action-guidance *within* the game, *for* the players, follows an unexceptional pattern: the status of play is described; the permissible moves are surveyed; the best move is found and recommended. What counts as the best move (within the game, for a player) is implicit in the game itself. That is, the best move can be inferred from the rules and current status of play. So the practical reasoning within the game is thoroughly ordinary – though of course hardly ever in a form directly testable for validity. Someone says: 'The Queen is pinned and castling is impossible. In fact, anything but Bishop to K-5 is mate in two. Move the bishop.' Translation into a testable form is tedious, but the process is a familiar one. The premises are exploded into a series of preliminary deductions, the preliminary conclusions compressed into generalizations, and the final argument constructed from them together with the relevant rule(s). A preliminary deduction would look something like this:

> *Rule*: A Queen cannot move onto a square occupied by one of her own men.
>
> *Fact*: White's QR-5 is occupied by one of White's own men.
>
> *Conclusion*: White's Queen cannot move onto QR-5.

And the final inference – constructed from the conclusions of many preliminary ones – would look like this:

> *Rule*: Each player must try to checkmate the other and to avoid mate by the other.
>
> *Fact*: Among the moves now permissible for White, only Bishop to K-5 will avoid mate.
>
> *Conclusion*: White must move Bishop to K-5.

Such inferences can be formalized and tested for validity by standard deductive methods. So what counts as a valid argument of this game-guiding sort is no different from what counts as a valid argument in logic generally.

What counts as a *sound* argument here, however, is instructively different from the standard case. Standardly, a sound argument is a valid one whose premises are true. But the rules of a game are neither true nor false. They do not describe; they define and *pre*scribe. What is true (or false) is not the rule itself but rather the statement that a certain rule is in fact a rule of the game. So a sound argument, here, is one whose fact-premises are true and whose rule-premises are accurate. (A rule-premise – call it R – is accurate for the game G if and only if the statement 'R is a rule of the game G' is true.)

Of course, even in the simplest game-guiding arguments, there may be difficulty in establishing the truth of the fact-premises or the accuracy of the rule-premises. (Are there really only three permissible moves? Do the rules *require* resignation, or is that just a custom among some players?) Preliminary arguments for dubious premises are probabilistic, and impart a commensurate degree of tentativeness to the final conclusion:

Rule: It might be the rule that players must resign when they believe they are about to be checkmated.

Fact: White believes there is probably no way for him to avoid checkmate.

Conclusion: It might be the case that White must resign.

What is true of game-guiding arguments is true of action-guiding arguments generally: insofar as they deal with a well-defined activity, and are made *within* that activity, *for* those engaged in it, soundness can be assessed with standard logical tools. I shall argue later that morality is a well defined activity. But for the moment, I simply want to explicate the concept of such an activity.

Rules and Definition

Consider the following limiting case: Call a game (or activity of any sort) *completely defined* if any possible act whatsoever is either required or forbidden by the rules of the game. In such a game there would be no room for discretion. There would be a determinable, deductively sound argument, about any proposed act, to the conclusion that a given player is either required to do it or forbidden to do it. Of course, that is so only *within* the game and *for* the players. Arguments drawn from the rules of a game have no necessary bearing on bystanders, or on players who want to know what to do with their winnings.

It is instructive to consider carefully just what kinds of rules it takes to make a game completely defined. To be completely defined, a game must satisfy these conditions:

i   Any act whatsoever is, determinably, either a play in the game or not.

ii   Any moment whatsoever is, determinably, either an opportunity for a given player to make a play or not.

iii   Every play is, determinably, either a good, bad, or indifferent move for each player.

iv   A move can have different values for different players, but a given move can have only one value for each player.

v   For any given player, at any given opportunity to move, there is at most one good, one bad, and one indifferent move available to that player.

vi   Players must make exactly one move each time they have an opportunity.

vii   Players must make good moves in preference to indifferent ones, and indifferent ones in preference to bad ones.

If a game fails to meet any of these conditions, then it will fail to be completely defined – that is, there will be times when there is either some uncertainty about what is to be done, or some latitude for the players.

What is instructive about this notion of a completely defined game (substitute 'activity', or 'project' or 'practice' if you like) is what it reveals about the types of rules required to define and regulate *any* activity. Most endeavors are, of course, *not* completely defined. (Not even as simple a game as tic-tac-toe is complete.) Yet they still support an impressive amount of sound practical reasoning. They can do this insofar as they have the same *sorts* of rules found in a completely defined game, even though the rules of each sort may be seriously indeterminate. In any move away from simple games toward complex social practices (education, for example, or the practice of a profession), the rules become increasingly indeterminate. The range of sound practical reasoning therefore shrinks significantly, and the precision of conclusions diminishes also. But that is not surprising. Aristotle's observation is sound: moral argument will not achieve the degree of precision appropriate to mathematics.

What we need is the concept of a *well-defined* activity – that is, a notion of the sort of incompletely defined activity in which it is still possible to get a good deal of sound practical reasoning going. (We can develop such a notion from examining the rule-structure of a completely defined game.) And then we need to assure ourselves that – under some plausible conception of it – morality is such a well-defined activity.

> The Table has rules. That isn't surprising. Without them, lunch would be chaos. Filled with dread.
>
> These rules are not written down, and they are intermittently in flux, and since the people at The Table never discuss them – at least not at lunch (that is one of the rules) – only the regulars are fully comfortable. Fully at ease.
>
> Take Matthew. He always sits at one end of the table – always the same end, as it turns out – the one facing the

double bay of windows out to the river, and closest to the Reference section, and nearest the stairs. (The tea room is squeezed into the second floor of a bookstore in Old Town. And it is not a room, really, just a one-step-up platform running from Reference out to the windows at the back of the store. There are six tables. The Room serves cold sandwiches and salads and pastries; coffee and tea of all descriptions. It is only a short walk from work.) The point is that Matthew doesn't have to sit at that end of the table. He just has to sit at one end, because he is nearly deaf in one ear and hard of hearing in the other ear and needs to read people's lips. So it is a rule that Matthew sits at the end.

Irregulars often misunderstand this. They think, illogically, that Matthew's end of the table is the head of the table, and that the table is therefore in some sense Matthew's table. That just isn't so. Matthew's end might just as easily be called the foot. And given his generally self-effacing nature, that would be a more accurate description. But all of this is nonsense. There is no rule about head or foot, and no rule about which end Matthew must choose. The rule is simply that he must choose one of the two. Within that set of options he is perfectly free to sit where he wants. Beyond that, it is out of his hands. (Humans don't want to have to crane their heads around to make sure Matthew can read their lips, after all. And besides, he does look a little like the solarized photo of him that Marta took for the cover of his new book of poems. The photo is a fair likeness of Shelley, and it is pleasant to see clearly, all through lunch, someone whose solarized photo looks like Shelley.)

It should be said that Matthew does have an ear trumpet – a red plastic one. But the earpiece looks like the glans of a penis. The trumpet is not permitted.

Here are some of the other rules: No more than two people at once may open mail at the table, and only Leslie may open a huge stack of mail. Any catalog must be passed around – unless it is the David Morgan one, which everyone already has. Any catalog with a page of teddies must be passed immediately.

No shop talk is permitted, except for brief bursts of appointment making, apologies for insulting behavior in

committee meetings, or exclamations of disgust, alarm, or
dismay.

Every Whole Table conversation begins with something
pointed and particular. (Marta tells about the public
humiliation of one of her dancers, for example, who went
white and faint the minute he stepped onstage. Mothers and
fathers were there. Seventh graders, too, and the whole upper
school.) There is then a general clamor for the floor, the
purpose being a) to ameliorate any unseemly effects of the
opening move (contempt, envy, fear, outrage), and b) to find
a general topic embedded in the story that everyone can fasten
on. Rob, for example, in this instance, reported that on his
first date he had continued to dance after the music to the first
song had ended.

Last year it was a rule that while Will was present, no Whole
Table conversation could last more than ten minutes. Three,
if it concerned computers or cats. But that seems to have been
relaxed. There was a conversation about the nature of time,
recently, that lasted most of one lunch and into another. The
issue concerned whether time is (was?) more aptly represented
by clocks with round faces than by digital watches. Matters of
scale were raised, and the nature of a discrete as opposed to
a continuous series, and the doctrine of eternal return. Lottie
was largely to blame for this, but no one much seemed to
mind, though it must be said that Will did sit quietly
throughout. There have never been any time limits on purely
private behavior.

It is hard to predict where The Table will go from moment
to moment. There is no agenda. In fact, if any of its rules
were ever written down (which will never happen) that one
would be in blood. It is the only one that is ever enforced
cruelly. People who come to The Table with an agenda are
shut out. Topics are something else. And carefully prepared
problems or special effects. There are no rules against those
things.

The Table has three possible states of being. It is often in
an uproar of private conversations, show and tell, rearranging
of chairs and plates of food to make more room, people putting
down a sandwich to dash to the post office or to get a book
to settle an argument, and the general turmoil caused by

arrivals and departures. Just as often it is perfectly still, with people reading, or eating quietly, or staring out over the river. There are those two states, and then there are the Whole Table times.

Under certain circumstances, people are allowed to brag to the Whole Table about their accomplishments. The conditions are that the brag must be in the form of a mere announcement – preferably non-verbal, and preferably (by prearrangement) made by a friend. It may only be made once, and people who happen to be away from the table at the time, or who simply fail to hear what was said, have to get the news some other way. Rob may say, quietly, that he won best in show. General admiration follows for a moment. Then someone, Judith usually, tells a gripping story of personal defeat drawn from the morning paper. She has perfect pitch.

Dress at The Table is casual, but controlled. It is true that Marta has been seen in a set of vampire teeth, and the women generally have more freedom than the men in these matters, but clothing is rarely an issue. Tweeds, corduroys, and jeans are all permissible for men. (Ties on Rob or Terry, however, raise anxieties.) Leslie's blouses are sometimes cause for concern. There is the matter of Lottie's hair, and Rob's cap, and Judith's shoes, but none of that much matters. Those rules are mostly in place by default rather than design.

Irregulars who are alert enough to be uncomfortable at The Table often make the mistake of thinking The Table is a club – a club that means to exclude non-members. Nothing could be further from the truth. There is, of course, a rule against active recruitment, but The Table has never wanted to exclude anyone. The desire for new members, when it surfaces, is poignant.

But lunch is lunch. It is not a time to do just anything you please. It is a time to sit with good friends, to be affectionate, to make them laugh, to be made to laugh, to fill out like a kite with the pleasure of small triumphs, to feel the pressure of a loving hand on a shoulder, to live in good company. And for that people have to have some understandings.

It doesn't always work. Judith may be immovable; Will may go too far; Marta may be morose; Terry may be angry; Matthew may be remote; Lottie may be curt; Rob may be bitter; Leslie may cry. Any of those things can disturb the balance. But mostly, lunch at The Table is just fine.

And that is not a comment about the food.

Types of Rules

An examination of completeness (for a game) yields the following suppositions about the kinds of rules an activity may have.

1 *Participation rules* define who is to be considered a participant and what counts as an act of participation. (Who are the players? What are the moves?) In medicine, for example, we need to know how to identify the professionals, and how to identify professional acts on their part. Physicians can legitimately prescribe narcotics; orderlies cannot. The musings of a physician are not prescriptions. And so on.

2 *Teleological rules* define the aims of the activity and any priority ordering or means-end relations among them. In medicine, again, it is crucial to know whether the primary aims are public health goals – with the treatment of diseased individuals being a means to reaching those goals – or whether those two aims are reversed. In the former case, should a choice have to be made, money might well be diverted from intensive care facilities to epidemiological research. In the latter case, the choice would more likely go the other way.

3 *Deontological rules* define the boundaries of permissible conduct and the extent of obligatory conduct in pursuit of the aims. Example: the American Medical Association has affirmed the rule that while it is never permissible for a physician, acting as a physician, to kill a patient intentionally, it is sometimes permissible for a physician to let a patient die.

4 *Valuation rules* define goods and establish priorities among competing aims, duties and goods. (Goods may be defined, for example, simply as things that are constitutive of, or instrumental in the achievement of, the aims.) To continue the medical example, triage rules are valuational in this sense.

5 *Procedural rules* define procedures for adjudicating disputes about the interpretation and application of the rules ('judicial' procedures), methods of enforcement ('police' procedure) and methods for getting closure on deliberation about what to do in a given situation ('parliamentary' procedure). And they define conventional styles, strategies and modes of conduct within the

activity. (A profession typically has an etiquette as well as a set of goals, duties, priorities and operating procedures.)

6 *Transformation rules* define the ways in which any of the rules may be changed (i.e., they define 'legislative' procedure).

7 *Recognition rules*, to borrow a term from H. L. A. Hart, define criteria of rule-legitimacy within the activity. That is, they define criteria for testing the truth of statements of the form 'The rule R is a rule of the activity G.'

Well-Definedness

Now it is clear that activities vary greatly not only in the content of their rules but in the extent to which they even *have* logically effective rules. Take a simple, customary game like tic-tac-toe and compare it with organized baseball. Baseball has elaborate, written rules of all the sorts mentioned above. Tic-tac-toe, by contrast, can appeal to little more than a dictionary definition of the game for any of its rules, and lacks entirely some sorts of procedural rules. Changes in tic-tac-toe occur in the ways changes in language occur, and not, as in baseball, through a regularized legislative procedure. Neither game is *completely* defined. But each game, in quite different ways, is *well* defined in the following important sense: *it has logically effective rules of all of the seven major sorts listed above*. For both games it is possible to know, in some cases, what counts as a rule, who is a player, what counts as a play, and what counts as a good play in terms of the object of the game. It is possible to know, in some cases, how the rules get changed. And it is possible to know enough about the procedure of playing the game to actually play it (time, talent and equipment permitting), or to recognize when it is being played. That much is certainly sufficient to give an activity a distinct identity, and to support a significant amount of coherent reasoning about how participants ought to act.

Note on logical effectiveness Define a valid argument in the usual way – as one in which, if the premises are true, the conclusion cannot be false. (Alternatively, as one in which, for any assignment of truth values that make the premises true, the conclusion is also true.) Then a logically effective premise of such an argument is one whose deletion from the argument would render the argument invalid. Similarly, a logically effective *part* of a premise is one whose deletion renders the argument invalid. Consider the following argument form:

P&S

P→Q /∴ Q

In that argument, S is *not* an effective part of the argument. If it were dropped, the argument would still be valid.

A logically effective rule is just a logically effective premise that happens to be a rule. But given the nature of practical reasoning, a logically effective rule would also, by definition, have to be one which is determinably relevant to a range of cases, and when used in a valid argument together with factual premises about those cases, yields a determinate conclusion about what some individual(s) must, may, or ought to do or be. This is so simply from the definition of a rule as a general, action-guiding utterance. If there is *no* range of cases to which a 'rule' applies in the sense just defined, then it is not a rule at all.

I shall argue, below, that *any activity is well-defined if it has at least some logically effective rules of participation, teleology, deontology, valuation, procedure, transformation and recognition.* The point now, however, is simply that the practical reasoning one can do within a well-defined activity is often imprecise and tentative, and often one can give no reasoned advice at all. There is too much uncertainty about the rules or facts. But that does not diminish the importance of the sound reasoning that can be done. Most significant human enterprises, after all, are at best only well-defined, not completely defined.

Moral Reasoning

I hold that morality is well-defined. That is, I hold that the activity of assessing human conduct in moral terms, and acting on such assessments, is an activity that has logically effective rules of all of the sorts required for well-definedness. But the argument for that contention depends on a distinction between what I shall call the general conception of morality and various special conceptions.

The General Conception of Morality

The general conception of morality, in a nutshell, is this: moral judgments are judgments about what rational agents ought to do or be, period. Moral acts and states of being are those that conform to moral judgments. Such judgments are not made in terms of the rules of an activity *within* our lives; they are not made in terms of an activity distinct from life itself. They are, rather, judgments made only in terms of living, period. They are judgments made, in principle, all things considered. That is what I meant at the outset when I said that moral judgments were made without special-purpose restrictions.

Special conceptions of morality, by contrast, hold that the moral point of view is just one among many that a rational agent might consider. According to this sort of conception, etiquette, egoism, altruism and so forth are all distinct points of view in terms of which one might choose to act. Morality is another. It is one which a rational agent could *in principle* reject, without self-contradiction. (Defenders of the special conception are therefore concerned to give an account of why one ought to be moral – that is, an account of why one ought to adopt the moral point of view rather than some other. Under the general conception, by contrast, the question 'Why be moral?' is, in effect, the question 'Why, all things considered, ought we to do what we ought to do all things considered?' That 'question' answers itself.)

Both the general and the special conceptions are concerned exclusively with the conduct of rational agents – that is, with getting action-guidance for beings who are capable of deliberation and choice. My contention is that the general conception is a better instrument for that job than a special conception.

Definitional note In what follows I use the term 'ought' to cover the whole range of prescriptive verbs: must, may, should, and so on. So ought statements may be judgments about values, about rights and duties, or about virtues and vices, ideals and horrors. I use the term 'rational agents' to refer to any beings capable of deliberation and choice, to whatever degree. Not all moral judgments, therefore, will necessarily apply to all rational agents. Differences in the capacity to deliberate and choose will guarantee that if nothing else does. *Moral* oughts are a special class of oughts – different in kind from prudential, technical, altruistic, egoistic and other sorts of 'oughts'. The task here is to say just how that difference is to be understood. I shall use the term 'morality' to refer to a certain rule-defined *activity* of assessing the conduct of rational agents and acting accordingly – in the same way one uses 'chess' to refer to a certain rule-defined game. A particular moral theory then, would be analogous to the rules that define a particular way of playing chess, and a list of moral judgments actually made by someone would be analogous to a play-by-play record of a particular chessgame. For simplicity of exposition, I shall ignore the complications of the past tense. I shall speak only of what agents ought to do and be, not of what they ought to have been and done.

Think again of the kind of guidance that occurs in a game: 'Bishop to K-5, idiot.' And now suppose the following insanity ensues:

> 'He's having a seizure! Get the nurse!'
> 'He said he didn't want to be resuscitated.'
> 'Well we're legally responsible.'
> 'I'm not talking about legality.'

Hidden among the more interesting things in that exchange is a series of shifts in the boundaries of relevance. 'Bishop to K-5' is rejected in favor of medical advice; the medical advice is brushed aside to honor the patient's wishes, then reintroduced on legal grounds, and finally rejected again. The point is this: reasoning about what chessmove to make, or what series of things to do in a medical emergency, or how to avoid legal liability, is radically restricted with respect to the range of relevant rules and facts. Each of these activities (chess-playing, the practice of medicine, the practice of law) is describable as a well-defined activity *within* our lives for which special purpose advice is available. It is special purpose advice in the sense that it is drawn purely from the facts and rules of a specific activity, and designed purely for participants in that activity, *all other considerations being held in abeyance.* Books on chess strategy do not deal with the question of what moves to make in a medical emergency. But in our lives *as such*, no special purpose restrictions apply. In life *as such*, the rules of chess alone do not ever settle whether anyone should move Bishop to K-5. That move might, all things considered, hurt someone's feelings.

Moral reasoning, as I use the term, is just this sort of *general* reasoning – reasoning about what we ought to do or be, period. No considerations are, in principle, held in abeyance. All things are, in principle, to be considered.

Of course, as a practical matter, we always ignore a great deal. We forget, or we are weary, or ignorant, or prejudiced. But those are defects – sources of failure to get the best reasoned guidance possible.

More to the point, we ignore things systematically, *in order* to get reasoned guidance. We have sweeping procedural rules designed to limit debate, get conclusions drawn and ensure timely action. But except for the time constraints, such rules are merely provisional. The important point is this: Whenever anyone can meet the burden of showing that an excluded consideration would make a difference in the outcome of a sound argument, we are bound to include it. That is just part of what it means to give a *moral* argument in this sense.

An example will help to clarify the point. Suppose a lawyer is trying to decide whether to represent a client she knows to be guilty. Professional ethics require it. The case has been assigned to her by the court and she has no cause, relevant to the code of legal ethics, for refusing. Still, she wonders whether, all things considered, she should do it. Notice what reasoning about such a matter would be like. She could not *actually* consider everything, and huge classes of facts and rules would normally not even occur to her. (The price of gasoline in Teheran, for example. Or the distance in miles to the sun. Or the rules of chess.) She would, typically, consider the consequences of such a refusal for herself, family, friends, clients and potential clients. She would consider what obligations – other than professional ones – she might have.

But there are circumstances in which even the rules of chess or the distance to the sun would be relevant to her decision. Suppose there is some question about her client's sanity, for example, such that if he were clearly insane, she would be willing to take the case. And suppose that some of the evidence for his insanity involves alleged delusions that he has concerning everyday affairs – e.g., the rules of chess. In that case the rules of chess are indirectly relevant to her decision, because they are relevant to deciding whether her client is deluded. Getting those considerations into the argument, then, *might* change the conclusion significantly – if not by flipping it from yes to no, then at least by altering its certainty. If that were the case, and if the lawyer were trying to decide what to do all things considered, she would (logically) be required to include them.

The process of moral reasoning, under this perfectly general conception of morality, is the process of finding all of the facts and rules that make a difference – all of them, that is, that we have the power to find – and then constructing the arguments. What makes a difference, morally, is anything that can be expressed as a logically effective premise in a sound argument about what we ought to do or be, period.

Elaborative note Recall that a premise is logically effective if, when it occurs in a valid argument, dropping it from that argument would render the argument invalid. Of course, what makes a difference – morally – is not just *any* logically effective premise, but only those that can be logically effective in *sound* arguments about what to do or be, morally. We are not concerned, for moral purposes, with the indefinitely large number of logically effective falsehoods in *un*sound arguments. Thus, if it happens that someone wants us to consider a fact or rule P in our moral deliberations, but it is clear that P cannot be a logically effective part of any *sound* argument we can construct (because it is false, perhaps, or because it is inferentially superfluous, or because it is irrelevant to any sound argument on the topic), then there is no reason in logic, for moral purposes, to consider P.

Special Conceptions

The alternative to adopting the general conception of morality is to treat morality as a distinct, 'special' activity within life. But then one is faced with two formidable problems (in addition to those that face any account of morality).

The Specialness Problem

The first is to define moral reasoning in a way that clearly separates it from other forms of practical reasoning. (Note that under the general conception of morality, moral reasoning is distinct by virtue of its inclusiveness.) I shall not attempt to survey the many subtle and illuminating attempts to solve this problem. I shall simply point out that all such attempts face the following quandary.

We all grant that moral reasoning must be distinguished, *somehow*, from mere prudential reasoning, advice to the lovelorn and so forth. But the question is whether we mean, by that distinction, to exclude these other forms of practical reasoning altogether from the moral sphere. Are prudential reasons, for example, *never* to be considered in moral arguments? If we insist on excluding them altogether – along with all the other special forms of practical reasoning (altruistic, egoistic, cost-benefit, etc.) – then it is very hard to get a grip on what moral reasoning could be. That is, it is hard to avoid the thought that what distinguishes moral reasoning from other sorts is just its *lack* of 'specialness'. If it is no *particular* sort of practical reasoning, but it *is* reasoning, then perhaps it is just practical reasoning as such. Or practical reasoning of the most thoroughly generalized and impartial kind. I confess to an inability to make further sense of this. It is thoroughly unclear as it stands, and every attempt I make to clarify it moves the notion either right back to the general conception of morality or over into quite a different sort of special conception. So I shall turn to the latter.

We may, after all, not want to exclude other sorts of practical reasoning entirely from moral reasoning, but rather to include them only under special conditions. Suppose, for example, that prudential concerns are often relevant to moral arguments, but just never, by themselves, *sufficient* to get to moral conclusions. Similarly for altruistic concerns, cost-benefit analysis, medical advice and so forth. All of those things may from time to time enter into moral argument, but never, by themselves, determine the outcome of a moral argument. Why not? There are two general sorts of answer.

UNIQUELY MORAL REASONS   The first is that there is some special sort of reason – a moral reason – which is wholly distinct from other sorts and which is necessary to every sound moral argument. This is one way of understanding 'supreme principle' moral theories such as Kant's or Bentham's: Every sound moral argument, no matter what other sorts of premises and subsidiary arguments may be relevant to it, must include, as a logically effective premise of the final argument, the appropriate instance of the supreme principle. E.g., Act X is permitted (or required) by the moral law; Act X is permitted (or required) by the principle of utility. But notice here that moral reasoning is not construed as *excluding* anything. Indeed, the substance of any sound moral argument will include much that is straightforwardly relevant to other sorts of action-guiding arguments. What makes moral arguments unique, it is said, is simply the necessary presence of the uniquely moral reason(s).

This appears to differ radically from the general conception of morality, but the appearance is misleading. To see why, consider the question: Is the use of the supreme moral principle required by reason (in a given case) or not? If the answer is *yes*, then this special conception of morality collapses into the general conception – for moral reasoning turns out to be reasoning about what to do, all-things-considered. We have simply found that a rationally necessary feature of practical reasoning in this case is the use of the moral law (or the principle of utility, etc.). On the other hand, if the supreme principle of morality is *not* required by reason as such, then the overridingness problem (discussed below) becomes especially acute. That is, it is hard to see why, from the standpoint of getting reasoned guidance about what to do, we should pay any particular deference to moral reasoning. It is simply one sort of practical reasoning among many, relevant or not as the case may be to deciding what to do, period. And again we are back to the general conception.

UNIQUELY MORAL STRUCTURES   The second sort of answer (to the problem of separating moral reasoning from other sorts) fares no better. On this view, moral arguments are distinct because they impose a special structure of priorities and weights on the sorts of considerations we use in action-guiding arguments. In morality (we say) prudence is important but sometimes subordinate to the welfare of others. Altruism is noble but one also has duties to oneself. And so on. A description of the moral point of view is a description, in all of its complexity and subtlety, of these rules of relevance and dominance.

That is surely a plausible line to take. But now notice the inevitable question: Is the moral point of view rationally defensible or not? That is, should we, all things considered, follow its dictates or not? If yes, then this special conception of morality also collapses into the general conception – for moral judgments turn out to be those that articulate what we ought to do and be, all things considered. If the moral point of view is *not* that, but rather something contrary to or merely coincident with what is rationally defensible, then we have no reason as yet to follow its dictates. Unless we are willing to discard reasoned advice altogether, then, as the ultimate arbiter of what we ought to do, we are led back to the general conception of morality – by whatever name we wish to call it.

The Overridingness Problem

The same conclusion is reinforced by considering the second major problem for special conceptions of morality. That problem is to give an account of why it is that moral oughts are thought to be overriding. If morality is just one point of view among many, why should we give it any more weight than any other? The possible answers to that question are instructive. They fall roughly into one of two forms: 1) the contention that the overridingness of morality is conventional, or 2) the contention that its overridingness can be given a reasoned justification.

CONVENTION   Suppose we have defined a special conception of morality – perhaps a complex system of priorities and weights for various sorts of considerations. Suppose, further, that everyone in our society accepts that description as the correct description of morality. Not everyone *uses* this point of view in deciding how to act, but that is beside the point. In practice, we accept that we *should* use it. In theory, however, we recognize that the overridingness of morality is purely a matter of convention. It is just conceptually attached, as it were, to the particular moral point of view we have, so that, for us, part of believing that something is the moral thing to do just *is* believing that that judgment should override any advice to the contrary. Yet this conceptual linkage is merely conventional. Other people, at other times, have defined the moral point of view differently – they have attached a different set of priorities and weights to prudence, for example. For them the idea of overridingness would not be conceptually attached to *our* concept of the moral point of view. It would, perhaps, be attached to something we would call prudence, or altruism, or even etiquette.

The question for practical reasoning, here, is instructive: Once we recognize all of this, what reason do we have for following the dictates of our moral point of view? The answer is clear: None as yet. We are, rather, right back to the question asked by the *general* conception of morality: What ought we to do and be, period?

JUSTIFICATION   The result is the same when we consider the possibility that the overridingness of the moral point of view might be rationally *justified*. Suppose, that is, that we can give a reasoned justification for holding that the special moral point of view is overriding – at least, whenever it is relevant to the situation. (Sometimes we are just playing cards, perhaps, and moral questions are out of place. When they are irrelevant, we must decide what to do on other bases.)

This sort of response also falls back on what is, in all but name, the *general* conception of morality. What we are to do, in each case, is what reason recommends. In some cases that will be something moral (in the special sense). In other cases, it will be something prudent or self-interested or altruistic.

OBJECTION: But surely it is absurd to think that moral arguments are all-inclusive. Aesthetic considerations, for example, guide our conduct, but they are very different from moral ones. *Style* is not a moral quality. And it is just disingenuous to argue that style can be relevant to moral arguments indirectly – and therefore must be, or can be, considered in moral arguments. Of course it can be relevant. But it is not itself a moral consideration. It only becomes relevant to moral arguments when surrounding circumstances give it a special significance – not a special *aesthetic* significance, notice – but a special *moral* significance. And the same thing surely applies to rules of etiquette and even prudence. These matters are in themselves quite different from moral considerations. Only when circumstances give them special moral importance are they relevant to moral arguments. So we are right back to the necessity of explicating a special conception of morality – one that illuminates the substantive difference between moral and non-moral action-guidance.

REPLY: When we are deciding how to act, all things considered, style matters. We care about the grace with which things are done, the beauty of our surroundings, the fittingness of our conduct, the elegance of our writing. We care about these things directly, and not merely because caring about them may be indirectly relevant to the fulfillment of our professional responsibilities, or business dealings, or social expectations. Similarly, we care about tact, 'the done thing', and prudence.

Take any act that is justified solely under a special conception of morality. For simplicity, suppose moral conduct is defined as altruistic conduct. Now imagine that there are two ways of doing the altruistic thing: one way has a certain elegance about it and is prudent besides. The other is rather flat-footed and involves a degree of personal risk. Which way should we choose? Clearly the first.

Partly, no doubt, this is true because others might appreciate our stylishness and not want us to take risks. So it would turn out to be even more altruistic to be stylish and safe while we go about our duties. But we would also make the same choice, all things considered, even if it did *not* affect the altruism quotient of the act. We would make it because we care about style and prudence directly, as ends. They are directly relevant to deliberation about what to do all-things-considered. And that is, after all, the sort of deliberation we must finally engage in. When all is said and done, what we want is what is best, period. Not what is best from some special point of view.

OBJECTION: Who is included in the scope of the word 'we' here? *Some* people, after all, *reject* the all-things-considered approach. They may hold, for example, that the controlling issue is obeying God's law, not figuring out what to do all-things-considered. And the same is true for defenders of a special conception. They are by definition interested in a more limited inquiry. So statements like 'What we want is what is best, period' only apply to those already committed to the general conception. What reasons can be given for adopting the general conception in the first place?

REPLY: Only the arguments already given: i.e., that any other choice will either collapse into the general conception or be unable to give an account of why we ought to be moral – why morality (or God's law) ought to be overriding.

OBJECTION: But suppose someone just rejects that task altogether? Rejects reason in favor of revelation or intuition? Holds that the quest for a reasoned defense of God's law or a special conception of morality is misplaced?

REPLY: If that is a rejection of reason *per se*, then there can be no reasoned answer to it – at least none the rejector will listen to. But if the rejection is instead a rejection in this special case, then a justification for treating this as a special case is clearly called for. Presumably, that justification (i.e., an adequate one) could only be given by arguing from the general conception. It would have to show that all things considered, we need not give a reasoned defense of adopting God's law, or a special conception, as an overriding guide. We may just adopt it. But of course, doing that would be tantamount to giving a reasoned defense of it in terms of the general conception after all.

OBJECTION: But suppose that moral considerations (e.g., altruistic ones) are just self-evidently *weightier* than non-altruistic ones. Suppose they can just be 'seen' to be generically superior to all others in the sense that, given a choice between doing an altruistic act and one that is merely (say) stylish, we can just see that we must ignore the matters of style.

REPLY: Why must we ignore them? Presumably because, all things considered, we can just see that style is less important. That is what it must mean to say that altruistic concerns are self-evidently more weighty than anything else. So again we are back to the general conception of morality.

OBJECTION: But now it is clear that this so-called general conception of morality presents us with a nightmarish problem of assigning weights to competing considerations – altruism against prudence, style against tact, etiquette against efficiency.

REPLY: *Life* presents us with that nightmarish problem. And any moral theory that ignores it is of very limited use. The general conception of morality faces the matter directly. That fact is a virtue, not a vice.

OBJECTION: Of course life is messy. That isn't the issue. The issue is that it is now clear that all the general conception does is to move the interesting questions 'inside,' as it were. Special conceptions must handle priority problems *between* morality and other sorts of considerations (prudence, for example). The general conception must handle exactly the same problems, but stated in terms of competing considerations *within* morality. So what have we gained?

REPLY: We have gained an account that places all sorts of supposedly non-moral concerns squarely in the middle of our moral deliberations – not out in the wings waiting to enter only when they conflict with our moral judgments. In that respect, the general conception gives us a more accurate picture of actual moral deliberation. We do not, in practice, ignore prudential concerns until we have concluded our moral deliberations. Those concerns are raised in the process. The general conception gives us a good way of understanding how that works – how prudence, for example, can be a necessary part of moral deliberation.

OBJECTION: But it is certainly a very odd way of understanding the process. It forces us to call all sorts of inconsequential choices moral ones, just as long as they are made all-things-considered. The general conception commits us to the absurd position that the choice of a breakfast cereal is a moral choice.

REPLY: Not unless the choice is made all things considered. And if it is so made, there is no absurdity in the *position*. The only absurdity might come from insisting on such an elaborate inquiry in the first place. We typically reserve such inquiry for 'weighty' cases, and the choice of a cereal is typically not weighty. But it could be (given food shortages, or allergies to some sorts of cereals, etc.). And when the choice is weighty, the general conception gives us a good picture of moral deliberation about it.

OBJECTION: But how good a picture of the process can it be until we actually work out the priority rules? Isn't that the crucial task, and isn't that what special conception theorists are really grappling with?

REPLY: It is of course true that the priority problems that plague special conceptions all arise, in different guises, under the general conception. The argument here was not meant to suggest otherwise. It was meant to suggest, however, that those priority problems could be more clearly articulated and clearly handled under the general conception. So far that is only a suggestion. In the next chapter I shall offer some argument for it.

In any case I submit that the general conception of morality is preferable to a special one. Its concern is with the ultimate question for practical reasoning – what we ought to do and be, all things considered. And that is, after all, the most plausible interpretation of the point of the whole enterprise of moral reasoning – *to get the answer that is overriding.* Moral oughts, under the general conception, are by definition overriding in the sense that they are 'final'. What we ought to do all things considered cannot possibly be superseded in the way that judgments from a special point of view can be. And as we have seen, if the overridingness of 'special' moral oughts is to be given an effective reasoned justification, it must be in terms of the general conception anyway.

So I shall adopt the general conception of morality here. It gives a clear picture of the sense in which other sorts of practical reasoning are both distinct from and connected to moral reasoning. It gives a straightforward defense of the notion that moral judgments override other sorts. And its choice is consonant with a commonsense view of the point of moral reasoning – to get an answer to the question of what we ought to do and be, all things considered. What remains to be shown is that this general conception of morality is well-defined.

The Structure of Morality

I suggested earlier that an activity might be considered well-defined if it has logically effective rules of participation, teleology, deontology, valuation, procedure, transformation and recognition. I want now to say something about why that is so, and then, finally, to show why it is evident that morality under the general conception has some rules of each sort.

Well-definedness

In order to get any reasoned action-guidance at all about an activity, we must at least know something about its aims, and the boundaries of permissible activity within it. Implicit in that is also the notion of a participant – that is, a definition of who can 'play' and what counts as a 'move'. Of course, rules of participation, teleology and deontology are often quite vague. But without at least some information of all these sorts, it is doubtful that we can even *identify* an activity as such. And it is certainly the case that, in the absence of such information, reasoned conclusions about what to do (within the activity) are impossible. They are impossible because no conclusion could conceivably be either ruled out or ruled in. The concept of well-definedness is meant to pick out those activities about which we can in principle get sound, reasoned, action-guidance. So having some teleological, deontological and participation rules is clearly a necessary part of the concept. And since, in order to identify any rules at all as belonging to a given activity, we must also have a recognition rule, it too is necessary.

Whether the same necessity attaches to valuation, procedure, and transformation rules is debatable. What is clear is that any complex activity that lacks them entirely will be significantly ill-defined. It will be ill-defined in the sense that we will have no way of getting any reasoned guidance within it on some urgent questions: How do we begin? How do we decide disputes? Can the rules be changed? For that reason it seems plausible to restrict the class of *well*-defined activities to those that have at least some rules of all seven sorts.

But is that enough? Might there not be some other sorts of rules that are important for well-definedness? And might there not be some specific forms of participation rules, for example, that are necessary or especially important? To both questions I must simply answer that I think not, but that I do not have a general argument to show it. What I have instead, and what is more to the point here, is an argument to show that morality is well-defined in the sense I have specified. That will be sufficient for present purposes.

Rules of Morality

Some activities are codified. They have a published list of rules that is more or less complete, supplemented by customs, understandings, tacit agreements and the like. Other activities operate almost exclusively in terms of unspoken understandings.

Morality under the general conception is uncodified, save for the canons of logic, but it has rules in the same clear sense that a lunch table has rules: it has common purposes and procedures. Some things are agreed to be good on its terms, and others not. Some things are out of place. And much of this can be described in a list of rules that the participants would agree is accurate. There is nothing mysterious about saying that such rules exist. (Nothing more mysterious, that is, than saying that about any rule – as opposed to a statement of it.)

Since morality is largely uncodified, the task here will be to articulate some of its unspoken understandings – its rule-structure. And a significant amount of its rule-structure emerges from what has already been said about the general concept of morality.

RECOGNITION   is controlled by the all-things-considered aspect of the general conception: a rule is a moral rule if it describes what rational agents ought to do or be, all things considered. More of this below.

PARTICIPANTS   are therefore also specified: moral action guidance is addressed *to* rational agents, *from* rational agents. But several things need to be said about the participation rule. Although it follows, from the general conception, that moral advice is addressed to rational agents, it does not follow that the advice is addressed to them *as* (purely) rational agents. Some moral theory reads as though what it recommends is a life 'purified' of the passions and habits that hamper reasoned deliberation. That is surely not the case here. Moral advice under the general conception is advice about what to do and be, period. Moral theory can in principle argue that we not act 'rationally' – that what is justified by reason is passionate conduct or unthinking habit. (There is something comic about a studious lover; something dangerous about a thoroughly deliberative driver.)

Further, the participation rule does not limit the class of rational agents to human beings, nor does it necessarily include them all. Moreover, the conduct that is required of rational agents may well involve other sorts of beings. Agents may have duties to non-agents, for example. And finally, the boundaries of the concept of agency are somewhat vague (with respect to the status of young children, for example, and some animals). But there are clear cases as well, and so the participation rule is capable of being logically effective in some arguments.

PROCEDURAL rules, at the level of moral theory, are the ones we use for reasoned theorizing generally – that is, the canons of deductive and inductive logic, criteria of relevance, standards of thoroughness in the search for data, and the definition of rational consensus characteristic of philosophy and science. It would take a set of books to spell these out, but I assume that that is not necessary for present purposes.

What is necessary here is rather to call attention to two things about these rules. One is that we have well-established streamlined versions of them for applied, rather than purely theoretical, work. Legal reasoning in a given case is a good analogy here. Second, there is of course significant vagueness in all of these rules – in both their theoretical and applied versions – and this vagueness sometimes leads to a significant level of uncertainty in the action-guidance they yield. But no one, I assume, would argue that because scientific revolutions are a messy business, or because at the most abstract levels of theory there are some seemingly perpetual debates among scientists, that the scientific method is hopelessly ineffective. It can yield provisional and productive consensus. Moral reasoning is capable of the same thing.

TRANSFORMATION AND RECOGNITION Of course such consensus is subject to radical change (e.g., the historic change with respect to forced slavery). And some moral disagreements arise from cultural lags with respect to such shifts. What causes these changes is not the issue here. It may well be that socio-economic, political, or religious factors come first and reasoned justifications tag along behind as rationalizations. That does not really matter for present purposes. What does matter is that until the reasoned justification is given, the change is not a change in *what is moral under the general conception* – any more than an unjustified change in a consensus about the shape of the earth would be a change in earth *science*. Further, as soon as the (sound) reasoned justification is given, there is a perfectly intelligible sense in which we can say that morality has been changed, even though the consensus has not. It has been changed in the same sense that science has been changed by a discovery that only one or a few people as yet believe.

The rule of transformation, then, under the general conception of morality, is this: the rules are changed by reasoned argument, in accord with some rules (procedural rules, perhaps), about which there is an existing rational consensus. It is quite like the way in which our science changes. It is quite different from the way purely conventional rules get changed. Pure conventions do not require reasoned justification.

Substantive Rules

When it comes to teleological, deontological and valuational rules, things are not quite so straightforward. These rules concern matters of substance rather than form, and it may appear to be a hopeless task to try to find rules of these sorts that are necessary to morality in the way that the object of chess is necessary to chess. Recall that the analogy to a game went this way: morality is analogous to chess; a particular moral theory is analogous to a particular way of playing chess; and a particular list of moral judgments about cases is analogous to a play-by-play record of a chessgame. We are looking, then, for rules that are definitive of morality as such – rather than definitive of a particular moral code.

There are such rules. They are not terribly interesting ones, any more than the rules of chess, abstracted from strategies and actual play, are interesting. But they are indispensable to moral reasoning, and they complete the point about the well-definedness of morality.

TELEOLOGY There is an aim implicit in the very notion of the life of a rational agent: goal achievement. We may fairly call this the ultimate, or defining aim of an agent's life as such. The justification for those assertions is as follows:

An agent's life is, in part, and by definition, one of deliberation and choice. Deliberate choice is a special kind of purposive activity. The defining aim of purposive activity as such is the achievement of particular goals. That is therefore the defining aim of morality – conceived as the activity of deciding what rational agents ought to do and be, period.

But note: The aim is the achievement of particular goals. Not any goals *in* particular. Not happiness, for example, or obedience to the will of God, or even survival. Those are particular aims *within* life – at most particular *ways* of life. It may be possible to argue that one of these ways of life is, all things considered, the best way for an agent to live. But that is an argument carried out *within* moral life; it is not definitive of the very concept of morality. The analogy to chess is again instructive: The definitive aim is to checkmate your opponent, but there are many ways of playing the game (tournament rules, lightning chess, correspondence chess and so on). It may be possible to argue that just in terms of the game itself, one of these ways is best. But that would be a judgment made *within* the activity and *for* players. It would not be a judgment about the very definition of the game. So too with morality. What is definitive of its aims is not any particular way that an agent might live. It is rather what is characteristic of agency as such: purposive activity in pursuit of particular goals.

DEONTOLOGY Prohibitions, permissions and requirements are part of the very language of action-guidance *per se*. And in the case of moral action-guidance, the bindingness of any such judgments – their overriding character – is given by the very form of the general conception of morality: its all-things-considered nature. So if the very notion of rational agency defines boundaries (permissions and prohibitions) for purposive activity, we must conclude that morality has constitutive deontological, as well as teleological rules.

And in fact such boundaries are implicit in the notion of the self-conscious, purposive activity characteristic of rational agency. Part of what it means to be self-conscious is to be aware of the boundaries that define things as 'other' – other than oneself or other than one's own. In combination with an agent's purposive activity such boundaries necessarily define some events (e.g., some acts by other agents) as *interfering, trespassing, intruding, welcome, invited,* and so forth – with all of the conative freight those terms carry. In our pursuit of particular goals we are disposed to reject what we see as interference and trespass; we are disposed to permit what we welcome and invite. In this sense, boundary-keeping activity is just a part of *being* a rational agent. Boundary-keeping rules are the deontological rules that define such activity.

It should be emphasized, however, that the conceptual connection here is not between agency and some specific set of boundary-keeping rules. Just as there is no particular purpose that is essential to agency as such, so too there is no particular set of boundaries essential to it. Particular sets of purposes, and particular sets of boundaries, are parts of particular *ways* of life. What is essential (teleologically) to agency as such is simply having *some* purposes. And what is essential deontologically is having – and 'keeping' – *some* boundaries.

It might be argued that if this is all that can be said about the teleological and deontological rules of morality as such, then it is fair to say that morality is still significantly ill-defined. It might be thought that the mere fact that agents have *some* goals and *some* boundaries (but not necessarily the same ones) does not give us enough to get moral reasoning started. It is as if we had been told, about a new game, 'There's no agreement about what you should try to do, except that you should try *something*. And there's no agreement about what moves are permitted and forbidden, except that some must be.' How could we even begin to construct reasoned advice for such a game? And how, similarly, can we get reasoned moral advice if all we know is that agents each have some aims and some boundary rules?

The answer is that the kind of moral reasoning these non-specific teleological and deontological rules define is a sort in which the fundamental task is to deal, in ways as yet unspecified, with the multiplicity of aims of agents who may have very different self-concepts – very different boundary-keeping rules. Think of a game in which the players make up the rules of play as they go along – under the constraint that play must always be according to *some* rules, and under certain procedural and recognition rules about rule-making. Reasoned advice is not impossible in such a game. In fact it can be a fascinating and challenging business – not to say riveting, if the stakes are sufficiently high. The same is true of morality.

VALUATION   The concept of rational agency also defines valuation rules for morality in the sense that the following preference rules for making choices among alternatives are constitutive of the notion of rational agency as such.

1   Correspondence of preference to value. A good thing is to be preferred to a bad thing, and more of a good to less of it – other things being equal. Such preference orderings are simply an expression, in practice, of value orderings – and values are by definition ordered in this way: good over bad, more good over less. Any other preference ordering would not be a logically consistent expression of the value ordering. Logical consistency is a defining characteristic of rational agency.

2   Transitivity of preference. Logical consistency also requires that preference ordering be transitive: If X is to be preferred to Y, and Y to Z, then X is to be preferred to Z. If that were not the case – if preferences were *not* transitive – we would get an incoherent result. Recall that preference orderings are to correspond to value orderings. Now if transitivity does *not* hold (that is, if X is not preferred to Z in the example above) then Z is either preferred to X, or is at the same 'preference level' as X. That is, in the corresponding value-ordering, Z is either superior to X or equivalent to it. We have either this situation:

$$\text{(i)} \quad X > Y$$
$$Y > Z$$
$$Z < X$$

or this one $$\text{(ii)} \quad X > Y$$
$$Y > Z$$
$$Z = X$$

Suppose we have (i). Then we would have said that X is both superior to Y and inferior to something 'below' Y. That is incoherent. And the result is similar if we have case (ii). There we would have said that Y is both superior to something (Z) and inferior to something else (X) that are of equal value. So logic requires transitive value orderings, and by extension, transitive preference orderings.

3   Generalization. A third valuation rule, entailed by the notion

of a reasoned argument, is that similar cases are to be treated similarly. If a set of action-guiding reasons justify a given act for any agent, then by definition they justify a similar act for any relevantly similar agent. The problem of deciding which things are *relevant* similarities is a notorious one, but the point that the similar cases rule is a *formal* constraint on reasoning about conduct (and hence a constraint on moral reasoning) is secure.

Summary

Morality, as I shall use the term here, is the activity of deciding what rational agents ought to do and be, all things considered, and then doing or being those things. That activity is well-defined in the sense that it is defined by some determinable rules of participation, teleology, deontology, valuation, procedure, transformation and recognition. Reasoned action-guidance within that activity, for the participants, is therefore possible in the same sense that it is possible for various well-defined activities *within* life. And it is subject to the same sorts of conditions for logical validity and soundness that are found in those everyday forms of practical reasoning.

CHAPTER 2

Moral Theory

The task of any moral theory is to define and justify some part of a way of life – to give an account of the things moral agents ought to do and be. The performance of that task, however, is always constrained by whatever general theory of morality lies behind the effort. In this book, such constraints are the ones imposed by the general conception of morality.

It turns out that those constraints, by themselves, block some conclusions and force others. Part of moral theory is therefore *a priori*, in the sense that its results are derived from the rules of the general conception alone, without further reference to experience. Most of the moral theory in this book, however, depends on empirical evidence as well as *a priori* argument.

The general pattern of argument will be to deal directly with the question of moral character. We will ask, first, what traits of character moral agents ought to have. Then and only then will we ask about conduct and the design of social institutions. The questions asked about conduct are these: If agents had morally justifiable traits, how would they decide to act? What would be the consequences, for their traits, of their acting otherwise? Would that be justifiable, all things considered? The questions asked about social structure are similar: Which structures promote good character traits? Which ones undermine them? Can the latter ever be justified, all things considered? In short, arguments about conduct will be made *by way of* arguments about virtue.

The point of doing moral theory 'through' the virtues is roughly this: Most of our conduct is controlled by dispositions – habits of thought, propensities to act, readinesses to respond – and that is just the way things ought to be, as long as our dispositions are good ones. But good dispositions can be either promoted or undermined by conduct and social structure. Thus the moral analysis of an act or a rule is seriously incomplete if its consequences for moral character are ignored. Conduct that is otherwise justifiable may be wrong just because it damages character. Furthermore, the relation between good character and good conduct is often problematic. At any rate, in some deeply troubling cases, it often *seems* as though good people cannot bring themselves to do what they ought to do (all things considered) precisely because they are justifiably disposed against that general *sort* of thing. Acting in character appears, sometimes, to be exactly the wrong thing to do, all things considered. The methodological point of doing moral theory through the virtues, then, is to make sure all these issues are addressed. Modern moral theory too often ignores them.

There is another point as well. Virtue theory yields some surprising and important substantive results. In particular, as I shall argue in the following chapters, it has a good deal to teach us about social obligations.

Experience and Morality

Because the moral theory to follow will depend on empirical premises at many points, it will be useful to make some general observations about those premises. I will try to be as brief and as banal as possible. The point is not to raise controversy but rather to describe some common ground.

The Social Self

We are social beings. Within the limits imposed by biology, our development is controlled by our interaction with the environment. We move against things, or with them, or in terms of them. They respond or not. We react, and act again. We learn.

These experiences are social if a) we are aware of them as *inter*actions and b) they involve others who are aware of them as such. The involvement with others may be direct (a caress) or indirect (struggle with an object created by others).

Initially, at least, through the long period of physical dependency in human infancy, most of our experience is social – either directly or indirectly. And some continuing social experience, at sometime during prepubescent years, is necessary for the development of those traits definitive of rational agency as such – namely, a sharply defined sense of self, and the ability to deliberate upon and choose a course of conduct. Without social experience, if we survive at all, we do not develop very well physically; we do not acquire language; our ideational abilities, character traits, and personality traits remain rudimentary.

In short, without the things we can acquire only through social experience, we do not become rational agents at all. We *are*, then, social beings in the strong and clear sense that our rational agency is the product of social experience, operating on the plastic and largely undeveloped biological stuff of which we are made. This observation will play a central role in the argument for reciprocity.

The Priority Problem

Apart from our social nature, perhaps the most obvious and morally compelling fact about our lives is the multiplicity of our aims, values, ideals and demands. If purity of heart is to will one thing, none of us is pure. Each of us is a fount of intentions, wants, hopes, habits, dreams, demands and expectations – all of which jostle for attention, and all of which lay claim to our limited personal resources. Each of us who lives with others lays claim to the attention of those others. When resources are scarce, we compete for them. Our demands upon each other, for help or forbearance, conflict. It follows that any moral theory under the general conception will find the problem of priorities to be a fundamental one. Problems of allocation and distribution abound.

There is an analogous problem with the various types of special-purpose reasoning that enter into moral argument. Utility may recommend one thing and etiquette quite another. Under the general conception of morality, we are to consider them both, unless there is some reason not to. Similarly, unless there is some reason not to, we are to give them equal weight. Yet they may conflict. Which is to take precedence and why?

Priority problems are notoriously hard to resolve. (That is one of the attractions of supreme principle theories. They lack one major source of priority problems: competing principles.) Moral principles which can be recommended on many grounds are therefore to be prized. I shall argue in the next chapter that reciprocity is just such a principle.

Ellen has lived alone since Johnny died, but she sees the other side of everything. She tells herself, for instance, that it was good he went quickly, that he was ready, that he hated retirement, that his best friends had died or moved away, that he no longer loved her. Comfort isn't love. Duty isn't love. Lack of alternatives isn't love.

Ellen tells herself that at least she doesn't have the house to worry about. For just a lot of reasons it would have been foolish to keep it. It took her all week to clean it, the ancient trees around the yard needed work, the trim outside would have to have been painted sooner or later. It was true she felt loved in the house, embraced by it even during the worst times. She wept when she saw it stripped after the auction, and again after the movers came to take what was left to her new apartment. She could not go near the old street now, for fear of seeing awful changes. And she was uneasy in the new place, slightly tense, half-expecting sudden noises, or loneliness.

But it was so easy to get distracted in the house. Johnny had kept everything — old radios, magazines, correspondence, broken staplers, rubber stamps, everything. Some of it could be used. Some of it couldn't be thrown away if you knew what it was. And there was cash — a ten here, a twenty there — tucked away in old billfolds, in the corners of old desk blotters, in unmarked envelopes. If she had kept the house she would have had to go through everything. So it was best to move.

People misunderstood, as always. They thought she was unfeeling, or shortsighted, or unprincipled, or just silly. She had long since given up trying to explain anything about her ruined life. She let people believe she was empty. That was what they wanted to believe: Tiresome Ellen. Empty-headed Ellen.

Tiresome old, sick old Ellen, she added. But every time she walked into her apartment, where everything was so easy to manage, she was sure she had done one right thing. You weren't supposed to move away from everything familiar all at once, and she hadn't. All her new neighbors were from the university, retired or nearly so. The compound of condominium apartments — in ninety townhouses — was a short walk from the campus, and she'd kept her memberships in the women's club, the concert series, and even the faculty club, though she was uncomfortable there without Johnny. True, the houses were nearly alike and very close together. She didn't like the siding of cedar shingles on them all, or the small patios and decks with uniform privacy fences, or the common carports. But there were lots of trees, some of them substantial. There were pleasant paths that wound among the houses, tidy expanses of grass in the common areas, and plantings that softened the sameness. The manager was a pill. Mary Worth in mufti. But the group activities she organized weren't so bad. Ellen usually went to the monthly cocktail parties. She liked the fact that there was more going on than she wanted to join, because it restored a part of the pattern Johnny's death had damaged. She had demands to fend off again, privacy to protect.

Ellen often took long walks. They were not aimless. She would go to the campus bookstore, or the bank, or the post office. But the purpose was often contrived, and she always took longer routes than necessary, so the walk would take more time. She answered the phone at the free clinic on Monday afternoons. She did fair linens for the altar guild on Tuesdays. She read for an hour before dinner every day – during the time she and Johnny would have been having drinks. She would not turn on the television before eight in the evening. It was important to fill up the days, to keep to a schedule. And it was important to hang on to the little things that gave her life shape in other people's eyes. Ellen was known for certain things. She didn't want to disappear.

People thought of Ellen as argumentative. She was, as Johnny said, disposed to disagree with everyone. Thoroughly disagreeable, he said. And it was true that she argued. It was true that her typical response to a flat assertion was to deny it. And it was true that at the moment she contradicted people she often had no clear idea of what might be wrong with what they had said. But the odds were she would find something. She saw the other side of everything.

The day she knew her life was ruined was the day she saw herself completely captured by a description. Disagreeable. That indicated nothing but a shell. Not a person but a form, a technique. Accept nothing. Transform everything by

negation. Let someone say, 'I wish I were a child again. No
cares. No responsibilities,' and she would say how miserable
it was to be that powerless, that confused and uncertain about
the world, that vulnerable. Let someone say, 'The summer
was wonderful, wasn't it? So much good weather,' and she
would say that too much sun was oppressive, that people
needed changes, clouds, and rain. Tiresome Ellen. Tiresome
old, sick old Ellen.

When she was young she was witty and more kind. She was
uncertain enough to be shy. She had the patience to make
her conversation appealing, and the energy to talk about
important things and to restrain herself. But thirty years in
the same small place takes its toll. Friends grow weary of each
other. Memories fuse into images, stories into epithets.

Ellen had a lot to live up to. She was tired, and sick at heart,
and bitter. But she didn't want to disappear. There wasn't
any other side to that.

Acting in Character

Much of our behavior is unmediated by deliberate choice. We
react reflexively, or spontaneously. We do things out of habit, or
unthinkingly. The relation of such conduct to deliberation and
choice is complex. We may anticipate a reflex and try to suppress
it (a sneeze). We may be aware of the habitual nature of an act as
we do it, and try to change it (a bad golf swing).

A disposition, as I shall use the term, is a persistent readiness to
respond and a propensity to act. It is a trait of character or personality. It may be innate or acquired, resistant to change or malleable,
weak or strong in relation to competing impulses and obstacles,
capable of a rich variety of expressions or not. It may be triggered
only by subliminal stimuli, or only by the most blatantly obvious
ones. It may operate entirely below the level of consciousness. (We
may speak, by analogy, of the dispositional properties of cells, or
organs, or even inorganic objects – e.g., a magnetized bar of iron.)
Some dispositions operate only when we are paying close attention,
both to the stimulus and the response the disposition produces.
(Example: the dispositions that make possible a witty conversation.) A disposition may produce pure motor responses, or kine-
sthetic ones, affective, cognitive, or decisional ones. It may produce

a complex array of such responses, simultaneously or in series. It may produce hesitation, alertness, anticipation. It may produce action, emotional reaction, or rejection. It may (and this is more to the point here) propel people to assess their circumstances in terms of particular aims, and then to act for those aims. Reciprocity, as I shall conceive it in the following chapters, is that last sort of disposition – one that is triggered by the receipt of goods or evils.

The immediacy of the conduct produced by dispositions has instrumental value of the highest order. Given the complexity and velocity of life – and human limitations – we could achieve nothing without basic physiological dispositions and very little without sophisticated motor and mental abilities. The immediacy has intrinsic value as well. Pleasures can be diluted or muddied by deliberation.

Unfounded Preferences

It would be convenient if our preferences corresponded to our considered judgments about what we ought to do and be, and if our feelings matched our beliefs. If that were true, then moral theory could devote itself exclusively to resolving conflicts among conflicting judgments and beliefs. The resolution of conflicting attitudes, feelings and preferences would follow automatically.

Unhappily, that is not possible. What people believe about something, as a result of their reasoned deliberations, is a notoriously poor index to their preferences or feelings about that thing.

Of course, it is true that affect and preference track belief in one sense: We would find it very peculiar if someone claimed to believe that a thing was good in some specified sense and at the same time claimed to disapprove of it *in that same respect*. Such a pair of statements borders on incoherence, because some sort of approval seems implicit in any claim that a thing is good.

Beyond that, however, people can and do approve of the same good things in very different ways, and to very different degrees. These differences in affect *may* correspond directly to differences in belief about the relative importance of goods, but then again they may not. Reason may rank-order things one way; emotion may give quite a different result. Our feelings and preferences may be, as we say, irrational or unreasonable or unfounded.

Some unfounded preferences are culture-bound. An example is the refusal to eat horsemeat or dogmeat – among people who can think of no moral objection to it and who are perfectly willing to eat other kinds of meat. Other unfounded preferences are purely idiosyncratic. The point is that there is often a disturbing difference between what we think we 'should' feel or prefer (as a result of our considered moral judgment) and what we do in fact continue to feel or prefer. If we act on our moral judgments we are uncomfortable, awkward, even miserable. If we act on our unfounded feelings or preferences we are similarly unhappy.

Moral theory under the general conception deals with this problem by addressing it as a second-level concern: Given that a feeling is unfounded, would it be better, all things considered, to act on it or not? A thoroughly predictable question, to be approached in a thoroughly familiar way. Clearly, however, other things being equal, moral principles that produce fewer of these second-level concerns are preferable to principles that produce more.

Unfounded Disturbance

An analogous problem arises with regard to equilibrium – both personal and social equilibrium. Some evils are disorienting, frightening, troubling, upsetting. They are, in a word, destabilizing. Others are not; they are understandable, manageable, expected. We can cope.

Among the evils that are destabilizing, there are matters of degree. The problem is that these differences of degree may be unfounded: our actual reactions may not correspond to what, on reasoned consideration, we think our reactions ought to be. What provokes the greatest personal and social turmoil is not necessarily the thing that is upon reflection the greatest evil.

The point is the same one made about unfounded preferences. We may have unfounded reactions of a destabilizing sort about various wrongs. In fact, we may even have them about things that, upon reflection, turn out to be right. (Consider the personal turmoil people go through when they begin to examine their racist or sexist beliefs.) Whether these unfounded reactions are culture-bound or idiosyncratic, they raise a second-level question about whether one should act on them. Moral principles that minimize such concerns are, *ceteris paribus*, preferable to those that do not.

Here is the weather from those stations reporting at 7 a.m.: Roanoke, cloudy and 65 degrees. Lynchburg, foggy and 63. Bluefield, obscure.

Virtue Theory

Excellence matters. It is one of the things moral argument under the general conception must consider, along with instrumental and hedonic values, aggregate welfare, efficiency, and so forth. To say that a hammer is an excellent one is to say it is *good of its kind*. Whether something is good of its kind is a relevant concern for moral argument because, other things equal, moral argument will favor the better hammer just because it *is* better, *as* a hammer. That just follows from the valuation rules: better, on any given scale, is preferable to worse, *ceteris paribus*.

The excellence of an object is assessed in a way that is conceptually distinct from assessments of instrumental value, efficiency and so forth. The assessment of excellence begins with a description of the *type* of thing the object is. A scale of values for things of that type is then constructed by reference to an ideal for the type, and the object is rated in terms of that ideal. How good it is, *of its kind*, is assessed by how closely it approximates the ideal.

The ideal for a type is ascertained by reflecting on the 'nature' of things of that type: their typical behavior under various conditions, their powers and propensities, the way they fit into their environments, the purposes we have for them, their own teleological properties, if any. Constructing a concept of an ideal for a type is like constructing an ideal for the all-round athlete. (In fact, that is just a special case of it.) We first try to get clear about the range of things various athletes do, *qua* athletes, and the traits needed to succeed in each. We then decide what combination of traits (levels of strength, endurance, agility, and so on) would allow a person to do all of those things at a level equal to what specialists in each can accomplish. If that combination of traits is inconsistent (great height for basketball, small stature for gymnastics) we revise the list until it is coherent, giving up those traits from inconsistent subsets whose absence reduces overall performance the least. If the remaining traits are still impossible for athletes to achieve, we may wish to reduce the list still further until we arrive at the highest 'possible' ideal. It will be quite different from the ideal for any particular sport. (Think of sumo wrestlers versus decathlon stars.) But that is understandable. It is itself the ideal for another special type of athlete.

There is, of course, no mechanical procedure for doing this properly – in part because there is no guarantee, in a given case, that there will be a unique set of traits that maximizes overall performance. We may, in a given case, have to choose between two or more mutually exclusive ideals, each arrived at in the manner just described. If no relevant grounds can be found for a reasoned choice in the matter, the choice will be arbitrary.

Nonetheless, the procedure for arriving at *some* reasonably defensible conception of the ideal is clear enough. It is a complex business, with a good deal of indeterminacy about it, but it is important to remember that it is an *everyday* business. Commodities, relationships, natural objects, talents, works of art, people and so forth are all rated in this way. It is a perfectly ordinary practice, no matter how extraordinary it may be to find it done in a philosophically defensible way. Calculations of social utility are similar, in that respect. They are common, but also commonly hasty, incomplete, and imprecise.

OBJECTION: This won't work. *Of course* it is an everyday business to define ideals for things like hammers. We make hammers for specifiable purposes, and it is in terms of those purposes that we can say which hammers are ideal. But there is no similar purpose specifiable for moral agents; no specifiable end toward which their existence and activity is working. At least, there is none that is philosophically defensible. We can *imagine* all sorts of *possible* ends – all sorts of teleological anthropologies – in terms of which ideals could be specified. Suppose the deity has given us these lives for developmental purposes; for 'soul making'. Or suppose the end toward which all human history moves is utopian communism. Or suppose the earth is something like an embryo, and human beings are something like bacteria necessary for the embryo's development. On any of those suppositions, sufficiently elaborated, we could construct some notion of an ideal type of human being. But surely those (and all the other teleological possibilities) are *merely* suppositions, or articles of faith. Surely we have no philosophically defensible account of such a teleology. And surely, without it talk of an ideal for our 'type' is empty.

REPLY: We need not appeal to a grand teleology at all. An ideal can be constructed for any type we care to define. The type need not be a 'natural' kind. It need not have a divinely or naturally given end toward which its individuals strive. It must simply be describable *as* a type, the individuals of which have characteristic powers and propensities, used in characteristic ways. If it can be so defined, it will yield the notion of an ideal, and individuals of that type can be rated accordingly.

Imagine a simple micro-organism, of no known utility or harm to us. Suppose it has a characteristic life cycle of three stages, during each of which there is a characteristic type of activity. The activity of stage one typically produces a result that triggers the transition to stage two; the activity of stage two is similarly connected to the transition to stage three; and the activity of stage three is reproduction. Now we do not need to assume some grand teleological scheme in order to determine which individuals of this type of organism are ideally suited to complete the three-stage career characteristic of the type. We may find, perhaps, that certain variations in size and shape are correlated with variations in rates of activity in each stage, and that certain rates of activity prohibit the change from one stage to another, or prohibit reproduction. It is not necessary to assume that reproduction is the organism's 'goal' to conclude that, *simply for the three-stage process we observe*, a certain size and shape is ideal (i.e., is most efficacious in generating this transition from stage to stage and the activity characteristic of each stage).

OBJECTION: But it is hard to see what connection any of that could have to the task of defining the moral virtues. There do not seem to be any activities characteristic of our species that would be relevant to such an undertaking. This is so because we are purposive individuals, and the multitude of human purposes will not even yield a single, coherent ideal for all the members of a given family, let alone the whole species. Some of us want to reproduce, others do not. Some of us are risk averse, others are not. Some of us prefer long, peaceful lives to short and glorious ones, others do not. Furthermore, we can deliberately alter other people's preferences and purposes. In principle (i.e., on a behaviorist's principles) we can generate nearly any set of purposes and preference schedules that we choose. So a theory of the virtues, in the way it is proposed here, would reduce to a series of relatively trivial assertions of the following form: Given that a particular individual has purposes A, B, and C, traits X, Y, and Z would be ideal. But of course, for other individuals, or for other purposes, those traits might not be ideal. And there isn't any way to determine, in terms of the sort of argument described here, what purposes people ought to have. Surely that is the primary question. Once we know what ends people *ought* (morally) to pursue, then no doubt we can construct an account of the traits they will need to pursue those goals. Those traits can then be called *moral* ones, or virtues, but *only* because they are ideal for purposes already known to be moral ones. Virtue theory is thus necessarily parasitic upon a prior determination of what counts as a moral way of life.

REPLY: It will be the burden of the next three chapters to show that that objection has no force. The general pattern of argument will be as follows:

Virtue Theoretic Arguments

Trivially, under the general conception, an ideal moral agent is one who can always do, and does always do, what is best all things considered. But saying that is no more useful than saying that a sedative is something that has dormative powers. What we want from virtue theory is an indication of the specific traits required for the general task of doing what is best all-things-considered. We want a theory of the virtues, plural.

The task of defining the virtues begins with empirical data about the species characteristics of beings whom we know to be moral agents. (Under the general conception, a moral agent is one who can make judgments about what to do or be, all-things-considered, as that enterprise is defined in Chapter One. A being who cannot act in this way would presumably have quite different virtues.) In principle, the scope of the inquiry is not limited to our own species. But given our limited knowledge about others, in practice the inquiry begins and ends with humans. The object of this first step, then, is to look for the features that define (human) moral agents as a type.

The next step is to look for the characteristic activities of the type: the way such beings develop and are sustained; the way they fit into their environment; the sorts of things they are impelled to do, and are likely to do; how they regard themselves and each other; what they demand of themselves and each other. The question of the virtues can then be addressed in the following way.

Given the type of being a moral agent is, and given the circumstances those beings are likely to encounter, the task is to describe the traits that would cause an individual moral agent who had them to excel at all of the morally justifiable things characteristic of moral agents as a type. (Recall the problem of defining the ideal all-round athlete.) Inconsistencies among traits will be dealt with later.

The next step is to take the list of traits so derived and find the ones that can be given a justification under the general conception of morality. That is, we exclude the ones that do not conform to the requirements of *a priori* moral theory, and among those remaining, we find the ones there are reasons to recommend, all things considered, for agents to develop and sustain. These traits are *virtues*, under the general conception.

The final step is to survey the set of virtues to see if the ideal they define (conjunctively) is logically and physically possible. If the virtues form an inconsistent set, we drop the ones (from inconsistent subsets) whose absence compromises overall performance least. Then, if the remaining consistent set is something actual moral agents would still find it impossible to acquire and sustain, we may wish to cut the list still further, to find the highest 'possible' ideal of moral character.

The argument in the following chapters is virtue-theoretic. Its aim is to show that a certain disposition to reciprocate is a part of ideal moral character, and that important consequences for moral conduct flow from that fact. The argument is about one virtue, and so it does not complete the pattern of virtue-theoretic argument described above. But it is a part of that pattern. It is rooted in empirical generalizations, from social science and commonsense, about the type of beings we are, what things we need in order to survive and thrive at the activities characteristic of us, in the circumstances we are likely to face. Reasons are then given for concluding that the disposition to reciprocate is one of the traits that will cause individuals who have it to excel at the things characteristic of moral agents. Reciprocity is, in that sense, one of the virtues.

OBJECTION: But how can an argument of that form possibly establish anything about the *morality* of the traits so defined? How does it entitle us to say that they are virtues? What it appears to do is simply to take whatever activities are *in fact* characteristic of human beings, then find whatever traits are *in fact* ideal for those activities, and conclude that those traits are moral virtues. But of course that won't do. Suppose murder is an activity characteristic of the species, and that ruthlessness and cunning are good traits to have for murderous activities. Does it follow that ruthlessness and cunning are moral virtues?

REPLY: Not unless the murderous activities characteristic of the species are themselves morally justifiable. Recall that that restriction was included in the argument form: 'the task is to describe the traits that would cause an individual moral agent who had them to excel at all of the *morally justifiable* things characteristic of moral agents as a type.' Presumably, murderous activity would not be justifiable, all things considered.

QUESTION: So there is an independent conception of goodness or rightness lurking behind this argument after all?

REPLY: There is a *provisional line of moral argument* behind it. We first consider the justifiability of an activity directly, without going through the virtues. Presumably, that will rule out some things. (E.g., see the section on *a priori* morality below.) We can then get a provisional list of the virtues. They may add factors relevant to the moral assessment of the remaining activities. If those factors rule out more activities, then the list of virtues will have to be revised again. And so forth. The process is recursive.

QUESTION: And open-ended?

REPLY: Not necessarily.

OBJECTION: But it might be. We can imagine that each recursive step forces a revision in the list, but doesn't reduce the number of elements in the list. And we can imagine an indefinite progression. Given A, then B, but given B, then A' and hence B', and A" and B" and so on. Is that tolerable?

REPLY: It is no less tolerable than the open-endedness of philosophical inquiry generally. Presumably we can achieve some reasonably settled results – that is, some conclusions about ideal traits that do not require cripplingly frequent revisions. Think of the concept of physical health. That is open-ended too in the sense that new diseases are identified from time to time, standards of nutrition are revised, and patterns of human life change in ways that cause us to revise our notions of physical fitness. Still, for practical purposes (e.g., insurance claims) we can get a reasonably precise and settled account of physical health. Just so, I shall argue, we can get a reasonably settled account of the traits moral agents ought to have *qua* moral agents.

OBJECTION: It is still not clear why we need to tie these arguments to the characteristics of the whole species. Why not just say that moral virtue, for every individual, will be whatever morally justifiable traits are ideal for whatever morally justifiable projects that particular individual happens to have?

REPLY: That is a legitimate extension of the argument form proposed here, but it is not directed at the same question. The question here is about what, if anything, can be said about the traits *all* moral agents, *qua* moral agents, ought to have. It is that question to which the rest of this book is addressed.

OBJECTION: But it is asking *that* question, rather than some other one, that needs defense. Why try to construct an account of virtue for *all* moral agents? Why not just pick some arbitrary subset? People over six feet tall, for example. Or risk-averse types. Or well-educated, urban, adult males. (That choice is familiar to moral philosophers.) The point is that the choice of moral agents *per se* as the type in terms of which a theory of the virtues will be constructed is a morally significant choice. It needs defense.

REPLY: The defense is this: Taking the moral agent *per se* as the type is the most inclusive choice we can make for present purposes. And if we choose any less inclusive type, moral argument under the general conception will quickly push us toward the most inclusive one anyway. After all, if we are going to prescribe conduct for all moral agents, we will have to defend those prescriptions with considerations that are relevant to all moral agents. Why, we will be asked, should everyone have the traits that work well for, say, adult males? Why should we raise every baby – or *any* baby – to have those traits? The answer to such questions will eventually have to be made in terms of the traits needed to flourish as a moral agent (with whatever additional characteristics a particular individual might have).

OBJECTION: Now the choice looks too restrictive. Why moral *agents*? Why not all sentient beings? Any being with identifiable interests? Agency, after all, leaves out some members of our own species, and many animals, who certainly are morally entitled to something from us.

REPLY: The questions at stake here are about conduct, not about passive entitlements. And the scope of the community to which moral prescriptions can defensibly be addressed is not the same as the scope of the community that has identifiable interests. The choice of the moral *agent* as the type for dealing with questions of conduct is therefore reasonable.

Skepticism about all of this is understandable, because the project looks suspiciously like a discredited aspect of Aristotelian ethics. In the abstract, there is no way to answer the skeptic further except to say that the arguments I shall make are not meant to be of the discredited sort. Showing that, however, amounts to actually making the arguments. That will be done in Chapter Three, and the skeptic's questions will be considered again there.

A Priori Moral Theory

The part of moral theory that derives its conclusions from the rules of the general conception alone is *a priori* moral theory.

Caveat

The whole enterprise of such *a priori* theory depends on getting an accurate account of the rules of the general conception, and the concept of moral agency implicit in it. Getting that account is analogous to finding the correct description of a customary game, or an adequate explication of a theoretical construct in science. In each case the problem is in part a conceptual one; it is resolved simply by thinking things through. Is 3-D tic-tac-toe 'really' tic-tac-toe? Is a virus 'really' alive? The answers to such questions do not come entirely from evidence about games played or viruses observed. The answers come ultimately from the meanings of the terms involved, and the purposes we have for them. But meanings and purposes change; the rules of customary games change over time, and what counts as a living thing may change as well. So the answers to conceptual questions about tic-tac-toe and viruses depend on when those questions are asked – that is, they depend on matters of fact about 'the rules' at the time of asking.

In an analogous sense, our account of the nature of agency is also conditioned by matters of fact. The concept of agency that we use, abstracted as it is from a simple set of social practices and expectations, is likely to change over time. Some of the changes may be rather superficial. The current penchant for including the notion of the transitivity of preferences, for example, may well be a matter of making explicit things that were there all along. But other changes may result from deep shifts in our understanding of the nature of human consciousness and conduct. Shifts, for example, in the connection we see between altruism and survival, or egoism and mental health. Moreover, our concept of agency as such, though we say it is in principle not limited to human agency, is drawn from evidence about our own species. And it is drawn from things we have either experienced ourselves or are able to imagine in detail and connect to what we have experienced. Intuitions fail, and conceptual arguments flounder in speculation about how moral rules might apply to some radically evolved descendant of our species, or to contemporaries in a strikingly different culture (the Iks) or a shockingly different setting (a concentration camp). What is true here of the application of rules to cases is also true of the use of the term 'rational agent'. Could it apply, for example, to a suitably high-powered computer? Or to one of the radically alien life-forms of science fiction?

In short, an *a priori* moral theory is *a priori* only subject to this important qualification: The concepts from which it is drawn are subject to change due to changes in our understanding of matters of fact, and our understanding of matters of fact is shaped by the range of available experience. That is no more limiting than the possibilities for *a priori* knowledge generally. But it stands as an important caution to the whole enterprise of getting an *a priori* moral theory.

Just listen, Jesse. Please. I'm better at examples. Listen to this. The people in my carpool think I'm divorced, no children, and seeing three men. Just listen. I used the word mistress to them. The mistress of three men. It's a metaphor. Does that make it better? My men are not supposed to know about each other, my life is very complicated, the balance is very delicate, and I make them pay for it. That's all true. See, you're laughing. The *story* is what interests people. They like the thought of it: the mistress. So when I say I'm edgy, or tired, or afraid I'm going to drop the pieces of my life, they have an idea they know what I mean. Does that make me a liar? David *betrayed* me.

Nobody tells the truth, Jesse. Those stories you tell get better every time, for instance. Is that an accident? Who would listen if they didn't? What kind of man would you be if you wouldn't make them better? I tell Anna stories to get her to talk. I don't see why that should upset you. That's not hurting anyone. Anna's unhappy and needs to talk. She's unhappy about you, and that's no secret. So I tell her it was always difficult for David and me too, that David is impotent and we just got tired of trying to make it work. And Anna will laugh, and that's a prize because she doesn't like rough talk. But she'll listen to a story like that, and she'll say, for instance, that she has the opposite problem with you. We know that's not true. But Anna and I understand each other. We know the truth is underneath the stories. That's not betraying anyone. That's not lying.

'How unlovely.' I don't think so. What's unlovely is your listening to stories that weren't meant for you to hear, and being so sanctimonious about them. I'll tell you something, Jesse. No one would listen to anything if it were exactly the truth. It would take too long and be too boring. I don't want to have another scene with you.

Just read the next paragraph. I'm going to write it and then go back and put parentheses around everything that's not exactly right – everything that's only partly true, or maybe overstated, or maybe just said for effect. See if you can rewrite

it, Jesse, so it doesn't lie. And when you do, ask yourself if
any human person would listen to it, Jesse. Whether it would
interest anyone.

I (hate) (you), Jesse. I'd be (just as happy) if you never
(spoke) to me again. And if you ever humiliate me again (in
public) I'll (kill) (you).

The Generalization Test

The conclusion of every reasoned argument is generalizable. If
premises A, B, and C justify an act for a given agent, then they
will by definition justify a similar act for any relevantly similar
agent in similar circumstances. This sort of generalizability is a
constitutive feature of reasoned justification as such, and therefore
of the general conception of morality.

What follows from this is a tantalizing possibility, imagined and
developed brilliantly by Kant: If an action-guide is justifiable, then
it is generalizable. It therefore follows (by contraposition) that if a
guide is ungeneralizable, then it is unjustifiable. Finding that a
guide is unjustifiable is tantamount to finding that the *conduct* it
recommends is unjustifiable.

The task is therefore to find the ungeneralizable guides. That is
the Kantian project, and however obscure its development may
have been, its strategy is clear and correct: To find the guides that
are in principle ungeneralizable, find the ones whose generalization
involves a contradiction.

> *Note* The following exposition is adapted from O'Nora
> (O'Neill) Nell's book, *Acting on Principle*. I do not,
> however, mean to imply her approval of my summary,
> and especially not of my rather breezy presentation of
> its limitations. Philosophers who already have settled
> opinions on the Kantian project will not find anything
> here to sway them one way or the other. I present this
> summary of the topic only because I use a modest
> version of the generalization test in some crucial places
> in the following chapters. I have tried to make sure that
> my use of it does not depend on preemptory judgments
> on deeply contested matters, but I have not concealed
> my biases against a more extensive use of it. Readers

may wish to follow out the references in the Scholium to work to the contrary.

The first step for the Kantian project is to say what it means for the generalization of an action-guide to involve a contradiction. The notion of a contradiction, as developed in standard logic, applies to descriptive statements – i.e., to sentences that can be either true or false. It does not apply – at least not straightforwardly – to the sort of prescriptive, action-guiding sentences we are concerned with here. But action-guides can all be 'projected' into descriptive language – into statements that describe what is the case when the guides are followed. If those projections are incoherent, then so are the action-guides they represent.

Take the action-guide:

i   I ought to make only false promises.

Suppose that part of what it means is that I intend to make only false promises. If that intention is justifiable by reasoned argument, then a similar intention, on the part of every relevantly similar agent, is also justifiable. Expressed in the form of a generalization, this would be

ii   Everyone ought to make only false promises.

Now *if* I intend to promise falsely I am in effect intending that the descriptive statement

iii   I make only false promises. be *true*.

That statement is a projection, into descriptive terms, of my intention as expressed in i. The projection of ii is

iv   Everyone makes only false promises.

Holding i commits me to holding ii – by the generalization rule. Holding i and ii is, in effect, to hold their projections iii and iv. So holding the intention expressed in i – as something for which there is a reasoned justification – commits me to all the rest.

So far so good. But in the case of this particular intention, there is a logical difficulty that develops as follows:

When I make a promise to other people, falsely or not, I intend to cause them to believe at least two things: a) that I intend to do what I say I will do, and b) that to some extent they can rely on the likelihood that I will do it. Without that sort of intention I simply cannot be said to have made a promise, falsely or not. (Without that sort of intention I could make a prediction with the words 'I'll do it.' Or I could negligently mislead people into believing I had promised. But none of those things is the same as making a promise, falsely or not.)

Now when I *intend* to cause something with my act (as opposed, for example, to merely *wanting* to cause it), I must believe that it is at least *possible* to cause it, in a sense of 'possible' that is stronger than mere logical possibility. I must believe that the relevant background conditions exist – conditions in the context of which my act will be sufficient to cause the event. Example: When I intend to ignite a match by striking it (and genuinely *intend* to do it as opposed to hope for the best) that implies my belief in the presence of oxygen around the match head – or rather, my belief in the presence of whatever background conditions my science tells me are necessary to make the striking efficacious. The presence of such a belief is just part of the difference between mere desire and intent.

But consider the state of affairs described by iv above – that is, by the statement that everyone makes only false promises. To intend that it be true would be to intend that there be no social practice of promise-keeping at all. It would be to intend that people never intend to do what they 'promise' to do.

Assuming that rational agents are by definition creatures who learn from experience, it follows that, *for them*, some promise-making intentions are impossible under the conditions described by iv. That is, under those conditions, a rational agent would not (for long) believe the 'promises' of others, nor believe that others would be fooled (for long) by his own. So since having an intention to promise falsely *requires* the belief that others can be fooled, the sort of intention expressed by i is impossible if iv is true. Statement i requires a continuing intention to deceive, and hence a belief that such deception could in principle continue. Rational agents who are attentive to their situation could not have such a belief (for long) under the conditions described by iv. (Inattentive or irrational agents are another matter, as are other versions of false-promising intentions. See below under *Three Limitations*.)

The conclusion is, therefore, that to intend that iv be true is inconsistent with intending that ii be true. Since holding i commits us to both ii and iv, i is incoherent. It cannot be generalized. It therefore cannot be justified, and the conduct it recommends is unjustifiable by moral theory under the general conception of morality.

This is merely one example – the most frequently discussed one.

The Kantian project is to apply the generalization test to every proposed action-guide, and it may be that many human projects can be shown to be unjustifiable in this way. (Breaking the law, for example.)

Three Limitations

There are, however, three things that suggest that there are significant limitations on the generalization test.

A   One is the fact that Kant's original statement of it, and the commentary on it since, is couched in terms of an agent's intentions or will. Yet some moral arguments are apparently not about intentions in the requisite sense, even indirectly. Take judgments about ideals. If I say that I ought to be faithful, I might not be saying, even in part, that I *intend* to be faithful. I might merely be saying that it would be ideal if I were, or that I hope that I can be. If such a judgment is justifiable under the general conception then it must be generalizable. But it is hard to see how generalization in those cases might lead to incoherence. Suppose I recommend that everyone *desire* to be unfaithful. That does not appear to lead to the sort of contradiction that a false-promising *intention* leads to. In order to say that it does, we must assert that intentions are somehow necessarily imbedded in desires. That obscures, I think, an important distinction. If so, then the generalization test may be significantly limited.

B   A second limitation concerns the fact that in many cases both a given action-guide and its 'contrary' are generalizable. There is nothing internally incoherent with the generalization of 'I ought to cultivate a garden', for example. Nor with its contrary 'I ought *not* to cultivate a garden.' It is perfectly possible to *intend* it to be true (under normal circumstances) either that everyone gardens or that no one gardens. In such a case the generalization test does not yield a determinate result: As far as it is concerned, both gardening and not gardening are justifiable. But, of course, one of the two may still turn out to be impermissible, all things considered, and if one of the two is impermissible, its contrary is obligatory. If it is impermissible for me to garden, it is by definition obligatory for me *not* to garden. So any generalizable action-guide whose contrary is also generalizable may still turn out – all things considered –

to be either forbidden, required or permitted. The generalization test, in those cases, is a necessary but not a sufficient condition for determining the moral status of an act.

C The third limitation is that the generalization test is indecisive for most of the moral issues we actually consider – or at any rate, the issues we would be forced to consider if we stated our intentions carefully. Take the argument about promising again. It establishes that making all of one's promises falsely (or all of some special sort of them) cannot be justified. But it does not establish that every false promise is unjustifiable. For example, 'I ought to make a few false promises, at my discretion' can be generalized, and is just the sort of claim that leads to moral turmoil. There is no contradiction between

> v I make a few false promises at my discretion.

and

> vi All people make a few false promises at their discretion.

Further, the contrary action-guide, 'I ought not to make any false promises at my discretion' is also generalizable. It yields the descriptive projections

> vii I make no false promises at my discretion.

and

> viii No people make any false promises at their discretion.

And again there is no contradiction. The moral status of these guides is as yet indeterminate.

The possibility arises, then, that agents who formulate their action-guides carefully enough would never fail to pass the generalization test, and that the moral conflicts among such agents could be chaotic. I think this is in fact the case – that the situation with regard to discretionary false promising, for example, can be duplicated for any sort of act one can define.

This result is neither surprising nor discouraging, however. As I noted earlier, it is not plausible to think that *a priori* morality could constitute the whole of moral theory. So it is not surprising to find that the generalization test must be supplemented. Moreover, the generalization test does force a careful formulation of intentions, and it is a formulation that eliminates special pleading. To be justifiable, one's action-guides must be coherent general principles for the conduct of rational agents. And that is a significant result.

Procedural and Valuational Commitments

A second significant source for *a priori* moral theory is a pair of rebuttable presumptions − one a valuational rule and the other a procedural rule − derivable from the general conception of morality. They come from the fact that adopting the general conception as a well-defined enterprise commits us to adopting devices for getting provisional closure on the process of reasoned justification. Without closure devices, we cannot come to any conclusions 'all things considered'. The reason is obvious. Limited as we are, we cannot actually consider everything. So as long as we intend to get to any conclusions at all with our moral reasoning, we must take second best: procedural and valuational rules that determine when we have considered enough to allow us to draw at least provisional conclusions.

Many such closure rules are adopted *a posteriori* − as a result of trial and error. Sampling rules are a case in point. How large a sample is needed for a given inductive generalization? Should the sample be random or structured? One develops answers to these questions empirically. But there are at least two important closure rules that can be established *a priori*.

The Presumption of Equality

Reasoned argument often confronts the problem of assigning weights to competing considerations. We weigh the interests of one person against the interests of another, or weigh rights against short run social welfare, and so on. Decisions about the relevant weights are crucial, and often generate arguments that are complex and inconclusive − inconclusive in part because they themselves involve disputes about the weighting of competing considerations. I follow Carl Cohen's remarks (on pp. 264−5 of his book *Democracy*) to the effect that part of a solution emerges from the following line of argument:

1) Assume that we have only this one miserably insufficient reason for thinking A and B are equal in weight − namely, that they are the same in the sense that they are both morally relevant considerations. Things that are the same in one respect just might

be the same in another. 2) Assume we have just one similarly insufficient reason for thinking that A and B are *un*equal in weight – namely, that they are *different* considerations. Things that are different in one respect might be different in another.

3) Note, however, that we have no reason at all, in this case, for thinking that A might be (say) *double* the weight of B, or half the weight of B, or any other particular weight that is unequal to B's. 4) The choice is simply between assigning equal weights (for which we have some reason) and assigning some undefined *un*equal weights (for which we also have some reason). 5) But we cannot, with reason, take the latter option: it is indeterminate. There is an indefinitely large number of unequal weights we could assign. Ex hypothesi, we have no reason to pick any one of them over another (or over equality, for that matter). 6) Any use we make of A and B in a reasoned argument will entail assigning weights to them. 7) So, in terms of reasoned justification, we must assign equal weights. That is the only determinate choice for which we have any reason, however thin it may be.

So the rule is simply this: In cases where there is no reason to assign any given unequal weight to competing considerations, we must assign equal weight to them. Without special justification, then, no agent's interests or welfare outweighs any other's – and in general, no consideration in favor of an action-guide outweighs one against it. This rule is, of course, a rebuttable presumption – in the sense that if we ever have reason to think two things are of a given unequal weight, that reason (together with the general reason for thinking they might be unequal) would presumptively outweigh one general reason for regarding them as equal. (I say 'presumptively' because such an argument itself assumes that two reasons are 'heavier' than one – an assumption which is defeasible in the way just described for assigning weights generally.) Yet the presumption of equality can be an important tool – not only as a way of getting closure, but also as a way of locating the burden of proof. The burden of proof – at the level of *a priori* theory – is on the inegalitarian.

Ultimate justification

The second closure rule is a procedural one designed to deal with the following sort of skepticism about ultimate justification: The rules of the general conception are themselves subject to change.

And reasoned argument always threatens to involve an infinite regress — first by giving reasons for a conclusion, then reasons for those reasons, and so on. The skeptic's demand for an ultimate justification of a given moral judgment seems doomed to go unanswered. Like a child, the skeptic can continually ask 'Why?' to any set of reasons we give, and 'So what?' to any descriptions we offer of the rules of the game.

There is an *a priori* solution to the problem. That is, one can show that there is a *form* of moral argument, within the general conception, that does not allow the skeptic to raise the question of ultimate justification in a damaging way. At the level of *a priori* theory it is *only* a form; only a type of possible argument. But that is nonetheless an important result — at least if it turns out that the empirical part of moral theory can construct arguments of this form.

The idea is to provide a 'ground' for a given moral judgment rather than a 'proof' of it. *Grounding* a judgment is putting a non-arbitrary stop to the endless process of reason-giving — to the endless process of 'proving' the judgment. The distinction between a ground and a proof turns on the fact that an argument can have a rational starting point which is neither an arbitrary assumption nor a conclusion from prior evidence. It may instead be something quite different, as follows.

Consider the principle of non-contradiction. It is not an assumption in the sense of being a proposition whose truth one actively assumes, and it is not a proposition for which one ordinarily offers proofs. There are certain metaphysical inquiries in which it is said to be challenged or 'adopted', and there are axiomatizations of logic in which it is derived as a theorem. But in our ordinary reasoning we cannot seem to get around it or 'outside' it. We can write out its denial, formally, but we cannot imagine an instantiation of that form. The principle of non-contradiction can be challenged (formally) but it is not in any ordinary sense a proposition we choose to believe, or adopt as our own, or assume to be true.

Now if no reasons can be offered for rejecting a principle such as that, then it may be said to be *grounded*, though unproved, in the following sense. If a principle has not been assumed or adopted in the first place, then *a fortiori* it cannot have been arbitrarily assumed. And if there is no reason to reject it, then it is not, from a reasoned point of view, *wrong* to use it. At worst, it is only a matter of indifference to reason. The burden of proof is ultimately on the skeptic, not on the defender.

This sort of argument can be turned to the purposes of moral theory. If one can find certain features of life that are simply 'built-in' – just *there*, unchosen by us – and if there is no reason to change those features, then the consequences that flow from them may be said to be *grounded*, though not, in any ultimate sense, *proved*. I shall argue that our purposiveness, for example, is just such a 'built-in.' And the consequences that flow from it are grounded in that fact; they do not stand in need of the sort of 'ultimate' proof the skeptic asks for.

It should be noted, of course, that grounded judgments are always challengeable. (Some Eastern religious doctrines challenge the legitimacy of purposiveness and consciousness of self.) And such considerations must be taken seriously; they could in principle defeat the grounding procedure in a given case. But if they do not defeat it – if, that is, they give us only skeptical questions rather than reasons – then it is perfectly justifiable for us to continue to use the challenged feature of our lives (say, our purposiveness or self-consciousness) as a ground for the ultimate justification of moral judgments.

I've always wanted to live alone. In the high mountains, for instance, or in the desert. Loneliness doesn't make me ache the way it's supposed to.

Of course I've never really been alone, so maybe this is all just talk. Maybe I couldn't live the way I want, or wouldn't like it. Anyway, it's no accident I'm so tied down.

I ran away a lot when I was little. Not away away, just 'off'. My parents worried, and tracked me down. We came to terms when I was nine or ten, one summer in the Colorado mountains. They always rented the same big, old frame cabin for the month of July. It was high in the mountains, above 8000 feet, where the ground is granite gravel covered with pine needles. Rustic. No electricity or running water. A privy, and spring water from a tap about thirty yards away. A shower house that served twenty cabins was a hundred yards away. One side of it was for men, the other for women.

My memory is that the shower house had smooth, worn,

slat board floors everywhere inside, even in the shower stalls. That's probably not right, but I remember the steam, and the laughter of the adults calling to each other through the partition, and the smell of soap and wet wood.

My uncle and aunt stayed with us for two weeks in early July. He taught me how to get away. We carried buckets of water every morning, first to the women, so they could make breakfast, then to the place by the side porch where my father and my uncle stood in the sun to shave. Do your chores first, he said. Be conspicuous about helping the women. Announce your plans when people are busy. Be definite. Be cheerful. Never come home late. Follow those rules, he said, and the women will let you do anything you want, if you're nine or ten.

This was in the late forties. Men wore undershirts when they stood in the sun to shave, and some of them (my uncle, for one) still used straight razors.

Where I went that summer was on top of the moraine four hundred feet above and behind our cabin. I could see the whole front range from up there, the east face of Long's Peak, Flat Top, Mary's Lake, and Twin Sisters. In one place there was a clearing, and a pile of boulders. Flat, smooth surfaces. Handholds and cracks for climbing. When I stood on top of them I could be seen from the cabin. The rules were that I had to show myself on the hour, every hour, and signal when I was going to start down. Those rules required me to carry my grandfather's pocket watch. I liked that part.

What I did up there was think about living alone on top of a mountain, in a firewatch station. I worked it out in detail. Supplies, daily activities, emergencies. It worried me that the work was only seasonal. I tried to imagine perpetual summer, but that felt like cheating.

I suppose I did a lot of other things up there, but the thinking is almost all I remember. It ended badly. A young couple looking for the trail suddenly came around the corner of one of my boulders out onto the ledge where I sat watching the lake. They yelled in surprise and I was thrown out into confusion so high that I might as well have been spinning out toward the lake. No one had ever been on the ridge with me.

I don't remember the rest of it clearly. I showed them the trail, led them down it, and never went back.

There aren't any mountains in the part of Wyoming where we lived. There are only hiding places. Eventually I found a good one – an acre of thicket and scrub trees fastened among the low grassy hills around the town. When I was eleven I built a fort in the middle of it, in a place so dense with low branches and brush I had to crawl twenty yards to reach it. There were no rules about it, because no one else knew I went there.

What I did in my fort was read and think about the sea. The hills were something like the sea – endless and undulating, with no way to get up high enough to get out. It was a mistake to tell anybody about that hiding place, but I told a friend. He liked the fort, and the lookout post. (I wanted a good view of the county road that ran along the edge of the thicket. I didn't want any surprises.)

One Sunday afternoon we spotted a car parked on the road. We hadn't heard it come. It looked empty, and there was no one in sight outside of it. We thought about criminals on the run, because my friend's father was a state policeman. We went to have a look.

Hiding in the ditch on the driver's side we couldn't see anything, so we crossed the road twenty yards behind the car. The passenger's door was open, and we could see the top of a woman's head. She was lying on the seat, face up. Sleeping, we thought. Her eyes were closed. Then the car started suddenly. A man had appeared in the driver's seat. He drove furiously down the gravel road, with the passenger's door still open, and stopped again several hundred yards away on top of a small rise. Then he began to back the car slowly back down the rise toward us. We scrambled for the fort. By the time we had crawled back into it and climbed into the lookout post, the car was gone. My friend said he would have to tell his father about it, because it might be important. We were forbidden to go to the fort after that.

I think I'm putting this badly. Making it too solemn. It's all comic stuff of course, and for a long time I thought it was trivia. All my obsessions. All the images that have a hold on me. It was so clear, I thought, that I was really driven by the desire to be connected. Nothing else, I thought, could explain the way I've lived so tied down. It's only rational that I'd think about the other side. Escapist stuff. Parents tie you down, so run away. Marriage ties you down, so think about the mountains or the desert. Business ties you down so think about some solitary triumph, some life that can be made entirely alone. The astronaut adrift in interstellar space. That's all clear enough, trite enough, comic enough. Walter Mitty stuff.

Well, I'm thinking now it's not so clear. I'm thinking I should try to tell the story as if the fantasies were what held it together. As if the desire to be alone were what really drives me and the rest of it – the obligations and friends and family – are the escapes. It's hard to express the thought that might be behind it. People spoil things.

Here is what I mean. It's the sort of thing that scares me now. Suppose someone told you that every time he ever made love in his life – every time – he had the same daydream. Being alone. Sailing alone in a wide, warm sea. I used to smile at that sort of thing. I used to think it wasn't even interesting.

Teleological Tendencies

A third source for *a priori* moral theory is a teleological tendency built into the very nature of rational agency – specifically, into its purposive nature, when that is combined with the generalization rule and the presumption of equality. Purposiveness is a constitutive feature of the life of a rational agent, and the level of our achievement of our goals is one dimension of our well-being. Since we are constitutionally committed to achieving our own goals, it follows that we are constitutionally committed to pursuing this aspect of our welfare. Under the general conception of morality, however, we are also committed (logically) to considering the welfare of others. This produces a tendency, in practice, to improve aggregate welfare – a 'teleological tendency.' The argument is straightforward.

We are committed, under the general conception, to a justification procedure that in principle considers everything that could be a logically effective premise in a reasoned argument about what to do or be, *simpliciter*. The teleological tendency comes from the fact that any agent's concerns about my acts are logically relevant to my moral decision in just the way that my own concerns are. I am therefore committed to considering the welfare of others in my moral reasoning.

An example should make this clear. 1) Suppose I want to do something, and my wanting to do it counts as a reason under the general conception for my doing it. (Nothing hinges on my having this particular reason. The argument will go through for any reason one names.) 2) How will that be so? Under the pattern of moral argument used here, the answer is that there must be a rule that connects wants to action-guides. The argument pattern is this:

> *Rule*:   Other things being equal, one may do what one wants.
>
> *Fact*:   I want to do X.
>
> *Therefore*, I may do X (other things being equal).

3) But then the question is, why are wants connected to action guidance in this way? The answer is evident: getting what one wants is a good. It satisfies one's purposiveness, and that is by definition a good. Not getting what one wants is in this sense a bad thing. 4) The next question is, Why is an act's being good logically relevant to the argument? And the answer can be only that, under the general conception of morality, there is a rule such as the following: Other things being equal, one ought to do the things that are good. Preferences must correspond to values. 5) Now what is it, in this example, that makes a thing good? My wanting it. But if my wanting X gives X a value, then the wants of any similar agents in similar circumstances must have the same effect. (By the generalization rule.) So 6) if my doing X is in this sense good because its presence is something I want, and bad because its absence is something someone else wants, then there are two values that I must consider. My act 'has' whatever values it is given by people's wants. 7) The rule is, again, that I must do the things that are good. So any all-things-considered argument must take into consideration *every* value for a proposed act.

The same sort of argument applies to any concern agents have about their acts. If their own concerns (values, rights, ideals and so forth) are logically relevant to their decisions about their own acts, then a similar concern about that act, on the part of any relevantly similar agent, will also be logically relevant. The general conception of morality commits us to considering them all.

Further, unless I can give some sound reasoned argument for

holding that my own concerns about my acts outweigh the concerns of others about those same acts, the presumption of equality commits me to assigning all these considerations equal weights. It does not follow, merely from the fact that the act under consideration is my act, that my concerns about it will be more important, all things considered, than those of some other interested party. In fact, quite the opposite may be true – as when I have a trivial, fleeting desire to injure someone else in a way that would do serious damage. In the absence of evidence about which way the balance should tip, we must presume equal weight.

That much is enough to give moral theory an *a priori* teleological tendency in the direction of improving aggregate welfare. If each agent must consider the welfare of others under the presumption of equality, the result is *likely* to be an improvement in the overall level of welfare. But it is important to note that this *a priori* tendency is not just the utilitarian principle in disguise. The utilitarian principle requires us to *maximize* aggregate welfare. The principle argued for here, however, only requires us to consider all the values there actually are for what we propose to do or be.

Deontological Commitments

A fourth and final source of *a priori* moral theory is the self-consciousness that is characteristic of rational agents. In the same way that the purposiveness of agents generates a teleological tendency, their awareness of themselves as objects generates deontological commitments. The argument goes this way.

1) Rational agents are by definition conscious of themselves as entities distinct from other things. They are, after all, defined as capable of deliberation and choice. They deliberate about what *they themselves* should do, and that amounts to being aware of themselves as objects. 2) This self-awareness is, in turn, defined in part by an awareness of the boundaries of the self. Awareness of one's distinctness from other things is an awareness – however vague – of the limits beyond which things are no longer (parts of) oneself. These limits are the 'boundaries' of the self.

3) Boundaries are, in principle, either moveable or not, and they are either permeable or not. If moveable, the question is whether they *should* be moved. (Should one insist on more privacy?) If permeable, the question is under what conditions border crossings

will be regarded as violations of one's boundaries, and what is to be done about such violations. (Am I violated by a slap? Do I turn the other cheek?)

4) Answering those questions amounts to what can be called boundary-*keeping*. One is deciding whether or not to retain or 'guard' the boundaries one has. 5) Such boundary-keeping is unavoidable for rational agents. Of course, a boundary that is both immovable and impermeable requires no keeping because it raises no questions about possible changes. And it may be that agents have some such limits – some deep recesses that can neither be enlarged nor diminished nor breached. Be that as it may, agents certainly do have the power to *set* boundaries that are moveable and permeable – for example, by insisting on new limits for permissible intimacies. So agents are always, in principle, involved in boundary-keeping – at least by default. To decide not to set boundaries is to keep them as they are. To ignore the issue is to leave them as they are by default.

6) The boundary metaphor captures this central feature of rational agency: The emergence of one's self-consciousness is, in part, the emergence of a set of dispositions to protect, defend, open, close, contract and expand oneself with respect to things that are 'other'. We do not, initially, 'adopt' these dispositions or assume their justifiability. We simply come equipped with them. 7) If there is no reason to change our dispositional equipment – no argument to show that it is unjustifiable – then it is not wrong to keep it. At worst it can only be a matter of indifference to reason. 8) If there is no reason to change the way we act out the dispositions we have, then it is not wrong to act them out as we do. 9) To act out our boundary-dispositions is to act deontologically. It is, in effect, to permit and require certain things of others. So we do *in fact* come equipped, as it were, with a set of deontological commitments – the things that our boundary-dispositions dispose us to permit and require of others.

10) The next step in the argument is to note that it is the task of moral theory to consider whether the things that we *in fact* permit and require can be justified – to consider whether there is, in fact, any reason to change them. And as we have seen, there are two powerful *a priori* restrictions on what can be justified: our deontological judgments must be generalizable; and the justific-

ation for them must operate in terms of the presumptive equality of the deontological commitments of others.

11) The final step for the time being is to see what follows, *a priori*, from the foregoing considerations. As it turns out, not much of a substantive nature does follow.

A Note first that it does *not* follow from any of this that agents will have the *same* rights and duties. For one thing, there is no guarantee, *a priori*, that agents will do the same sort of boundary keeping. Indeed, it is clear from experience that they do not. Some people are much more demanding than others, much less 'open' to interference, and much more self-protective. Of course, the mere *fact* that an agent keeps a certain set of boundaries does not entail that those boundaries are justifiable. But they might be. And there is no reason to think, *a priori*, that different sets of boundaries might not turn out to be equally justifiable. It might, for example, be a matter of indifference to reason whether one is withdrawn and zealously self-protective or outgoing and unguarded.

B Note also that it is not yet clear what degree of dominance these deontic commitments, if justified, will have over competing values or ideals. By definition, requirements take precedence over permissions, goals and ideals. But we commonly hold that there are differences of degree among rights and obligations. Some are thought to be relatively trivial; others are of the first importance. The same is true of values and ideals, and important considerations of these sorts are often thought to outweigh individual rights. In national emergencies, for example, we often suspend some civil rights. It is not yet clear what system of priorities on such matters is defensible.

C Finally, there is a more positive result, but it too is limited in an important way. It concerns the coherence of our system of deontic commitments. Start with the true but trivial: moral theory, since it rests on reasoned justification, cannot justifiably contain contradictions. So, *a priori*, it can never be the case that I have a right not to be murdered (meaning that you have a duty not to murder me) and at the same time that your murdering me is permissible. It is also true, however, and not quite so trivial, that moral requirements must be compossible, subject to a significant limitation. The argument goes this way.

Suppose the following requirement is justified – say by a promise that I made.

ix I am morally required to be in Roanoke now.

Suppose further that part of what we intend to do by imposing that requirement is to make its descriptive projection 'I am in Roanoke now' *true*. Then suppose that I have foolishly made a second promise (both were some months ago) which yields

x I am morally required to be in Palo Alto now.

Its projection, which we intend to make true, is 'I am in Palo Alto now.' Clearly, since I cannot be in two widely separated places at once, we cannot coherently intend both that I be in Roanoke and simultaneously that I be in Palo Alto. There cannot coherently be any conflicts of requirements in this sense. (There can be conflicts in other senses, however. See below.)

In short, moral theory must have a set of priority rules that resolves all such conflicts. In the case of conflicting promises, for example, we might rule that the second one is void. (Let the law on bigamy be the model.) But notice that this is a purely *formal* result. Nothing follows *a priori* about which priority rules to adopt. All we can conclude, *a priori*, is that there must be some, and that they must resolve all of the cases in which contradictory intentions seem to be justified. [Note: To the extent that the priority rules do not resolve all conflicts, they are theoretically unsatisfactory. But given the complexity of the task, complete satisfaction is too much to ask for. See the discussion in the 'Reasons for Reciprocity' section of Chapter Three.]

The reference to intentions in this argument brings out a limitation, however. The limitation comes from the fact that it is not *necessarily* self-contradictory to impose impossible requirements on agents. This is so because the point of imposing a requirement need not be to have it fulfilled. The point may be to create a situation in which an agent must necessarily fail, morally. (Those of us with Calvinist upbringings are all too familiar with such requirements.) So if the point is to make me fail, then requiring me to be in two places at once will certainly do it. It may be perverse, but it is not self-contradictory, and such perversity cannot be ruled out *a priori*.

Summary of *a priori* Results

Some of the moral theory that can be deduced *a priori* from the general conception, then, is this: The very notion of reasoned justification gives us the form of an answer to the problem of ultimate justification – namely, the grounding procedure that puts the burden on the skeptic to show why existing dispositions and values are not justifiable. It gives us the generalization test; and it gives us the rebuttable presumption of equality. The notion of rational agency yields a teleological tendency to improve aggregate welfare, through the logical requirement that others' welfare always be considered on a presumptively equal footing with one's own. And it yields the result that the requirements we impose, if we intend them to be fulfilled, must be compossible.

A few substantive results can be forced *a priori*, then, but by themselves are rather meager. To reach the matters of most importance, the arguments must be enriched by reference to experience. It is not that *a priori* theory is unimportant. On the contrary, it is necessary – defining as it does some criteria any moral principle must meet. Those criteria are indispensable to the argument for reciprocity.

CHAPTER 3
Reciprocity

Gifts and goods pervade our lives. So do evils and injuries. Everywhere, in every society of record, there is a norm of reciprocity about such things. Returns are expected: good for good received, hostility for hostility. The details differ strikingly from place to place, time to time, and every society is profuse with forms. There are rituals of gift giving, unspoken understandings between lovers, patterns of family life, expectations among friends, duties of fair play, obligations of citizenship, contracts – all understood as reciprocal. There is an intricate etiquette for it all, and it is connected (both in theory and in practice) to prudence, self-interest, altruism, basic human needs, social welfare, notions of desert and duty, justice and fairness.

Much moral theory about reciprocity is misplaced. It tries to justify *acts* or *rules* of reciprocation – to justify them directly by reference to their utility, or their obligatoriness. It then stumbles over the most fundamental issue: What can there be, in the very act of giving a gift, that requires a commensurate return on the part of the recipient? How can a benefit, *unasked for* by the recipients, obligate them to make a return? The justification for such 'noncontractual' obligations is obscure, yet it is the crux of the matter. We do not need the notion of reciprocity to get an account of voluntary agreements. If it is to have a useful place in moral theory at all it will be for an account of nonvoluntary obligations – the kind we acquire whether we ask for them or not. Ethnographers, social anthropologists, historians, and sociologists report in unison that people everywhere do 'feel' such obligations. In particular, they feel them toward benefactors. The mere recognition of a benefit seems to generate a sense of obligation to repay. That sense of obligation may be oppressive or exhilarating, the source of resentment or delight, of volatile social practices or stable ones. But it is a pervasive feature of human social life. It will not go away.

Injustice will not go away either, of course. The persistence of a practice does not make it morally defensible, and explanations for it (claims, for example, that it is a structural feature of the human psyche) are not justifications. But there is a justification for reciprocity, from what I shall call virtue theory – from an account of the traits of character people ought to have, all things considered. I shall argue that we ought to be *disposed*, as a matter of moral character, to make reciprocity a moral obligation.

Thesis

Consider the following maxims.

1 Good received should be returned with good.
2 Evil received should not be returned with evil.
3 Evil received should be resisted.
4 Evil done should be made good.
5 Returns and restitution should be made by the ones who have received the good or done the evil, respectively.
6 Returns and restitution should be fitting and proportional.
7 Returns should be made for the good *received* – not merely for good accepted or requested.
8 Reciprocation, as defined by 1–7, should be made a moral obligation.

The thesis of what follows is that we ought to be disposed, as a matter of moral character, to act in the ways outlined by those maxims. In outline, the argument will be as follows:

> Premise 1): Normally formed human beings, in the normal course of their maturation into moral agents, develop a disposition to reciprocate.

That is an empirical claim, and it is restricted in two important ways. First, it is only the claim that agents have *some* version or other of a disposition to reciprocate, not that they all have the same version. Second, it is a claim about results only. Nothing in the argument hinges on a particular hypothesis about the origin of the disposition – e.g., whether it is 'structural' or learned.

Premise 2):   There are good reasons, under the general conception of morality, for concluding that moral agents ought to have some sort of disposition to reciprocate, and there is no countervailing reason for concluding that they ought not to have one.

Premise 3):   It follows, from 1) and 2), that if any existing reciprocity disposition is justifiable under the general conception, then it is also *grounded*, as that notion is defined in Chapter Two.

Premise 4):   One version of the reciprocity disposition is justifiable under the general conception – namely, the version described by the maxims above.

Premise 5):   Contrary versions of the reciprocity disposition – that is, ones whose maxims deny any of the maxims above – are not justifiable under the general conception.

Premise 6):   It follows, from 4) and 5), that the version of the reciprocity disposition described by the maxims above is the one agents ought (morally) to have.

Premise 7):   The justification given for 4), 5), and 6) implies that, under the general conception, the reciprocity disposition as defined by the maxims above constitutes a part of excellence in moral agents *qua* moral agents. That is, the justification offered for reciprocity is given in terms of what one needs in order to become a moral agent and to flourish *as* a moral agent – to become and be a good 'thing' of that type.

Conclusion: The disposition to reciprocate, as defined by the maxims above, is a moral virtue.

That bald outline may suggest a degree of certainty not to be found in the arguments to follow. Those arguments – like most in moral philosophy – are necessarily tentative at many points. Some of this is due to tentativeness in the empirical data on which the arguments depend, and some of it is due to considering reciprocity in isolation from other virtues, as well as in isolation from the more purely teleological and deontological aspects of moral theory. So the arguments here will *support*, rather than 'establish,' the propositions in the outline. But the support is very strong, and it puts a heavy burden of proof on any moral theory that does not include reciprocity as a central element.

In 1961, when I was 30, I went to the rehab center in Georgia. I'd gotten worse again, and it didn't look as though there was going to be another remission. Couldn't walk at all. Spasms very bad. Couldn't push my own wheelchair. Could barely feed myself. I thought it was going to be that way or worse until the end.

The Center looked like the campus of an expensive private college. Two hundred acres in the country, the major buildings arranged in quadrangles connected by colonnades, housing for the professional staff on the grounds. There was a golf course for the staff, tennis courts, a swimming pool, and a stable – all at a discreet distance from the hospital, and off limits to patients. There was a carillon that chimed the hours and was played on Sunday mornings, shaded lawns, and a quiet dining room with whitecoated waiters. The misery inside the buildings seemed unreal from the lawns.

Connor stayed with me. She introduced herself to people as my sister-in-law, which was almost true. We didn't explain further, and weren't asked to, at least not directly. The southerners didn't press for answers that could raise matters of honor. Northerners, and midwesterners like ourselves, thought they already knew what they needed to know.

Connor rented a small house on the grounds and I spent most evenings there. She found people we liked among the staff, and patients' families, and gave dinner parties to keep our spirits up. Mornings she played golf, or rode, or read. In the afternoons she did business – things for our farms back home. I don't know what she did at night, when I was back in the hospital. She said she had trouble sleeping. I know she drank too much, and lost too much weight. A bag of bones, she said. Bones and breasts. Freckles and red hair.

We didn't like the South. We didn't like my illness, and my melancholy, and her anger. We didn't like our situation.

Our situation was that my brother had been married to Connor's sister, but that they were no longer civil. Connor and I, on the other hand, couldn't get free. The more divided they became, the more we were forced into their parts. From birth they had been decreed to be the perfect lovers, the political alliance between the two families. Connor and I, however, had been allowed to grow up despising each other – to adopt the contempt our fathers felt for each other rather than their passion for merger. There was still some of that childish hostility in us, but we bore the weight now. We had the farms, and would get the rest eventually. David and Elizabeth were divorced. That disqualified them from family life. Connor and I were merely sinners, incorrigibles, eccentrics. We hadn't done anything unpardonable.

That was the situation. What we didn't like about it was the dishonesty, begun in Connor's bedroom after her sister's wedding. Connor thought she herself was pregnant. She was being tough about it, and secretive, but she needed an ally against her parents, and against the child's father. We agreed on a strategy. It wasn't needed, finally, because it turned out Connor wasn't pregnant after all. But we kept the alliance, and when we found, little by little, that we were good at intrigue, good at making money, good at taking the families by surprise, we went on the offensive. The Second-Born-Usurpers. Cheerful, harmless deceptions. Then David and Elizabeth started to go sour. Then Connor and I became lovers. Then our harmless intrigues succeeded. David was out. We were in – both of us, as we had planned, because we refused to get married. Then my illness. It was all a sickening shambles.

What we didn't like about the South was the open segregation and concealed passions. The Colored Only signs. The explicit Rightful Place arrangements. The stares of the whites, the averted eyes of the blacks. We were used to chafing against our own forms. They were just as rigid but not (we thought) as oppressive, not as gratuitously insulting, and not as dangerous. In our world the hostilities were more evident than the signs, and we could feel less guilty. We were not deep thinkers.

My roommate was a sullen paraplegic from Atlanta. Robert. Twenty-five, married, with two small children. A lineman who'd broken his back in a stupid accident on the job. It had been his fault, as he told the story, and his offhandedness about it made me furious. He wasn't interested in my blameless disease and I wasn't interested in telling him about it. He just sucked on his resentments: My catholicism, my education, my money, Yankees who stirred up trouble, and fancy breeders who called themselves farmers. I refused to use his name. Everybody called him Buster, he said. I called him Robert. Or sometimes Lineman Bob.

Lineman Bob and I didn't have much to say to each other. When the conversation turned away from his physical problems he went mute. When Connor came to get me in the evenings he glowered. He was self-absorbed, obsessed with his upper body strength, tormented by the loss of his sexual powers. (Connor was interested in that part.) He cried sometimes late at night after the curtain was pulled between our beds.

When I turned on the television, he usually left the room. He didn't want to hear about freedom rides, or the Kennedys, or anything else the network news might show. The day-shift orderlies, all of them black, would come in when he left. Twos and threes would stand near the doorway, or make work for themselves in the room while they watched the noon news. They never spoke to me about it.

The day shift worked very hard. Therapy schedules were grueling, and the rule was that patients were not allowed to waste their energy getting to and from the tanks, tables, gyms, pools, and brace shops. The orderlies had to get us there on time and take us back to rest between sessions. Pushboys, they were called, when they did that part of the job. And there were constant changes of clothing. T-straps for the pool, shorts and shirts for the weight room, T-straps again for the stretching tables, full armor (braces, clothing) for functional therapy. They did all that in addition to the usual medical chores.

Connor's dinner parties were on Saturdays. I was too tired

for anything like that during the week, and on Sundays we wanted a private meal. A few times she invited patients, but usually not. The old polios were all right – cheerful, at least – but in general other patients depressed me. Depression made Connor angry.

There was one I liked. John – the one I roomed with later. His wife Joan came down from Raleigh most weekends, and Connor got along well with her. We would have had them to dinner more often, but it was too hard for John – or rather for everyone else. He was a quadriplegic, and getting his motorized wheelchair into Connor's cramped little house was an ordeal.

He had been a surgeon before his accident. He didn't want to talk about anything connected to medicine, and neither did I. Neither of us had to explain. We talked money, mostly, because he was thinking about how he might make a living in investments. Joan asked me to try to persuade him to stay in medicine – to teach or write – but I didn't want to raise the issue with him.

I don't know what the women talked about. Connor, as I said, was interested in certain medical problems – details she couldn't find in the Center's library. Joan was a nurse, and married to a quad, so maybe they talked shop. I don't know.

One night, about two o'clock, I heard a woman whispering with Lineman Bob. On the other side of the curtain. I'm sure it was Connor.

After I moved in with John I went into remission. Inexplicable. Spasms diminished to tremors, muscle control came back, first in my arms and then in my legs. It was gradual, and I was very weak at first. The therapy changed and intensified. People were friendlier. My mood changed to wary relief. I got interested in the farms again, and took the double load off Connor. I helped John make some money.

The first time I walked alone to Connor's house, and sat in a normal chair for dinner, she cried with pleasure. She promised not to be so angry. She promised not to drink so much.

We got out of there. That's the story.

Reciprocity is a complex notion. The account here will reflect that fact in the wide assortment of arguments it uses. But complex arguments are not necessarily subtle or profound. And in fact, at bottom, each of the arguments here is quite straightforward. The subtlety, if there is any, is in arranging them so as to make the overall justification clear.

Moral Agents as a Type

Moral theory about the virtues begins with description: a description of the characteristic capacities, abilities, propensities, and activities of moral agents *qua* moral agents. Call that a *type description*. The purpose of this first step is to lay the groundwork for judgments about what counts as being good as a moral agent — being an excellent individual of that type. The virtues will be the traits necessary for, or productive of such excellence, subject to the constraints of moral theory generally.

Getting an accurate, *comprehensive* type-description for moral agents would be a vast undertaking. Mercifully, only a small part of it is relevant here. Only one trait (reciprocity) is being considered, and only a few of the things typical of moral agents are directly relevant to its justification as a virtue. Some of the relevant factors have already been discussed: e.g., the purposiveness of moral agents and their boundary-keeping activity. Further, the general constraints imposed by moral theory have been discussed: the generalization rule and the presumption of equality; the teleological tendency and the 'rules of morality'. Those things will control, in part, what can be justified as a virtue. If a given trait involves an agent's having intentions that cannot coherently be generalized, for example, then that trait will not be justifiable under the general conception. It will not be a virtue. Similarly, if it arbitrarily fails to satisfy the presumption of equality, or the teleological tendency, or the purposiveness and boundary-keeping activities of agents, it will not be a virtue. Much of the argument of this chapter will be devoted to showing that reciprocity, as defined by the maxims above, is justifiable in the respects just mentioned.

But in addition, there are these further features of our lives as moral agents that help to justify reciprocity as a virtue: There is the existence of a universal social norm concerning reciprocity, and there is the fact that reciprocity is psychologically linked to certain primary goods. [A primary good is a state or object or disposition that is necessary (logically, physically, or psychologically) to the conduct of rational agents as such – that is, to deliberation and choice, or to goal satisfaction *per se*, or to boundary-keeping *per se*.] The primary goods linked to reciprocity are equilibrium, self-esteem, and reliable expectations.

Exchange and the Norm of Reciprocity

Social life is thick with exchanges – transactions that involve, for each party, both receipts and disbursements. Some of these exchanges are economic; others concern things that the parties are unwilling to treat as commodities. (Acts of love, for example.) For all of these exchanges, in all societies of record, there is apparently a norm of reciprocity, the form of which can be stated thus: Good is to be returned for good, but not necessarily for evil.

What is universal is only this vague form. Societies differ markedly in their norms about retaliation, for example, so it is not possible to say that the form includes something like 'Evil must (or must not) be returned for evil.' And there are striking differences as well in how various cultures have worked out matters of proportionality (think of the potlatch), voluntariness (i.e., what one's obligations are if one did not ask for a given benefit), and the type and directness of the required return. (Consider the highly ritualized, roundabout character of the Kula exchange in the Trobriand Islands.)

In short, what is universal is merely exchange under some sort of requirement that good be given for good received. Other considerations are needed to give definition to the requirement.

> *Note* The norm of reciprocity is not equivalent to the Golden Rule – found in Confucian, Talmudic and New Testament texts. That rule concerns more than exchanges, for one thing. It proposes a criterion for initiatives one might take: Do to others only what you would have them do to you.

Equilibrium and the Norm of Proportionality

Primary goods are the things necessary for the life of a rational agent as such. Equilibrium – as defined here – is one of the primary goods, and it is linked to reciprocity.

Human life is possible only within the ambit of a tremulous balance of physical conditions. The homeostatic mechanisms that control body temperature are a good example. Within a certain range of ambient temperatures, and a range of internal conditions as well, these mechanisms keep body temperature at non-destructive levels. They balance certain internal states (e.g., the flow of blood to the extremities) against ambient temperature and body conditions. The result is not static body temperature, but rather oscillations within a certain range. Within that range, one's body temperature is in equilibrium.

There are similar equilibrium mechanisms at the level of consciousness. Some of them are reflexive (e.g., adrenaline surges in response to fear). Others are more or less under conscious control (e.g., various psychological 'defense mechanisms'). In any case they function to preserve the balance of internal conditions under which consciousness itself, and various states of consciousness, are possible.

Finally, and more to the point here, social exchanges are governed by equilibrium preserving dispositions. We soon learn that we cannot, as a matter of fact, get what we want from others (sustenance, love, freedom) without giving something back. Even infants have a crude, faltering awareness of how to please, and what connection that has to getting what they want. By the time we are aware of ourselves as moral beings, the disposition to reciprocate – to sustain the sort of equilibrium necessary for productive social intercourse – is deeply ingrained.

I am, of course, describing the course of (statistically) normal human development. Some children, for whatever reason, do not acquire the disposition. They may, like the autistic, be unable to return the attention of others. Or they may, like some severely abused children, give more and more to the very people who give them the least. But those are statistically abnormal states – described by those who do such describing as pathological states.

The point here is that in a crude form, the disposition to reciprocate is in fact acquired in the course of normal human development. I say 'in crude form' because all that can be said about this 'normal' disposition – that is, all that is common to the remarkably diverse versions of it found in the normal range – is merely a tendency to expect to get and give good, roughly in proportion to the good one gives and gets. People may hope for more (something for nothing), or fear getting less. They may define very narrowly the range of those to whom, and from whom, reciprocity is expected. (That is one way of characterizing a 'criminal' disposition.) People may think that it is inappropriate to respond with the same *type* of good. (An example is the so-called slave mentality, in which slaves are said to feel that masters can only be 'repaid' by obedience.) All of these are variants of the disposition to reciprocate, as it is connected to the primary good of sustaining social equilibrium. If there is some reason to think it a good disposition to have, and no countervailing reason to think it a bad thing to have, then it is not wrong (under the general conception of morality) to have it. It is grounded.

Self-Esteem and the Norm of Restitution

Once the disposition to reciprocate is acquired, it gets linked with the need for self-esteem. This is not a logical necessity, but it seems to be a psychological one. And it adds a further feature to the disposition: the need for restitution. The connection is this.

It is commonly observed by psychologists, and confirmed by everyday experience, that a sense of self-worth is psychologically necessary for a productive life. ('Productive' is defined here as neutrally as possible. It refers to goal fulfillment in general, not any special sort of goal fulfillment.) Low self-esteem correlates directly with depression, and depression correlates with the inability to deliberate, choose and act. Low self-esteem is not the only cause of depression, and through it, of psychic paralysis. Nor is any given level of self-esteem sufficient for a productive life. But it does seem to be a necessary condition. That is, there is some vague and variable threshold below which the lack of self-esteem induces a paralysis that defeats any enterprise an agent can construct.

The sources of self-esteem are, roughly, the attitudes of others and the extent to which people believe they meet their own standards of excellence. Both of these sources are connected to reciprocity. Once the disposition to reciprocate is acquired, and becomes a socially important equilibrium device for social intercourse, acting it out becomes crucial to self-esteem. Others expect it to be acted out, and an agent's failure to do so diminishes others' sense of his worth. Agents who have the disposition will expect to act it out, and failure to do so – failure to live up to their own standards – will damage their self-esteem. The need for self-esteem thus reinforces any existing disposition to reciprocate.

The desire to make restitution for the harm one has done is intimately connected to all of this. We soon learn (again, in the normal course of development) that we will suffer – in others' eyes and consequently in our own – if we do not make amends. By the time we reach moral maturity, some sort of norm of restitution is built into our inventory of dispositions. In the absence of good reason to abandon it, we have a ground for this further aspect of the disposition to reciprocate.

Expectations and the Norm of Enforcement

As social intercourse approaches chaos, productive life (for rational agents) approaches impossibility. In order to deliberate, plan, choose and carry out our intentions we require some assurances as to the conduct of those around us. We require reliable expectations as to the general nature of their behavior – expectations about what sorts of initiatives they are likely to take, how many they are likely to take, how much they are likely to respond to our own behavior.

Notice that it is not uniformity or constancy that we require in the conduct of others. It is only predictability – and not exact predictability at that. It is enough to know the general range of possible outcomes. But we must know at least that general range if we are to carry out our projects. Given uncertainty about how others will act if their conduct is uncontrolled or uncoordinated, we have a powerful motive for enforcing at least some fundamental norms. And in fact, in the course of normal human development we acquire dispositions that amount to norms of enforcement. We often coerce compliance with what we believe to be justifiable requirements on others. We act somewhat less coercively to get compliance with norms that fall short of being requirements. We often do not accept, passively, what we believe to be evil in the conduct of others. We resist it, or avoid it, or retaliate. There are vast differences in these enforcement dispositions across cultures and even within large, complex societies. But by the time we come of age, morally, we have them. If there is no reason to alter or eliminate them, then it is not wrong to have them.

What we need now are some reasons for thinking that such a disposition is a good one – and for thinking that the particular version of reciprocity outlined at the beginning of the chapter is the best one.

Moral Imperialism

OBJECTION: There is a disturbing arrogance about this project – about trying to go on to specify *in detail* what form of reciprocity everyone ought to exhibit. Social exchanges are always deeply embedded in a particular cultural context. It is that context from which they draw most of their social significance. It is the context that determines what counts as an appropriate return. Surely anthropology teaches us the foolishness (and the horrors) of wrenching a practice from one culture and trying to impose it on the patterns of life in another. (Consider recent efforts to introduce bottle feeding formula in some developing nations.) No doubt there is some sort of norm of reciprocity in every culture, but the idea that there could be a particular *version* of it that is best for every culture is absurd. For example: Societies differ markedly in the extent to which their fundamental ritual exchanges are competitive. Think of the potlatch among some Pacific Coast North American Indians. Compare that to the ritual gift giving at Christmas in our culture. Then compare both of those practices to the round-robin Kula exchange in the Trobriand Islands. Each of those practices is embedded in a rich tradition that has great significance for social life in its culture. It is preposterous to believe that there is some lofty vantage point from which we can survey them all, isolated from their social significance for a particular culture, and say, 'This one should be adjusted so, and that one should be abandoned in favor of another.'

REPLY: First, it is no part of this project to isolate the details of reciprocity from the social contexts in which they operate. Moral judgments under the general conception are to be made all things considered, and the social significance of a practice in its full particularity – what other things stand or fall with it, for example – is obviously a matter of moral concern. That is part of the reason for the tentativeness of the arguments to follow. They support the justifiability of a certain *schematic* version of reciprocity. They do not specify the details (e.g., what particular goods may be substituted for others). And even the schematic version is, in principle, subject to revision – both on the basis of considerations drawn from other parts of moral theory, and on different assumptions about the human condition. If, for example, the conditions of human life with respect to the scarcity of resources were to change dramatically, then so might the virtues. But the arguments here assume the general outlines of the existing world – a world, for example, in which scarcity is at least a threat for us all, and we are not omnibenevolent. So, second, within the existing conditions, it is plausible to hold that the basic human needs and wants to which reciprocity is addressed are common to all moral agents. Agents are, after all, *similar* as well as different. If they were not, they could not intelligibly be considered a *type*. The project here is to define, schematically, the elements of reciprocity that would be ideal for beings of that type. That project is analogous to defining some ideal of nutrition for human beings generally. It would be absurd to specify particular recipes, but it is not absurd to specify certain schematic constraints. No doubt many societies thrive, and many individuals in them flourish, with less than ideal versions of reciprocity – e.g., ones that include retaliation, for example. But the same can be said for societies in which disabling nutritional diseases are epidemic. *Other things equal*, surely it would be better to eliminate those diseases. Just so, it would be best (other things equal) for moral agents *qua* moral agents to cultivate the version of reciprocity argued for here.

OBJECTION: Extraordinary. The medical model of moral philosophy. The moral philosopher as mental hygienist. That certainly has unpleasant associations. And it reveals the poverty of the whole project. There are circumstances under which we should *not* force nutritional ideals onto a people's pattern of life. (Think again of the bottle feeding case.) Likewise for their pattern of reciprocal exchanges.

REPLY: Certainly. But that does not mean that we are unable to *specify* an ideal in each case, or that it is unimportant to *know* the ideal. It simply means that other considerations sometimes justifiably crowd out efforts to pursue the ideal.

OBJECTION: This analogy is specious as well as distasteful. People's nutritional needs, after all, are physiologically *fixed* in a way that their social and psychological needs are not. People can be conditioned into virtually any pattern of behavior – virtually any set of *felt* needs and wants. They need not ever develop the characteristics of moral agents in terms of which virtue theory here operates. So at best the arguments here are only for an ideal relevant to a pattern of life we have already decided (via our cultural conditioning) to adopt. Why adopt it? is the prior question.

REPLY: The arguments here are for an ideal relevant to a pattern of life that normally formed human beings in fact *exhibit* as they develop under the very wide range of 'normal' conditions – and in fact under (almost?) all existing abnormal conditions as well. No doubt we could, in principle, pursue a conditioning regime for children that would prevent their development into moral agents – a regime that would extinguish every vestige of their teleological and deontological behavior, for example. But we should be clear about how huge an effort that would be. (One wants to say monstrous, but leave that aside for the moment.) Surely the burden of proof is on anyone who would propose adopting such a regime, and surely that burden of proof has not (cannot?) be met. Until it is, there is nothing arbitrary about noticing the characteristics of what *exists*, describing its virtues, and then looking for arguments *against* recommending those virtues. If no countervailing arguments are forthcoming, then the virtues so described are grounded. It will be my contention, in what follows, that a particular version of the disposition to reciprocate can in fact be justified.

Material For the Arguments

Anything that is justifiable under the general conception of morality will (presumptively) exhibit the teleological tendency described in the previous chapter. That is, it will tend to increase aggregate goal satisfaction. This is a rebuttable presumption, drawn from the *a priori* requirements of generalization and presumptive equality, as they operate to produce moral theory about the purposiveness of rational agents. Without special justification, then, anything that tends to *reduce* aggregate goal satisfaction is *not* justifiable, other things being equal.

Further, the valuation rules of the general conception require that more of a good be preferred to less of it (again, other things being equal). So if one version of reciprocity tends to promote more aggregate good than another, it is the version theory must take, *ceteris paribus*.

There is a similar opening for argument with regard to the deontic commitments the general conception generates. Moral theory requires that an agent's boundary-keeping be generalizable, and operate with a presumption of equality concerning the boundaries kept by all other agents. The deontic demands agents make in keeping their boundaries need not be uniform, but they must form a compossible set of requirements and permissions. That is, sets that fall short of compossibility are theoretically unsatisfactory. But given the complexity of human life, the density of human population, and the velocity of human activity, getting a moral theory that fully satisfies the compossibility requirement – satisfies it with mathematical precision – is an unlikely prospect. Conflict *reduction*, however, is certainly part of the task of moral theory. And it generates the following justification principle: Anything that generates deontic conflicts is presumptively unacceptable, whereas anything that harmonizes deontic claims, or tends to reduce conflict, is justifiable, *ceteris paribus*. Note that this is again only a rebuttable presumption. If it can be shown that some claims are more weighty than others, a principle that increases conflict among low-level claims might be preferable to one that merely reduces the sheer number of conflicts.

Several empirical realities, mentioned in the preceding chapter, also provide material for the arguments. Moral theory under the general conception recommends courses of conduct that can be given a reasoned justification by and for rational agents. Even if it recommends that agents ought to act impulsively, or unthinkingly, or spontaneously – indeed, even if it recommends self-annihilation – moral theory must *first* recommend what is necessary for the development of the kind of rational agency that makes such 'opting out' possible *as the act of a rational agent*. It must, in short, recommend the sorts of social interactions necessary for the development of rational agency.

Further, given the multiplicity of human projects in competition for scarce resources, moral theory is faced with a severe conflict-management problem. Other things being equal, things that increase such conflict are unacceptable; things that reduce such conflict are justifiable.

And finally, there are the difficult second-level problems generated by passions that do not square with reasoned judgments about what the passions ought to be. Dispositions that reduce such conflicts are also preferable, *ceteris paribus*, to those that do not.

Acting in Character

If *reciprocating* is justifiable, then a *disposition* to reciprocate is also justifiable. Exchanges come thick and fast, and people often expect spontaneity. ('If you have to think about it, don't bother.') In all of this, we need the kind of speed and reliability and ease that only can be had by acting in character. Acting on principle is not enough. We ought to be *disposed* to act on it. That seems secure enough not to need further argument.

Elements of Reciprocity

I turn now to arguments for each element of the proposed disposition.

1 Good received should be returned with good

More precisely: We ought to be disposed to return good for the good we get from agents who are trying to produce benefits for us. The reasons are not hard to find.

For one thing, reciprocal exchanges (of good for good) are typically a potent source of pleasure in themselves. That is, the mere transactions are a source of pleasure, independently of how highly the participants prize the things that are exchanged. (We often mean it when we say it's the thought that counts.) Even infants seek reciprocal transactions and delight in them for their own sake. Characteristic sorts of infant–adult interactions – various sorts of hand play, vocal responses, gesture matching, and hiding games

– illustrate the point. By all evidence, infants actively seek such interactions, just for the immediate pleasure of them. And it is clear that the same sort of behavior is typical of human beings of every later age. The games may change, or at any rate become more subtle and complex. (Think of smiling.) But the point is that taking pleasure in returns of good for good is typical of us. Of course a wide variety of things can prevent or dilute the pleasure. Personal 'cost' is a factor, as is timing, satiation, the history of a particular relationship, and matters of etiquette. But the same is true of other pleasures. That does not compromise the point that such pleasures are characteristic of human life.

The next thing to note is that the pleasure we take in reciprocal exchanges is enormously fecund. By prompting us to act reciprocally, it generates many of the conditions under which the sustained pleasures of social relationships are possible. It is therefore an instrumental good.

The reciprocal transactions themselves, moreover, are instrumental necessities in our lives. Whether the frame of reference is the development of initial social attachments between parents and infants, or the development of friendships, good working relationships, or common decency and civility, the reciprocal element is a crucial factor. Indeed, as the studies of blind infants bring out starkly, it is a crucial factor in cognitive, affective, and social development *per se* – as well as in the development of a self-concept. Blind infants struggle to act reciprocally, but do so in ways that are difficult for sighted adults to 'read'. If the adults who care for the infant are unable to read the infant's behavior correctly, the results are tragic – a self-fulfilling prophecy of autism or retardation for the child. (See the references in the scholium.)

Strictly, of course, *taking pleasure* in reciprocal exchanges for their own sake is not necessary for prompting the sort of reciprocal behavior we need for our development. It will suffice if we are simply *disposed* to return good for good, with whatever affect prompts others, in particular situations, to take part. Taking pleasure in it all belongs to the virtue of conviviality, rather than to reciprocity. (See Chapter Four.) So here I shall simply state things in terms of bare necessities. As follows:

We all need help – in becoming what we want to be, in achieving our extrinsic goals, in keeping our boundaries. Reciprocation for that help – *if it is a general feature of social interaction* – reinforces helping behavior. It is a powerful element in sustaining the help we need. That is just a fact about the way human beings behave.

Not reciprocating, on the other hand, if it were a general feature of social interaction, would quite likely extinguish helping behavior. (Lasting unrequited love is rare.) Certainly, if *evil* were typically returned for good, the help would cease. We must have the help to become mature rational agents. And moral theory under the general conception must recommend it (the help) for agents – even if the point is only to put them in the position of being able, as rational agents, to take a self-destructive course of action. So under the general conception, only a disposition to reciprocate – and not its negation – is justifiable.

There are, however, many possible variants of the disposition. Should we be disposed to make 'full' returns, or only partial ones? What about responses to mixed blessings, and evil? Most of those details will be addressed in the sections to follow. But I want to say something here about the issue of *selective* reciprocation.

Resources are scarce, and time and energy are limited. Reciprocating for *every* good received may well be impossible – or at any rate so costly that it would cripple further social relationships. It might be self-defeating, in the sense that it would compromise the very efforts at further social intercourse that reciprocity is supposed to promote.

It does not follow, however, that people ought to adopt a *disposition* of selective reciprocity – i.e., a disposition to make returns for only some of the good they receive. Quite the contrary. It seems evident, all things considered, that we ought to be disposed to reciprocate for everything, and to work out the necessary compromises with competing demands case by case. The reasons that lead to that conclusion are as follows.

The number of possible selective dispositions is indefinitely large. The problem of picking just one of them – to teach or learn – is consequently very difficult. Even if whole ranges of them can be ruled out on some non-arbitrary ground, that still leaves an indefinite number of alternatives within the remaining range(s) – alternatives whose differences from one another may be minuscule. The only workable procedure in that case would be to choose one candidate as a sort of paradigm, permitting any variant of it that meets some criterion of 'family resemblances'. No matter how clear the justification for the paradigm is, then, the permissible variant problem will be a messy business.

Further, *a priori* morality requires that the selectivity produced by the disposition be non-arbitrary – that whatever principle of selectivity we adopt be sensitive to all the differences relevant to a decision about who, in a particular case, ought to get a reciprocal return. The project of trying to build all of the potentially relevant differences into a selective disposition is preposterous. It is preposterous for the same reason that it is preposterous to think that one could write a law that would never require interpretation. Clearly, the only reasonable course here is to adopt some sort of *presumptive* disposition – that is, one that prompts people to reciprocate (in a select range of cases) subject to an assessment in each case of whether such selectivity is justifiable. We could cut down the extent of such considerations by adopting rules of thumb about priorities (e.g., between reciprocity and other moral demands; between friends and strangers). But practice in accord with those rules would also have to be sensitive to exceptions, case by case.

At this point it seems clear that there is no special advantage to choosing a selective disposition. A perfectly general disposition to reciprocate in *every* case – subject to priority rules and considerations case by case about competing demands – is much more straightforward. It obviates the need for finding a paradigm and inventing a family resemblance rule, and such a general disposition will be able to handle exactly the problems of overburdening that raised the (apparent) need for selectivity in the first place. Furthermore, one of the objects of the argument of this chapter is to show that reciprocity is a *fundamental* moral requirement. The notion of a general disposition, occasionally compromised on behalf of other pressing demands, is more appropriate than a selective disposition to a fundamental requirement.

So the disposition to return good for good should not be selective. It should instead prompt us to make returns for all the good we receive.

Note The choice of the term 'receive' as opposed to 'accept' or 'request' will be argued for below.

OBJECTION: Sometimes the point of a gift is pure benevolence. People do things for us out of love, or out of a desire to please or help. In those cases reciprocation would be an affront. Reciprocation makes pure benevolence impossible. Surely the appropriate response to pure gifts is simply gracious acceptance and gratitude. So it cannot be justifiable to be disposed to return good for all the good we receive.

REPLY: That does not follow at all. The only thing that follows from this objection is that sometimes – e.g., in cases of pure benevolence – it is not appropriate to be disposed to make a return immediately, or directly, or in kind. 'I love you, too,' may be an awkward response, but there are others. Acts of love are surely not made *impossible* by reciprocation *per se*. If they were, love and friendship could never be mutual. If my friend surprises and delights me, may I not – at some suitably remote and unguarded moment – surprise and delight him in return? Part of what we mean by love or friendship is the disposition to give freely – without thought of return. But just as surely, another part of love and friendship involves the disposition to be *moved* by the receipt of such gifts – to be *disposed* (by receiving them) to do like things in return. A 'friend' who is not moved in this way – who only 'takes,' no matter how sweetly – lacks exactly the sort of reciprocity disposition that makes genuine love and friendship possible.

OBJECTION: Unconvincing. We want room for pure benevolence – in which nothing is expected in return.

REPLY: Reciprocity is a *recipient's* virtue. It is the way people ought to be disposed to *respond* to others. It says nothing about how people ought to behave, or feel, when they *give* a gift. Perhaps friends ought to give without thought of a return. But how should we receive gifts from our friends? Surely we should not respond to them with *evil*, or with indifference. And surely we should make our responses fitting and proportionate. That is reciprocity.

OBJECTION: Alright. Suppose reciprocity is the recipient's virtue and pure benevolence is the donor's virtue. The two are incompatible. If I am trying to be benevolent, but I know that you will *return* every gift I give with some reciprocal gift of your own, my gift will be tainted. How can I be *purely* benevolent if I know you are disposed to reciprocate?

REPLY: That is one reason so much rests on matters of fittingness. (See below.) If your act would be tainted by an overt response from me, I must find some other way of showing my friendship. Perhaps just by accepting the gift and suppressing (out of friendship) my desire to do more. *That* will be, in the circumstances, a fitting return.

OBJECTION: But love and friendship are by definition reciprocal. The point here is also that there are some acts of benevolence that are *not* embedded in reciprocal relationships and which would be undermined by the attempt, on the part of a recipient, to force them into the pattern of a reciprocal transaction. Think of a stranger on the street who helps pick up some papers you've dropped. Should you pursue her? 'Wait! Let me help you in some way!'

REPLY: Of course not. But such impersonal benevolence is (or could become) part of a *pattern* of social life – a pattern to which it is certainly appropriate to contribute in return. Such patterns get started and are sustained in part because people are disposed to reciprocate for the goods they receive (or could receive) from them. They get started and are sustained because people are disposed to reciprocate *appropriately* – not by pursuing their own anonymous benefactors but by doing the same *sort* of thing their benefactors did. This will be discussed further under the heading of fitting and proportional benefits.

2 Evil received should not be returned with evil

More precisely: We ought not to be disposed to return, with evil, the harm done to us by agents who are trying to harm us. And *a fortiori*, we ought *not* to be disposed to return the harm done to us unintentionally. The argument for this can be quite short.

Moral evil, under the general conception, is conduct (or its consequences) that is unjustifiable all-things-considered. It is, by definition, precisely what we ought not to do. So whether we have suffered evil or not, it would be self-contradictory (under the general conception) to recommend unjustifiable conduct. Reciprocity, if it is to be a moral virtue, cannot dispose us to act unjustifiably – to return evil for evil. On the contrary, if it is to be a disposition that yields justifiable conduct, it must dispose us *not* to make such returns.

It is important to note, however, that the argument just given does not support the conclusion that we ought to be disposed to return *good* for evil, or to 'accept' evil. Reciprocity is not the Christian virtue of loving forgiveness or turning the other cheek. Further, it should be held firmly in mind that there is a difference between doing harm to someone (e.g., a wrongdoer) and doing something that is unjustified all-things-considered. (See the discussion, below, of resistance to evil.)

Retaliation is of course a widespread practice, and the desire to retaliate is even more pervasive. If it were to turn out that a disposition to retaliate were universal – perhaps even a species characteristic – and if we could find no reason, on balance, for opposing it – then we would have to regard it as grounded, morally. But in fact we have the most decisive reason imaginable, under the general conception, for opposing it. Retaliation, defined as returning evil for evil, is by definition unjustifiable. It is by definition an instance of acting immorally.

OBJECTION: The definition of retaliation used here is simply designed to fit a tidy *a priori* argument. A *proper* view of retaliation is that it is returning an unjustified injury with a *justified* one – and that the initial injustice is all that is needed to justify the return.

REPLY: That definition fares no better. Under the general conception, the receipt of an injustice cannot be *all* that is needed to justify doing an injury in return. We are to do what is justifiable all-things-considered, and it is clear that the social *effects* of such retaliation, for one thing, will always be a relevant concern. We must consider the interests of all the agents who might be affected, on a footing of presumptive equality with our own. (See Chapter Two.) Injuring the wrongdoer may turn out to be justifiable, but not merely by virtue of the fact that the wrongdoer injured someone.

OBJECTION: Well then, let us use the device of a rebuttable presumption. Let us say that an unjust injury creates a rebuttable presumption that a return injury (to the wrongdoer) is justified. Then we can get all of the other considerations into the picture before we decide, but the point would be that reciprocity should *dispose* us to return injury with injury.

REPLY: But what conceivable warrant could there be for holding that an unjust injury creates such a presumption? Any such injury is by definition an evil for the person injured. So even if doing it is a good for the one who retaliates (because, for example, it is 'satisfying'), it is by no means clear that the good will outweigh the evil done to the wrongdoer. Further, there is a significant probability that the retaliation itself will be received by the wrongdoer as unjust. And if everyone is disposed to retaliate for perceived injustice, the prospect of self-perpetuating cycles of revenge is also significant.

In sum, there is no reason to think retaliation is a justifiable moral precept under the general conception, nor that it should be built into a disposition to reciprocate. The original maxim stands: If reciprocity is to be a moral virtue, it must dispose us *not* to return evil for evil, or injury for injury.

OBJECTION: We are apparently going to be told below that we should be disposed to resist evil, and that that may involve doing injury to the wrongdoer – in the form of self-defense or punishment, for example, or as a general deterrent. But in that case it looks as though the present maxim is empty. It says we are not to return evil for evil, but virtually anything can get back into the picture in the guise of a deterrent or an effective punishment – even malicious motives. 'Let him *see* how much you hate his crime, how much you enjoy his suffering. Let him hear the mob.'

REPLY: It is hard to imagine in detail how *evil* motives toward wrongdoers could be a genuine good, and how the intention to act on them could be generalizable. It is one thing to retaliate; quite another to match the evil motives of the one you punish. Such an 'evil for evil' response would have no particular advantage as a deterrent. (It is a commonplace of criminal law history that the viciousness of the punishment is not the operative factor in general deterrence. It is the certainty of punishment, and the fact that it imposes an unacceptable cost for a given crime, that is the relevant factor.) And it is plausible to suppose that malicious infliction of injury on the wrongdoer would only exacerbate the problem. But suppose, for the sake of argument, that it would not. Suppose, in fact, that it would be a more effective method of resisting evil than any other. Reciprocity (and doubtless other virtues as well) would still forbid it. The maxim to the effect that we ought to resist evil does not hold that we ought to resist it at any cost, or in the most effective way regardless of other considerations. And reciprocity is not the whole of virtue. To wit:

3 Evil received should be resisted

If we are not to return evil for evil, how should we be disposed to respond to it? The options are what might be called active or passive acceptance, and active or passive rejection. By active acceptance I mean actually returning *good* for evil received. ('Love thine enemy.') By passive acceptance I mean merely standing mute, as it were, making no protest at all – implicit or explicit. (Turning the other cheek, perhaps, although that seems a bit too active.) Active and passive *rejection* are distinguished in a similar way. At the extremes, the difference between them is the difference between fighting or struggling against an evil and merely refusing to submit to it.

The usual problems of classification arise for both the active/passive distinction and the acceptance/rejection one. (Is a rent strike active or passive?) For present purposes, however, classification does not matter. What counts is the general *aim*, not the choice of methods. Under the general conception of morality, the aim must be the reduction or elimination of evil. That conclusion comes directly from the valuation rules implicit in the notion of rational agency as such: that is, a preference for good over evil, more good over less good, and less evil over more of it. Rational projects (aims) must conform to those rules, which means that when confronted with the choice, we must opt for efforts to reduce or eliminate evil as opposed to those that either increase it or leave it constant. The only disposition consistent with that requirement (of rational agency *per se*, under the general conception) is that we be disposed to 'resist' evil – that is, work to reduce or prevent it – *in some way*.

But note that this result is indeterminate with respect to methods.

Assuming equal effectiveness, it is a matter of indifference to this part of moral theory whether we choose active or passive acceptance, active or passive rejection. Given the right circumstances, turning the other cheek can be very coercive. What counts as a justifiable act of resistance is therefore left to case by case considerations. (See the sections on civil disobedience in Chapter Eight.)

Further, given the 'responsive' nature of the reciprocity disposition generally, it seems appropriate to restrict the disposition to the aim of resisting the evil we actually receive. That may seem unconscionable when we think, for example, of passive bystanders during an assault. Reciprocity, as restricted here, would apparently do nothing to propel such people to act, even if they could prevent the evil at no risk to themselves. But such criticism is not cogent. For one thing, acts of aid or rescue, *to the extent that they are acts of reciprocation*, are covered by the maxim of returning good for good. We act on behalf of the victims – either out of some knowledge that we owe them a return, or on the assumption that we do. So resistance to evil is not the relevant maxim, here.

But reciprocity does not yield a full account of giving aid, because giving aid (as we usually conceive of it) is an altruistic act, not an act of reciprocation. And even if altruism is thought of as 'reciprocal' – i.e., something volunteered in the expectation that one will *eventually* get a return – it is outside the ambit of reciprocity as that notion is defined here.

Reciprocity is not the whole of virtue, and it would serve no good purpose to expand it to cover the territory of other virtues such as altruism. Reciprocity as it stands will give us a partial account of the proper response to evil, but we will have to look elsewhere for the considerations that complete the account. Whether, for example, it is part of another virtue to go looking for evils to fight is not properly a part of this inquiry. Here, I will stay with this restricted maxim: that we must resist the evil we receive.

Richard woke suddenly, heart pounding, his back damp against the sheet, at six-twenty on Thursday morning the eleventh of September. He lay very still, so Ginny wouldn't waken, and the tension in his upper body gradually eased. He dozed.

Ginny woke him again at seven-fifteen, tugging him toward

the edge of the bed, ducking away from his clutch. She was wet from her shower, smelling of soap and coffee. She was gone for the day by the time he got to breakfast.

There was a note – a list of reminders – on his placemat. He started to use the back of it for the symptoms, but stopped in fatigue. The day spread out like a dirty sail.

The timing of his arrival at the office was a small private joke – designed by him to be an emblem of his status. He could not control it day by day, but in general he arrived well after the secretaries and paralegals and associates-on-the-make, well before any of the partners who happened to be going through the change, and just moments before any serious work got started. It had been that way for a dozen years, and he hoped it had been noticed.

On that Thursday people were crowded around the desks and counters in the secretarial pool, ridiculing the Thought for the Week. The Thought came from a senior partner, forced into retirement by senility. He was writing a Book of Thoughts, and distributing copies every week to everyone at the office.

Emmy was leading a responsive reading. The chorus included some partners, and even mailroom people. Everyone was laughing and cheering her on.

'Beware the man who thinks competence is enough,' she read.

'*For he is a fool and will fail.*'

'Beware the man who thinks appearances are everything,'

'*For he is a cynic and an idiot in the technical sense.*'

'Take to your heart the man who is bright,'

'*And who is not afraid to hide it;*'

'The man who is careless of appearances,'

'*But always well turned out;*'

'The man who . . .'

Richard raised his hand abruptly, stopping Emmy in midsentence. By common consent it was his job to give a halfhearted rebuke at the end. (He thought the ridicule was cruel, and everyone knew he felt disloyal listening to it.) He didn't usually interrupt. In fact, he usually stopped to listen. Emmy thought he had been rude.

Richard was the chairman's secretary. Administrative

Assistant, as Emmy insisted. She was office manager, and wanted the chart to be clear.

Emmy's chart said that Richard's job was a notch below her own, but she made it clear to everyone that she wanted his job, and she was gradually nibbling at the edges. She now took the minutes for the partners' meetings, for example, which was something Richard had always done, and she was hinting she would like to handle arrangements for them too — travel for the overseas people, and scheduling, and things like that.

She put it to Richard as a mutual benefit. He would have a promotion. She would have a job more suited to her talents.

'I don't handle people very well,' she said to Richard. To the chairman, who liked intrigue, she said that God did not intend for men to keep appointment books.

Richard sat at his desk and hated her. He hated intrigue. Before Emmy, he had been comfortable. Before Emmy, he had kept the office out of his life.

In his life, he played the tuba in a band in outdoor concerts. In his life, he sailed with a friend on a racing yacht. He sang often, and badly, to applause from Ginny. He refused to cook. He loved to eat. He traveled. As a matter of principle, he would not read books unless they had pictures in them. (Everyone, as he said, had to have principles.) And on principle, he would not take work home.

In his life, Ginny was the one who worried and worked — first to make her furniture, then to establish her shop, then to get recognition. She had problems with apprentices, and with floorspace, and with dealers. In his life, Ginny was the one who worked, and he was the one who helped. Ginny listened only to music composed before 1910 (and anything for the tuba). Ginny drew lines and Richard crossed them.

Emmy cheapened him, and forced the office into his life. Emmy threatened him, and forced him to think about self-defense.

By five-of-ten that Thursday all of the partners had gathered for the meeting, and he served coffee. He raised his eyebrows at Emmy's skirt, which was slit halfway up one thigh. She was aware of his notice, and annoyed.

At ten-twenty-five, without warning, after the partners had all gone into the meeting and the coffee had been cleared, his chest went tight and he began to sweat. The pain grew and spread. His breath got short. He tried to get out to the hall for help, but failed. In shame he watched the fingers of his right hand crawl toward the intercom.

He could not answer. He simply kept pressing the button until he saw a face in the doorway. He managed to get the confidential letter in his typewriter covered. He managed to get the cap onto his pen before three men lifted him to the floor and opened his collar. Blinding light, hard floor. He gagged and couldn't breathe at all, head held under water while he thrashed in silence.

Emmy's long hair fell around his face. She put her open mouth on his, and his head and neck and lungs all bulged with the pressure of her kiss. He had one moment of lucidity and relief, and in that moment the only thing he wanted was to get away from her. He died the following Tuesday.

4 Evil done should be made good

More exactly, we ought to be disposed to make restitution for the wrongs we have done. The details are difficult to work out, because restitution involves fundamental questions of reparative justice and comparative value. But the general rationale for this maxim of reciprocity is fairly clear:

The wrongs we do to others typically undermine their dispositions to deal with us freely and reciprocally. Unrequited love is rare, and beyond a certain point, pathological. Given the importance of reciprocal exchanges it is unjustifiable, *ceteris paribus*, to make them less likely. It is therefore unjustifiable to undermine people's dispositions to make them. If a wrong has already been done, however, the problem is to find a way of repairing, or if possible avoiding, damage to the victim's reciprocity disposition. It is implausible to think that that can be accomplished, routinely, by hiding the wrongdoer. In fact, that will produce even more damage if the victim then becomes generally wary. The damage can, of course, be averted by hiding the very fact that a wrong has been done. (Persuading people that the injury was a necessary – and hence a justifiable – evil, for example.) But such conduct does not pass the generalization test. Or rather, the generalization of such conduct, as required by moral theory, is incompatible with the very form of social life it is ostensibly designed to sustain – reciprocity. For what such generalized lying would accomplish is not the sustenance of reciprocal exchanges as defined so far, but the creation of a new practice: returning good for hidden evils. Its intentions are incoherent.

The only remaining possibility (at least the only one I can think of) is restitution. That practice does help to restore the confidence required for free and reciprocal exchanges. I say 'helps'. In a sense, the damage done – as long as it is remembered by the injured party – can probably never be completely undone. (If that is so, it is a psychological truth, not a logical one.) But some help is better than none, and a great deal of human experience suggests that restitution is an extremely useful practice – useful for sustaining productive social exchange.

It is also useful for sustaining self-esteem. As pointed out earlier, self-esteem is psychologically linked to the regard of others. Insofar as their damaging regard is avoided or ameliorated by making restitution, self-esteem is helped, and self-esteem is a primary good.

In addition, for those wrongdoers who feel guilt or shame for their deeds, restitution has a therapeutic effect. And its usefulness as a device for moral education is generally acknowledged. So we have many good reasons for holding that restitution ought to be a part of the reciprocity disposition.

The type and amount of restitution to be given is often a difficult issue. Some losses cannot be restored at all. Others can be made whole only at a cost that exceeds the loss. The appropriate maxim here, as for returns of good for good, is fittingness and proportionality (see 6) below). The disposition to make restitution must be to make whatever sort of return 'matches' the type and scale of the harm done. Measurement in these matters is a problem, as is scaling the restitution to the wrongdoer's ability to repay. But these problems are not unique to the virtue of reciprocity. They occur in everyday assignments of legal sanctions, compensation, and damages. The only thing that may be special here is the extent to which the 'receiver's' values control what counts as a fitting and proportional return. But that is best discussed below.

Note The arguments here apply to unintentional wrongs as well as intentional ones. But a wrong is not just an injury or a harm. A wrong is an *unjustified*

injury. The maxim defended here does not require restitution for injuries justifiable under the principle of
double effect, for example – assuming that principle is
a part of moral theory.

5 The returns should be made by the one who has received the good or done the evil

More accurately: We ought not to have a disposition that permits
returns by proxy, though it ought in some cases to permit, and in
others to require, indirect returns and returns made by collective
efforts. The justification for this element of the disposition is
stronger in the case of making restitution than it is in the case
of returning good for good, so I shall deal with the two cases
separately.

A In the case of restitution, the reason for a no proxy rule is
clear. In cases where restitution serves as moral education (for the
wrongdoer or others), or is therapeutic for the wrongdoer, proxy
returns are useless. And in general, proxies complicate matters.
The proxies have not violated social norms. The 'returns' they
make, therefore, will be seen as acts of benevolence which, under
the norm of reciprocity, one must return. So instead of restoring
the balance, they aggravate the imbalance.

Indirect returns are quite a different matter. They are sometimes
inappropriate, given the warrants for making restitution, but at
other times they are precisely the sort of returns that ought to be
made. The reciprocity disposition ought to be sensitive to these
matters, as part of the project of making fitting and proportional
returns. This will be discussed below but it is worth going over
briefly here.

Indirect returns can be out of place when paying through an
intermediary is offensive to the recipient and does little to clear the
debt. ('Don't send your lawyer. I want it directly from you.') And
again, when restitution is meant as moral education or therapy,
indirect methods may be inappropriate.

Similarly for 'collective' methods – such as payment through
pooled funds (e.g. insurance), or through a business or government
agency. People sometimes gain little confidence from such repayment. ('What do they care? It's not their money. They'll just go on

doing the same thing.') And the effect on moral education, or the psychological health of the wrongdoers, may be damaging. The diffusion of responsibility in complex social structures is dangerous.

On the other hand, however, there are times when only indirect or collective methods will do. Restitution through an agent can be a courtesy if the recipient does not want to face the wrongdoer. And the knowledge that people are insured and thus *able* to make restitution, or make it without disproportionate sacrifices, may be exactly what is required to sustain free and reciprocal social transactions.

The result is, therefore, that while we ought to be disposed *against* restitution by proxy, the choices between direct and indirect, individual and collective returns should be left open – to be decided in each case in terms of the fittingness criterion.

B In the case of returning good for good received, the justification for the no proxy rule is less decisive, and in fact may be thoroughly culture-bound. There is certainly nothing incoherent about a system in which each person makes only proxy returns, or some combination of proxy and personal returns. And to the extent that making such returns personally would violate social expectations, we would, I suppose, want to insist on proxies. The only problem is that the use of proxies would itself come under the control of the reciprocity principle, so that an additional level of things would have to balance out in the long run. Your proxy return on my behalf is a good which I must return. But how? By arranging for a proxy when you need one? Or by acting as a proxy for someone else, who in turn, as in the Kula exchange, passes the favor on? Such an arrangement has a pleasing delicacy, but it seems unnecessarily complex. Economy, insofar as it contributes to achieving the purpose of the enterprise, favors the no proxy rule.

Indirect returns, or collective returns, are a bit easier to deal with. They sometimes satisfy the reciprocity requirement, or are even necessary to its satisfaction. A man who has been helped by a charitable organization may not know who contributed, and the contributors may want anonymity. Returns in that case must be indirect. If they are made by helping to sustain the charitable organization, they are collective. On the other hand, indirect or collective returns sometimes fail to satisfy. ('She says the gift is from her whole family. I love *her*, not her family.')

In short, this aspect of the disposition to reciprocate must reflect

the subtlety and complexity of human reactions to reciprocal exchanges. The controlling idea, for the justification of its details, is
to find the methods that best satisfy the aims of the practice of
reciprocating – methods sensitive to matters of fittingness and
proportionality. Those methods are then balanced against other
considerations (e.g., moral education and therapy).

QUESTION: What about affect? And tact, and style? Everything
reciprocity aims for will be lost if the return is fumbled, and it can
easily be fumbled by ungratefulness or clumsiness. ('Well *of course*
it was a beautiful dinner. But they were so awful about it – so
obvious about paying us back. *Never* again, George.') Shouldn't
the reciprocity disposition include something about the 'spirit' in
which the return must be given? We don't want obsequious gratitude, but neither do we want contemptuous payoffs.

REPLY: In general, it *cannot* be said that we ought to be disposed
to make returns in any particular 'spirit', or with any particular
affect. The range of cases is too varied, and people's preferences
differ so thoroughly in this regard that it is a hopeless task to try
to say anything – at this level of generality – about the 'required'
affect. (Suppose your mother dies. One friend writes a long,
eloquent and impassioned letter about the pain of a parent's death.
Another, just as carefully, writes this: 'I heard with sorrow the
news of your mother's death. My own mother died twenty-three
years ago today. I still dream about her often.') Which is best?
Surely there is no *general* answer. Everything depends on the
circumstances of the particular case – the relationship you have
with each friend, your own emotionality, and so forth. In particular
situations these things are usually clear enough, and it is a part of
practical wisdom, discussed in the next chapter, to be alert to such
things. But there does not appear to be any useful general maxim
about the matter.

> 'You dance like a feather.'
> 'A feather?'
> 'Well, a bear, then.'

6 Returns and reparations should be fitting and proportional

Or, as I shall sometimes rephrase it, returns must be commensurate.
More fully: We should be disposed to make returns and reparations

that are appropriate as to type and quantity. What counts as appropriate is any return or reparation sufficient (given the existing background conditions) for satisfying the ends of the practice of reciprocating.

The general warrant for this maxim is not hard to see. Within the confines of any project, the only rationally justifiable choices of means (for that project) are ones that will or might work – ones that are, or might be, sufficient (given the background conditions) to achieve the project's ends. Further, under the general conception, only those means that are justifiable all-things-considered may be adopted. The end, here, for which one must find effective means, is implicit in the general line of justification for reciprocity: namely, the maintenance of the sort of social equilibrium that makes productive social exchange possible. The notion of 'balanced' exchange is implicit in the notion of equilibrium. And unless an exchange involves *commensurate* goods – i.e., commensur*able* and proportional ones – it cannot be said to be balanced. That much is definitional, but is only enough to establish the general point that returns and reparations must be proportional.

The general requirement of fittingness, however, is also easily established. In part, it is simply a restatement of the notion of commensurability required for determining that a return is proportional. The goods we exchange out of reciprocity must be of sorts that can be compared as to value. We must be able to determine, at least roughly, when a return is equal to the good we have received, or when our reparations are equal to the harm we have done. If the goods we return are not commensurable, they are not fitting.

But there is also another aspect of the fittingness requirement, one that comes from the fact that reciprocal exchanges are typically meant to sustain a particular practice or institution rather than productive social life *per se*. In that case, returns that are irrelevant to the special purpose so defined are not fitting, no matter how valuable they may be generally. (When someone needs help with the rent, an invitation to join a discussion group on the mating behavior of free ranging vervet monkeys will not do.)

In general terms, then, it is not difficult to establish that returns must be fitting and proportional. The more difficult task is to establish some useful general rules for deciding, in specific cases, what will count as fitting and proportional. Must it be 'in kind'?

Must it be direct? How is its value to be assessed? Most of these matters will have to be worked out case by case, but there are a few useful general principles.

A Fittingness

Clearly, since the whole idea of reciprocity is to return *good* for good, the return of evil for it will by definition be unfitting, as will be a return of something valueless. Further, since the point of being disposed to reciprocate is to create and sustain balanced social relationships, the good returned will have to be good *for the recipient*, and (eventually) *perceived* by the recipient both *as a good* and *as a return*.

To explain: If a return is not *actually* a good (but only, perhaps, an apparent one) then it necessarily fails to be a return of good for good. Similarly, if the thing is not a good for the one to whom we owe a return, it necessarily fails to be a return at all. Finally, if the return is not *perceived* as a good by the one who receives it, and is not perceived *as a return*, and not perceived as such *in time* to have an effect on future social transactions, then the act will have no point *as an act of reciprocity*. (It may, of course, have some other point – e.g., an altruistic point.)

So it is clear that the fittingness condition means that we should be disposed to return things that are genuine goods *for* those *to* whom we owe a return, in ways that make it possible for the recipients to *perceive* that those goods are good *for* them, and returns *to* them. This is what we should be disposed to do, even though ignorance and vice and circumstance will often prevent us from actually doing it. (We will sometimes think a thing is a good, for example, but be mistaken; or think the recipients understand our intentions when they do not. That is why we need practical wisdom – and luck – to go along with reciprocity.)

These observations help to answer two important questions about fittingness. One is whether returns must be 'in kind,' and if not, what controls the principle of substitution. Clearly, there is no reason to think returns *must* be in kind – whatever that might mean (money for money; service for service). In fact, tying the return too closely to the kind of good received can defeat the purpose of reciprocating, either by creating a stultifying series of pointless trades or by insuring that the return will not be a good at all for the recipient. ('I don't *want* a popcorn popper. That's *why* I gave you *mine*.') In general, anything that contributes to the welfare of the recipient will qualify as fitting, provided it can be perceived as such by the recipient, and perceived as a *return*. (Further restrictions will be imposed by proportionality. See below.) That much, however, is enough to make it evident that most of the details about what counts as fitting will have to be worked out case by case. They will depend, in each case, on a great many factors special to that case – including the history of the relationship between the parties. ('Well, if you want to know why we were a little cool about the silver bowl you gave us it's because that bowl was what we gave you for your wedding.')

A problem does arise when the two parties have irreconcilable differences about what constitutes a genuine good, and when the initial benefactor is not willing to accept anything that the recipient is willing to give in return. In such a case the recipient has a dilemma. On the one hand, she is disposed to return something that is a genuine good for the benefactor, but if she cannot bring herself to believe that what he wants is a genuine good for him, giving it to him will not satisfy her disposition to reciprocate. On the other hand, if she returns something that *she* perceives as a good, but which he will not *accept* as a good, then the point of the exchange – as a reciprocal one designed to sustain productive social transactions – will be lost. ('If you patronize me that way we're through. Let me be the judge of what's good for me.')

Under the general conception, the solution is as follows: Since the point of reciprocating is to engender and sustain productive social exchanges, and since that can only be done in this case by completing the transaction in some way that satisfies the benefactor, that should be the controlling concern. Of course there are many times that such a maxim will have to be overridden, all things considered. Benefactors may make evil or impossible demands, and in such cases justice, benevolence, prudence, or concern for our own integrity and self-esteem may require us to refuse the demand. Not every exchange should be completed, all things considered. Not every relationship should be sustained. But we are discussing the maxims of just one of the virtues here. Its point is to dispose us to complete transactions and sustain them. To that end it should first dispose us to try to do that in ways that satisfy both us and our benefactors. Failing that, it should dispose us to satisfy our benefactors, unless there are some overriding reasons (from other virtues or values or duties) not to do so. That is as much as we can say at this level of abstraction. The details must be worked out case by case.

OBJECTION: But that tells us exactly nothing. It says, in effect, 'Do whatever your benefactor wants, unless you shouldn't.' Some guidance.

REPLY: Exactly. *Some* guidance. Conflicts like this prevent fully satisfactory answers. That is what defines them as genuine conflicts rather than merely apparent ones. And the abstract level of the analysis prevents a more detailed response. But the analysis here *does* make *some* progress toward a decision. It instructs us, in cases of irreconcilable conflict, to use our benefactor's conception of a fitting good rather than our own – subject always to all the other relevant considerations, such as justice, benevolence, self-preservation and so forth. That may not be an elegant and decisive recommendation, but it's better than nothing.

OBJECTION: It's just about what Aristotle said about these conflicts, without the weaselly *ceteris paribus* clause. And it's just as unconvincing. What it does is make us vulnerable to the whims of our benefactors. They can simply stick us up by refusing to accept anything that isn't exactly what they want – by refusing to acknowledge anything else as fitting.

REPLY: We are always subject to the whims and dishonesty of other people in the sense that, if we don't spot it, we sometimes make costly errors. Reciprocity by itself is no help with this. (Neither is conscientiousness, or trust, or benevolence. It is part of prudence, together with practical wisdom, to protect us against such things.) But once the deception is spotted there is no special problem about reciprocity. We see that the refusal to accept alternative goods is insincere, and we are therefore not bound by it.

OBJECTION: But suppose the benefactor *is* sincere, just eccentric. Suppose his conception of a fitting return is bizarre. Not that our making that return would be unjustifiable. (Let's not squirm out of this by saying that we don't have to yield 'all-things-considered.') Let's just say that making that particular return would be repugnant to us, yet it is the only thing he will accept. We are still, then, at the mercy of sincere benefactors who have strange tastes and perverse desires.

REPLY: Yes. That's one of the charms of social life, and there is no point in trying to deal with it further at this level of abstraction. It is a matter for case by case deliberation.

Abstract considerations of fittingness do contribute at least one more important element to theory, however. That element concerns the question of how direct the return must be. Gifts and goods come to us from people – from individuals – but they often come by way of institutions. Think of a blood bank. The blood is contributed by individuals who, typically, do not know who will receive their blood. It is taken by medical personnel, transported and stored by technicians, and administered by a separate set of medical people. Suppose my life is saved by a transfusion. To whom do I owe a return? To the donor, surely, and (at least) to any others who, in the process, did more for me than they were morally obligated to do. Must I track them all down and give each one something in return?

Considerations of proportionality aside, it is important to see how the fittingness consideration alone helps to answer that question. My return must be something my benefactors will perceive *as* a return, and *as* a good. Most of those benefactors are unknown to me. And it is a fair assumption, in our culture, that they would not find my tracking them down for some sort of personal encounter to be a good. All I know about what they value – what they would consider a good for themselves and a return for the benefit they have provided – is that, in all probability, they will want others to help them sustain the blood bank. As long as the bank *is* sustained, they will feel 'repaid', whether they know who is responsible or not. We who have benefited can obviously make a fitting return in *that* way. (Matters of proportionality will be considered below.) We would probably not be making a fitting contribution by tracking them down, and we cannot be sure we would be making one by giving to another charity – the March of Dimes, for example. Everything points in the same direction – toward a contribution to sustaining the blood bank. It need not be 'in kind'. But it should be to that institution.

Notice, however, how circumstances may change that result. If a special appeal is made for five pints of blood for me, and five donors come to the hospital in the knowledge that I will learn their identities, what counts as a fitting return might be very different. The donors might, for example, welcome some expression of gratitude from me, and an assurance that I will try to emulate their example.

What controls the 'fit' here is the nature of the act of benefaction. If it is meant to be a personal exchange then a personal response is probably called for. (Giving blood to the Red Cross is no way to answer a love letter.) But if the benefit is not aimed at a specific person at all, but aimed instead at sustaining a social structure to provide such benefits to many people, we may conclude (in the absence of evidence to the contrary) that a return aimed at the same purpose will be fitting.

B Proportionality: Equal Benefits and Sacrifices

What counts as a proportional return? Assuming that the return is fitting, what counts as enough? Enough means enough to equal the good received, of course, because reciprocity is meant to produce 'balanced' exchanges. But there are two dimensions to the notion of a balanced exchange. One concerns what it costs the participants to make their 'gifts', the other concerns the benefits they derive from their 'receipts'. An exchange can be balanced in one of these ways and not in the other. Moreover, it is sometimes impossible to balance it in both ways. Consider:

Suppose an affluent mother gives her son his first bicycle. She gives it casually, with little thought, at little or no sacrifice. The price means nothing, the bike is ordered by telephone, delivered fully assembled, and so forth. In one sense, a commensurate return from the boy would be one that equals the mother's negligible sacrifice. We may suppose he has very little money, so he buys her a clever greeting card he has heard her admire. In terms of comparative cost, then, he has made a fitting and proportional return.

It is clear, however, that in terms of the comparative *benefits* involved, the boy may *not* have reciprocated, and perhaps could not possibly do so. Perhaps the bike looms very large in his life. To him it is a huge benefit; a treasure. The greeting card is, on the other hand, a momentary, minor pleasure for his mother, doubled by the thought that it came from her son, but still nothing to match the value to him of the bicycle. So the exchange of *benefits* has *not* been proportional.

Further, it is quite possible that the benefits cannot be made proportional without skewing the sacrifices. What is it, after all, that would be of comparable novelty, usefulness, and delight to the mother? (Assume, for the sake of argument, that it would have to be an immediate return, in the form of a piece of merchandise.) Isn't it likely to be altogether beyond the boy's reach?

That sort of situation is an everyday occurrence. A gift of negligible cost (a pint of blood, a timely telephone call) has life-saving benefits. The repayment of a small debt, of insignificant value to the donor, is a crushing cost to the debtor. The problem for moral theory here is how to define the disposition to reciprocate in such situations.

The answer comes from considering the purpose of reciprocity, as it is justified under the general conception. Its purpose is to sustain mutually advantageous exchanges. Balanced *benefits*, therefore, must be the leading concern. From a purely selfish point of view, one would try to maximize one's own benefits and minimize one's own sacrifice. Altruistic concerns would generate the same efforts on behalf of others. Either point of departure must be universalized (under the general conception), and that would yield the maximal-benefit minimal-sacrifice rule for everyone. Efficiency and social welfare considerations give the same result. There are, of course, occasions when perceived inequality in the level of sacrifice affects the level of benefits. ('I worked so hard for that and what she did was so easy for her. I feel exploited.') But in such cases, it is the connection to benefits that makes the level of sacrifice a relevant issue. When the benefits at stake are *derived*, in whole or part, from equality of sacrifice, then equating the benefits will entail equating the sacrifices. In any case, it follows that we should be disposed, *first*, to return commensurate benefits with as little sacrifice as possible.

In cases where equating the benefits would mean making a significantly larger sacrifice in return, it seems clear that the level of sacrifice should be controlling. The alternative to that would be to preserve equality of benefits no matter what the cost (or some cushioned version of that rule). And that would lead to self-perpetuating and increasing inequalities. The disadvantaged would become progressively more impoverished as they struggled to return equal benefits. The result would be antithetical to the sort of social equilibrium reciprocity is designed to sustain. An equal sacrifice rule in these cases is clearly preferable, since it would not compromise the ability of either party to make further exchanges. It is clearly a second-best option (second to equal benefits at equal or less the sacrifice) because it may well have a chilling effect on exchanges among unequals. The wealthy may withdraw. ('I'm not getting enough out of this. He tries, but he just doesn't have the resources. We're going to have to let it drop.') But second-best is often the best we can get.

In all of this it should be remembered, however, that the tremendous variety and subtlety of human preferences, and the remarkable range of human abilities, often makes equal-benefit returns possible in cases where – to an outsider – they look impossible. Reciprocities are not, for the most part, money matters. Returns need not always be in kind, and they need not always be immediate. A son may return his mother's gifts with kindness and obedience, or with care when she is old. The important point is merely that the exchange be balanced to the satisfaction of the participants. It seems clear that the disposition best suited to achieve that end is one that tries first for returns matched to the benefits received, at no net loss, and failing that, for returns matched to sacrifices.

C Proportionality: Joint Projects

Jointly produced benefits raise a special problem. Suppose a hundred friends combine to set up a newly married couple in housekeeping. How is the couple to reciprocate? The benefit is very great, and we may suppose that they can give nothing comparable in return – either to the group as a whole or to even one of their friends. Moreover, equal sacrifice (e.g., by their giving small gifts in return to each friend) would put them right back where they started, as an impoverished pair of newly-weds. And we may suppose their friends do not want that. This sort of situation confronts us all with respect to corporately produced goods – public health and safety, educational, charitable, and cultural institutions, and so forth. The problem is what sort of reciprocation to make when we seem unable to do anything that equals either the benefits we have received or the sum total of the sacrifices that have gone into producing those benefits.

Here it is important to remember that such benefits typically come to us by way of people's participation in on-going social institutions (e.g., rituals, voluntary associations, governments). What is *fitting* is reciprocal participation in those institutions. It is only that sort of return, generally adhered to by recipients, that will sustain the institutions. Returns directly to the participants, *in lieu* of participation, would not be fitting because if generalized, they would undermine the institutions. Similarly, general refusal to participate in the *very* institution from which the benefit came would undermine it. The fittingness rule for these corporately produced benefits, then, is to make a return to the very corporate enterprise that produced them.

A proportional return is a 'proportional' level of participation. And since (by hypothesis) one cannot match the benefits received, one can only take the second-best option and make an equal sacrifice. But equal to what? Equal, evidently, to the sacrifices made by others who have comparable abilities and resources, and who have benefited in a comparable way. A plausible technique for deciding on the amount is to find out (roughly) what the average contribution is from people like yourself (i.e., people of roughly comparable age, income, aspirations, time available, special talents, and so on), and then to adjust that up or down in terms of the benefits you have actually received – i.e., in terms of how far above or below average – for all recipients – those benefits were.

This technique has several virtues. First, notice that although we do not typically confront all of our benefactors in cases like these, we do usually confront a variety of representative benefactors – people of various levels of ability, income, and benefits received. Contributions from us, scaled in the way just described, are likely to be perceived by those people as proportionate – as our fair shares – since they are explicitly equated to what similar people in similar circumstances are doing. If they are so perceived, these contributions from us will promote the general purpose of reciprocity. Second, the sort of calculation required here is familiar to us all – to human beings generally. We just are, typically, aware of where we stand, relative to our fellows, with respect to a wide variety of socially important factors. (And our acquaintances are equally aware of our standing.) So the use of this technique calls for the application of information we already have, in ways that are thoroughly familiar. Third, the technique provides for relatively simple adjustments to be made in case total contributions fall short of (or exceed) the amount needed to sustain the enterprise. We can simply issue an appeal for everyone to increase (or decrease) their contributions in a way that preserves the ratios. Fourth, there is a straightforward trial and error extension of the method for getting new enterprises off the ground. (This is not, strictly, the concern of reciprocity, but rather of its related virtues.) One sets fair shares initially by analogy with comparable enterprises, and then adjusts them in the way just mentioned on the basis of what people actually contribute. And finally, this technique conforms at least to the spirit of the controlling idea of proportionality. By hypothesis, we cannot return either benefits or sacrifice equal to the sums given by our benefactors. But everyone else is in the same situation. We can all, however, scale our contributions to what similar people in similar circumstances have done for us – where 'similar circumstances' makes reference to both the relative level of benefits received and relative level of ability to make a return.

A fair share, so defined, is a fitting and proportional return for the benefits provided by social institutions we want to sustain through reciprocity. It is fitting because it is calculated to fulfill the purpose of reciprocating in the given case (i.e., by determining how much it will cost to sustain the institutions and by raising shares to generate that amount). It is a proportional return in the sense that it represents the same sacrifice other participants are expected to make. It is, in that sense, a mutual but indirect exchange of commensurate benefits.

OBJECTION: Suppose some beneficiaries do not contribute their fair shares? Must we raise the assessment again? Doesn't that invite freeriders and won't it eventually impoverish the people who play fair?

REPLY: Reciprocity involves making returns to benefactors – in this case, to the participants in the institution providing the benefit, not to the freeriders. So the fair share is not calculated for all the beneficiaries (i.e., for participants plus free riders). It is calculated for participants only. And that is, after all, what is fair. It is they – not the freeriders – who have provided the good for which we owe a return.

OBJECTION: But what if that is just too costly? There does not seem to be any mechanism here for limiting increases in 'fair' shares. If, for example, the number of freeriders goes up, so will the cost to the remaining participants. Are we to keep increasing assessments until everyone reaches maximal sacrifice?

REPLY: These matters cannot be isolated from other concerns. Institutions die, in part because people stop participating and the cost of carrying on becomes too high for the remaining few. And people have competing obligations. But the disposition to reciprocate is essentially retrospective. We owe a return for benefits already received, and are to make that return based on the *current* fair share. Reciprocity does not dispose us to make prospective contributions. And in any case, under the general conception, the virtues must be sensitive to circumstances in which what they dispose us to do is unjustifiable, all things considered. So if the cost is unjustifiably high, we ought not to make the return. It is justifiable, all things considered, to be *disposed* to reciprocate. It cannot be justifiable to actually *do* so, if doing so is morally wrong. And not every institution should be propped up by increasingly costly returns.

OBJECTION: All the talk about institutions has diverted an answer to an important aspect of the problem that opened this section: What are we to do about benefits that come from groups of people who do not form a continuing institution? Such benefits may present us with the same problem of scale – that is, an inability to make a return in proportion to either the benefit we receive or the aggregate sacrifice that produced it. And since there is no institution to sustain, there is no way to calculate a fair share as you define it.

REPLY: An answer can be found by an analogous route. What is *fitting* will be determined by the *point* of the exchange. If it was not part of a continuing practice or institution, we first need to know what purpose the benefit was meant to serve, and for what purpose a return is expected. Assuming those purposes are justifiable, a fitting response would be one that serves the same sort of end – one that follows the same moral rule, as it were. And a proportional return would evidently be one that involves a sacrifice equal to that of one of the participants. So if, for example, the purpose of the benefit given to me was simply to relieve my distress in an emergency, with no expectation of a direct return to the people involved, then a fitting and proportional return from me would be participation in a similar act of altruism when the need arises. That is one way continuing practices and institutions get started. And the method of calculating a fitting and proportional return for the initial benefit is analogous to the method used in the institutional case.

In seventh grade Margaret had long brown hair and cold hands. She was very slender. She invited me to a square dance, which is where those things impressed me. So did the trapped feeling I had when she asked me to go. We were already friends of sorts. Small town, same schools, same age. I aspired to someone else – the best girl in the class. But I was only second best, and Margaret was second best too, so there was really no choice.

She doesn't remember the dance. She now claims to remember a great deal about our grade school days instead. I remember almost none of it, and certainly nothing much about Margaret. She says I was arrogant, and legendary in a grade school way. I am supposed, for example, to have often trailed off into a murmur when reading aloud in class. The story is that I was deeply interested in the text.

My memories of that time are more of emotions than of events (confusions, for example, and embarrassments and cowardices), more of myself than of anyone else (she has the arrogance part right) and nothing of Margaret except that she was the only Democrat in the third grade – the only one ready to vote for Truman over Dewey. She took a lot of cruelty for it – on the gravel playground where such things usually ended in scraped knees and elbows. No one came to her defense, least of all me, but I didn't actively taunt her, and she must have taken my silence as a form of help. (People repeat their juvenile mistakes, and she has made that one again and again.) I admired her courage but thought she had stupid opinions. She doesn't remember being a Young Democrat for Truman.

In the summer after seventh grade Margaret put me into a trance – stunned me into a three-month dream of desire, exclusively and explicitly sexual. I saw her only once that summer – sitting on the shaded steps of her house in the early morning, early in June. Long, bare legs. Long, brown hair. Eyes closed, face turned away. It was enough.

I wanted to see her again, of course. And wanted is not a strong enough word for my obsession. I rode my bike by her house four or five times a day, ready with openings. (It would not have been right to phone or go somewhere everyone knew she would be.) The summer was very hot, very dry, very still, even by Great Plains standards, and what I remember most (aside from every detail of the naked body I imagined for her) is the constant, aching disappointment of those empty porch steps, and the constant, soft sound of the wind through the cottonwoods that lined every street.

Margaret doesn't remember sitting on the steps. In fact she believes that the sighting, as she calls it, was part of my trance – a way of blaming her for the rest of it. But she was unhappy that summer, preoccupied. Her family moved east a hundred miles in the fall.

I don't remember being upset about it. Margaret says I was (her girlfriends wrote her that I was insufferable), but I think I was too exhausted to care. Sometime in August I burned out. All summer, during the week, I had sold ice cream from a peddle cart from ten to three, then done my paper route, then sold again from seven to nine. On Saturdays I collected for the paper route, played tennis, delivered papers, and played tennis again under the lights. On Sundays it was church, swimming, and tennis. All in a dream about seeing Margaret, being seen by Margaret, lying with Margaret, teasing Margaret, running away with Margaret, defending Margaret, pleasing Margaret, making Margaret cry. (Contrition is one of my best acts.)

I've never had story fantasies about her again. She is not sure she likes that, and for a while did not even believe it. She thought, at the time I told her, that the remark was a maneuver for moral advantage. It may have been. But it was also true.

Two years after she moved away she wrote me a letter. It was like seeing her on those steps again, after an age in which the old fantasies had become childish, and all the old, careful evasions of honest feeling had become pointless. They had not become pointless, of course, for anyone we had to deal with in person. But in the letters we began to write we felt free, and floated on a thick cushion of confidence that we could not harm ourselves, ever, in each other's eyes.

In tenth grade our mothers limited us to one letter a week. We were silently satisfied because that was the number we had agreed on anyway. (Or rather that was the limit I had announced. Margaret said I had a genius for restraint.) Postcards didn't count – not, we assumed, because they were ontologically distinct (Margaret had an unusual vocabulary), but because their contents were public, and usually consisted of little more than chess moves.

The letters, however, were intensely private. We ached for them and sweated writing them. Margaret can even remember things we wrote – the most intimate things, she says, she has ever written to anyone. I remember only the sight of her handwriting on the identifiable envelopes, and the sharp, anticipatory pleasure of coming home every Friday to find the letter waiting. (She insisted then that she had to write on Wednesday night, though I knew, and she knew I did, that she was also trying to complicate my Friday nights. Not spoil. Just complicate.) We wrote a lot to each other, she says, about ways to enrich things by complicating them. And Lord knows they were complicated for us. How to be faithful to someone else (we were both going steady); how to be honest to our parents (we had sworn to say as little as possible); and mostly – most difficultly – how to write exactly what we wanted the other to understand. We got very good at it in the seven years we wrote. Margaret has an exact count of the letters – I've never asked how. Three hundred seventy-one each way, she says. Not counting the ones after the sundering, as she calls it.

Bitch. Invited me to her high school graduation. Arranged for me to stay with Zoe's family. (Zoe was her best friend. Margaret's parents did not approve of her invitation to me.) We double-dated with Zoe and a guy I despised – mostly for the fact that he regularly whipped me in interscholastic tennis. Rob.

Rob and Zoe had a lot of quiet, sudden fun that night in

the front seat of a Buick Roadmaster, while Margaret kept
her purse on the back seat between the two of us and watched
the movie in misery. There was more sport, and more misery,
at Zoe's house afterwards.

It crossed my mind that Rob was somebody I knew by other
names from the letters. Old Acne and Face, for example. Bill
the Conk. William One-Muscle. He Who Will Not Be Denied.
But I couldn't bring myself to believe it because Zoe was so
careless. God only knows what Rob was thinking. Maybe he
was just dumb.

Zoe came to my room that night about three. I wasn't asleep.
She got into my bed (her parents' room was right across the
hall, so you can understand, even if Margaret can't, why the
protests I might have made were too subtle for Zoe to notice),
and lay chastely next to me, her night gown up around her
waist and one bare leg over mine, talking about Margaret
and Rob. Hinting that Margaret wasn't a virgin. (I knew that.)
That Margaret wasn't honest. That Margaret was going to
let me down.

Some best friend, I said.

Yes, said Zoe. *The* best.

That was the night before the graduation. I didn't stay for
the formalities.

Margaret's letters that summer were very dark – like a heavy
perfume. Mine must have been strange, too. I must have
accused her of setting the whole thing up with Zoe to test me
for some private purpose of their own. That's what I think,
and Margaret has never denied it, though neither of us now
remembers what was said about it that summer.

We went to different colleges. Margaret had to stay at home
– for financial reasons, she said, though I suspected that her
parents just wouldn't let her go anywhere else when there was
a college right there in her home town. (I imagined that her
mother, whom I had never met, was psychotic, and that her
father was an alcoholic. Margaret was hurt by those fantasies.
There were limits.)

In college Margaret cut her hair and pierced her ears and
majored in French. Her breasts seemed to get heavier. (She
said it was the language.) She came for weekends three or four
times a year, and of course we wrote. Once a week, every

week. My family was in love with her. She stayed with us sometimes at holidays, or for a week in the summer. She made my junior high school age brother ache in a way I recognized, and my sister, when she was a senior in high school, began to copy the way Margaret dressed. My father and mother just assumed she was their daughter-in-law.

I don't know when it was exactly – probably when we were juniors in college – that we began to write about our earlier letters. Metaletters. And we wrote (and destroyed) a novel together over two years of the four. The middle two? Margaret cultivated a literary persona, and I learned to do a fair imitation of the scientist. We think now that those things were decisive.

Margaret went to graduate school in English. I went to medical school. It was a sign of what was coming, I suppose, that it did not occur to either of us to compromise our choice of schools to be together. (Margaret said once that it occurred to her, but that she dismissed it. I think she lied to me then, and has since come to believe the lie.)

In graduate school we wrote very different letters. Terse. Just as long, but compressed. She says I was melancholy the first year. (Unhappy, yes. And frightened that I had made the wrong choice. And it is true that I played the sad young man for the women at school. But it couldn't have shown in the letters to Margaret. She was ruthless about that pose.)

Margaret was a coward. That angered me. She wanted to quit when she got scared, and quitting meant getting married. She came to visit in the fall of the second year. An all-night ride on the train, arriving in mid-afternoon. I was irritated at the interruption, nervous about what she wanted, and helpless, as usual, when I saw her. Long, brown legs. Long, brown hair. The familiar, long embrace.

She was tired, but I ignored it. We went to the Art Institute, to dinner, to a concert, to a bar where one of my friends made an ugly pass at her, and back to her room. We said next to nothing of importance. (On the contrary, she says, everything that was important was said that night.) I provoked her into a series of very cruel, and very funny, lies about the man she was dating. Something she has never forgiven me for. And she said she needed my help in deciding whether to marry him. (As she said this, she was in the bathroom, with the door open, in full view, looking into the mirror. I do not remember feeling anything.) The genius of restraint went back to his room for the night.

She left the next day, after a long, tiresome fight about courage, and career, and marriages that fail. The genius wrote her a letter of absolution. There was no answer – no letter at all, no postcard, no *word* – for three weeks. No word for the first time in seven years.

When the letter came it was gracious and formal. She thanked him for being so considerate and understanding. She thanked him for being so honest about his egoism. She thanked him for not using the advantage he had – the leverage of the three hundred seventy-one letters each way. And she guessed she would marry the man she had lied about so brutally under inexcusable provocation. Consider her engaged.

He wrote a vengeful, cunning reply, announcing that he had destroyed her letters (he had) and demanding that she do the same to his. There was also a good deal about betrayal, and cowardice again, and infantile obsessions with security. She sent him a vicious gift in return – a carefully marked copy of Thomas Mann stories. And then there was silence for nearly a year.

In his third year of medical school he received a series of letters that frightened him. The familiar envelopes induced a specific, hysterical, and complete inability to read – to *see* – her handwriting. Only her hand. Nothing else. He could not ask anyone to read the letters. (He thought his career would be lost – that it probably *was* lost.) He finally wrote to ask her to type them. He did not explain.

She typed everything she sent him for the next four years. One of them, inevitably, was a pleading invitation to her wedding. It would be more elaborate than he would like, she said, but surely he could forgive that. At an inconvenient time, but would there ever be a convenient one? Back in the town he despised, among strangers except for Zoe, but at least Zoe wouldn't be a nuisance. She was eight months pregnant with her second child, and her father – a Lutheran minister – was doing the wedding service. Even Zoe wouldn't dare.

So two days after he graduated from medical school
Margaret was married. His family was bewildered and angry
for him. (He had said nothing to prepare them or to explain.)
Her family, he found out later, was also bitter – not on his
account, but apparently because the only son-in-law they had
ever wanted was old William.

He brought his gift to her house, by prearrangement, on the
morning of the wedding. Outside, on the sidewalk that was
already hot from the early summer sun, he tried to imagine
the house as the one in the other town, in the seventh grade
summer. He tried to imagine the ache of the empty porch steps,
and the hot wind in the summer trees. He tried to feel sorry
for himself, and anger at what he knew Margaret would say
about the effort.

Inside, Margaret was waiting with the long embrace. Her
parents were not there. The groom emerged from one of the
back rooms, fly half-unzipped, and stood partly behind her.
He took the gift and put it on an end table. (Margaret knew
it was poisoned. She didn't want to deal with it.) There was a
little feeble conversation. Another embrace. A handshake for
the groom (whose zipper was now closed). And that was that.

Zoe was the matron of honor, uncomfortable and sullen.
Margaret's father refused to walk her down the aisle, so her
brother filled in. He was twenty years older than Margaret and
she hardly knew him. I was sorry, then, about the gift – or
rather the letter with the gift. I don't remember what the gift
itself was (Margaret says it was 'useful'.) But the letter, from
a purely technical point of view, was one of my best – a hymn
of hope for their life together, gracious and loving to every
eye but Margaret's. To Margaret it read, as I had hoped, as
an exquisite denunciation of the compromise she had made.

In the receiving line she kissed my cheek, squeezed my arm
just hard enough to hurt and said softly that I had hoped too
much for her. As she said it she turned to greet the next guest.
I loved her for that for most of the two hour drive home.

Margaret and Jerry went to Spain for their honeymoon. His
family is old money by mid-western standards, and big money
by Great Plains standards. He is witty, and urbane (he wrote
me a couple of letters, now sadly lost, and phoned me when
their first child was born, and another time when Margaret

was seriously ill). He has the kind of ambition I've always aspired to – the kind that takes no notice of conventions, or familial obligations. I went to visit them once, but was overcome by what seemed to me a parody of an Ibsen play. (The tame single friend theme.) We wrote only at Christmas.

Margaret did not come to my wedding. (I think I invited her.) She sent a cheerful, condescending letter asking for a detailed description of my bride. I think all four of us were embarrassed.

Three years ago, in her Christmas letter, Margaret embedded an oblique reference to her sanity. I cannot recall the exact words, but the gist of it was that she had been a trial to her husband and teenage children, but that their patience had pulled her through. (I hope that captures the mock nineteenth-century tone.)

It took me a week of effort to write back – to write something adequate and true and loving. I'm afraid what came out was the honorable physician offering help as a professional courtesy. Which, in truth, is all I had to offer.

There was no response for two years. Then in the card this Christmas, in fair copy in her best old high school hand, were two poems I can never show to anyone.

I have not replied. I will never.

7 The returns should be made for good received, not merely for good accepted

More completely: We ought to be disposed to make fitting and proportional returns, not only for the good we solicit, and not only for the good we explicitly accept, but for all the good we are aware of having received. The reasons are as follows.

Much of the good we receive from others is not actively solicited by us. For each of us, some goods are wholly unexpected, of types we do not actively promote, produced by people we do not know. Inventions, perhaps, or works of art, ideas, and initiatives. And much of the good we receive is not of a sort that we must make an effort to accept. Certain public goods – clean air, for example, or public health and safety – are in this category. With effort, we can reject them (e.g., by suicide). But it is the rejection, not the receipt, that characteristically requires the effort.

Sustaining the efforts that provide such goods is crucial. Many of them are necessary to our very development as rational agents; we need them before we can ask for them or accept them contractually, and we therefore need the social structures or personal virtues in others that will sustain the production of such goods. Further, even after we reach 'contractual' age, we need these noncontractual goods. The velocity and complexity of our lives prohibits anything resembling contractual negotiations with all the parties involved in the production of necessary public goods, for example. Insistence on a contractual model of these exchanges forces us toward the comical idea that with every breath we take we tacitly 'accept' – in a contractual sense – the benefits of the cooperative efforts that keep the air clean. It is clear that we do nothing of the sort, at least in most cases. We 'accept' these goods, for the most part, only in the sense that we *receive* them, make use of them, need them, or want them.

The question, then, is whether we ought to be disposed to reciprocate for such goods, once we realize their sources and values. Suppose we are *not* so disposed. Then by definition reciprocity will give no support to their production. To get them, we would have to depend on other sources of non-contractual obligation (duties of care, so to speak) to sustain the necessary social practices. Or perhaps we would have to rely on others' altruism and acts of love. On the other hand, if we *were* disposed to reciprocate for these non-contractual goods, we would have an additional, powerful means of sustaining their production. Just as reciprocity helps to sustain other sorts of social transactions, it would help to sustain these. (That is an empirical claim, but it seems a secure one.) We therefore have at least some warrant for defining the disposition to reciprocate so as to include returns for all the goods we receive, rather than merely the ones we accept. The remaining issue is whether support from reciprocity is *needed* for the production of these non-contractual goods.

The question of need is essentially an empirical matter. There is certainly no reason in principle to oppose a system in which the production of these goods is controlled by altruistic duties or virtues. But there is some reason in fact for thinking that such a system, *without* support from reciprocity, would be unreliable. Self-interest is not an eliminable part of our concerns. We can learn to let altruism dominate self-interest in many areas of our lives.

We can be disposed to discount our selfish motives generally. But we cannot rid ourselves of them. It seems safe to say, then, that social practices that rely *solely* on altruistic motives among participants are vulnerable. They will satisfy people's self-interested concerns only accidentally, and when that accidental connection is broken, it may be difficult to hold people to the practice. If people are disposed to reciprocate for the goods they receive, however, the connection to self-interest is not accidental. Participants can expect help in return for the help they give, benefits in return for the benefits they produce. That should make the continuance of the practice more secure, and given the importance of the goods at stake, such added security – no matter how strong the altruistic motives of participants – is surely to be prized. The reasons are ample, then, for holding that we ought to be disposed to return good for good *received*, not merely for the good accepted.

OBJECTION: There may be *some* reasons in favor of it, but there are *overwhelming* reasons against it. For one thing, such a disposition would create an unrelievable sense of debt. We receive benefits, after all, from millions upon millions of people who contribute to the public goods we enjoy. And we receive benefits from inventors, artists, production workers, managers, and clerks who produce many of the private goods we enjoy. Most of them do not even know that we exist. The notion that we should be disposed to make some sort of return to *all* of them is absurd. How could we ever finish such a task? How could we even begin? It would be all-consuming. And since we could not possibly accomplish the task, the disposition to try – to think that we ought, morally, to try – could only lead to a sense of moral failure. That would be destructive of the very sense of self-esteem reciprocity is supposed to help sustain.

REPLY: Recall again the arguments above about fittingness and proportionality. The sort of return it would be *fitting* to make is something comparable to the type of thing our benefactors did: E.g., make a contribution to the common stock of public goods; make a contribution to the private goods others may enjoy. The sort of return it would be *proportional* to make is a 'fair share', as that is defined above. A fair share is by no means an unrelievable debt. It is scaled to the benefits we actually receive, and then adjusted in terms of our ability to repay. Being disposed to return a fair share, so defined, is hardly an impossible burden. It need not lead to a sense of moral failure. It need not do anything to compromise self-esteem. If anything, it ought to enhance self-esteem by prompting us to carry our weight in the social life from which we take so much.

OBJECTION: On the contrary. What this reply makes clear is an invidious threat to self-esteem. If we were disposed to make these returns – 'fair' shares or not – we could no longer have the sense that we control our own destinies. It would be palpably clear to us that we were at the mercy of anyone who happened to thrust benefits upon us – benefits we did not ask for and could not refuse. That sense of vulnerability, that loss of autonomy, would hardly be conducive to self-esteem. Suppose you just want to live in peace, doing your fair share as previously defined, but your neighbors keep upping the ante? Do you have to keep upping your response? Do you have no control whatever over the situation? Here is a case, after one developed for other purposes by Robert Nozick in *Anarchy, State and Utopia*. Call it the benevolent neighborhood case.

Suppose you move into a quiet neighborhood. You are sociable and cooperative, and so are your neighbors. But for you, a house is just a shelter. You don't feel great pride of ownership. You don't 'identify' with the neighborhood. You just live there, doing the things necessary to keep your neighbors happy: keeping the exterior of the house presentable, loaning tools to your neighbors, helping them when they are sick, letting their children play in your spacious front yard. It is all nicely balanced, and not at all burdensome. Just the sort of arrangement you wanted when you moved out from the city. True, several things could be better about it. There are no streetlights, for example, making it hard for visitors to find your house. There is an unkempt field along one side of the neighborhood, and the owner of the field regularly tries to get it rezoned for light industry. Still, it is a lovely place to live. You like the streets dark at night because you are an amateur astronomer. You like the overgrown field aesthetically, from a distance. And most of all you like the lack of demands entailed by living in the neighborhood. But things suddenly change. Your neighbors form a neighborhood association. You decline to join, making it clear you like things the way they are, and don't have the time to go to association meetings. They go ahead without you and negotiate the installation of streetlights. (You have to admit that, on balance, they are an improvement. You benefit.) The association then incorporates itself and assesses dues. It buys the overgrown field, clears it, plants grass and trees, and makes part of the field into a playground. Again you benefit. (Your investment is now safe from the rezoning threat; the children don't have to play under your study windows, and so forth.) *But you didn't ask for any of this, and you don't have any choice about accepting or refusing the benefits your neighbors have created.* You just receive them. Why should you be disposed to make a return for them? Your neighbors knew your sentiments. We can suppose they are quite understanding – quite unconcerned about your being a free rider. Perhaps they even feel a little awkward about putting you in this position. Why should you be disposed to make a return? Why can't you opt out? Suppose your neighbors get giddy with success and start all sorts of other projects. Are you to have no control at all over these things? Are you to be entirely at the mercy of their benevolence? Where does this sort of thing *end*?

REPLY: It ends where the *goods* end. What lurks behind all these objections is the spectre of a *loss* – a loss of control over our lives and resources. But if that actually *happens* – if the 'benevolence' of meddlesome people results in a net loss to us – reciprocity will *not* dispose us to make a return. The *fear* of such a loss should not be confused with an *actual* loss. Reciprocity protects us against the latter. It is by definition an evil, and reciprocity disposes us to resist evils, not return good for them.

OBJECTION: That is far too quick and superficial. The *fear* of the loss may well be what makes life miserable. Everything our neighbors have done may *in fact* have been a net benefit for us, but we just wish on balance that they *hadn't* done it, because it makes us apprehensive about what they might do in the future – especially if they are encouraged by our reciprocation. If we were disposed to reciprocate as defined here, we would not be able to stop the cycle before we suffered 'actual' losses. We would be disposed to keep making returns, in effect egging our neighbors on, until they finally went too far.

REPLY: If their 'benevolence' makes our lives miserable, then they have *already* gone too far. And in general, even if we still receive *net* benefits – in a way we do not like – reciprocity will dispose us to do two things: resist the method (as an evil), and make a return for the actual benefit received. So in the case of the benevolent neighbors, if what makes us miserable is the openendedness of their activity and the tiresome, time-consuming methods they have chosen for doing it, then reciprocity will dispose us to tailor our returns to discourage those methods.

OBJECTION: Why not discourage the methods by not making a return for the benefits? Why not do the tailoring on the disposition to reciprocate? If we were disposed simply to make returns only for the good we *accept*, then these problems would not arise.

REPLY: There are two separate questions here. The first is about tactics. It may, on occasion, be a good *tactic* to refuse to make a return. That is consistent with reciprocity if the motive is to prevent imbalances and to resist evil methods. But changing the disposition itself is another matter. The objection behind that suggestion, after all, was about methods, not about the goods received. We *need* many of the public goods that we receive (receive as opposed to ask for and accept). Reciprocity should promote the production of those goods. It will do that only if it disposes us to make returns for them.

OBJECTION: There is still the matter of control. There is something objectionable, here, about the extent to which it is *other* people who control the extent of what we owe. It is one thing to grant the existence of natural duties – duties attached to our stations in life, for example. They may be beyond our direct control, but they are also beyond the direct control of others. Here, however, with reciprocity, others do have direct control. All they need to do is produce something that is genuinely good for us. We will then be forced to make a return. Surely it is natural to resist that. Surely that resistance is something that lies behind all of these objections.

REPLY: Other people's conduct is always controlling – no matter how we define reciprocity – in the sense that it constitutes a large part of the circumstances in which, and in terms of which, we must conduct our lives. The moral question addressed here is simply how we should be disposed to respond to an important *type* of circumstance – the one in which other people produce goods that we enjoy. My argument has been that we ought to be disposed to make a fitting and proportional return for the good we receive. Such a disposition will promote one of the most important circumstances imaginable, after all – the one in which what we get from others is good, rather than indifferent or evil. Such a disposition will not prompt us to participate in projects that do us harm; that is prevented by the fittingness requirement. And this sort of reciprocity will not overwhelm us with burdens; that is prevented by the proportionality requirement. So it is hard to see what the source of this objection could now be. People who are disposed not to reciprocate may of course object out of their contrary disposition – out of their contrary intuitions about the way we ought to behave. But to treat that sort of resistance as an objection to these arguments is to beg the question. These arguments are normative ones aimed at showing why people ought, morally, to be disposed *not* to object. Another source of resistance is of course the reluctance we all may feel about doing something we perceive to be onerous, or not in our immediate interest. But that begs the question also. The arguments here are designed to show that whether we intuit it to be true or not, or want it to be true or not, we *ought* to be disposed to return good for good received, all-things-considered. The empirical claim here is that to live otherwise is to promote a progressively impoverished life.

8 Reciprocity should be made a matter of retrospective obligation

More exactly: We ought to be disposed to reciprocate, in the way defined, and to treat failures to do so (retrospectively) as failures to fulfill requirements. We ought to be disposed to *make* reciprocation a requirement.

To be disposed to make reciprocation a moral requirement is to be disposed to ascribe blame to people who do not reciprocate, or to coerce them into reciprocating, or to punish them or extract compensation from them for their failure to reciprocate. That is just definitional – just part of what it *means* to treat reciprocation as a requirement rather than an ideal, a good, or a permissible option. It seems reasonable to call such requirements obligations, rather than duties. 'Obligation' typically carries the sense of a requirement that was generated by a social *transaction*. (E.g., a promise; a contract.) 'Duty' does not so regularly carry that sense. Some duties are said to be 'natural' – simply attached to one's 'station'. (E.g., the duty not to commit murder.) The requirement to reciprocate is clearly something that is generated by a social transaction.

Of course the 'requirement disposition' is typically quite complex. We excuse people from blame under certain circumstances. We sometimes blame, or coerce, or punish only very slightly, or very subtly. We sometimes refuse compensation. The details cannot be worked out here, however. The sorts of 'enforcement' that can be justified vary too much from case to case. Moral theory can only handle such issues in the context of much more specific considerations – e.g. discussions of familial obligations, or citizenship obligations. At present, the very general definition above must suffice.

Note I shall sometimes speak of 'treating' or 'regarding' reciprocation as required. Those locutions are meant to be synonyms for 'making reciprocation a moral requirement.'

There is often good reason to insist that people not have a 'sense' of obligation as they reciprocate, because that sense of obligation would diminish or destroy altogether the goods they seek. In continuing relationships, for example, acts of love usually have a reciprocal character, but they would be spoiled for the lovers if they were undertaken as obligations. In some other sorts of dealings, the opposite is true: things go much more smoothly if each party is acting out of a sense of obligation, and each perceives that in the others. (I like to know that the people to whom I have loaned my car feel *bound* to take good care of it and return it to me, as promised, with a full tank of gas.) Just *when* people ought to reciprocate out of a sense of obligation and when not is a topic best left for considerations of specific sorts of relationships. Here, at the most general level, the appropriate maxim merely leaves the matter open.

What cannot be left open, however, is that reciprocity should be treated — at least in retrospect, when people fail to give it — as a moral requirement. That is, there are good reasons for concluding, all things considered, that we ought to be disposed to regard it as such, at least in retrospect.

The reasons for concluding that reciprocity should be a requirement are these: Social equilibrium and productive social exchange are necessary for the generation of primary human goods. Reciprocity generates and sustains those things, and there is reason to conclude that it is indispensable for that task. (This is an empirical claim about human social psychology. See the scholium to this chapter.) Yet two tendencies pull us away from reciprocity. On some occasions we try to dominate exchanges — to tip the balance in our favor. On other occasions we tend toward altruism — we tend not to count the cost or ask for anything in return. These tendencies, given free rein, are likely to produce entrenched inequalities of a sort that damages primary goods. Such inequalities are injustifiable under the general conception.

Here is a familiar scenario from the human history of dominance struggles: Winners in initial contests gain advantages that make further victories easier. Victories are exploited to gain status and power. Status and power become entrenched — gradually institutionalized in hierarchical social class and political structures. Those structures are then closed against further competition, and challenges are suppressed. The wealth and welfare of the underclasses are then systematically plundered. Aggregate welfare is sacrificed on behalf of the privileged few.

The corresponding scenario for altruistic exchanges is more subtle but no less devastating. Initial imbalances occur gradually, inadvertently. Altruists do not count the cost, and things just do not always balance out. Moreover, altruists disguise their own sacrifices so as not to trouble others. But they are open about their delights, so as to please their benefactors. The gap widens, still concealed. When the disparity is finally recognized, it produces a tragicomic impasse (for pure altruists) in which the worse-off one tries to help the other retain the advantage and the other tries to refuse. More likely, self-interest asserts itself and a mismatched, bitter conflict ensues.

We are vulnerable, then, to tendencies that destroy our potential for balanced exchanges, and the primary goods reciprocation generates. The *capacity* for balanced exchanges must be preserved, against the effects of opposing tendencies, by insisting that overall *actual* balances in exchanges be preserved. (Recall that it was the actual imbalances that were at the root of the problem in the scenarios above.) In this sense, insisting on actual balances means making them required. Reciprocation, then, ought to be made (treated as, regarded as) a requirement.

If it ought to be made a requirement, then we ought to be *disposed* to make it such. After all, if we were disposed otherwise, we would not enforce actual balances, and hence not protect our capacity to reciprocate. But as noted above, a *prospective* sense of obligation in reciprocal transactions is not always justifiable. So what is left is a retrospective sense – a disposition to regard failures to reciprocate as failures to fulfill an obligation. Corrective measures can then be taken in time to prevent the entrenchment of unjust advantages. Reciprocity should be a 'retrospective deontic' virtue'.

Note It may also be that we should be selectively prospective – that is, reciprocate out of a sense of obligation in some sorts of cases but not all. But the prospect of constructing an argument that generates the necessary discriminations is daunting.

That leaves the question of stringency, and that question must be left for now. There is no general answer to it, as far as I can tell. It is obvious that the intricate exchanges in an intimate relationship call for very different sorts of constraints than the arm's length dealings of adversaries. The disposition to reciprocate must be sensitive to those things, but the details are best left to discussions of the specific types of relationships involved.

Objections

The remaining step in the justification is to consider possible reasons to the contrary. I shall do so by posing a series of objections to the arguments so far, and replying to each in turn. Some of these objections and replies are restatements of issues already considered. But the repetition has a purpose: It is to acknowledge the persistence of certain lines of objection and to show that even in their starkest forms they can be answered.

Power, Inequality, and Totalitarian Demands

OBJECTION: If we are disposed to reciprocate, as a matter of moral obligation, for every good we receive, then most of us will soon be slaves. Those who gain an initial advantage in scarce goods (through luck or natural ability or industry) will be able to increase and institutionalize their advantage by forcing reciprocal exchanges. They will be able to overwhelm the disadvantaged with benefits. Reciprocity will require commensurate returns. But what goods will the disadvantaged be able to offer? Service. Deference. A share of their product large enough to insure that they can never dig themselves out of the hole. The point is simply that temporary inequalities among people are inevitable. An obligation to reciprocate allows the unscrupulous to perpetuate and enhance those inequalities. And once the wicked acquire sufficient reserves, inequality can be institutionalized – through agencies designed to 'provide for' the disadvantaged. If these people are required to reciprocate (with service, which is all they have to offer that is proportional in value), their liberty will be eroded. The slide toward totalitarian government will be hard to stop. And it will have been engineered through the obligation to reciprocate.

REPLY: It will *not* have been engineered through reciprocity. Recall that commensurate exchanges are to be measured in terms of both benefits received and sacrifices made, with the final assessment to be made in terms of what best achieves the purposes of reciprocity. Those purposes are the promotion of the social equilibrium, self-esteem and social exchange required for a productive life – a productive life for all rational agents, under the presumption of equality. The only returns people are required to make are those that promote these goods. And, of course, we are not required to return good for evil. We are rather required to resist it. So cynical attempts to engineer overwhelming debts will fail – *if reciprocity as defined here is observed.*

OBJECTION: The manipulation of returns need not be *wicked*. It might just be entrepreneurial. An obligation to reciprocate for the goods we *receive* (as opposed to invite or accept) puts too much power in the hands of others. Enterprising people can shower us with unasked-for benefits – not to enslave us or to enshrine inequalities but simply to get benefits in return. ('It's more fun when it comes from you.') Or to store up reciprocity credits for a rainy day. Do we really want a principle that puts the extent of our obligations so thoroughly in the hands of others?

REPLY: The most direct rebuttal to this objection is to point out its underlying assumption: that the 'goods' these entrepreneurs shower upon us are, on balance, not *good* at all. (Otherwise, what is there to object to?) But if they are *not* good, reciprocity does *not* require a return. In fact, it requires us to resist the practice. So what is the problem?

OBJECTION: The problem is the *control* others have over the extent of our obligations.

REPLY: But we should be clear about the scope of that problem. We are not talking about malicious acts, or 'goods' that are not really good. Those cases have been dealt with. So what is left? Cases in which people of good will produce something that is genuinely good for us in the hope we will reciprocate. That is exactly the sort of behavior that is needed for a productive social life. A disposition to reciprocate for it is thoroughly justifiable.

OBJECTION: And if we *cannot* reciprocate? Suppose we are so ill, or so poor, that we cannot make a commensurate return. Yet we receive great benefits from others – perhaps life-saving benefits. If we had to feel *obligated* to make a return in those cases we would be under a terrible burden. One that would surely produce resentment.

REPLY: Commensurate returns in those cases are commensurate *sacrifices*, not commensurate *benefits*. As long as we are able to have social interactions at all with others, we can make such returns. And if we lack the power to have social interactions altogether, presumably we lack the sense of obligation as well.

Obligations to the Undeserving

OBJECTION: The reciprocity requirement is still too broad. It apparently requires that we make returns to people who benefit us only accidentally – and to those who do not intend to benefit anyone, but just do. This brings out the trouble with all the talk about indirect benefits. Much of the good we rely on (the conscientiousness of airline mechanics, for example) has nothing *specifically* to do with us. It is not produced specifically for us – perhaps not specifically for anyone. Why, then, should it create anything other than gratitude or relief on our part? Why are we required to return a benefit? In what sense do these 'accidental benefactors' deserve a return?

REPLY: Much of the good *we* produce is itself only accidentally beneficial to others. It is the fitting return we should make. (We return accidental, indirect or impersonal good for the accidental, indirect, or impersonal good we receive.) And if the return we make is commensurate as well, then the obligation to reciprocate has been fulfilled.

OBJECTION: What about people who try to produce benefits for us but fail? What do we owe them? Think of the friend who brings a fragile gift and breaks it accidentally in the process of handing it over. What are we supposed to do – break a comparable gift on her doorstep?

REPLY: The warm intentions and the attempt are gifts we *do* receive in that case. Surely we ought to be disposed to return those. And as for our dashed expectations, those were not goods received. Reciprocity either fails to engage them at all or, if they are evils, instructs us not to return them with evil.

OBJECTION: *And* it instructs us to *resist* such evil. That conjures up a comical spectacle: a session of moral education on the doorstep. 'Clumsy fool. Look what you've done.'

REPLY: There is nothing wrong with being disposed to help people to be less clumsy. There are oafish and ludicrous *ways* of doing that, but nothing in the notion of reciprocity suggests we should act in those ways.

OBJECTION: But doesn't the very structure of the disposition promote oafishness? Suppose three friends in a golf foursome help you look for a lost ball. One of them looks assiduously. The other two wander over to help half-heartedly, urging you to drop a new ball and take the penalty. One of the two spots the ball. Or change the case to something more important – a lost wallet, for example. The friend who *finds* the wallet is the one from whom you receive the good – or at any rate, the *most* good. Yet it doesn't seem right to let the *consequences* control our reciprocal response. Their *conduct* should be controlling. The one who looks the hardest deserves the most credit whether he finds the wallet or not. Yet reciprocity apparently suggests otherwise. It requires a return proportional to the benefits received – proportional to the consequences. The reluctant friend who actually finds the thing will get the lion's share of the reciprocity because he produced the lion's share of the benefits; the really helpful friend will get (by comparison) an empty handshake.

REPLY: Intentions *are* controlling, in the sense already explained. Benefits produced accidentally or grudgingly generate (at most) an obligation to make a comparably motivated return. Willing helpfulness, unlucky or not, gets something similar in return. There is nothing counterintuitive about that. And if it happens that the willing friend is clumsy or inefficient or inept in the help he gives, then we are back to something analogous to the broken gift case. We'd rather not have that kind of help; it's not (much) good to us. Reciprocity disposes us to discourage it.

Bookkeeping

OBJECTION: One of the bothersome aspects of the disposition to reciprocate is the fact that it requires people to keep score. That sort of thing may be all right at arm's length, but it is not the sort of thing friends and family and lovers do. (Or at least, not what they *should* do.) In fact, it is the sort of thing we stop doing when we make friends, or fall in love.

REPLY: The disposition to reciprocate does not require explicit or exact accounting. In fact, where such bookkeeping interferes with the practice of other virtues, it is unjustified. It is, after all, only a means, not an end in itself. And it is rarely even necessary once the habit of reciprocating is well ingrained, any more than sounding out the syllables is necessary for fluent readers. We just learn to keep relationships in balance without the sort of calculations that destroy spontaneity. But the importance of the equilibrium should not be forgotten. And the disposition to reciprocate is crucial to it.

OBJECTION: Still too cold-blooded – and wrongheaded. Balancing the books is not the point of an act of love. No matter how subtly or subconsciously it is done.

REPLY: Of course it's not the point. But it can be one of the *results*. And it is important to get that result. The equilibrium that reciprocity establishes is a means – something that enables us to *sustain* productive (justifiable) relationships.

OBJECTION: But the sense of 'obligation' here is still bothersome. In intimate relationships it is out of place. Perhaps we should be disposed to treat reciprocity as an ideal in those cases, and as an obligation only in more impersonal dealings. No doubt I *should* return my friends' dinner invitations (or take a gift with me when I go). But to say I should be disposed to think it my *obligation* to do so is quite a different matter.

REPLY: Agreed. And the arguments here do not say that we should be disposed to think of it as an obligation *while we do it*. They assert only that we should be disposed always to treat it as an obligation in retrospect, and only occasionally as an obligation in prospect. In intimate relationships it may well be that we should ordinarily reciprocate out of other motives (e.g., out of love rather than duty). The 'expectation' of reciprocity would arise (psychologically), then, only when something goes wrong. That is a very common feature of dispositions: They sometimes operate without our being conscious of them, and at other times we are quite aware of their presence. The important point here is not the awareness of the disposition, but the stringency of it. And it seems to me that it is precisely in intimate relationships that we should most expect reciprocity (in this retrospective sense) because it is precisely in those relationships that the failure to reciprocate can be most subtly disguised and be so subversive.

No Room for Pure Gifts or Pure Contracts

OBJECTION: Reciprocity now threatens to swallow up all social transactions. It looks as though every time I give or receive a good it will trigger someone's disposition to make a return. But surely we don't want that. Surely we want to preserve a place for pure benevolence or altruism on one side and pure contract on the other. We want to be able to give a gift without evoking a sense of obligation in the recipient, and we want to preserve the sort of 'We're quits' contractual relationship in which the exchange obligates neither party to continue the transaction. It looks as though reciprocity won't allow this – that it will govern all transactions.

REPLY: It will not govern them all from the *benefactor's* side. Reciprocity is a recipient's virtue. A benefactor's motives may be as purely altruistic as you like. The gift may be given with no expectation of return; no desire for a return; a desire that there be *no* return.

OBJECTION: But if we *know* the recipient is virtuous then we know we'll get a return. We won't be *able* to give a 'free' gift.

REPLY: Virtuous recipients will be sensitive to our motives – sensitive to what counts as a good for us. We can make it *plain* whether or not we will accept a *quid pro quo* return. We can say, in effect, that the pleasure of seeing our gift enjoyed is all the return we want. We can make it clear that acceptance of the gift is all we want. This sort of thing is a common practice. People have a large repertoire of ways of communicating such things, and we think people deficient if they cannot respond to such signals.

OBJECTION: But deficient in reciprocity? Why not just deficient in sensitivity, or social grace, or tact?

REPLY: That too, probably. But if we want no reciprocal reaction from our beneficiaries – then we will have to disguise the very fact of the gift – disguise it so completely that they are not aware of having received anything. That can sometimes be managed. (Edith Wharton is said to have disguised a large gift of money to Henry James as a publisher's advance.) If we just want to be anonymous, that too can be managed. But if not, if we want to delight a friend and take pleasure in his delight, how will we want that friend to be disposed to respond? I suggest we will want him to read our intentions and respond in a way that completes them. *That* is a reciprocal response.

OBJECTION: But recipients will still, then, be looking for some way to reciprocate – even if it is only by giving us the benefit of their delight or gracious acceptance. They *must* do so, in this theory about reciprocity, if they are disposed to make a return for all the good they get. The question is *why*? Why must they always feel this way? It taints the gift for both parties. I give out of a desire to please you, but I know that my gift will prompt you to try to make some sort of return – indirect or not. You receive the gift with pleasure, but that won't be pure either – even if I let you know your pleasure is all I want. Your desire to make the appropriate return will intervene. What a grim life.

REPLY: No. That fear is based on a confusion. We mustn't confuse the disposition to reciprocate with the disposition to *consider, consciously*, every act of reciprocation. Virtues are much more complex than that. Think of the analogy to linguistic ability. Our use of language is controlled by complex dispositions too, but we do not consciously consider the rules of syntax every time we read a sentence. Living out a life in which we are disposed to return good for good received can be full of spontaneity and unconscious mental processes.

OBJECTION: That brings us right back to the problem of contract. There it would be the unconscious part of the disposition that would be likely to cause the trouble. There ought to be a place for one-time transactions, but reciprocity – at least as an unconscious motive – will tend to perpetuate serial transactions, or perhaps leave people with a vague feeling that they should carry on.

REPLY: Not if the transactions are perceived as balanced. And I take it that we ought to be alert to the possibility that even our most carefully considered contracts might be, or become, unbalanced. When that is true, the disposition to reciprocate can make a useful contribution to the process of adjusting the contractual obligations.

Freeriders

OBJECTION: In large-scale societies, the failure of a few people to reciprocate is not damaging. And since reciprocation is costly to the recipient, it looks as though it would be rational to be a freerider for as long as you can get away with it. In fact, at most, the argument here justifies only this freerider version of the disposition to reciprocate. We ought to be disposed to reciprocate only to the extent that it is effective in preserving social equilibrium, etc. The intention to adopt that disposition is generalizable. (If everyone were disposed to do only the minimum required, we would still reap the benefits.) And it would allow each of us, then, to 'ride free' – as long as enough others were reciprocating to sustain productive social exchanges.

REPLY: Such a disposition is inconsistent with the goal of sustaining social exchange. It leads to the following dilemma. Every agent would presumptively be justified in having the freerider disposition. (By the generalization rule and the presumption of equality.) Each agent who had it would reason as follows: At any given moment, there will either be enough reciprocation to sustain productive social exchange or there will not be enough. If enough people reciprocate, then I will not. (My help would be superfluous and costly, and my freerider disposition would operate to keep me from giving the help.) On the other hand, if not enough people reciprocate, then I will not do so either. (The probability is very low that my contribution would put the effort over the top. The contribution would be costly for me, and futile. My disposition to reciprocate only when it is effective – only when doing so would produce good that I could not otherwise obtain – would again operate to keep me from reciprocating.)

In either case then, when generalized, the disposition to be a freerider would be self-defeating. 1) We must have the goods reciprocity produces. They are necessary for satisfying the requirements of the general conception of morality. (Specifically, the development of rational agency and the satisfaction of the teleological and deontological aspects of the general conception.) 2) There are good reasons for adopting a reciprocity disposition in order to satisfy those requirements. 3) But any version of the disposition that puts us into the dilemma just outlined will not allow the disposition to satisfy those requirements. 4) *Ceteris paribus*, any such version is unjustifiable. 5) The freerider version is such a version. 6) Therefore the freerider version is unjustifiable.

OBJECTION: Here is another version of the disposition. Call it the criminal version: We ought to be disposed to reciprocate only when we cannot get away with doing otherwise. That is, as long as others don't notice it or care, and yet go on reciprocating themselves, there is no need to participate.

REPLY: Some people have the criminal version, and some of them profit from it. Others suffer. But in theory the criminal version cannot be justified. Moral theory cannot justify something whose general adoption would *decrease* the degree to which its requirements are satisfied – all things considered. And the general adoption of the criminal version would presumably do just that. It would decrease the extent to which reciprocity would satisfy the requirements. Therefore: If reciprocity is to be one of the ways we use to satisfy the requirements, then it is hard to see how the criminal version could be justified. To be justified, it would have to be required by some *other* feature of moral life – one that outweighed the damage done to reciprocity. Without a showing that there is such a feature, the criminal version of the reciprocity disposition is unjustified.

Priorities

OBJECTION: The relation of reciprocity to other features of moral life has not been discussed. It has not been established that a disposition to reciprocate is compatible with them (whatever they may be). And even if it is in general compatible, there is no guarantee that the specific details of the disposition proposed here are compatible.

REPLY: There is no denying that the results of this inquiry are provisional. Further considerations, say of topics like friendship or altruism, may force revisions in some of these results. But that is true of all moral theory under the general conception. It is always subject to review in the light of further relevant considerations. So it is no objection to the arguments here to point out that they *might* have to be revised. Of course they might. Absent a *specific* objection – that is, reference to a specific feature of moral life that can be justified and appears to be in conflict with reciprocity – there is no objection to answer, here.

OBJECTION: But what about priorities? The argument is that reciprocity is in effect an obligation. Obligations presumably take precedence over mere ideals, or prudence, or whatever. But what kind of precedence? That is, how much of our own welfare must we sacrifice to satisfy the obligation to reciprocate? Surely a justification of reciprocity must give a general answer to these priority problems.

REPLY: Reciprocity is a fundamental concern, in the sense that its justification is given in terms of things necessary to moral agency as such. And since it is a deontic norm, reciprocity is fundamental in another sense. But until we compare it with the details of other elements of moral life, it is very difficult to say what it has priority over, and how much weight it should be given. As a matter of definition, it outweighs any single ideal or value that conflicts with it. Given the presumption of equality, it is equal to any single deontic consideration that conflicts with it. (And outweighed by two or more of those considerations.)

But how many values ought to be sacrificed for a duty? How many ideals ought to be compromised? I do not know of a way to answer those questions in general. As far as I can tell, they can only be addressed by restricting the inquiry to a specific priority problem, in a specific context. (Example from Rawls: The priority of equal liberty in industrialized democracies.) And that is the way I shall deal with priority problems in the remainder of this book – by addressing them in the context of specific problems.

The Indeterminateness of it All

QUESTION: Your contention, then, is that this whole enterprise is provisional and incomplete. That the details of the disposition may have to be revised when other moral principles or virtues are considered. That the priority rules must be found case by case. And even then they cannot be settled in a general way, since new circumstances may arise that could change the outcome. By implication, the same is true of moral theory as a whole. It is as changeable as the conditions of human life. It is as indeterminate and unfinished as it is partial. And since we cannot do it all at once — hold it all in view at once — it will always have the sort of indeterminacy that these arguments about reciprocity exhibit. Do you actually want people to *accept* that vision of moral theory — and the consequent uncertainty for moral life?

REPLY: Yes.

CHAPTER 4

Virtues and Priorities

Under the general conception of morality, we must expect the inventory of virtues, and the way those virtues are ordered, to change with the conditions of human life. Drastic changes in the human condition would produce comparably drastic changes in the account of the virtues. There would be little need for justice, for example, in a world of perfect benevolence and abundance; little scope for generosity in a world of extreme scarcity. Cultural differences might also be reflected in the account of the virtues. The relative importance, say, of courage and conscientiousness might be very different now than it was in Homeric Greece. Moral theory is thus tied to facts about the human condition generally, and to the various societies in which people live.

A complete moral theory would give an account of how the various virtues fit together, given existing conditions, and how they fit with teleological and deontological concerns. Can courage, properly defined, conflict with prudence? If so, which should be controlling? Can benevolence, properly defined, conflict with a duty to tell the truth? If so, which should yield? Can reciprocity, properly defined, conflict with self-interest in a given case? If so, how should we decide what to do in that case? A complete moral theory would answer such questions – either by showing that morality is a perfectly *seamless* whole, in which there are at bottom no separate elements that could conflict with one another; or by showing that morality is a perfectly *harmonious* whole, in which there are at bottom no genuine conflicts between the separate elements; or by showing that morality is a perfectly *ordered* whole, in which all genuine conflicts are effectively resolved by a set of priority rules.

This book is not an attempt at a complete moral theory. My conviction is that such a theory would have to rely on priority rules – that moral values, duties and virtues are irreducibly plural, and irreducibly in conflict in the absence of priority rules. But I will not argue that point here. Instead, I will focus on some practical realities: In practice, we reason in terms of a plurality of conflicting moral principles. In practice, we have conflicting moral dispositions.

This chapter gives some reasons for thinking that the claims of reciprocity have a high priority when they come in conflict with other elements of morality. It also outlines some virtues that are closely related to reciprocity in the sense that, without them, being disposed to reciprocate might not be a virtue at all. Succeeding chapters, or sections of them, will also comment on these matters. The cumulative effect of these discussions is meant to establish that reciprocity is a fundamental virtue, in a sense presently to be defined.

Note on terminology In what follows I shall use the terms 'reciprocity,' 'generosity,' and so forth to refer to the *dispositions* to reciprocate, act generously, etc. I shall use related terms (e.g., 'reciprocation,' 'acts of generosity,') to refer to the acts that flow from the dispositions.

Reciprocity as a Fundamental Virtue

It is plausible to think that some morally justifiable dispositions are less important than others – in the sense that, in most cases of conflict, moral theory will conclude that they must yield to those other virtues. We can easily imagine cases, for example, in which tact is justifiably sacrificed for efficacy, and *if* it is true that in *most* cases tact *ought* to be subordinate to efficacy, then we may say that the disposition to be tactful is a less important, or a less fundamental, virtue than the disposition to be effective.

Pairwise comparisons like that, however, are not a very feasible way of establishing the priority of a given virtue. Aside from the difficulty of surveying an adequate range of cases for each pair, the 'winner' of each comparison would then have to be pitted against each of the other virtues in a sort of round-robin tournament to determine overall rankings. And before we could even begin such a process we would have to have an adequate inventory of the virtues – something that is itself a daunting task. For present purposes, something considerably less will have to suffice.

What I propose to do is to outline a set of criteria that it seems reasonable to think any disposition would have to meet in order to dominate others regularly in the theoretical resolution of conflicts, and then show that reciprocity meets those criteria. My purpose will be to show that there are good reasons for granting reciprocity a presumption of priority (subject always to countervailing argument) when it comes in conflict with elements of moral theory that do not meet those criteria – or do not meet them fully.

Note I shall say that elements of moral theory (the maxims of a virtue, or teleological or deontological principles) conflict in a given case if the prescriptions they yield for conduct in that case are mutually exclusive. To say that one of the conflicting elements has presumptive priority over the others is to say that, in the absence of sound argument to the contrary, its prescriptions for conduct in that case are the ones moral theory will yield.

Criteria for a Fundamental Virtue

1 *Deontic character* Deontic principles and maxims, by definition, set boundaries for permissible conduct. Nondeontic principles and maxims are meant to operate within those boundaries, and (*ceteris paribus*) yield to deontic ones. Deontic virtues, therefore, have presumptive priority over nondeontic virtues. Reciprocity is a deontic virtue.

2 *Connection to primary goods* Primary goods are those necessary for life itself, and for agents' ability to generate goods within their lives. Some dispositions (e.g., pain avoidance; need reduction) are directly instrumental for creating and sustaining primary goods, while other dispositions (e.g., a preference for corn over lima beans; a fondness for vocal music) are not. Further, among the directly instrumental dispositions, some are necessary for producing and sustaining primary goods; others are not. It is reasonable to hold that the necessary dispositions

ought to have presumptive priority over those that are either not directly instrumental for primary goods, or not necessary for them. Reciprocity is necessary for creating and sustaining the primary good of a productive social life.

3 *Inclusiveness* Among the deontic virtues necessary for primary goods, some set boundaries for a wide range of activities and institutions, while others have a relatively narrow focus. The disposition to be just, for example, is triggered only in social situations of a special sort: i.e., those in which agents have competing or conflicting interests. Reciprocity, by contrast, is *not* confined to situations of social conflict; it is meant to operate in all social transactions. In that sense, reciprocity is a more inclusive virtue – a wider virtue – than justice. Now presumptive priority rules are devices for placing the burden of proof in moral argument – devices for eliminating duplicative argument and getting closure in disputes about conflicting maxims or principles. Other things equal, it makes sense to give presumptive priority to the more inclusive virtues, as a way of simplifying moral argument. The reason is this: The more inclusive virtues, since they apply to large areas of our lives, are likely to come in contact with, and need to be made compatible with, a considerable variety of more narrowly circumscribed virtues. Absent sound argument to the contrary, if each of the narrower virtues is adjusted to be compatible with the more inclusive ones, it is plausible to think that that would also reduce conflicts between the narrower ones. So ordering presumptive priority rules to match relative inclusiveness seems a sensible strategy.

[*Caution*: Such ordering is a sensible strategy *within* the class of virtues that satisfy criteria 1) and 2) above. But there would be obvious objections to extending this priority principle to the virtues generally. Prudence, for example, is probably more inclusive than justice. Though prudence is confined to situations in which there is some risk to the agents involved, it is not confined either to social situations generally, or to situations of social conflict. Yet because justice is deontic and prudence is not, or at least not usually thought to be, it would be implausible to hold that the disposition to be just should be trimmed to fit the disposition to be prudent.]

Reciprocity is Fundamental

It was argued in Chapter Three that reciprocity is a deontic virtue, and that it is, given the conditions of the lives of moral agents as we understand them, necessary for creating and sustaining the primary goods summarized in the phrase 'a productive social life'. In addition, it was argued in Chapter Three that we should be disposed to reciprocate in *all* social transactions involving goods (and by implication, evils). Thus reciprocity's claim to being a very inclusive virtue seems secure as well. Reciprocity therefore satisfies the three criteria here proposed for a fundamental virtue. It is fundamental in the sense that its prescriptions for conduct justifiably take presumptive priority over prescriptions derived from virtues that do not satisfy the criteria.

This result, while it does not entail that reciprocity has priority in any *particular* case, does establish – at least with respect to all the virtues that do not meet the criteria – that in conflicts with reciprocity it is they, absent sound argument to the contrary, that must give way. Considering the list of virtues involved here (e.g., courage, self-control, prudence, kindness . . .), this is a significant result.

That leaves the question of presumptive priorities *within* the class of fundamental virtues. Here it seems plausible to assume that reciprocity is one of the *most* fundamental virtues – that in fact its only serious competitor for sole possession of the title is justice. (This is, however, largely an assumption, because in the absence of an analysis of all those other virtues – an analysis structured like the one given for reciprocity – it is difficult to make the comparisons.) Other deontic virtues – such as truthfulness and fidelity – appear to be either less inclusive or less directly connected to primary goods than either reciprocity or justice. Assuming equal deontic weight, then, both reciprocity and justice would dominate the others.

The priority relation between justice and reciprocity is a difficult thing to assess even in a preliminary way. I have only two observations to offer, neither of them very helpful. The first is that at least one element of reciprocity, the fittingness and proportionality maxim, is probably also a constituent of justice. But I am uncertain whether that has any general importance for the priority question.

I will have some remarks in Chapter Eight, however, about its importance with respect to obedience to law.

The second observation is that reciprocity appears to be more inclusive than justice, while justice might well turn out to be the more exacting virtue – the more stringent of the two. But because the two overlap, and are both so directly connected to primary goods, it is hard to see how an adequate *general* case for the priority of either one could be made. I will have more to say about this matter in Chapter Six, in the discussion of another sort of priority problem.

Nevertheless, this much is clear: Reciprocity is *a* fundamental virtue in the sense specified here, and *if* it is subordinate to any other virtue, it is probably subordinate only to justice. That much will be enough to serve the arguments in succeeding chapters.

Related Virtues

Reciprocity, taken by itself, is insufficient for its own purposes. That is just trivially true in the sense that any intention or effort or inclination will fail in the absence of the means to carry it out. But it is also true in a more interesting sense: virtues come in mutually supportive clusters. Any disposition, in the absence of the appropriate support, is more likely to be a vice than a virtue.

Intellectual abilities are good examples. Quickwittedness is no virtue unless it is reasonably accurate, and accurate analysis is often useless without imagination. But the same general point applies to the moral virtues: Fidelity and courage, courage and prudence, prudence and generosity, generosity and temperance are familiar pairs. In general, the virtues are interconnected. They come in clusters or not at all.

Reciprocity is at the center of such a cluster – a set of traits whose presence with reciprocity enhances productive social interaction, and whose absence compromises the effectiveness of reciprocity. The reciprocity cluster includes many of the standard virtues in thoroughly predictable versions. I shall not rehearse these matters. It seems pointless, for example, to go over the ways in which honesty and fidelity and courage are required.

There are, however, four virtues that have especially important connections to reciprocity. They are generosity, conviviality, empathy, and practical wisdom. I shall make some remarks on each of them in turn. The discussion of each will center on the sense in which it is necessary for, or supportive of, the effectiveness of reciprocation. The compatibility of each virtue with the formal requirements of moral theory will be addressed, as will the fact that each can be argued for on grounds that are independent of its connection to reciprocity. Such considerations help to shape the version of each that is finally justifiable.

This is, however, a book about reciprocity. I will not attempt a full account of any of its related virtues, and I hope readers will be tolerant of the terse and perhaps even dogmatic tone of what follows. What I am striving for is an economical presentation of ancillary matters. I do not mean to suggest that I think these related virtues, considered separately, would be any less complex than reciprocity, or any less beset by philosophical problems. For the most part, I will simply assume that the version of each that best supports reciprocity will also turn out to be the one, or very like the one, that is justifiable all things considered. That assumption is plausible because reciprocity is a fundamental virtue, in the sense previously discussed. It is therefore plausible to assume that while other versions of the related virtues may be better for other things, on balance the ones best for reciprocity – or ones very like them – will prevail. But this *is* only an assumption; I will not argue further for it.

This is Lacey's story. I shouldn't tell it, but it's too good to keep. She'd been in the studio all afternoon working in plaster. Pretty hot and messy. She was in those overalls of hers with nothing underneath. Sarah was sitting for her. Sarah. The one with the hair. Yes, well, they decided to go out for a beer. I know, I know. Just wait till you hear the rest. Lacey put on a tee-shirt and they took her motorcycle. You know Lacey's helmet? Well, she's got a better one for the rider. Captain Gross. They went to that place down on South Creek – the one with all the pickups and shotguns. It's closest, and it was only four in the afternoon. Practically nobody there. They walked up to the door and this giant lime green woman meets them. Blocks the door. Lime green double knit pantsuit. Blond beehive hair. Lacey and Sarah take their helmets off. Sort of a reflex, Lacey thinks. Well, they know it's their clothes, and the motorcycle and so on, but Lacey thinks what the hell, I've got a tee-shirt on and shoes too. So she says to the woman, We'd like to come in for a beer. The woman just looks at Lacey for a minute, and then shakes her head. She says, Do you look like me? Well, Lacey doesn't catch it. I mean, she remembers now she did hear it, but didn't think she did. She thought maybe she wasn't hearing too well because of the motorcycle. So she says again that they want to come in for a beer, and the woman takes a step outside the door this time and very slowly says 'Do, you, look, like, me?'

Well, Lacey goes automatic. She doesn't know why this next comes out. She says, very carefully to the woman, No, I don't look like you, I'm an *artist*.

Everything is *soundless* for a second. Suspended. Lacey says she couldn't hear a thing until Sarah started to giggle and the woman started to laugh. Lacey just broke up. You know how she is when she gets started. All three of them, this time, laughing at themselves. They thought they'd never get stopped.

There was never any question of their getting in to that place, but the pantsuit woman brought them some beers to go.

I wish I'd been there. I wish I'd seen that.

Generosity

To reciprocate is to respond to a benefit or harm in a way that restores and sustains social equilibrium. But reciprocity does not initiate social exchanges, it completes them. Other dispositions are needed to get the process going.

Generosity, as its Latin root suggests, can *generate* social exchange – at least among people who are already disposed to reciprocate. For that reason alone, generosity is an important adjunct to reciprocity. Furthermore, a particular version of the disposition to be generous reinforces reciprocity.

Elements of Generosity

INITIATIVES Given that some forms of social interaction are necessary goods, it is clear that initiatives are necessary *as means* to those goods. (A situation in which each person does no more than wait for another to start is a situation in which no one will start.) So the intention never to take the initiative is not generalizable. That is, its generalized form 'No one ought ever to take the initiative' is inconsistent with the prescription to achieve the necessary goods of social interaction.

On the other hand, the contrary principle 'I ought *always* to take the initiative' has problems of its own. To intend that 'Everyone ought always to take the initiative' is to intend it to be true that 'Everyone always takes the initiative.' In many situations that is impossible. (Only one player is allowed to open a chessgame.) And in others, while it is not impossible for everyone to take the initiative, their doing so is incompatible with the achievement of intended goods. (Think of drivers at a four-way stop.)

A *disposition* to take the initiative, subject to the constraints of right-of-way rules, solves the problem nicely. If everyone were so disposed, and knew the right-of-way rules of a given enterprise, that enterprise would always get started. Whether it would then be sustained, and whether it is justifiable in the first place, are separate issues.

Assume the enterprise is the achievement of the necessary goods of social interaction. Social exchange, of the sort governed by reciprocity, is a necessary means to these goods. Exchange requires an initial proffer of goods. If everyone were disposed (subject to the right-of-way rules) to make such proffers when exchanges were necessary, then we would have the following result: Whenever someone knew the exchange was necessary, and was able to initiate it, it would get started. To the extent that such a disposition is lacking (i.e., is weak, or restricted in scope, or entirely absent in some agents) there is a corresponding inability to generate the necessary goods. To the extent that the disposition is restricted to 'necessary' exchanges – as opposed to justifiable exchanges generally – there is a corresponding diminution in the ability to generate goods *per se*. On the valuational principle that more good is better than less, moral theory will favor the presence, in everyone, of a disposition to take the initiative in all justifiable exchanges (subject to right-of-way rules).

Generosity is such a disposition. In part, it is a readiness to give – a readiness to proffer goods to others. That element of it is clearly justifiable. (It should be noted, however, that generosity is not the only complex disposition that has this 'initiatives' component. An entrepreneurial disposition might also have it, as would an experimental one, or an altruistic one.)

OPENHANDEDNESS   Generosity is also liberality in the proffering of goods. Generous people are unstinting. They are not disposed to do just the bare minimum, and they are not disposed to keep exact reciprocity accounts. ('We've had them over twice this year. They've only invited us to dinner once. The museum trip doesn't count. So they owe us.') Further, in reciprocal exchanges, generous people tend to give the benefit of the doubt, about how much is owed, to the other's estimate.

This aspect of generosity reinforces the value of reciprocal exchange. The generalization of the contrary intention ('Everyone ought to give only the bare minimum') is not *inconsistent* with the intent to achieve a productive social life. We could manage if everyone kept exact accounts. But liberality reduces conflict in the following way: people often differ about how much is owed – and differ over very small amounts. Moreover, they may feel cheated by an exact accounting that proves their initial estimate wrong. Generosity prevents some of this. A disposition to ignore small differences in favor of the other person reduces unproductive conflict and unfounded ill-feeling. At least, it does so if it is quite generally present in the population, along with the disposition to reciprocate. If not, then others are not likely to return the favor, and the small differences one continues to ignore may add up to something significant – something that, in terms of the rationale for reciprocity, ought not to be ignored.

This raises an important point. Generosity, as defined here, is meant to contribute to the ends we seek through reciprocity. No doubt the initiatives generous people take, and the liberality they show, put them somewhat at risk. But the sort of generosity that is compatible with reciprocity is not imprudent, or extravagant, or altruistic. It operates in the expectation of *a general pattern of* reciprocal exchanges. Should that general pattern be absent, generosity would not be justifiable – at least not on the grounds here offered for it. Within that general pattern, however, and constrained by an agent's own disposition to reciprocate, the risks are not imprudent. The benefits are considerable.

MAGNANIMITY   The final element of generosity is the willingness to lay aside resentment – the readiness to forgive injuries.

Reciprocity requires restitution. But once restitution is made, there remains the matter of restoring the pattern of productive social exchange. Restitution is often inadequate for the task. This is so in part because, for some things, full restitution is impossible. (Think of compensation paid to survivors for the wrongful death of a family member.) In such cases, a continuing sense of debt can cripple both victim and wrongdoer. It can, to put it crudely, diminish the prospects each has for a productive social life – either with each other or with others. And even in cases where full restitution *can* be made, the making of it may not dissolve the *feelings* of resentment in the victim or guilt in the wrongdoer. Such feelings also compromise a productive social life.

Generosity – in the sense of a disposition to lay aside residues of resentment – is therefore an important adjunct to reciprocity. Notice that it is not, here, defended as a substitute for restitution; that would be incompatible with the moral requirement of reciprocity. But *after* restitution is made, *after* the obligation to reciprocate is met as fully as possible, a disposition to forgive the remainder of the debt, and to ignore one's lingering resentment or guilt, is a very useful thing to have. It makes an important contribution to a productive social life.

Conviviality

I shall use the term conviviality to refer to the disposition to participate in and take pleasure in social life. A complete unwillingness to enter into any social interactions whatsoever is incompatible with the requirements of moral theory. That is, its generalization is inconsistent with the attempt to achieve necessary goods. But just as evidently, many of the goods produced by social interaction are not necessary to rational agency as such, and the disposition to produce them cannot justifiably be treated as a moral requirement on that ground.

Elements of Conviviality

SOCIALITY   The goods necessary to produce and sustain rational agency as such can only be produced through social interaction.

Moral theory under the general conception therefore imposes a moral requirement on everyone to act so as to enable those goods to be produced – to be disposed to act so as to produce them. But depending on the circumstances, fulfilling that requirement might involve very little in the way of social interaction, and the corresponding disposition to participate in social life might be as minimal as a mere willingness to live alongside others (perhaps at a great psychic or physical distance) and to interact with them only when it is 'necessary'. In any case, at least this minimal version of the disposition, given the appropriate definition of 'necessary', can justifiably be treated as a moral requirement.

A more robust version is justifiable as a matter of supererogation, however: the willingness to *contribute* to enterprises that *enhance* a productive social life. Note the implicit restrictions: this is a disposition to contribute. It is not a disposition to take over, or exhaust oneself in the effort. And it is only justifiable enterprises that are involved. A disposition to participate in injustice, or to be meddlesome, or to join in anything that anyone happens to propose, is hardly a virtue. But the readiness to contribute, suitably restricted, *can* significantly enrich the lives of individuals. The more widespread this disposition is in a given population, the better the results. Since the results are not necessary to rational agency as such, the disposition that produces them cannot be treated as a moral requirement. But on the valuational principle that more of a good is better than less, it is certainly justifiable as a supererogatory element of moral life.

SOCIABILITY   A further element of conviviality is the disposition to seek and give pleasure in the company of others – *to be and to live in good company*. The ability to take pleasure in the company of others, to give others pleasure, and the disposition to seek out and sustain such company, has obvious benefits. Intrinsic values aside, it obviously reinforces reciprocity.

It does so in two ways: For one thing, it provides an additional motive for the sort of social equilibrium reciprocity is designed to sustain, and hence for reciprocal exchanges. That sort of equilibrium is important for self-esteem, and for the esteem of others. Both of these things are connected causally with one's success in convivial pursuits. So people who are disposed to be convivial in this sense will thereby have an additional incentive, beyond the sense of obligation engendered by reciprocity, for reciprocating. Conviviality thus reinforces reciprocity.

For another thing, sociability reduces the 'cost' of reciprocity. Reciprocal exchanges among convivial people are occasions for taking pleasure in social life. But making a return is often felt as a 'cost', and may in itself be quite unpleasant. A disposition to be sociable can generate pleasures in social transactions as such, and hence offset the felt costs of reciprocating. In that way sociability can reinforce reciprocity. Moreover, *whatever* pleasure one can take in justifiable exchanges is – *ceteris paribus* – all to the good. Conviviality can produce such good.

> I got the strangest telephone call today. Touching, really. From Mr. Fullerton, the newspaper carrier. Thanking us for the Christmas gift we sent.
> We sent?
> A ten-dollar check, I think. I don't remember exactly. Anyway, he said he just wanted to thank us. I said we appreciated his service. He said he tried to give good service but not everyone seemed to appreciate it. I said well, we did, and especially the fact that he never missed a day, even in the worst weather, and we were so far out in the country.
> So?
> He said he had a lot of customers out our way, but we were so generous, and every year it was more.
> And?
> And I said it was nothing, and he said it was something special, I didn't know, and back and forth and back and forth. It just seemed to be an endless conversation. Finally I just said thank you, but if that's the way he felt about it, next year I'd cut it back to five. To stop these damn phone calls.

Empathy

Empathy is a form of vicarious experience. It is having a facsimile of another's psychological state – particularly the emotional and conative elements of that state. It is feeling what another feels – in the knowledge that one's experience is vicarious.

As a virtue – that is, as a disposition that is justifiable under the general conception of morality – empathy is precarious and subtle.

It is precarious because the belief that one has 'the same' feelings as another is always suspect. And it is precarious because it is always balanced on a narrow rail between too much and too little. (Bleeding hearts; cold fish.) The subtlety of it comes from the delicate perceptual abilities required to read people's emotions accurately, and from the intricate inhibitions and propensities we must have to regulate how often, and how fully, we empathize. ('Not in the car, please.') This subtlety, combined with the utterly familiar place empathy has in our lives, makes it difficult to say much about the topic – at least in general terms – that does not sound either foolish or trite. Fortunately, what needs to be said here does not need to be said at length.

Empathy and Reciprocity

Empathetic understanding of another's point of view is sometimes useful in reciprocal transactions. For one thing, reciprocity requires us to consider the size of a good or evil from all the relevant points of view – that is, to consider the values attached to a thing by all the relevant agents. This is part of the process of finding the size and type of return to be made. Sometimes – but only sometimes – empathy is important to that process.

Consider: For the most part, the velocity of our lives and the size of our society force us to operate in terms of assumptions about whole classes of people – assumptions about what people in general regard as good, and about their preference schedules. We have neither the time nor the need to try to 'sense', empathetically, how each of the relevant agents experiences the thing in question. But there are other cases (in one-to-one dealings, for example) in which reciprocity requires the kind of fine tuning for which global assumptions are inadequate. We need to know how a particular individual regards the thing in particular, and we need fairly precise information. Empathy – assuming its accuracy – can provide some of that. It is quick. It reduces the need for tedious and exasperating inquiries. (E.g., the TV sportscaster's mindless 'How do you feel?' asked of an exhausted marathoner.) And it forces one in the direction of giving *equal* consideration to the experience of others. Our own vivid desires, laid against a mere belief about how others feel, tend to acquire an unfounded importance in our moral deliberations. Empathy can reduce that. In short, it has cognitive value.

.Empathy also has some emotional effects that enable and reinforce the disposition to reciprocate. Feeling the forgiveness of another can help one to eliminate unfounded guilt; feeling the repentance of another can enable one to lay aside residual resentment. Empathy can motivate the return of good for good. (One has a fuller sense of the value of the return.) It can motivate the refusal to return evil for evil. And it can strengthen the resolve to exact restitution.

Empathy can have value for reciprocity only under fairly severe conditions, however. In general terms, those conditions are as follows.

ACCURACY   Inaccurate facsimiles can generate moral error. Our empathetic powers must be *reliable* if we are to be justified in using them in the ways described above. Perhaps an artist's empathy need not be accurate – insofar as it is used to generate the raw material of a work of art. But inaccuracies in the estimation of another's values defeat the purpose of reciprocal exchange.

COMPLETENESS   Similarly, incompleteness in the range of empathic powers can produce moral error. Empathizing with only some of the relevant agents can be worse, for purposes of reciprocation, than empathizing with none of them.

APPROPRIATENESS   Completeness in scope is not completeness in number. We cannot hope to empathize with everyone whose interests are morally relevant to our conduct. Nor would it be appropriate to try. We can only hope to be able to empathize with all the relevant 'types' of people, and to be alert to the times when empathizing with some one person is necessary – as opposed to the times when it is merely beneficial, or the times when it is not beneficial at all. Sometimes it can be disabling.

SELF-AWARENESS   In the form justifiable for reciprocating, empathy is not a sort of psychic fusion. To lose oneself in another's world is to lose touch with one's own place in the reciprocal nature of social life. That is not a loss that is compatible with reciprocity.

SPONTANEITY   Finally, the emotional value of empathy – for reciprocity, again – is diminished insofar as one's empathetic responses are consciously fabricated. Spontaneity increases the power of empathy as a motive for reciprocation, and as an antidote for unfounded guilt or resentment.

These few remarks should suffice to indicate the sense in which empathy is a supererogatory virtue supportive of reciprocity.

Practical Wisdom

There is a master virtue – a complex disposition that mediates all other virtues. 'Practical wisdom' is an apt name for it. In its absence all the other virtues are defective.

Practical wisdom, as I shall use the term, refers to a set of traits that helps to translate intentions into effective conduct. The traits are purely instrumental; they can translate unjustifiable intentions into unjustifiable conduct as well as the reverse. Practical wisdom, in this sense, is the propensity to deal effectively, out of habit, with conflicting impulses, and effectively time and tune the gratification of desires. Reciprocity, without such wisdom, is inept.

Elements of Practical Wisdom

The connections between the most fundamental virtues are difficult to trace out. In particular, the connection between practical wisdom and self-control (temperance, *sophrosyne*) is a vexing question, as are the connections between wisdom and courage, or wisdom and prudence. Some of that difficulty comes, I think, from the effort to define practical wisdom as something more than a purely instrumental thing. Considered purely as an instrumental virtue, however, practical wisdom has a fairly clear outline.

ALERTNESS TO AGENDAS   A good motive is not much use if the conduct it generates is misplaced. Teachers, for example, must learn to listen – to sense the context of a question, and the purpose behind the asking. When they do not do that – when they are not alert to their students' agendas – they often make comical mistakes. The same is true for efforts to reciprocate. Misperception of a benefactor's purpose is often fatal for those efforts, while correct perception of the purpose is necessary for determining what will count as a fitting and proportional response.

ALERTNESS TO POSSIBILITIES   Wasted effort and wasted opportunity both compromise a project. An element of practical wisdom is the ability and propensity to avoid such waste by correctly perceiving *when* it is possible, and how it is possible, to accomplish one's ends. The connection to knowledge here is quite close. Obviously, the more we know in general terms about the way relevant things work, and about the relevant characteristics of the agents involved, the better our judgment is likely to be. But that is not necessarily because that knowledge is used *explicitly* in deliberation. It may rather be, and perhaps usually is, because such knowledge controls what we expect to see, and therefore, to some extent, what we do see as possibilities. Practical wisdom is, in part, the ability to put knowledge to use in this way.

TIMING AND TUNING A closely related element is the ability to time and fine tune acts so as to achieve the desired effect most fully, easily, economically, or elegantly. This involves both self-control and a refined appreciation of how the possibilities for action are related to one's purposes. The self-control required is of two sorts: the control needed to delay gratification, and the control needed to act in spite of uncertainty, or disinclination, or fatigue. The similarity of this to courage – which is in part the ability to act in spite of *fear* – is obvious. So is its similarity to determination and persistence. But that is simply because a different sort of self-control is an element of all these things.

The other part of the ability to fine tune one's conduct is a refined appreciation of the possibilities – an awareness of how well each of the available options serves auxiliary purposes. Suppose there is an obligation to reciprocate in a given case. Suppose there are several ways in which it can be done, and that they are equally effective for reciprocity purposes. An element of practical wisdom is the ability to identify the most effective one for the purposes of efficiency, and style, and all the other relevant considerations.

COORDINATION The final element of practical wisdom is closely connected to the previous one. It is the ability and propensity to adjust projects so as to make them compossible. This obviously requires both the self-control and the appreciation of possibilities just discussed. Long-range goals must be weighed against short-range satisfactions, for example. (At least, they must be if we are to make choices all-things-considered.) Doing that, and acting on the outcome, often requires a good deal of self-control.

But dealing with the welter of claims and inclinations and inhibitions that compete for our attention is more than just a juggling act. At any rate, the element of practical wisdom that deals with such matters must be more than a mere propensity to satisfy as many urges as possible. It must also be the readiness to abandon or destroy possibilities when doing so is necessary as a means to enhancing one's life overall. To see this, consider: Contracts and promises limit people's options, but they also enhance important projects. It is part of practical wisdom's purely instrumental function to apprehend – as if by perceptual awareness – when coordination requires sacrificing some possibilities, and when it requires preserving them.

There is a tempting train of thought that connects this aspect of wisdom to temperance – to moderation and self-restraint. That temptation should, I think, be resisted. Those things may well be virtues, but wisdom in its purely instrumental function does not entail them. What it entails is not 'moderation in all things', but rather whatever is best all-things-considered. That is *sometimes* moderation, but it could also be immoderately intense passions, exuberance, extreme effort, extreme sacrifice. The object of this aspect of practical wisdom (the coordination aspect) is to make the passions compatible with our projects. That does not entail – at least, not *a priori* – blunting or forfeiting them.

Concluding Remark

In the absence of some other virtues, reciprocity cannot make a contribution toward the sort of productive social life in terms of which it is justified. That is by no means an unusual situation. Virtues generally come in mutually supportive clusters. The reciprocity cluster includes some virtues in fairly standard versions and for fairly obvious reasons (e.g., honesty, fidelity and courage). And like every other virtue (and vice, for that matter) reciprocity requires a certain sort of purely instrumental wisdom. But it also requires, or at least is enhanced by, generosity, conviviality, and empathy. These virtues will enter the arguments of the following chapters at some important points.

CHAPTER 5

Virtue, Social Structure, and Obligation

Social structure shapes moral character. If it damages virtue, then it ought to be changed; if it promotes virtue, then it ought to be sustained. Furthermore, the virtue of reciprocity generates obligations that have an important bearing on what social practices and institutions can be justified. That is the gist of this chapter, stated without the elaborations and qualifications that make it true, and without the argument that makes it plausible. Those things follow.

The Problem of Structural Conformity

The virtues are learned, not innate. It may be that the rudiments of some of them are inborn, or emerge automatically in the normal course of maturation, but the fully articulated dispositions under discussion here are traits we acquire – traits we learn. That much is evident enough not to need argument.

Moreover, the social structures we inhabit are fundamental factors in moral education. (By 'social structure' I mean any well-defined activity that involves social interactions.) The range of activities available to us, the rules of those activities, and the practice of them develop dispositions in us. Initially, we may be driven by innate impulses and steered by brute circumstance. (Think of an infant rooting for the nipple.) But when we begin to participate in well-defined activities – even the earliest, simplest games we play as infants – we add a powerful new determinant for our conduct. Such activities habituate us to patterns of expectation, affection, cognitive and conative activity. They determine, in part, what we are disposed to do. That too seems unarguable.

It follows that virtue theory must concern itself with social structure. The virtues are dispositions. To say that we ought to acquire and sustain them is to say implicitly that we ought to use the means necessary to acquire and sustain them. If, in principle, social structures can either engender or destroy the virtues, sustain or damage them, enhance or inhibit them, and if such structures are an inescapable feature of our lives as moral agents, to say that we ought to have a certain virtue (say reciprocity) will be to say, implicitly, that we ought to have the social structures necessary for it.

Those general propositions must be used cautiously, however. It is not a matter of logical necessity, after all, that because we participate in some activity our virtues will be affected by it, or be affected in some fixed way. The connections between behavior and dispositions are empirical matters, subject to significant individual variations.

Furthermore, moral theory in general has a complex connection to social institutions. On the one hand, its finality requires social structure to conform. The rules of morally justifiable institutions must themselves be justifiable. On the other hand, theory justifies arrangements that shelter people from explicit moral concerns, and some evidently good institutions have at least a few rules that are, in the final analysis, arbitrary or inefficient or objectionable in some way. That complicates matters.

Some obvious examples of this complexity are escapist entertainments, games, sports, rituals, and all the social settings that license us to drop the effort to be fully moral. We indulge ourselves. We talk irresponsibly in the company of friends. We are caught unaware in love. Surely much of that is good.

Similarly for the structures we invent to focus attention and concentrate effort. ('I can't think about that now, I have to go to work.') We move from compartment to compartment in our lives. We divide the labor. That cannot be all bad.

As a result, it will not be possible to conclude *a priori* – or flatly – that activities whose rules force conduct contrary to virtue ought to be avoided, or that the social structures that promote those activities should be changed. The conclusions here will have to be more carefully qualified. For one thing they will have to be tied firmly to what we know about the empirical realities. The crucial thing here is what will *actually happen* to the virtues, not merely whether we have matched the rules of a structure to the maxims of the virtues. For another thing these conclusions must acknowledge that while the rules of a given social structure might well be bad for virtue, we still might have overriding reasons, all things considered, for adopting them.

The Argument for Structural Conformity

Nevertheless, the following commonsense observations suggest an important line of argument for insisting that the rules of social structures ought to conform to the maxims of the virtues. The argument depends crucially on empirical premises, but these premises appear to be amply confirmed by the behavioral sciences.

The observations that suggest the argument are these. First: Some structures are 'comprehensive' in the sense that they directly influence a large portion of our activity, at least as a background against which other things are assessed. The legal order is an example. What it requires and permits, how it is enforced, and the extent to which others comply with it all directly condition a great deal of our conduct, whether we actually attend to that influence or not. There are other structures that are quite different – structures that are 'isolated' in the sense that they directly influence very little of what we do. (Tic-tac-toe, for example.) The distinction between comprehensive and isolated structures admits of degrees, of course, and a good deal of individual variability. Work, for some, may become increasingly comprehensive as the years go by – first a job, then a career, then a life. For others, it may maintain a relatively stable place on the continuum.

The second observation is that participation in a structure sometimes engenders a sense of 'legitimacy' in participants – a sense that what they are doing is good, right, or noble. Some activities are expressly designed to do this. (Marine boot camp is an example.) Others – such as playing with a Rubik's Cube – takes whatever legitimating effect they have from the social context. Context is important in any case, of course, as are the dispositions an individual brings to the activity. What is important, for present purposes, is not to work out the details of these effects, but simply to notice that participation sometimes produces them and sometimes is expressly designed to do so.

The third observation is that some structures are 'integral' to an agent's self-concept, while others are not. Self-esteem is often a barometer here. Suppose that playing badly at chess involves no loss of self-esteem for me because I do not think of myself as a chess player, much less a good one. So while I may be disappointed when I lose, I am not disappointed *in myself*. I do not feel ashamed, or embarrassed, or diminished. I have no need to redeem myself. On the other hand, suppose performing poorly in class *does* involve a loss of self-esteem because I *do* define myself in part as a teacher. I *am* disappointed in myself when I teach poorly. I *do* feel the need to redeem myself. In that sense teaching is integral for me; chess playing is not.

Those commonsense observations help to frame the following definitions, and in turn the empirical hypotheses necessary for connecting virtue theory to questions about social structure.

Definitions

First, let us say that the *participants* of any well-defined activity (any structure) are all the agents who are *defined* as participants by that structure's participation rules. It is clear, then, that merely *being* a participant has nothing necessarily to do with the agent's awareness of it, or consent to it. (Think of the subjects in a deceptive experiment, or the inmates of a prison.)

Second, let us define *passive, conscious participation* in any structure as simply *being aware* that one is defined as a participant by that structure's participation rules.

Third, let us define *active participation* as conduct that is *intended to satisfy* one or more of the rules of the structure (other than its participation rules). That is, active participation is conduct intended to satisfy one or more of the teleological, deontological, valuational, procedural, transformational, or recognition rules of the structure.

Fourth, and finally, let us define *successful* participation as active participation that actually does satisfy one or more of the structure's rules.

Hypotheses:

I *The compliance effect*: *Ceteris paribus*, passive, conscious participation tends to produce active participation when it is called for by other participants in conformity with the rules of the structure. Call this the compliance effect. The prediction here is that people who are aware that they are participants in some structure are thereby more likely than not to comply actively, on demand, with some of the rules of the structure.

II *The multiplier effect*: *Ceteris paribus*, active participation that is perceived by the actor to be successful tends to increase either the frequency, scope, or self-initiatingness of subsequent (active) participation. Call this the multiplier effect. The prediction here is that when other factors are held constant, people who perceive an increase in their success rate are *thereby* more likely than not to increase their active participation rate.

III *The potency effect*: *Ceteris paribus*, the more comprehensive, or legitimate, or integral a structure is for a given agent, the stronger (for that agent) are the compliance and multiplier effects of participating in it. Call this the potency effect. The prediction here is that, when other factors are held constant, increases in a structure's perceived *potency* (i.e., its comprehensiveness, legitimacy, or integralness) will be directly correlated to increases in its participants' rates of active participation.

IV *The internalization effect*: *Ceteris paribus*, the more successful and potent and prolonged participation in a structure is, the more likely it is that such participation will engender or enhance participants' *dispositions* to conform to the rules of the structure, and to weaken or inhibit their dispositions to deviate. Call this the internalization effect. The prediction here is that, again holding other things constant, increases in the extent to which active participation in a structure is successful, potent, and prolonged will correlate directly to increases in the extent to which the rules of the structure are internalized by those participants – i.e., to the extent to which those participants develop dispositions whose maxims match (i.e., are the same as) some of the rules of the structure.

Now my contention is that those four hypotheses – or rather, the versions of them science has dealt with – have been widely confirmed in empirical studies. In particular, I think here of the literature on deviance and conformity, submission to authority, the development of role relationships, self-concepts and narrative patterns for conduct, and the general material on socialization and educational processes. Some of the relevant literature is cited in the scholium to this chapter.

There is a great deal of disagreement among scientists about the underlying mechanisms here, the strength of the predictable effects, the exact range of circumstances in which confident predictions can be made, and so forth. But the use I shall make of the empirical material does not depend on the resolution of those disagreements. It depends only on some things that I take to be generally agreed upon among social and behavioral scientists – and it is that that I have summarized in the hypotheses above.

Conformity to Virtue

The line of argument that connects virtue theory to moral theory about social structures can now be stated as follows:

> *Premise 1*:   If people have the dispositions that they ought, morally, to have, then they ought to do the morally justifiable things that will sustain and enhance those dispositions.

> *Premise 2*:   If people do *not* have the dispositions that they ought, morally, to have, then they ought to do the morally justifiable things that will generate those dispositions.

I take it that those premises follow directly from the valuation rules of the general conception: more good is preferable to less. If there is a course of otherwise justifiable conduct that will increase or sustain the level of good, then that is preferable to courses that do not do this. Having the dispositions we ought to have is by definition a good. If we can do something, justifiably, to acquire or sustain them, then we ought to do so.

> *Premise 3*:   Potent social structures whose rules match (are the same as) the maxims of a virtue will tend to generate and sustain that virtue in those whose successful participation in the structure is prolonged.

> *Premise 4*:   Potent social structures whose rules are contrary to the maxims of a virtue will tend to weaken and inhibit the development of that virtue in those whose successful participation in the structure is prolonged.

Those premises (3 and 4) follow from the empirical hypotheses discussed above.

CONCLUSION FROM 1, 2, AND 4: *Ceteris paribus*, any potent social
    structure in which moral agents do in fact have prolonged,
    successful participation ought to be fashioned so that its rules
    are not contrary to any maxims of any virtue.

The *ceteris paribus* clause here is meant to cover at least four things, each of which could render the argument invalid. One is the possibility that the *potency* of the structure could be eliminated; a second is that *prolonged* participation could be eliminated; a third is that *successful* participation could be eliminated. If any of those things could be done without changing the rules contrary to virtue, and if doing so was as or more justifiable than changing the rules contrary to virtue, then the conclusion above would not follow. And the fourth thing, of course, is the possibility that all-things-considered it might be better to live with the damage to virtue than to try to change the structure. Thoroughgoing arguments to the sort of conclusion above, then, must give reasons for concluding (or assuming) that none of these four things obtains. I shall try to do that, in the chapters of Part Two, when I make arguments about refashioning social structures.

CONCLUSION FROM 1, 2, AND 3: *Ceteris paribus*, social structures
    sufficient to generate and sustain the virtues of every moral
    agent should be created and sustained.

Several things about this conclusion need to be noted. First, it does not assert that any or all structures should be open to every agent. That would be an absurdity. (Think of a family.) And in any case that absurdity does not follow from 1, 2, and 3. Second, the conclusion does not assert that the same *sorts* of structures must be available for everyone. Different structures may do the same job with respect to the virtues. (Some people get along very well without religion.) Nor, third, does this conclusion imply that every moral agent must develop the same set of virtues. The phrase 'of every moral agent' is meant to indicate that what virtues are possible may vary from agent to agent. (Consider what might be possible for a brain-damaged child.) Finally, the *ceteris paribus* clause is meant to cover at least two things: One is the possibility that there may be some equally good or better way to generate a given virtue than by the route recommended above. And the other is that even if there isn't another route, it still might be better, all things considered, *not* to create or sustain a social structure to do it.

Even with all its provisos, however, it should be clear that this form of argument gives virtue theory an important connection to the task of designing social structures. And when the virtue involved is a deontic one, like reciprocity, which ought to guide our conduct generally, that connection is even more important. It will be the task of subsequent chapters to show what the connection between reciprocity and the design of some fundamental social structures is.

Virtue as a Source of Obligations

Henceforth I shall use the term 'reciprocity' to refer to the disposition – the virtue – defined in Chapter Three. I shall also often speak of the obligations of reciprocity, or the acts of reciprocation that the virtue makes obligatory. I want now to say more exactly what such talk of obligations means, and what the warrant is for speaking in this way about virtuous conduct.

The Obligations of Reciprocity

It is often noted that virtue-theory has a look that is quite different from that of value theory or duty-theory. Virtue-theory tends to speak of ideals rather than requirements, exemplars rather than principles, shortcomings rather than wrongdoing, and so forth. But as the arguments of Chapters Three and Four made plain, some virtues have deontic aspects. To have those 'deontic virtues' is to be disposed to make some conduct obligatory. If the disposition is morally justifiable – i.e., if it is a moral virtue – then presumably the obligatoriness of the conduct it yields is also justifiable, in some sense. But in what sense? Can virtues justify obligations, period? Or do they rather justify having a 'sense' of obligation, as distinct from the obligation itself?

I shall address these questions by explicating a form of argument for obligations. The argument-form will be framed in terms of reciprocity, but in principle it is applicable to any justifiable disposition that has a deontic component. Virtue-theory thus has general consequences for the theory of moral obligations.

1   We ought (morally) to be disposed to reciprocate, as defined in Chapter Three.
2   To be so disposed is to be disposed to make reciprocation a matter of moral obligation.
3   To be disposed to make something a matter of moral obligation is to be disposed to regard doing it as being one's moral obligation – at least in the sense that one looks back on failures to do it as failures to satisfy moral requirements. In some cases, regarding it as one's moral obligation also involves thinking of it prospectively as an obligation.
4   If a given disposition is morally justifiable, then the acts it disposes us to undertake, and the ways in which it disposes us to regard those acts, are also morally justifiable, *ceteris paribus*.
5   If it is morally justifiable to be disposed to *make* an act one's moral obligation, then that act *is* one's moral obligation.
6   To be disposed to reciprocate, as defined in Chapter Three, is to be disposed to make reciprocation a moral obligation in situations like X.
7   Y is a situation like X.
8   Therefore, reciprocation in Y is a moral obligation.

   Most of the premises in this form of argument were defended in Chapter Three. Specifically, I there gave arguments for 1–4. Premises 6 and 7 are purely schematic. Filling them in will be the task of subsequent chapters.

   At the moment, then, it is premise 5 that needs some comment. It is, again,

> 5   If it is morally justifiable to be disposed to *make* an act one's moral obligation, then that act *is* one's moral obligation.

   At first glance, that seems deeply dubious. For one thing, the notion of something's 'being' an obligation is as yet undefined, so it is hard to assess the asserted connection between being and making. (Recall that 'being disposed to *make* reciprocity an obligation' was defined in Chapter Three as being disposed to ascribe blame to people who do not reciprocate, or to coerce them into reciprocating, or to punish them or extract compensation from them for their failure to reciprocate.) Just intuitively, it seems that it could be justifiable to act *as if* something were an obligation when in fact it is not. An example, perhaps, is the law of quasi-contract. There the law will sometimes make something obligatory by acting as if there had been an explicit contract between the parties. And of course it is in principle possible to justify having false beliefs, so it may sometimes be justifiable to both believe that something is obligatory and to act as if it were, even though it is not. Thus premise 5 seems false.

The reply to that objection begins with the observation that all forms of pretense – acting 'as if' – can plausibly be distinguished from actually *making* something obligatory. The notion of pretense implies that there is something lacking. Either the thing is known not to be obligatory, or we suspect it isn't, or don't care whether it is, or are unwilling to treat it as obligatory in every respect. Under such circumstances, we may decide to go ahead and act as if the thing were an obligation (and thereby make it one for others), but we have not thereby 'made' it one *for ourselves*. The sense of 'make' that I want to use here is stronger. It entails no such reservations, mental or otherwise. (We *may* have them, but need not. In order to pretend, we *must* have them.) The inference in premise 5 depends on a stipulative definition, then, but it is a plausible one. I am simply stipulating that the conditions for asserting justifiably, all-things-considered, that we ought to *make* x obligatory include the conditions for asserting justifiably that x *is* obligatory, all-things-considered. I am assuming that if it is justifiable to *be disposed* to act in *all* the ways appropriate to something's *being* obligatory, then one can conclude that the thing is an obligation. There is no point in trying to define a more stringent sense for something's 'being' an obligation.

At any rate, that is how I shall speak in the chapters to follow. If I can show that reciprocity disposes us to make a thing obligatory, then I shall say that it is obligatory. But the ontological claim involved in that way of speaking amounts to no more than what has just been described.

PART 2
PRACTICE

Introduction to Part 2

.

The following chapters assess some important social structures in terms of reciprocity. The topics to be considered are families, providing for future generations, and obedience to law. The controlling assumption here is that these structures ought to have rules that match the maxims of reciprocity, in the sense required by the arguments of Chapter Five. These structures are potent. People's participation in them is likely to be prolonged and successful. And reciprocity is a fundamental virtue – not an ornament, but an essential component of our capacity to construct and sustain a productive social life. Potent social structures ought not to damage or inhibit reciprocity; they ought rather to engender and enhance it.

The choice of topics here was controlled by theoretical rather than practical concerns. My purpose was to test the results of Part One against a variety of cases in which it seemed likely that pressing the reciprocity arguments would have theoretically interesting consequences – interesting either because they help to move moral theory around some notorious dead ends, or because they help to answer some lingering doubts about the arguments of Chapter Three.

I do not mean to imply, however, by aiming this set of practical chapters at theoretical goals, that I am uninterested in applications. On the contrary, if I thought the theory here had no important consequences for moral life, or that the chapters to follow made no contribution toward producing those consequences, I would not have written them. But applied ethics needs something to apply, and in particular it needs a richer set of substantive considerations than it typically uses. The chapters in this part, while directed to a theoretical task, should also suggest how the theory can be put to some significant use.

A reminder, however, about that use: A very common form of

moral theorizing tries to get closure on moral questions by appeal to a single principle, or ordered set of principles. (Think of utilitarian theory.) The caricature that lurks behind it is the idea of mechanical jurisprudence: Give us a law, and we will find a clerk to apply it. That *is* a caricature, of course, because these theorists recognize the complexity and uncertainty involved in any real-life applications of their principles. But the effort behind the theory is the reduction of that complexity and uncertainty – the simplification of moral deliberation. The suspicion seems to be that if moral theory is as complicated as moral life, it will not help us.

The general conception of morality is hostile to simplification. It insists that moral theory reflect the full complexity of moral life, in all-things-considered deliberation. The caricature that lurks behind this is the idea of intellectual paralysis: Give us one thing to consider before we act, and we will give you ten thousand more. That too is a caricature, for deliberation under the general conception does have closure rules. But the effort is to be inclusive, to represent the intricacy and ambiguity of moral situations. The suspicion is that a theory that simplifies will foster the sort of deadening, totalitarian uniformity that characterizes most utopian thinking.

Readers accustomed to single principle theories may find the rest of this book frustrating. Everything is conditioned upon expanded deliberation – not just about the facts of a situation, but about other virtues, values, and requirements. But that is just because reciprocity arguments do not capture all the considerations relevant to any moral choice. They cannot complete the inquiry. What they can do, however, is to show us what we will be disposed to do if we have this one central virtue, and what some social structures must be like if we are to engender and sustain that virtue. I submit that that is a practical result of some significance.

CHAPTER 6
Families

Families are potent. According to the reciprocity arguments of Part One, then, families ought to be structured so that they engender or enhance reciprocity, and if they damage or inhibit it, they ought to be changed. That means, apparently, that we ought to bring the rules of familial activities into accord with the maxims of reciprocity. This chapter is a general exploration of that idea.

Since reciprocity generates obligations, the questions raised in this chapter predictably concern familial obligations – spousal, parental, and filial. The focus is therefore narrow. Most of what is valuable and much of what is philosophically interesting about families lies outside its scope.

Inside its scope, however, there are at least five topics of fundamental importance. One concerns balance in intimate relationships. The fundamental question there is whether reciprocity is a virtue at all in such relationships, or whether they ought to be controlled by other traits. I will consider this issue in the context of marriage, and will argue that reciprocity is fundamental to it. The argument can then be applied to other familial relationships, friendships, and intimate relationships generally.

A second topic of importance is parental obligations. Reciprocity, while not the only source of them, contributes importantly to their scope, in ways that are somewhat surprising and unsettling. In particular, it has implications for cases in which children cannot or do not reciprocate. A related (third) topic is parental authority. Here the reciprocity arguments provide the framework for an account that can be applied to political obligation as well, and I will extend it to that topic in Chapter Eight. Fourth, there are important issues about priorities. Commonsense morality gives more weight to the interests of intimates than to strangers, but moral theory has had difficulty justifying that priority. The reciprocity arguments have implications for that issue.

Finally, there is the question of 'the debt that cannot be repaid.' Particularly in familial relationships, it may seem that the disposition to return good for all the good received imposes an impossible requirement. That issue will be considered both in this chapter and Chapter Seven (Future Generations).

At three that morning, Thanksgiving Day, clouds began to rise in the west. The Jensens' house was luminous in the moonlight – a solid block of white-painted brick surrounded by ancient trees and twenty acres of level pasture lands. It looked deceptively small from the highway two hundred yards away. The house was square, undecorated, two and a half stories, with twin exterior chimneys at each end, the parallel verticals of which, running from ground level to three feet above the ridge of the roof, made the house look narrow, compressed.

The several small outbuildings, also brick, were as old as the house itself and in good repair, but the two brick barns that had stood on the property for nearly a hundred years were gone, as were the Quarters – a row of small frame houses, first for slaves and then for wage laborers, that had connected the barns. There were no crops now, no hired help, no horses or dairy herd. It was a holding action. At three a.m. there was still a light on in one of the upstairs bedrooms.

Margery's alarm was set for five, but she was awake for half an hour before that, curled on her left side, covers to her chin, staring at the lighted numbers on the clock radio. She'd expected to have back pain again, but didn't. Instead she was deeply comfortable and warm. Last night's dread was gone.

As the minutes went to 59 she thought about letting the alarm wake Carl, somewhere out of touch on the other side of the bed. Petty, she thought. Let him sleep. She looked at the hollow palm of her hand, ten inches from her face. The station she listened to wasn't on until six and she wondered which way the radio would sweep, what kind of music it would find. She reached the button just as the clock reached 5:00. Safe.

By six she had the stuffing made for the turkey, and the late night glasses and ice cream bowls in the dishwasher. It had started to snow. Roddy was in the kitchen, sleepy and cold, wearing nothing but the jockey shorts he'd slept in. She wished he wouldn't do that.

He asked if she had brought his bags in from the car. He wanted to run before breakfast.

The sight of him so sleepy, and the diffidence in his voice, made Margery flush with memories of the two of them together in the kitchen, in the early mornings, when Roddy was in high school. He would have gotten up early to finish his homework. The younger children would still be asleep, and after Carl had gone at seven she and Roddy would have half an hour together. Mother and son against the world. She felt, just for an instant as he moved close to her, the shock of her first discovery, years before, that he was taller than she. Not just a fraction taller, but several inches. How could she have failed to notice?

Roddy read her mind. 'Once a baby, always a mother,' he said, and put an arm around her shoulders.

'Get some clothes on, please.' She was smiling, folding a dish towel with abrupt, precise motions. 'Be back by seven. I'm not running a short order kitchen this morning.' She looked up at him and patted his cheek with the tips of her fingers. 'Your bags are in the front hall.'

A few minutes later, on his way out, dressed in a sweatsuit, he looked forty again. His rumpled hair was thin, and his face was rough. He handed her a half-empty bottle of bourbon.

'This was in the living room. Maybe we should lock up the bar.'

Margery put the bottle behind the cleansers under the sink. So many things could go wrong.

Breakfast was quiet. The three of them had talked the night before about Roddy's separation. Margery was reassured; Carl relaxed. Roddy's presence always dissolved their questions and anger and disappointment. His Barbara would bring the children for dinner. That much would be the same at least. And there wouldn't be a scene.

'I don't want those children hurt,' Margery had said. She had said it with what she meant to be intensity and authority. Instead it sounded petulant to her ears, and both men said of course you don't. No one does. And that was the end of it.

So breakfast was comfortable. The three of them sat for
nearly an hour over coffee, looking at the light snow falling
outside, planning the day, trading news. The smell of the
Thanksgiving turkey began to fill the kitchen.

By ten-thirty, when Lynn and Hal drove in, it was snowing
heavily. The roads were still mostly clear, but the yard was
covered and the small pastures surrounding the house were
uniformly white. The big maples in front of the house were
bare. Through their low limbs, and through the falling snow,
the encroaching subdivisions on every side looked benign.
Roddy and Carl were splitting wood. They had been in and
out of the house several times – to get gloves, then caps, then
light jackets. The temperature was dropping. They came
around to meet Lynn's car, and motioned again and again,
windmilling their arms, for Hal to park alongside the jeep.
Carl tried to shout through Hal's window, pointing to the
place. Hal finally understood and backed his Datsun
alongside the jeep. Lynn rolled down her window and spoke
to her father, who had to lean down to hear.
'We got all the way up to Roanoke last night. Afton
Mountain was scary this morning. Snow and fog. Jack and
Katherine here?'
Carl shook his head.
'Are they coming down 81 and over? That mountain is going
to be a mess in another hour.'
Lynn saw her mother standing in the doorway, and got out
of the car to wave. Roddy put his arm around his sister and
she hugged him at the waist. They didn't speak or look at each
other.
Lynn left the unloading to the men, and followed her mother
into the kitchen. Shopping bags of food came in one by one.
She and Margery unwrapped apples, bags of nuts, jars of honey
and preserves, and two dozen pint jars of homemade root
beer. They told the men where to put things, but it was hard
to get their attention. Roddy and Hal were talking computers
and Carl seemed distracted. He did most of the work, even
taking the suitcases upstairs, and when Roddy and Hal sat
down in the living room, and Roddy took off his cap and
gloves, Carl went back outside by himself.

For the moment, mother and daughter had nothing to do. They sat at the kitchen table, watching the snow. Margery's appraisal of her daughter was critical, as usual, but she kept it to herself. Lynn's long hair was flat against her head, straight and stringy. She was very thin and trembly. In her jeans and bulky sweater it was not so painful to see, but Margery could not have suffered her bare arms and legs in silence. It was foolish to be so thin, she would have said. It wasn't healthy. Hal too. Always so agitated, both of you.

Lynn pushed back her silver-rimmed glasses, still staring out of the window. She rarely looked directly at anyone.

'Daddy looks tired,' she said.

'He was up late last night.'

The women listened for the sounds of conversation in the living room.

'I'll bet he was,' Lynn said. She pushed at her glasses again. 'I was hoping to see some fall color up here.'

'Nothing's ever perfect,' said her mother.

Jack's station wagon pulled in an hour later. Katherine was driving – because Jack's left wrist was in a cast – and Steven, their eleven-year-old, was between the five-year-old twins in the back seat. He looked exasperated. Jay and Katie, the twins, had their doors open the second the car stopped, and dashed around to the back of the wagon, which was loaded with open cartons. Steven went into the house.

The wind was strong by then, and visibility was poor. There was over an inch of snow on the ground, blowing into deeper drifts along the shrubbery. The twins hugged everyone by turns, and tried to help unload. Lynn and Margery stood in the open doorway, enjoying the spectacle of the four grown men and two children jostling for position.

Hal asked about the trip over the mountain. Jack said they had crossed the Blue Ridge at New Market, ahead of the storm, and come down 29. Even that way the last twenty miles had been bad. He handed a box, one armed, to his older brother.

'Where's Barbara staying?'

'At her sister's,' Roddy said. 'What happened to your hand?'

Katherine picked her way carefully along the snow-covered brick walk, holding her arms out slightly from her body for balance. She was dressed like Margery – tweed skirt, soft sweater, stockings and low heels. She waited just inside the front door and took the carton of food Roddy was carrying. The two of them were still formal with each other, reluctant to touch, slightly wary, even after fifteen years. They had once been lovers.

Katherine took the food to the kitchen – three pumpkin pies and two jars of homemade cranberry sauce. Her older son was there, talking earnestly to his grandmother. Every move was ritual, predictable. Steven went to the library to watch the parade on TV. Roddy and Hal made most of the trips to the car. The twins, inside now, hanging on Jack, begged their grandfather to set up the model trains in the basement – in the big pine-panelled room that came as close as the old house could to the abomination (Carl's word) of a family room. It was the room where Roddy had been put every night he brought Katherine home. She was given his room, and Margery made up the sofa bed in the basement for him. Now when Katherine came here, she slept in Jack's boyhood bed.

Jack told the twins that the basement was probably too cold to play in. He said they had games and books anyway; that the parade was on TV.

'It's all right,' Carl said. 'I turned on the heat down there an hour ago.'

Jack did not reply, as though nothing were expected. He looked down at his children, and absently smoothed Katie's straight brown hair. She moved closer to him. Jay, on his father's left, edged out of range of the casted hand.

'We may have to stay overnight.' Jack said finally. 'We brought sleeping bags for the kids.'

The four of them stood in the wide center hall that ran the length of the house, with the kitchen and dining room on one side, the living room and library on the other. Carl said they might as well bring the bags in. The roads would be impassable by late afternoon.

The three women joined them in great good humor. Margery announced merrily that one of the root beers had sprung a leak. The men gave a small cheer. She said she was afraid some of the other jars might burst, so she'd put them all on the

back porch, up against the house. They probably wouldn't
freeze, but they would need watching.

The twins were ready to watch. They ran to tell Roddy and
Hal, then into the library to tell Steven, then back through
the hall on their way to make the first safety check. They
promised not to go too close to the jars.

The adults were suddenly happy. Sudden glory. The root
beer was always a disaster, no matter who made it, and Lynn
was formally exonerated. She feigned wounded pride. It
wouldn't be Thanksgiving without a root beer disaster. Now
it was.

Hal and Roddy joined the group, and there was talk (from
Hal and Katherine) about *buying* root beer next year, or
maybe even *this* year. A & W tasted pretty good, didn't it?
And it was reliable.

'You don't understand,' said Roddy. (This was his line. It
had been his line since he uttered it spontaneously at the age
of seven.) 'Root beer is a sacred drink.'

There were ritual cheers for Roddy the little boy. Carl, seized
by a spasm of laughter, gripped Katherine's arm so fiercely
that she turned and hugged him in self defense. He reached
out to touch Hal through her arms.

Steven came out of the library. 'Hey,' he said. 'There's some
football on.'

Barbara phoned at one o'clock. Margery answered in the
kitchen. By then there was a blizzard outside – snow falling at
an inch an hour, high winds, temperature in the low twenties.
The twins came back and forth, reporting on the weather
and the root beer and their grandfather's efforts to set up the
trains. The old house had fireplaces in all its major rooms,
and Roddy had laid fires in the ones on the first floor – living
room and library, dining room and kitchen. The meal was
almost ready.

Margery pressed the phone hard to her ear, and sat at the
kitchen table, speaking quickly, urgently. There wouldn't be
any problem, she said. There was plenty of room. Jack and
Roddy could pick her up in the jeep, and she could bring
overnight things. She and the boys could have Lynn's room.
There was so much food, and so much room. It would be

better for the children than that empty apartment on
Thanksgiving. Jennifer wasn't even there, was she? Hadn't
she gone home with her boyfriend for the weekend? What if
they got snowed in for a day or two? Jacob's cousins were
here. Grandpa had set up the trains for Jacob and the twins.
And even if little Adam was too young to understand, they
all wanted to see him. And her. Please, Barbara. Margery was
weeping.

Lynn took the phone. Her mother went to the sink to catch
her breath and stop her tears. She ran cold water on her
fingers and pressed them to her eyes.

Lynn listened, and agreed. Yes, it was emotional blackmail.
No, it wasn't meant that way of course. Yes, they understood
how difficult it was, and that Barbara should do what was
best for herself. It couldn't be good for the children if
everybody was miserable. All of this was said by Barbara while
Lynn responded in single syllables. Finally she turned her
back to her mother and spoke softly.

'You know how much they count on Thanksgiving. It's hard
for everybody. But Barb. You don't *have* to do *anything*.
They'll live.'

Katherine took the phone and asked Barbara how she was
holding up, whether she had enough money, whether her
sister's place was all right. They could help – she and Jack.

Margery worked grimly at the stove and spoke bitterly to
her daughter, keeping her voice low. 'Those two have a lot
in common,' she said. 'That one dropped him when he gave
up medical school and now the other one is doing it when
he's leaving the Army.'

Lynn first decided to let it pass, then changed her mind and
said her mother should be fair, that Roddy didn't give up
medical school and he wasn't just leaving the Army, either.
He'd flunked out of school and he'd been passed over twice
for promotion and everybody knew that was just the tip of the
iceberg. She said she loved her brother but couldn't imagine
how anyone could live with him.

'We lived with him,' Margery said angrily.

Lynn forced a laugh and put her long thin arms around her
mother's shoulders. '*You* lived with him, mother. The rest of
us just survived.'

Roddy was furious. He took the stairs three at a time to get to the upstairs telephone. When he came down he said he was going to get his wife. Katherine signalled Jack. He got his coat and followed his brother to the door.

They were gone for over an hour. Everything slowed down. The children were pacified with crackers and cheese. The men moved a rollaway bed into Lynn's room and Margery made up the sofa bed in the basement. Roddy would sleep there. Lynn put her hair up, and changed into a long wool skirt. Her mother approved. They waited.

When they heard the jeep coming up the access road they all went to meet it. Roddy drove straight across the yard and right up to the front door. Barbara was laughing against her will, covering her eyes in horror for the benefit of the family. Jack carried the baby, fast asleep, into the living room, and Jacob, the six-year-old, disappeared with the twins. Steven and Hal unloaded the suitcases. Barbara carried the baby's things. She was wearing jeans and a sweatshirt.

Once inside the front door she cried a little on Margery's shoulder. 'This won't change anything,' she said into Margery's ear.

'No,' said Margery, rubbing Barbara's back. 'But that's no reason not to come.'

Barbara caught Lynn's eyes. 'You fink,' she whispered. 'Why did you have to dress up this year?'

Lynn shrugged helplessly, arms outstretched, and smiled.

Ten minutes later they sat down to dinner. The children quieted, and Carl had drawn a breath to offer a prayer when he saw Margery look at him and shake her head just slightly. He let his breath out, carefully, through set teeth.

'Let's just have a moment of silence, then,' he said. Heads bowed.

Familial Obligations

In families, where equilibrium can be so precarious, social life so intense, and transactions so frequent, subtle and intimate, reciprocity has sweeping consequences. Moreover, because our early family life typically forms so many of the fundamental elements of our moral character, the patterns of reciprocal relationships in the family will have significance for social life in general.

What follows will be restrained by potential conflicts with other matters of moral concern – other virtues, values, and obligations. What reciprocity requires may not be what a full scale moral inquiry would recommend – what we ought to do all-things-considered. But that should not be allowed to obscure the central role reciprocity must play in moral deliberation.

Spouses

OBJECTION: Love stands as an implicit rebuke to the business of reciprocating. That business is crass by comparison – simplistic, superficial, singleminded, overly concerned with obligations and with getting even. The reciprocity arguments claim to capture something fundamental about human life, but it is questionable whether they are even *relevant* to a discussion of good loving relationships – the sort we have in deep friendships and good families. It is true that when something goes wrong in love we often try to patch things up by imposing requirements on people. But when things are going well, talk of obligations is out of place, and so is getting even. If that is right, then reciprocity may not be a fundamental virtue after all, because it does not, or should not, operate in what ought to be a large and precious area of our lives.

REPLY: That is *not* right, but it points to the fundamental problem reciprocity theory has with what might be called *profound* relationships, where the term profound refers to matters of both depth and obscurity. Depth, here, is a metaphor for relationships that are intimate, intense, intricate, encompassing, and filled with strong feelings. Obscurity is a metaphor for relationships that are particularly resistant to description and analysis – in which motives, feelings, aims, hopes, expectations, and beliefs are either so darkly tangled or so purely transparent that we cannot see them clearly; in which what we know about the relationships is so rich that we cannot hold it all in view; and in which the most deeply satisfying experiences seem ultimately inexplicable. The fundamental theoretical problem is this: How can reciprocity operate in profound relationships without doing damage to them? How can a deontic virtue like reciprocity – one that is so attentive to detail, so 'correct', so insistent – be anything but antithetical to love, for example? (Some analogous oxymorons: A conscientious lover. A temperate lover. A prudent lover.) If reciprocity necessarily damages profound relationships, and if those relationships are good ones, all-things-considered, then reciprocity will have a limited scope. It will be confined to superficial relationships.

Some marriages are meant to be profound – or just *are* profound, whether they are meant to be or not. But so are many other relationships: parental ones, and deep friendships, for example. They all raise the same fundamental problem for reciprocity. It is worth remembering, however, that the source of the problem is not marriage, or parenthood, or friendship *per se*. The source is a particular type of relationship that *can* occur, but does not *always* occur, in those contexts. Marriages are not necessarily profound. An example is a marriage of convenience in which the spouses live separately and have very little to do with each other. Such marriages may be charged with social significance (status, entitlements) and still not raise any special questions about reciprocity – questions that are not raised, for example, about contractual obligations generally. Similarly for friendship, parenthood, and love relationships. They are not always profound, but when they are, they raise the question of whether the virtue of reciprocity is excluded from them.

I contend that reciprocity is not excluded from them. The reasons come directly from the discussions of virtue theory in Chapter Two and 'retrospective' obligation in Chapter Three. Briefly, they are as follows: Acting in character is not necessarily a matter of consciously acting on principle. Acting impulsively, for example, is not typically a matter of deciding to follow a principle of impulsiveness. Rather, acting in character can be so routine, so automatic, so unconscious that the actor is not aware of its being 'in character', and perhaps not even aware of it – or able to remember it – at all. (Which shoe did you put on first this morning?) Further, *good* character sometimes necessarily obscures motives, aims, and principles. We cannot be wholehearted while we are toting up the pros and cons. And that is true of reciprocity as well. We sometimes necessarily fail to act reciprocally if we are aware of our conduct *as* reciprocal. That is why we should be disposed to act out the maxims of reciprocity unconsciously in some cases, consciously in others. In that respect reciprocity is neither more nor less complex than some other important virtues. It can operate every bit as obscurely, spontaneously, and surprisingly as benevolence.

I have argued, however, that we should take stock of the reciprocal nature of even intimate relationships in retrospect – not after each 'transaction', of course, but regularly enough to prevent the growth of destructive imbalances. In profound relationships that kind of regular retrospective assessment is crucial. Without it, we are likely to fall unawares into patterns of dominance and submission that are unjustifiable, and into suffering that is bewildering. We are especially vulnerable to those things if the 'rules' of the relationship damage reciprocity.

Consider: Suppose that a profound relationship is defined in a way that imposes significant inequalities on the people in it. (Say that one of them is defined as 'master'.) Next suppose the rules impose a rigid division of labor, along lines that make the master's labor increasingly important, while the other's, over time, becomes less so. (Perhaps the husband-father's career blossoms as he ages, while the wife-mother's tasks diminish in importance as the children become independent.) Then suppose that the rules implicitly discourage even retrospective evaluation of matters of reciprocity, and discourage renegotiation. ('If you loved me, you wouldn't even *think* such things. Love is forever.') That is a fair statement of one form of marriage idealized in our culture. It is also a recipe for producing exactly the sort of destructive imbalance reciprocity is meant to prevent. In that case either the relationship is changed, or reciprocity is compromised, or the lives of the parties become increasingly miserable.

Reciprocity should not be compromised – not if the arguments of Chapter Three are sound. And there is surely no reason, under the general conception, to submit to misery that is avoidable. That leaves changing the relationship, and the general lines of the needed change are clear. Since it is also clear, however, that it is very difficult to make deep structural changes in a profound relationship once it exists, it is preferable to start with a structure that is consistent with reciprocity.

In general, what this means for marriage is this: In marriages that are profound relationships, structural inequalities should be avoided, both in the initial and the prospective positions of the spouses, and the 'rules' should encourage reevaluation and renegotiation in conformity with reciprocity. For marriages that are not profound, no special restrictions are imposed by reciprocity, beyond those that apply to social relationships generally. More specific conclusions on each of these matters follow.

Structural Equality

For purposes of reciprocation, there are at least three areas in which damaging inequalities can be built into the structure of a marriage: in the distribution of usable resources; in the depletability of those resources; and in the prospects for developing those resources. Reciprocity requires structural equality in all three areas.

DISTRIBUTION   Here the reciprocity arguments are concerned with net overall equality in the value, quantity, variety, and accessibility of the spouses' usable resources. People can vary enormously in the types and amounts of things they bring to a marriage and still be roughly equal overall. But if the overall positions are unequal, reciprocal transactions that conform to the maxims of reciprocity will have to follow the equal sacrifice rule. That is second-best to the equal benefit rule – which governs exchanges between equals – and to some degree the second-best rule works against sustaining a relationship. Moreover, the *extent* to which the equal sacrifice rule will work against the relationship will likely correlate directly with the size of the net overall inequality. Spouses who are vastly superior to their mates will face the choice of either giving very little or getting very little in return, either of which tends to drive a profound relationship toward a superficial one. Marital arrangements that often raise this problem are those that involve pronounced disparities in age, authority, status, wealth, needs, and powers.

At this level of generality, the reciprocity arguments can only offer cautions, however. We observe that some types of marital structures are likely to be unstable in terms of reciprocity, and it is therefore clear that we should not encourage them, and certainly should not force people into them. (We should not, for example, promote social expectations that one spouse must be master.) But ultimately, of course, it is the net overall positions of particular spouses in particular marriages that count, and it is obvious that people can in principle be 'matched' for reciprocating precisely *because* of their inequality along some dimension. There may be objections to such matches on other grounds, but not just in terms of the distribution of resources.

A final caution on this topic. It is equality of *usable* resources that is at stake here. It is no help to have equal resources if we are prevented by social convention from using some of them (e.g., intellect, aggressiveness, nurturance). The reciprocity arguments will not be satisfied by a showing that the spouses are 'formally' equal. Effective equality is the concern here, and the structure of a marriage – its 'rules of resource usage' – are an important element in deciding whether there is the necessary equality in resource distribution.

DEPLETION   A second important factor for any lasting relationship is the direction in which reciprocal exchanges are likely to drive the net overall balance of resources. People may start with equal positions and be driven into very *un*equal ones if one spouse's resources are more quickly depletable than the other's. Suppose (to continue the example begun earlier) that some society's conventions dictate that the *usable* resources a woman brings to marriage are childbearing capacity, housekeeping skills, willingness to submit to her husband's authority, ability to satisfy his sexual needs, and a certain ornamental value. Suppose the same conventions dictate that a man's primary resource is his ability to provide socio-economic and physical security for his wife and family. Let us say that the spouses initially contribute equally to the marriage in these respects. Now suppose that the man's ability as a provider increases steadily up to the point of retirement – say at 65. Will the woman's ability to contribute to the marriage do the same? It is unlikely. And marriage structures are objectionable, in terms of reciprocity, whenever they do not take into account this aspect of the spouses' prospects – the extent to which the spouses' usable resources are differentially depletable.

DEVELOPMENT   A third concern about structural equality is this: If convention requires that one of the spouses (say the woman) may not pursue activities that increase her resources, but at the same time require her husband to 'better' himself (perhaps with her help), the result is not hard to predict. Marriages that are meant to be both profound and lasting, then, must not impose this third kind of structural inequality either.

Structural Change

In any reciprocal relationship, profound or not, changed circumstances may force us to choose between abandoning the relationship entirely, or changing its 'rules'. In a marriage, that choice is often forced when one spouse is permanently injured, or has a long illness, or is thrown out of work. It is also forced when people go through crises in adult development – radical changes in their desires, hopes, aspirations, priorities, and sources of self-esteem. (That catalog is not meant to be exhaustive.) Such changes do not necessarily strip people of resources or produce a net overall imbalance of resources. That may happen, but not necessarily. The point here is not about resources, but rather about the circumstances under which marriage partners may justifiably change some of the fundamental rules of their relationship. There are, after all, some clear cases of this sort. When spouses are no longer physically capable of carrying out their parts of 'the bargain', for example, then something must change. If marriages are to last through such changes, they must have effective transformation rules – effective ways of changing the fundamental structure of the marital arrangement. Note the 'if'. Reciprocity does not require that marriages *be* enduring. It only requires that *if* they are, they be defined so that they can cope with major changes in the spouses' circumstances.

What that means for marriage, in general, is this: On the assumption that we want marriages to be lasting reciprocal relationships, it follows that their structure should not be defined as static – as forever fixed by vows and conventions at the time of the wedding. Rather, the marriage contract should have a well-understood set of transformation rules adequate to deal with the sorts of changes we know often occur in the spouses' circumstances. More specifically, marriages should have transformation rules that deal with both incapacitation and what might be called transfiguration. To explain:

Incapacitation provides the clearest case for a need for transformation rules, and also requires the least comment here. There are ambiguities, of course. ('He could find a new job if he really wanted to. He's just taking advantage.') And there are matters of degree. ('I know it's tough, and I'm willing to make some adjustments, but I don't see why we have to change *everything*.') But in our culture at any rate, people are able to see that a marriage *can* be changed when one or both of the spouses are incapacitated in some way, and are able to see *how* it can be changed. They are not always able to see the need for such changes in a particular case, or to make the changes themselves, but that is a different matter. Again, recall that reciprocity by itself does not require people to opt for continuing their marriages. The point here is simply that lasting marriages should, and generally do, have transformation rules that deal with incapacitation.

I make this point for two reasons. One is that these generally recognized transformation rules exist in spite of a good deal of conventional pressure to think of marriage in static terms. The standard vows certainly imply that the major teleological and deontological rules are fixed, and domestic relations law tends to underline that notion. Popular culture also helps to reinforce the static conception with advice about how to keep 'romance' alive, where 'romance' refers to sexual desire, tenderness, thoughtfulness, and the level of risk, novelty, intensity, and desire to please characteristic of the early days of a courtship. All of this prompts us to think of marriage as something that should always be 'the same', even while we recognize some circumstances under which it should not be. It seems to me (but I claim no special probity for the observation) that this tension between conventional expectations and the rules we actually employ in marriage is counterproductive. It would be better, all things considered, if we abandoned the rhetoric that suggests marriage ought to be a static structure within which people grow and change, and within which relationships deepen but otherwise remain essentially the same.

The other reason for making the point about incapacitation is to contrast it with what I called transfiguration – by which I mean a radical change in a person's goals, priorities, or boundaries. Some transfigurations are idiosyncratic. Conventional definitions of marriage cannot be faulted for failing to anticipate them in detail. But we have reason to believe that other transfigurations are not idiosyncratic – that they are instead predictable features of adult development. If that is so, and if these transfigurations result in predictable changes in what spouses want in a marriage, and are willing or able to give, then reciprocity requires that the structure of a lasting marriage be able to track them. In order to keep such a relationship in conformity with the maxims of reciprocity, we need to have transformation rules that allow us to adjust the rules of the marriage as the spouses mature. Reciprocity supports what might be called a 'developmental' form of marriage.

In the absence of a detailed account of adult development, it is hard to say what such a developmental form of marriage should be. But the idea of such a form is no different, in principle, from the developmental conception we have of parenting. Children mature. As they do, parental and filial obligations are expected to change. People often have difficulty *making* the changes, but there is consensus (culture bound, in part) about the broad outlines of the changes that ought to be made. There ought, for example, to be a gradual reduction in parental caretaking responsibilities and an increase in filial ones as normal children mature.

The observations here about structural changes in marriages are no more startling than this: spouses mature. As they do, marital obligations, institutionalized in the deontological rules of the marriage, should also be expected to change. People will likely have difficulty making the changes, but we should have some consensus about the broad outlines of the changes that ought to be made. We ought, for example, to have a more settled conception (however culture bound it must be) of the extent to which, and the directions in which, marital obligations should change at identifiable points in the course of a marriage.

OBJECTION: We already have it. Or rather, various subgroups in our society have somewhat different 'settled conceptions' on the matter. There are, for example, elaborately defined social conventions about who does what for the wedding and initial establishment of a household, and later for child care, and still later when the children are independent. Groups and individuals vary widely – e.g., about the proper division of labor – but it is wrong to imply that people do not have settled convictions on these matters.

REPLY: People have more or less settled convictions on sex roles – with respect to division of labor and perhaps sexual activity. But the question is not about role relationships *per se*. The question is whether people have a genuinely *developmental* conception of those roles, specifically tied to a supportable theory of adult development and designed to sustain and enhance the reciprocal character of the marriage. That is an empirical question, but since the general wisdom in the human sciences seems to be that we do not yet have an adequate theory of adult development, the answer to the question appears to be no, on that score alone. And in any case, it is clear that some of the most powerful conceptions of marital roles (the so-called 'traditional' ones) are not well designed for purposes of development – for reasons already mentioned. There is no reason to think that, under the general conception of morality, moral theory will justify only *one* pattern of role relationships. But it will require that, other things equal, all the patterns selected satisfy the developmental requirements of reciprocity.

OBJECTION: But that tells us both too little and too much. It is too little in the sense that it merely points to a deficiency. We are not told anything about how this deficiency should be remedied. *How* are we supposed to obtain this developmental conception of marriage? Is it supposed to grow up spontaneously, once people are aware of the need for it? Absurd. But what is the alternative? Legislation by psychologists? That absurdity points to the sense in which this theory – vague as it is – is already too much. This theory suggests that there should be a sort of lock-step career to marriages. ('Well, now that I'm thirty-five I guess the rules have changed.') Surely that is antithetical to profound relationships.

REPLY: Is it antithetical to a profound parental relationship for a parent to say (or think) 'You're too old for me to have to do that for you'? No. And parenting isn't objectionably lock-step because of it. *If* there are predictable developmental changes in adult life – predictable transfigurations in goals, boundaries, and priorities – then those things can and should be reflected in the structure of the marriage relationship. Its transformation rules, for example, can be designed to be responsive to these changes *as they occur*. That is not a lock-step arrangement. It does not *force* change. It simply accommodates change.

As to how we can achieve the necessary consensus about these matters, it is instructive to continue the analogy with parent-child relationships. How did we achieve the consensus we now have about the broad outlines of child development? Surely the current consensus in our culture grew out of explicit, sustained intellectual attention to the topic of child development, the wide dissemination of theories about it, the 'testing' of those theories – in the public

forum – against ordinary experience, and the subsequent refine-
ment of the theories. It is an ongoing process.

OBJECTION: It is an ongoing series of fads about prenatal care,
methods of giving birth, methods of feeding, nutrition, methods of
toilet training, discipline, education, activities . . . And opinions on
these things swing back and forth between the same familiar poles.
Each time the fashions change people think they are on to something new and important. Then it doesn't work any better than
the 'old' way, which is soon 'rediscovered' at great expense. The
analogy is not reassuring. The prospect of oscillating fashions
about 'marital development' is just comical – something fit for
satire.

REPLY: We already *have* those satires, both about parenting and
marriage, precisely because we have those comical, oscillating fads
about them. We have fads precisely where we do not have
adequate, settled theory. But it is a mistake to suppose that we
have no good theory about any aspect of child development. We
know a great deal more than our predecessors did, for example,
just about the physiology of growth in children. We know significantly more about their perceptual and cognitive development, and
there is important preliminary work being done on moral development. Those things get translated into our behavior toward children – sometimes with farcical results, but sometimes, too, with
deeply satisfying ones. There is no reason to think that analogous
attention to adult development, translated into conduct with regard
to marriage, could not yield comparable results. Comparably
farcical ones, of course. But also comparably satisfying ones.

> Evan had a sudden laugh – other kinds too, but sometimes
> just a single, explosive sound and then a quiet convulsion
> that twisted his narrow face, squeezed shut his startled eyes,
> and shook his thin blond hair. His children, when they were
> small, and Audrey, when she was still married to him, would
> laugh too, when he laughed like that, and flush, and watch
> him warily. He might then cry with pleasure, for no apparent
> reason, and cover his face with his linen handkerchief. He
> might jump in the air and shout. He might swing little Jenny
> over his head, or put Jamie on his shoulders, or wrestle

Audrey, and tickle her, and kiss her until the children, choking
with glee at their mother's helplessness, would scream for
him to stop. He needed an audience – an astonished and
delighted one. He might, if he was at the table with friends
at dinner, take a pork chop in both hands and gnaw his way
to the bone in two quick bites, looking straight at little Jenny,
who always toyed with her food. (The children were always
at dinner with the adults. 'It's their house too,' Evan would
say. 'Why should my children be shut up in a closet when my
friends come for dinner?' He didn't ask that question in a
way that called for an answer.)

Evan was sudden, in these moods, and they came from such
a rush of tender, childlike love in him that stopping him was
out of the question. 'I'm an artist, by God,' he would say when
they teased him. 'I make my living on these lovely impulses.
Why shouldn't I service them?'

'So it's you that does the servicing, is it?' Audrey said to him
once at the table. Evan folded his napkin and placed it
delicately on her head.

In these sudden moods he might sing, or play the piano. He
might pack them all into the car and drive them out into the
open country. Or he might just go into a secret exuberance –
one that bore watching, in self-defense.

Audrey was six feet tall, big-boned, and broad-shouldered.
Her hands were long-fingered and strong. Her hair, thick and
straight and dark brown, with long streaks of gray she had
had since she was twenty, fell halfway to her waist. She was
a cellist – a teacher and a performer. Sometimes, when she had
an audience she liked, she played for them after dinner, after
the children were in bed. It often aroused her – the pleasure
of giving food and music to her friends, the deep string sound,
the resonance in her body. She would settle into the chair, so
Evan would notice.

He would slouch dangerously in his chair then, legs stretched
out almost to where she sat, eyes closed, daring her to make
him respond. The music room was crowded with instruments
and books, music stands and straight chairs for students, a
small concert grand, padded benches, and Evan's armchair. He
and Audrey liked to tease each other in front of friends.

Once Evan told her that while he listened to her play like

that he imagined – so vividly he had to swallow to keep from choking – the taste of a raw, red, resinous warm wine, served from a cup of beaten gold. The cello was all wrong then, he said. Too tame. What was wanted was something to match the wine. Something Mycenean. Bare-breasted girls vaulting over the backs of horses.

'Or sitting at your knee,' Audrey said. (She often sat that way, head on his thigh, listening to him read. Little Jenny, recently, sitting on his lap, had walked her fingers slowly up his chest and over his chin to his lips, then kissed him on the ear. Audrey had watched in wonder.)

'Yes,' Evan said with satisfaction. 'At my knee.'

'Servicing.'

Audrey meant it (did she?) to be taken lightly, but Evan stumbled up from his chair violently. They were alone, at the dining room table, with tax records spread out to sort. She saw his stricken face and reached out involuntarily to touch him, to take back whatever he had heard in her voice. Her fingers found the inseam of his trouser leg; her hand slid round to cup his thigh.

'Well, it's the same thing, isn't it?' he said. He sounded winded. 'Playing the cello for me.'

It took them a long time to understand what had happened – how they had gotten so brittle that a few light words could craze the whole surface of their lives.

'I always thought of them as gifts,' Evan said to her, months later. They were in bed, exhausted and sweaty, tired of touching, unhappy with each other, resentful. 'Impulses.'

'I don't know what they are,' Audrey said. 'But they're better than these damn obligations to let you make me happy.'

Evan changed. He would give that sudden laugh and then his startled eyes would open to see the faces of his friends or his children, and Audrey's hands. Wary of me, he would think. Bracing themselves. And then nothing. He would brood.

Audrey finally found a line of thought that brought him out of it – at least the worst of it. She said he was too old to change. That his neural pathways were ruts. That he was an unregenerate old dirty old chauvinist old sot and that deep down he would always just want a woman at his feet. To go with the wine. Audrey said she didn't care about deep down.

She said it several times, at unexpected moments, after she saw how he was beginning to take to it – beginning to build a story around it. 'I don't care about motives, Evan,' she would say. (Or dreams, or desires, or impulses. She used his name because he liked to hear her speak it, and she rarely did, unless she made a special effort. Evan was preoccupied. He wasn't aware of her effort; her desperation.) 'Just the surface, Evan.'

Evan thought she was a genius. 'Well hell,' he began to say softly. 'I can manage the surface.'

He managed it for a while with farce and deception. He went underground – covered everything with a thick layer of cheerful, metaphorical projects meant to express every dark impulse that every dark theory of human nature said he might have. He was eclectic about theories, as always. He judged them mainly by aesthetic standards. But that was what had shocked and sickened him in the first place. The image of the master beckoning the slave; the way that image suddenly reorganized his perception of himself – his understanding of his desires. He set out, with overlaid comic intent, to get a series of those reorganizations.

'Sicken by theory,' he would murmur, 'then heal by theory too.'

'Evan,' Audrey whispered to herself. 'Oh, Evan.'

Audrey was excluded – not because he withdrew, or kept her away. If anything he was more often at home, more often attentive, more often lively. But he was suddenly opaque to her. His actions were so heavily encoded, so cryptic, that she rarely had the sense that she knew what he was doing at all. On the surface he had hardly changed, she thought, except that he was less alarming, less impulsive, less demanding. She didn't understand why he spent six months learning how to grind a telescope mirror, or why he ran (and lost) in an election for the county board of supervisors, or why (after that election) he joined a church for the first time in his life (his devotion lasted three months), or why he spent weekends of another year, on and off, getting a pilot's license. None of those things seemed either desperate or random. But none of them seemed to lead anywhere either, and Audrey didn't like to ask. (Well, the pilot's license led to an initiation. One of Evan's students at the college – a bright, ethereally naive freshman boy – had never been up in an airplane. Evan took him flying one clear afternoon in October, and then brought him home to dinner. Audrey was wrenched into helpless laughter by the boy's still astounded and frightened face. Evan told her later, when she asked, that it was part of his virgins project. That was the last time she asked for details.) She thought sometimes that he was sinister, or perverse, or sick, and at other times that he was exactly what he said he was, a comic figure struggling with a demon.

They had gone through the business about disproportion – how it was irrational to let an image change so much. Erase the image.

'The image of what?' Evan said. 'For the next ten minutes, please don't think of a grizzly bear.'

And besides, he explained, that one image was just the trigger, not the whole cause. It was the surprise that was at the heart of it – the discovery that he could be so surprised about himself.

Audrey told him he thought too much, that he expected too much, that he was suffocating – she was suffocating – in his introspection. She told him she was tired of being the heavy, tired of being the butt of his vengeful private jokes. She wished to God he wouldn't *think* so much.

'I'm a writer,' Evan said. 'That's what writers do. And people always take revenge – so I do that too.'

What Evan did, finally, was to write a savage book about self-deception. In the middle of the writing, in the middle of the year, in the middle of his life, his old exuberance caught him by surprise. The children were too big by then for him to swing them to his shoulders; and Audrey, he was sure, would pin him if he wrestled her. But she dared him happily with her eyes, and the children giggled and demanded that he try. Evan would then sometimes cry with pleasure, his eyes wide open, groping for his linen handkerchief. (If they were at dinner he would get bombarded with linen napkins. Three of them.)

'Why did you lie to me, love?' he once asked Audrey. 'About not caring about what was behind everything.'

They were lying in bed, sweaty and sleepy, still touching, deeply pleased with each other.

'Because I thought it would work,' Audrey said.

'Well, hell,' Evan answered, 'Just look at us. It did.'

Parents

The typical account of parental obligations is organized around two ideas: the parents' voluntary assumption of care for the child, and the child's long period of dependency. The thought is that the parents' *causal* responsibility for the helpless child is somehow the source of parental obligations. The parents chose to have the child, knowing the child would be dependent for a time. They thereby created a perilous situation, and ought to see it through.

I say only that the typical account is organized 'around' those ideas, because it is quickly amended to cover cases where parenting is not fully voluntary, or children are not fully dependent. Suppose, for example, that a pregnancy is the result of rape, and abortion is out of the question because it is unsafe and counter to the woman's moral convictions. Or suppose that the pregnancy was intended, but that an improperly done amniocentesis persuaded the parents to have a damaged child that they would have aborted had they gotten an accurate diagnosis. If those cases are to be brought under the heading of voluntary assumption of care, then 'voluntary' has become a term of art far removed from ordinary use. If, on the other hand, any of those cases (e.g., the rape cases) are not to be brought under the voluntariness heading at all, then the typical account lacks the means for dealing with them.

Similarly for the notion of dependency. Once the discussion moves away from the strict physical dependency of infancy and early childhood, it becomes harder and harder to make the case that children are 'really' dependent. Or rather, as the children mature, their dependency dissolves into something more properly called felt need, and the potentially unlimited scope of felt need is troublesome. (What of the felt need of some adults to continue living with their parents? Does that sort of need enter into sound arguments for parental obligations? Does it enter in the same way, say, as does the need of an eight-year-old for education?)

There are, in addition, some other troubles with the typical account of parental obligations. One is that it seems designed to produce only fixed-term obligations. Its reference to the child's temporary dependence suggests this, as does its typical resistance to treating felt needs as an indication of dependence. Yet where families maintain close ties, their members do not always *behave* as if parental obligations were all of a fixed length. Children continue to expect help from their parents, and parents feel obligated to give it. Of course, such behavior might be unjustified, all-things-considered. But the typical account of parental obligations seems to make a ruling on the question too quickly. Surely there is more to the matter than dependency.

Another troublesome feature of the typical account is that it suggests that parental and filial obligations have entirely different sources. Parents who grow old and feeble become as dependent as children, but their children do not have the causal connection to this situation that figures so prominently in the typical account of parental obligations. So on the typical account, the children's obligations cannot be justified by the same considerations that justify the parents'. Yet surely there is a common source for some of these parental and filial obligations – not only in agreements between parents and competent children, but also in the reciprocal exchanges that are so frequent in family life.

Finally, there is a cluster of connected questions that arise about parental obligations to diseased or damaged children. On the typical account, because the children are so dependent, parental obligations should be even more extensive for these children than they are for healthy children. Yet in practice, many people reject that conclusion, and many more are uncomfortable with it. In practice, some defective fetuses are. aborted; some defective newborns are allowed to die; and some retarded children are placed in institutions – not for their own good so much as their parents'. The typical account suggests that all of this is unjustifiable. It suggests that parental obligations are entirely a function of the child's needs and the parents' abilities construed strictly. A line of argument based on reciprocity suggests otherwise.

Reciprocity and Parental Obligations
Assume that parents have the virtues of reciprocity, generosity, conviviality, and empathy. Then healthy children will enter into the social relationships that engender and sustain those virtues soon after they are born. Their abilities and needs will elicit generosity. Their efforts to respond – to cope, to adjust, to help, to answer – will be goods for those around them. (Objects of

intrinsic pleasure, as well as conveniences.) The children's playfulness will be a pleasure to watch; their pleasures will engender the same in others.

Further, hopes and expectations are brought to the parents by each new developmental task the child accomplishes. These are, in effect, gifts to the parents. How much their lives will thereby be enriched depends on many things, not the least of which is the kind of world the child has entered. If it is one that the parents believe will doom the child to a life of misery, the hopes and expectations may be agonizing. But the parent's perception of the child's potential is also an important determinant. A child's development is valuable in part because of where it will *lead*. For example: A retarded child's triumph with his shoelaces will likely be both bitter and sweet for the parents. The bitterness will come from remembering how relatively little instrumental value such accomplishments can have for the child, compared to what they can have for the child with normal prospects. The sweetness may be all the more intense by contrast, but the experience will be significantly mixed.

Finally, as a healthy child matures in the context of a family whose members have the reciprocity virtues, a parent–child relationship of unique powers is likely to emerge. It is a relationship unlike any other that the people involved can construct. In it, some things that would be insignificant in any other context are profoundly important. In it, some things that would be terribly significant in any other context have very little importance.

The consequences for the scope of parental obligations are of some theoretical importance. The considerations above, together with the reciprocity arguments, make it plain why it is justifiable to take a more tentative attitude toward parental obligations in some cases than in others. It is not that we lack reasons for thinking that the parents are obligated – say in the case of a catastrophically defective newborn. It is merely that *one* powerful source of parental obligations is either missing or diminished. Consider:

Parental obligations of reciprocity arise only when the child enters the social life of the family, and continue as long as the child continues to participate in that social life. The extent of those parental obligations, moreover, is governed in part by the extent of the child's participation – in the same way that the extent of our obligations generally is governed by how much others do for us. So it is clear that some parental obligations, at least, are functions of the capacity of the child to enter into reciprocal social relationships.

It is not entirely clear when, in human development, such relationships first become possible. Some parents insist that the starting-point is well before birth (e.g., soon after quickening). Others construe such purported relationships as imaginative projections on the part of the parents. Developmental biology reports the fetus' growing responsiveness to stimuli throughout pregnancy, but does not settle the question of whether any of that responsiveness is social. (A social relationship, recall, is characterized by *mutual* awareness of the relationship.) What is generally agreed upon is that healthy newborns exhibit the beginnings of reciprocal behavior almost immediately, given certain conditions for the delivery, and that reciprocal behavior that is clearly social (again in a rudimentary sense) soon follows. Parents who do not perceive this social behavior in their (healthy) infants are deficient – either in intellectual or moral virtue.

The same cannot be said, however, about parents who do not perceive social behavior in the fetus. It seems clear that there just is none to perceive in the early stages of pregnancy, and there is significant uncertainty about the matter throughout the prenatal period. (Though as the pregnancy approaches term, it becomes increasingly plausible to believe that social behavior is possible, given the behavior of newborns.)

Uncertainties (and certainties) on such matters are quite properly reflected in our moral judgments about parental obligations: Insofar as a child is clearly a participant in the reciprocal social life of the family, then it is clear that the parents have obligations of reciprocity. But insofar as it is not clear that the child participates, the existence of parental obligations of reciprocity is also unclear.

Further, the *extent* of these obligations of reciprocity is governed in part by the extent of the child's reciprocal social behavior. (This is a general consequence of the reciprocity arguments. See Chapter Three.) And the extent of the child's social behavior is a function of the extent to which the child and others can 'recognize' their intentions as social ones – that is, as ones characterized by mutual awareness. This, in turn, is controlled in part by the degree of 'alienness' between the parties – the degree to which it can be established that the parties can have similar psychological states. Note that this question of alienness is not stated as a question about how alien one might feel or believe another to be, but rather about what can be established by reasoned inquiry about the matter. This is required by moral theory under the general conception of morality, because its object is to discover what we ought to do all-things-considered. A part of that inquiry is the discovery of what we and others *can* do – not just what we happen to believe they can do, but what (all-things-considered) we conclude they can do. To the degree that a child is alien – so undeveloped or deformed that we cannot be sure we can establish contact – reciprocal social relationships with the child are impossible. Parental obligations of reciprocity are therefore limited in such a case.

In general, then, considerations of reciprocity lend some credence to the view that the extent of parental obligations to fetuses is less than it is for newborns, and less for catastrophically defective newborns than for healthy ones. These considerations do not actually *establish* that conclusion, because they only show that one source of parental obligations can be absent in some cases. The fact that this is not the whole story is evident when one considers that as children's ability to enter into social relationships increases, the extent of their physical dependence on others decreases. It would be an odd result if *all* parental obligations varied inversely with need. But however partial the result may be, reciprocity arguments add important elements to the theory of parental obligations.

When I was eight years old I fought the toughest kid in fifth grade and broke his nose. There was blood. That shocked me; that and the way he keened and cupped his face in his hands and tried to get his breath. He ran in tight little circles, with tight little steps, hunched over. *Like me*, I thought. Like me after the car door slammed on my fingers. I shook with pity and ran away ashamed.

For days I dreaded arrest. (I had an exacting sense of justice.) But when that didn't happen I began to worry about reprisals. I was only a third grader, a year ahead of my age, and he was *big*. Billy something. Probably Big Billy something. And I had to go onto his playground – across his part of it to the third grade corner – every day before school, and during recess,

and after lunch, and again on the way home. I had a lot of
time to think about what was coming to me.

When it didn't come – when I finally could believe he wasn't
going to get back at me – I decided it was because I'd kept my
mouth shut. No one but the two of us knew about the fight.
He wasn't telling, and when he decided I was just a little kid
with nothing more than third grade ambitions he left me alone.
The whole thing had been a fluke anyway.

What happened was this. He came riding up behind me on
his bike very fast, without a sound, on a deserted sidewalk
several blocks from school. For no reason at all, he punched
me in the back as he went by – hard, with the heel of his
hand between my shoulder blades. It knocked me flat onto the
grass beside the walk. I still remember the feel of it against
my face. He skidded and stopped astride the bar of his bike,
half-turned toward me with one foot on a pedal, twenty or
thirty feet away. It's a vivid image – an extreme low-angle
shot, almost from ground level. It was a warm, leafy
afternoon. I remember he was wearing a longsleeved checkered
flannel shirt, like one I had, cuffs turned up, and there were
empty canvas newspaper bags wrapped around the handlebars
of his bike. There was a long, still moment when we were
both too surprised to move. He looked a little scared. I don't
remember hurting, or even being winded. I just remember
charging him in a rage. He got tangled in his bike, and by the
time he kicked free his nose was broken.

I ran home.

That was the year my father was away, and that was the
year I learned not to give my mother much in the way of
detail. Just the news, she'd say. Just the emotional news, kiddo.
That was also the year I got a grip on some fundamentals –
why 1952 cars and trucks came out in 1951; exactly when
people did and did not want you to imitate the way they
wore their gloves or gunbelts; why you stood half-way to first
base when you'd been sent out to play second. Those
principles were generalizable.

My mother was cheerful and interested and generally reliable
but dangerous about fundamentals. If you blurted out
questions she'd answer them and then go straight to the coach
or the principal. Best not to blurt, kiddo.

My father came home from Korea when I was nine-and-a-half — almost ten. I had a canvas ammo belt I'd bought with my own money at the Army Surplus Store. He didn't say anything about it one way or the other, and I took that message pretty hard.

He looked me over for several days — watched me do things. It made me nervous. Then suddenly he bought me a Brownie Hawkeye camera. (How did he know I wanted it? I hadn't told anyone. And if he knew that, why didn't he also know I wanted a Gilbert chemistry set?) The same day he bought me the camera he took me out in the street in front of our house, where the trees wouldn't get in the way, and taught me how to punt a football. It's the only time I remember my father deliberately teaching me anything.

It was a revelation. I'd been getting mysterious results all the time he'd been gone. Sometimes I would kick the ball halfway as high as the big elm trees along the street. Other times, nothing. It turned out that everything depended on how you stood when you started — where your weight was and which foot you were on when you dropped the ball. It's a universal principle. I made the inference to baseball and tennis by myself. My mother taught me about metaphors.

I told her once, when I was in high school, that when Dad came home from Korea he studied me for three days, checked me against some standard in his head, bought me a camera, taught me to punt, and then left me alone. She practically strangled herself trying to say something about Dad and herself and her washer-dryer. I had to get her a glass of water and a Kleenex. You can never tell when something like that is going to be really funny.

When I was ten I got an afternoon paper route. I didn't want it, but my mother took a tough line. She said I could do it. She said she knew most of the other boys were older, but there were some little ones too.

I didn't like that one bit. Aside from the insulting reference to my size, there was an awful lot that woman didn't know about the situation. Some of what she didn't know was this: The only little guys in the whole operation were the scraggly kids who did street sales, and they got their papers upstairs at the front desk. They didn't have to go down to the basement where you could get killed. It was hot as Hades down there, so hot no one could stand it, and so noisy from the presses that nobody could hear you scream. The part of the basement where the paperboys folded their papers was dark, too, because the cheapskates who ran the paper thought the light from the press room was enough. That meant that nobody could see you bleeding, either. Also, you had to get there right after school – before four o'clock for sure – and then hang around until the high school kid who handed out the papers called your route number. Then you had to give him the code for the day. It was well known that he called the route numbers any way he wanted to, and that nobody would tell anybody else what the code was. If the high school kid didn't like you, or you didn't know what to say when he asked you for the code, you'd always be last. Then you wouldn't even get your papers until four-thirty, and wouldn't get them folded and get out to do your route before five. In the winter that was after dark. Men would yell at you from their front porches because their papers were late. Also, if the older paperboys didn't like you, one of them would chase you around while you were trying to fold your papers and while you were gone someone else would steal papers from your bin. Then if you didn't count exactly right while you packed your bags you'd be short at the end of your route twenty or thirty blocks from the Herald Building. Furthermore, it was obvious that a ten-year-old who couldn't remember the nines on the times-tables could not possibly remember one hundred and twenty-three street addresses. And last but most of all, there was the initiation. It was a fact that sooner or later all the new boys got beaten up and had their pants pulled off and were locked into the huge storage room with the newsprint. Sometimes they stayed there the whole night before they were found. There was so much noise nobody could hear them pounding on the door, and nobody would tell. You could never be sure when this was going to happen to you. It might be the first day or the first week, or it might not. All of this was *common knowledge* at my grade school. It made me mad that my mother was so ignorant about it and still willing to send me into it. My father wasn't any use either. I couldn't tell either one of them the truth, because my mother would just go straight to the owner of the paper, and my father would just look at me. Probably teach me to box.

I just had to face it.

(That year I also had to face learning to swim at the Y, where my parents didn't know we weren't allowed to wear swim suits and where the older boys who ran the tadpole class and had hair on their peckers laughed at the little kids who didn't.)

So I faced it, and nothing happened. First of all, nobody messed with me, because the kid whose nose I'd broken told somebody I was a real sonofabitch. That was his gift to me for keeping my mouth shut. The word got around. So there was no initiation, and nobody touched my papers. My route number was always called early, because I always got there on time, stayed in the caller's line of sight, and never hesitated at the window. (I figured out the code the first day. When you went up to the dutch door at the press room – the window – you had to tell the caller how many papers you wanted. But he wore earplugs because he worked inside near the presses. You could hear him when he shouted into our room but he couldn't hear you unless you were right at the window. So he wanted you to give him a hand signal on your way up to the window, after he'd called your route number. Palms-down meant you wanted the same number of papers you'd had the day before. Two fingers on your left hand meant minus two; two fingers on your right hand meant plus two. And so on.)

The first night I did the route by myself, without the boy who was training me, I was long by five papers at the end, and threw them away before I remembered, first, that I should have taken them back for credit, and second that I had missed a whole block.

I went home.

I was sick to my stomach with shame, but I was not going to ride all the way back down to the Herald Building. Circulation, however, had already called my mother. People had complained. I was trembling and cold. My mother told me to go back and finish the job. She wasn't even looking at me.

It seems to me now that finishing the route that night was

the hardest thing I've ever done. At the time it seemed impossible. The kitchen was warm and supper was ready. Mother had made my favorite meal – the thing nobody else liked – mashed potatoes with creamed hamburger. The kitchen smelled of fried onions and browned meat. They wouldn't wait for me because my older brother had to go back to high school for band practice. They were all ready to sit down around that brightly colored table and because of my stupidity I had to go out in the cold. I wasn't ever going to get the whole route right. I was too little for it. It was dark outside now, and my bicycle had no headlight. Only reflectors. It had started to rain and I didn't have a slicker. Only a windbreaker. The Herald Building was miles away. I'd have to go to the front office, where I'd never been, and find the night circulation man. He hated route carriers. He only liked the street sale boys, and he swore at you if you missed part of your route. He was a drunkard. I was afraid of him, and afraid of getting initiated – the next day, or the next week – and ashamed of being afraid. My mother wasn't even looking at me.

But the Herald Building wasn't really that far, I found the night desk without any trouble, the clerk there was matter-of-fact, and nobody yelled at me when I delivered the late papers. (The rule was you had to knock on their doors.) By the time I got home I was exhilarated with relief.

Mother was indulgent. She let me wash off the ink and newsprint grime in the kitchen sink. She and my father had waited supper. My brother had eaten alone. At the table, my mistakes were ignored. Form. Anything could be mastered with good form.

'I think someone needs more mashed potatoes,' my mother said. She stopped to rub my shoulders on her way around the table.

She never used my name unless she was angry. In the imperative mood the name was understood, not spoken, and in the indicative she favored pronouns. 'Somebody needs to be more careful,' she would say. 'You make me very proud.'

I've never understood that. I suppose she had her reasons.

Children

I turn now to some general remarks about filial obligations of reciprocity.

Many children who are raised by their parents have, as a result, lives that are on balance good because their parents are generous, convivial, empathetic and reciprocal. These fortunate children have extensive filial obligations of reciprocity. No special argument is needed to establish that general point. It was argued in Chapter Three that we ought to reciprocate for all the good we *receive*, not merely the good we accept or ask for. Fortunate children, whether they 'accept' it or not, have received from their parents not only the genetic endowment that is a condition of their good lives, but also a large measure of what was required for them to develop and sustain their lives. Surely this set of facts fits directly into the argument-form for the obligations of reciprocity. The problem is then not whether any such obligations exist. It is rather how they can be discharged. They often seem like debts that cannot be repaid.

Less fortunate children – or children whose parents are less responsible for caring for them – have less extensive filial obligations. At the extreme, children whose lives are on balance bad, and whose parents abuse them, may have no such filial obligations at all. And in general, the less extensive or effective the parental care, the less extensive the filial obligations of reciprocity. The reciprocity arguments cut both ways: They generate obligations for good received, but also a justification for resistance to evil. And they fail to justify obligations in cases where the parents reject or abandon or are indifferent to their children.

Two things need to be noted about this conclusion. The first is a caution about the positive side of the principle – that is, that in general the *more* extensive or effective the parental care, the more extensive the filial obligations. The caution concerns what counts as a *good* for the child. There is a saturation point for many of the things children receive, beyond which more of those things is *not* a good. (Think of the smothering parent.) Children have obligations for *good* received, not for things that go beyond the saturation point. Further, considerations of marginal utility enter the picture as well. The second overcoat may be a genuine good, well below the saturation point, but it may not be as valuable as the first, just because one is all that is needed for comfort. The arguments for filial obligations are affected by such considerations.

The second thing to note about these general conclusions is connected to the proportionality principle. Recall that we are to reciprocate in ways that are proportionate and fitting to the goods received. Parental care that is *indirect* (e.g., given through the hiring of servants) will likely produce only filial obligations for some sort of equally indirect reciprocation. And in general, the type of response the child is obligated by reciprocity to make will reflect the type of good received. Of course, no one is morally *limited* to a 'matching' response. It is merely that nothing more is morally required *by reciprocity*. So parents who distance themselves from their children may expect equally distant reciprocation. Those who maintain close ties may justifiably expect something comparable in return. Great variety in the character of filial obligations is therefore possible, and the options are controlled to a large extent by the preferences and conduct of the members of each family.

In general, it seems clear that many of the details of reciprocation in a parent–child relationship will be worked out in the same *sorts* of ways these details are worked out in any other relationship of mutual care and concern. The parent–child relationship may well have extraordinary complexity, intensity and devotion. But such differences in degree rather than kind merely generate differences of degree rather than kind in the obligations of reciprocity.

Parental Authority

There is, however, one important area in which filial obligations seem to have a special character – quite different in kind from that found in friendships. (Though not so different, as Socrates evidently saw, from an aspect of our relationship to the law.) That area concerns parental authority, and the source of children's obligations to obey their parents. Arguments drawn from reciprocity have some contribution to make to this subject – though I do not claim that they can give a full account of it.

Consider: Reciprocity will often dispose us to comply with the demands of our benefactors, meet their requests, respond to their needs, act on their preferences, and follow their instructions. We will be disposed to do this when we understand it to be justified for making a fitting and proportional return to them, and it will be a matter of moral obligation for us. But nothing in this, so far, warrants the title of obedience. Following instructions is not necessarily obedience, as we ordinarily understand the term, and neither is doing what people ask. Questions of obedience arise in situations of conflict – situations in which the parties are at odds about what ought to be done, if only in the minimal sense that one has made a decision on the matter and the other has not. People obey in those situations when they comply *against* their own desires or judgment. Their obedience may or may not be justified, and if justified, it may or may not be obligatory. (It is often justifiable to obey a doctor's orders, for example, on the assumption that she knows what is best for one's health. But such obedience is not necessarily obligatory.)

Authority, as I shall use the term, is the power to create *obligations* of obedience. Authority in this sense is sharply distinct from the power (justifiable or not) to demand and get obedience. Hobbes saw, for example, that it might be justifiable to allocate certain powers to the sovereign, but justifiable also to hold that citizens were under no obligation to obey. Capital punishment, he supposed, was one such power. For good reasons, as rational contractors, we might want the sovereign to have a legal entitlement to impose the death penalty, but also insist that those condemned to die be under no obligation to cooperate in their own executions. In such a case I would say that the state had a justifiable power (a legal entitlement) to carry out certain acts, but no authority in the matter – no power to create an *obligation* of obedience in the matter.

I adopt this narrow sense for the term authority because it addresses the crux of the moral issue here. It is no great challenge to show that parents (or government officials) ought to have certain decision-making powers, and effective means of carrying out those decisions – if necessary against the wishes of others. Even anarchists will agree that the exercise of coercive power is sometimes morally justified. And they will agree that those on the receiving end may well have a moral obligation to do what they are being forced to do. What anarchists deny is the existence of any conceptual link between those two notions – justified coercive power and an obligation to obey. What they deny is the existence of a power to create obligations of obedience. The question about parental authority that I wish to discuss, then, is not whether parents are ever justified in controlling the conduct of their children. (I shall assume that sometimes they are justified in doing this.) And the question I wish to discuss is not whether children are ever morally obligated to obey their parents. (Again, I shall assume that this is sometimes the case.) The question here is rather whether parental power and filial obligations are ever *linked* – whether parents can create filial obligations; whether parental power ever constitutes parental authority. ('Because I say so. That's why.') Specifically, the question here is whether the reciprocity arguments support the notion of parental authority.

The arguments do support that notion, in the following way: 1) *Ceteris paribus*, parents have justifiable, if limited, powers to define the sort of life the family will lead, and to get obedience from their children. 2) Children, in the normal course of events, acquire obligations of reciprocity to their parents. 3) Under some circumstances, parental powers include the power to specify that filial reciprocation must take the form of obedience. That power, *together* with preexisting filial obligations of reciprocity, constitutes parental authority.

That is the outline of the argument. I will fill it in a bit in a moment, but first it is important to note that parental authority of the sort I am discussing depends on the prior justification of *both* parental power of a specific sort and filial obligations of reciprocity. In the absence of either, parental authority cannot be justified – at least not by way of the reciprocity arguments. As children mature, for example, we may think the scope of justified parental power narrows. If it does, then parental authority wanes correspondingly, for that reason alone, even though filial obligations of reciprocity may increase. On the other hand, if parents abandon or abuse their children, filial obligations of reciprocity will wither, and parental authority along with them. It is the conjunction of the two elements – justifiable parental power and filial obligations of reciprocity – that constitutes parental authority. (Social relationships *per se*, then, do not necessarily generate authority, even if they do generate obligations of reciprocity which we can only satisfy by doing what our benefactor asks. That situation often arises in friendships, but unless one of the parties justifiably has exclusive power to set the terms of the relationship, there is no 'authority' involved.)

PARENTAL POWER   Families are not voluntary associations, and they are not associations of equals. People may marry and have children voluntarily, but they do not choose their natal families. Children grow strong and parents grow feeble but something of the initial inequality between them will be preserved. People may choose to sustain family ties, but something of the initial involuntariness will also remain. I assume, here, that the initial inequality and involuntariness is justifiably reflected in the moral demand that parents be responsible for protecting and nurturing their children, and be the ones who initially define (within limits) the rules of family life. That allocation of responsibility is in part, by definition, the allocation of power to the parents – the power to make decisions for and get obedience from their children. It is not my object here to discuss the scope of parental power, except as it connects, in principle, to obedience rules (see below).

FILIAL OBLIGATIONS   Similarly, what is needed for the argument here is not a discussion of the scope of filial obligations *per se*, but simply the observation already discussed that reciprocity generates them for children who receive good from their parents, and fails to generate them otherwise.

RECIPROCITY, POWER, AND OBEDIENCE   The crucial issue is the link between filial obligations and parental power. Consider: Parents may impose rules upon, and insist on obedience from their children for at least two reasons: for the children's benefit (safety rules), or for the parents' own benefit (quiet zones). Obedience to these rules is often presented to children as something that is *obligatory*, not merely something that is good, or wise, or prudent, and considerations of reciprocity do support that claim, in the following way.

A Suppose parents insist on obedience to some rule, for the purpose of promoting the child's own good. Their imposition of the rule is thus an attempt to provide a benefit – a good – for the child. Suppose they succeed in getting the obedience, and it is in fact of benefit to the child. (Think of safety rules for crossing streets; or rules about doing homework.) The child then has in fact been provided with a benefit, and has an obligation to reciprocate. What would be fitting? A clever child will see an opening here: Forcing the *parents* to obey a rule for *their* own good seems fitting. (And in fact children often do just that, in the full awareness that they are 'returning the favor.' People say 'I didn't really want to go to that thing, and I wouldn't have if my boy hadn't insisted. But I guess I'm glad I did.' Or, 'When I light up a cigarette now, the twins try to put it out. They're pretty officious about it.') But that course is often not available, or not a proportionate good. What is available, and often proportionate, is doing what the parents *want*. Obedience, in other words, *can* be a fitting and proportional response.

Of course, it is not fitting and proportional in just any case. Questions of the genuineness of the benefits arise. A rule necessary for a young child's health or safety is one thing; rules designed to make the child act out a parent's idiosyncratic vision of perfection are another. But if on balance it is good to act in accord with the parents' rule, and if on balance doing so voluntarily would be good (or at least not harmful), then if that is what the parents want for their trouble, that is something that is fitting. Whether it is the *only* thing that is fitting has not yet been settled. If it is the only thing that parents will *accept*, or the only thing the child can offer, then it may be.

B A similar sort of argument applies to cases in which parents impose rules on children for their own (the parents') benefit. Here the children are being asked, in effect, to reciprocate in a specific way for other benefits their parents have provided. ('I don't think it's too much to ask, when your mother isn't feeling well, for you to play *quietly* in the house.') Some such demands may of course be unjustified – out of proportion to what the children owe. When they are, reciprocity gives no support to the claim that children must obey. And in cases where obedience would inhibit, or damage, or conflict with reciprocity – *in anyone*, including the parents – these considerations would support disobedience by the child, *ceteris paribus*.

In the cases, however, in which obedience would be a fitting and proportional return for the child to make, *and in which parents may justifiably restrict children to that option*, parental authority exists. Children then have an obligation to obey, created by their parents – both because the parents, by their benefaction, provided the goods which generated the child's obligation to reciprocate, and because they then (through the exercise of a justifiable power) restricted reciprocation to obedience.

OBJECTION: If that is true, then every benefactor has authority, because in cases where the parties differ about what counts as a fitting and proportionate return, reciprocity disposes us to satisfy the benefactor's conception of the good. Benefactors, then, if they are sincere about it, will be able to create obligations to obey – just by refusing to recognize anything but obedience as a fitting and proportionate return.

REPLY: Not so. Not unless those benefactors have a justifiable power to establish the rules of the exchange unilaterally, and nothing in reciprocity itself entails that they do. Reciprocity simply disposes us to return genuine goods – not whatever subclass of those goods a benefactor insists on. It is conceivable that, in isolated cases, the only genuinely fitting and proportionate good will be obedience, but if so, that will not be because the benefactor *decided* to accept only obedience. It will rather be because there happens to be no other available good. Even so, reciprocity will not obligate us to make a return if the 'obedience strings' attached to our receipt have turned the 'good' into an evil. ('If I'd known that was the price I would never have accepted.') And nothing in reciprocity by itself binds us to continue such relationships in the way, for example, that parents and children are bound, at least for a time, to continue familial relationships. Parental authority arises in a special institutional setting – one in which continuing parental power is justified.

OBJECTION: But unilateral power to establish the rules of an activity cannot in principle be restricted to parent–child relationships. It certainly appears, for example, to be a part of very many institutional arrangements.

REPLY: Yes. And when it *is* a part of those arrangements – *an independently justifiable part* – then the appropriate benefactors will be able to create reciprocal obligations to obey. But there will be two major steps in the justification of such authority: the justification of the allocation of rule-making power, and the application of the reciprocity arguments.

The Priority Problem

When hard choices have to be made, we are typically expected to rank family members above friends, friends above neighbors,

neighbors above acquaintances, acquaintances above strangers, and so forth. The expected preference order follows expected differences in the 'closeness' of the social relationship involved.

There is not much disagreement – either in theory or in practice – about *whether* we should have some preference ordering. It is generally agreed that we should. But there is a great deal of disagreement about the details. For one thing, our practice in these matters is riddled with exceptions along several dimensions. One is special obligations: I may have made agreements with strangers that override ordinary commitments to family. Another is a sense of scale: The trivial interests of a friend are not supposed to outweigh the survival needs of an acquaintance. And still another dimension of exceptions takes account of deviations from the 'standard' pattern of 'closeness' in our relationships: If my family has thrown me out, whereas some friends have taken me in, I may be expected to reverse the usual preference order. ('Those people are my *real* family.')

In addition to the exceptions, there are perplexing conceptual questions. Who is my neighbor? Is it a matter of geography or social organization? Is a family a biological unit or a sociological one? Where are the lines between friendship and mere acquaintance?

And finally, there are deeply troubling questions of distribution: How much should we give to famine relief, for example, or disaster relief, or medical research, or refugee organizations? Enough to lower significantly the standard of living we provide for our children? Who comes first: Aging parents, or children? A healthy child, or a terminally ill one? A close friend, or a distant relative?

The fact that there are hard questions like these – questions for which a comfortable answer seems impossible – is not surprising. What is surprising, and discouraging, is that moral theorizing about these issues often seems to make matters worse, at least in terms of reconciling the results of considered moral judgment with some of our most persistent and profound convictions.

Consider: If we try to justify priorities on the basis of human needs, or human rights, or human welfare, then it is clear we will have great difficulty justifying the 'typical' priorities. The usual accounts argue that we know the needs of those closest to us best, and that they are the most accessible. As a general rule, then, the argument goes, the typical priorities make sense. In general, it is most efficient and most effective if we all order our priorities according to the 'closeness' of the relationships involved.

The trouble with that sort of account is that the exceptions immediately swallow the rule – at least in the world we now live in. Communication and travel are swift and efficient. Cases abound in which the choices we must make are between the survival needs of strangers and the relatively inconsequential needs of our families. And the inefficiency of the typical, family-centered priorities is revealed in cases of catastrophic losses – losses most efficiently handled by spreading them over a large group of people (e.g., through insurance schemes).

The usual accounts of these matters, in short, tend to yield conclusions that conflict with the typical pattern of priorities. Before we simply say so much the worse for the typical priorities, we should consider reciprocity arguments. They generate a powerful defense for both the typical priorities and the standard exceptions to them.

Virtue and Social Distance

In outline, the reciprocity arguments on the priority problem go this way: Reciprocity and empathy are traits of character people ought to have. Those traits will in fact order priorities by 'social distance' – that is, they will generate preferences for those who are 'closer' to us, when we must choose between those closer and those farther away. Social structures that enforce other priorities may inhibit or damage reciprocity. To the extent that they do, they are unjustifiable, *ceteris paribus*. That is the outline of the argument. Here is how it can be filled in.

Social Distance
Relationships differ along several dimensions that are commonly described with spatial metaphors. Specifically, the scope, covariance, frequency and duration of people's interactions – taken together – can be described that way.

SCOPE   We say, 'We're not close. We never talk about anything but business, and he acts as though he'd crack if someone actually touched him.' We say, 'There are just certain subjects that are out of bounds. Certain moves you can't make. At this rate, we'll never even really be friends, let alone lovers. It's just too much of an arm's length arrangement.' Such statements indicate something about the scope of a relationship – how much of the full range of human interaction it involves. The level of intimacy, the intensity of emotional involvement, and the extent to which we share our lives with others are all parts of this element of closeness.

COVARIANCE   We say 'I know everything about him, but we might as well be strangers in one sense. We're not really *connected*. We don't really *care* much about each other.' We say, 'When she travels I always worry. Because she hates to fly, I get as nervous as she does.' We say, 'I can't stand to see that child suffer anymore. If I could just go through it *for* him it would be a blessing. And I'm not being noble. It would be easier for *me* that way.' Such statements indicate something about the extent to which people's experiences are causally linked – the extent to which they are covariant. Some relationships have great scope but fail to be 'close' just because they are not covariant. We can break them off without looking back. We can pay attention to other things at will. We are relatively unaffected by the fortunes of the other person.

DURATION   Close relationships take time to develop, and (other things being equal) the longer they last the closer they become. We say, 'I feel like an outsider with her family. We've only been married a year, and when they start reminiscing . . .' The sheer quantity of shared experience is an element in what we call the closeness of a relationship, and that is connected not only to scope but duration.

FREQUENCY   The quantity of shared experience is also connected to the frequency of interactions. We say, 'We've always told each other everything. Been very open. And we've known each other a very long time. But how close can you be when you only see someone two or three times in ten years?' Taken by itself, frequency is no more indicative of social distance than any of the other elements. Familial relationships, for example, often have a covariance that makes us call them close even though the people involved live far apart and communicate infrequently. News of an adult son's distress brings turmoil to the father; a mother's pride in a grown daughter's accomplishments is as intense as the pride in her first few steps. Desire for a former husband or wife persists.

The concept of social distance as I shall use the term, is meant to encompass the enormous variety of ways in which relationships can be described as 'close' or 'distant' in terms of these four elements. Precise measurements are not needed for the arguments to follow. What is needed is merely attention to the way social distance is in general connected to reciprocity arguments. That will be enough to generate some important conclusions about the priority problem.

Reciprocity and Social Distance

The smaller the social distance between people, the more intricate and pervasive are the exchanges between them. Consequently, the difficulty of deciding who is in debt to whom, or when equilibrium has been achieved in a relationship, varies inversely with the distance. Exact calculations are virtually impossible within a nuclear family, and extremely difficult even for close friends. In such relationships it would nearly always be reasonable for everyone involved to feel either in debt or cheated no matter what choices were made. At least that would be so if people tried to keep a strict accounting of who owed what to whom. The potential for continuous ill-feeling and the consequent breakdown of close relationships is obvious. With good reason, therefore, we ought not to cultivate 'reciprocity accounting' in close relationships, as long as those relationships remain stable and roughly balanced.

The situation changes as social distance increases, however, partly because the potential for reasonable disagreement over credits and debits decreases. Many exchanges with strangers are discrete and of assessable value. And many of the benefits we receive from strangers are so indirect that reciprocity for these can be equally indirect (e.g., by our being law-abiding, productive citizens.) So the stability of relatively distant relationships is not threatened by a more calculative approach.

Further, we are, typically, *always* more 'in debt' to family than to friends, to friends than to acquaintances – if for no other reason than the sheer frequency of exchanges. The more transactions there are in a relationship, the more likely it is that there will be 'loose ends'. When all of this is put together it follows that it is always reasonable for virtuous people to think that anything they have to give is more likely owed to those closer than those farther away. Distributional preferences, given the disposition to reciprocate, will therefore be ordered by social distance.

Something similar may be said of empathy. We identify most fully with those closest to us. That is, their interests are 'real' to us in a way that the interests of more distant people are not. Empathetic identification with the suffering (or pleasure) of people whose very existence we know about only indirectly (through the descriptions of others) cannot help but have an imaginary, dilute, and dubitable quality. In contrast, the interests of those close to us – the interests communicated to us directly – have a vividness, immediacy, and indubitability which imaginatively constructed empathy can never match. It is certainly plausible to suppose that, insofar as empathetic identification produces conduct 'for' the interests of others, it will produce preferences for those with whom our empathy is strong over those with whom our empathy is weak. The consequence, again, is preferences ordered by social distance.

Virtue and Priorities

If people have the traits they ought to have (i.e., the virtues of reciprocity and empathy), then they will order their priorities in the typical fashion – according to the social distances in the relationships they actually have. If the traits are justified, then so (*ceteris paribus*) are the priorities they dispose us to have. Note that nothing said so far entails that everyone will (or should) put their families first. The priorities appropriate to each person will be controlled by the nature of the relationships in that person's life. Sometimes families are destructive. Sometimes pets assume more importance than people. Such facts are justifiably reflected in our priorities. (Unfounded beliefs on these matters, however, are not. See below, in the discussion of racism and sexism.)

OBJECTION: Even if reciprocity disposes me to order my preferences by social distance, it does not follow that it permits me to *act out* those preferences – to the disadvantage of people who happen to be 'farther away' from me than family or friends. If a judge, for example, or the captain of a sinking ship, or a physician forced to distribute scarce life-saving resources, is faced with putting the welfare of a friend before that of an equally needy and deserving stranger, we would expect the judge (or captain, or physician) to *prefer* the friends, but to *act* impartially. Virtue is complex in this respect, sometimes forcing us to act in ways that go against our sentiments and preferences. So the argument may establish that it is virtuous to *prefer* the interests of those close to us, but it has failed to show that it is virtuous to act out those preferences.

REPLY: The objection here is plausible only because its examples are drawn from 'public' morality. They are cases in which people in their roles as officials or professionals are required to be impartial – to suppress their social distance preferences.

Impartiality may be a virtue in public life – that is, we may have good moral grounds for wanting officials and professionals to develop such dispositions. (Even that is a dangerous doctrine.) But in private life matters are different. Friends who never *act out* their preferences, or family members who never act out their special love for one another would fail to be what we mean by friends or family. In private life, at least, the dispositions to reciprocate and empathize – as parts of moral excellence – must produce not only preferences ordered by social distance but conduct based on those preferences. To prohibit such conduct is to prohibit one aspect of (private) virtue.

OBJECTION: Not necessarily. Impartiality may be a form of saint-liness in private life. Something like asceticism or self-denial. That is, impartiality might be the sort of 'perfect' virtue that we cannot expect of ordinary folk but by which we identify the very best among us. If so, then we cannot say that virtue *per se* entails preferences and conduct ordered by social distance, but only that imperfect or ordinary virtue does so.

REPLY: I think there are good reasons for rejecting this – for arguing that saintliness (of the sort under discussion) is not a perfect virtue at all but rather an awe-inspiring amplification of one or a few of the elements of virtue – to the detriment of others. (The perfectly impartial 'saint' is more like a body-builder than like an all-round athlete. It can be argued that body-builders are athletes, but there is some question about it, and they are certainly not candidates for athletic perfection.) But even if it were true that perfect impartiality were the perfection of virtue, it would not follow that we either could expect or would want that perfection in very many people. If not, then the argument I have given for the priorities ordered by social distance still stands — at least for ordinary people.

OBJECTION: Well, for ordinary people the social distance argument proves too much. Ordinary people are often racists or sexists, for example, on the grounds of perceived social distance. ('They're just different from us.') If reciprocity tells us we should institutionalize preferences ordered by social distance, then it tells us, in effect, to institutionalize whatever racist and sexist preferences we have.

REPLY: Reciprocity does nothing of the sort. Racism and sexism are based on false beliefs — beliefs about the range of people with whom it is possible to have productive social transactions. Those false beliefs lead to unfounded preferences. The reciprocity arguments, like all the other aspects of moral theory under the general conception, treat unfounded preferences as obstacles to be surmounted, not things to be engendered and sustained by social structures. Among the preferences that we do in fact order by social distance, the only ones we *should* so order are well-founded ones. A general preference for intimates does not rest on false beliefs.

OBJECTION: But a specific set of preferences might. People do, for example, systematically develop their circle of friends on the basis of all sorts of prejudices — prejudices about race, sex, education, appearance, taste, manners, speech. . . . Once we acquire a circle of friends, for whatever bizarre or reprehensible or amusing reasons, reciprocity apparently instructs us to give priority to their interests. And it will therefore legitimate our prejudice — our racism, for example — once it is embodied in the pattern of our acquaintances.

REPLY: Reciprocity will not legitimate the *prejudice*. It will only legitimate the priorities for particular people that arise from the particular relationships we happen to have. Those will not have the general form 'any white over any black.' Their general form is instead 'any intimate over an acquaintance.'

OBJECTION: But the point is that racist preferences will mean that those intimates will *in fact* always *be* whites, or blacks, or men, or women. And reciprocity will then work to sustain those relationships and hence those unfounded preferences.

REPLY: Reciprocity will work to sustain the particular relationships if they are justifiable ones. It is a conservative virtue in that respect. But particular relationships can be severed from the prejudices that get them started, and nothing in the maxims of reciprocity is consistent with encouraging the evil aspects of a friendship. Reciprocity is not the whole of virtue. It does not, for example, dispose us to search out our prejudices. We need other virtues for that, just as we need other virtues for being courageous or benevolent. Reciprocity imposes priorities, but it does not impose or reinforce relationships that are themselves unjust.

OBJECTION: But doesn't the whole argument rest on simply *defining* elements of virtue in such a way that they yield these priorities? For example, if we can find good reasons for thinking that strangers have *rights* comparable to those possessed by our friends, then isn't it *irrelevant* that we typically give priority to our friends because we feel closer to them? Wouldn't we then have to *redefine* the traits of character constitutive of virtue so that they would *not* yield these priorities? After all, the disposition to be just (e.g., to respect rights and to treat similar cases similarly) is also presumably a part of virtue. Any trait of character which encouraged us to ignore equality could not be a part of virtue – because it would not be consistent with the disposition to be just. So what we would need (for virtue) would be dispositions to reciprocate and to empathize which subordinated themselves to the demands of justice. And that seems correct in any case. Feelings of 'closeness' should not control our conduct; *principle* should. And if our moral principles tell us that we should sacrifice the interests of family and friends on behalf of strangers who are starving, then that is how we should act.

REPLY: The general form of an adequate reply here is something like this: The disposition to be just is certainly a part of virtue. And the priority problem arises in part because of the connection between justice and equality. But at the very least that still leaves the question of how to decide conflicts between people with equal rights. The argument here supports deciding the conflicts along the lines of social distance.

The conflict between virtue and principle raises much more fundamental and difficult issues. We want people to act in character and at the same time be sensitive to changed circumstances; to act immediately, spontaneously, out of inclination and yet to be influenced by moral deliberation. We want people to develop robust, stable traits of character but still be able to change rapidly. This is the stuff of paradox and tragedy. (Also, thankfully, comedy.) The occasional consequence – to take an extreme case – is a tragedy like Oedipus'. Oedipus had the traits that constitute excellence in a king (e.g., decisiveness, honor, the willingness to sacrifice self-interest, trust in those closest to him), and those traits brought him down. The result is close to paradox when it turns out that moral theory itself recommends the development of such traits. But I do not think that there is any straightforward way of concluding that it is the traits that ought to be abandoned.

The Problem of Limits

Familial obligations often seem oppressive – at least to people who are rightly disposed to reciprocate, and be generous, empathetic and convivial. If the family is a close one, its (virtuous) members will rightly expect family matters to receive high priority. And in a close family, there are a lot of family matters. The sheer quantity of reciprocal transactions can be consuming.

There is also the problem of term. Familial obligations, whether chosen or not, seem bounded by nothing short of the destruction of the familial relationships (e.g., by death, divorce, or distance). In a close family, there is no way to repay everything you owe, and no way to start fresh.

There is no theoretical 'solution' to these problems; no tidy argument that limits obligations whenever they begin to be oppressive. Family life for good people just is oppressive at times, in ways that cannot (rightly) be eased. It is tragic that the very traits that make a good life possible can also sometimes force destructive burdens on the people who have those traits. But virtues are not like suits of clothes, to be changed for comfort as often and as quickly as we like. And families are not machines, with interchangeable and easily repairable parts.

There are, however, some features of the reciprocity arguments that should be given careful attention in this context. They serve to limit familial obligations in much the same way they limit the obligations of reciprocity generally. These features have been discussed earlier, so I shall only mention them briefly here.

One is the fact that the obligations of reciprocity are generated by the receipt of *goods*. What counts as a good will vary with our needs, circumstances and purposes, which in turn will vary with our capacities, abilities and prospects. Those things, in their turn, are in part determined by our place in the life-cycle (infant, child, etc.) There is a good deal of *unfounded* oppressiveness in family life – oppressiveness that comes from mistakes about the genuineness of the goods we proffer to others. Not everything a parent does for a child is a good for that child, and vice versa. People who are not alert to changes in the lives of others (and, indeed, to changes in their own lives) lack an important ingredient of practical wisdom. The disposition to reciprocate, in the absence of practical wisdom, is not a virtue.

Another feature of the reciprocity arguments that should be attended to is the degree of control we can have over the nature of our social relationships, and hence over the extent of our obligations to reciprocate. Along some dimensions such control varies *inversely* with social distance: It is often easier to 'renegotiate' with people we are close to than with strangers. So familial relationships – in terms of their pattern of reciprocal exchanges – need not be fixed entirely by things outside our control. Learning when to go away is as important as learning when to stay. Learning how to let go is as important as learning how to hang on.

In short, the reciprocity arguments, properly understood, do not necessarily generate overwhelming familial obligations. Much depends on circumstances and the choices made by the members of the family. To ask for more – to ask for immunity from the *possibility* of oppressive familial obligations – is to ask for a very different moral theory.

Friends

OBJECTION: This whole chapter is a bad idea. The desire to write it is just the desire to say something about the subject because it is an important subject (or rather because friendships are an important part of social life), and because people would be puzzled if a treatise on reciprocity ignored it. (Aristotle himself, after all, regarded reciprocation as central to friendship.) And it wouldn't be difficult to write a workmanlike chapter on the subject, with intricate classificatory schemes and arguments with numbered sentences. (Analysis in search of an idea.) But theoretically interesting ideas are another matter, and the truth is that a discussion of friendship, *at this point*, wouldn't contribute any. The underlying issues (e.g., proportionality) have already been treated at length. A consideration of friendship is not likely to add anything of importance to those arguments – in the way, for example, that the arguments about families did with respect to the priority problem. And now that spousal relationships have been discussed in terms of their profundity, the connection between reciprocity and friendship can be extrapolated very easily. We choose our spouses or not, as the case may be. It is the same with friends. There is great diversity in the possible forms of marriage. The same is true of friendship. The way reciprocity ought to work in a marriage (the way it should handle matters of proportionality, for example, and bookkeeping, and substitutivity of goods) depends heavily on the purposes of the marriage and the resources and values of the partners. The same holds for friendships. In both marriages and friendships we face problems about equilibrium, priorities, and limits. If the marriage or friendship is a profound one, then those problems ought to be resolved by bringing the structure of the relationship into conformity with the maxims of reciprocity. There is a presumption in favor of structural equality, a need for developmental forms, priorities that conform to social distance, and so on. None of this is surprising – or at this stage of the treatise even interesting. Unless a discussion of friendship would add significantly to moral theory about reciprocity, or unless that theory yields some novel thesis about friendship, there is no need to write a chapter about it.

REPLY: Fair enough.

CHAPTER 7

Future Generations

Here are some common moral exhortations: We must provide for the future – make sure there *is* a habitable future. We must preserve and transmit the best elements of human culture and achievement, enhance the lives of those who follow us, and give our children a better start than our parents were able to give us. We must leave the world a better place than we found it. We must do these things even if it means making significant sacrifices. We must do them *for* posterity, because we have *obligations* to future generations.

The substance of such rhetoric is not new, but the urgency in it may be. Certainly the context in which we face these matters gives them an apocalyptic character. The spectre of nuclear war, the wholesale despoliation of the environment, the rapid depletion of some non-renewable resources, and – if we are spared the war – the prospect of a crushingly overcrowded planet are warrant enough for the urgency.

Moral theory on these matters faces some baffling problems. In what sense, for example, can we be said to have obligations 'to' the non-existent 'persons' in future generations? How are such obligations connected, conceptually, to the obligations we have to do things now for the future benefit of our contemporaries? (Are those latter obligations also effectively obligations to 'future persons'?) Assuming that we can in principle have obligations to our successors, what grounds are there for thinking that we do in fact have them? Contract, rights, and utility theories all have notorious problems here. Nonexistent 'people' do not have either rights or interests, and cannot make agreements. On what grounds, then, are we to include their potential rights, probable interests, and likely choices into deliberations about what we must do? And even if we should include them, what weight should we give them, and how far into the future should our considerations reach? (To the tenth generation, with the interests of each succeeding generation discounted at a specified rate?)

Perhaps the whole problem is misconceived. Perhaps the only obligations we have are to contemporaries, but some of those obligations 'concern' the future. Perhaps the only rights and interests we must actually consider are existing ones, but some of those also 'concern' the future. Then, perhaps, it will be the case that we should act *as if* we were acting for our successors, when in fact we are only responding to our contemporaries. That, of course, would tie the fate of future generations to whatever rights and preferences our contemporaries happened to have.

The reciprocity arguments have important consequences for moral theory on these topics. For one thing, reciprocity gives a ground for obligations in these matters that does not raise ontological questions about potential persons and future interests. Those questions do not thereby disappear, of course, but their importance for moral theory becomes somewhat more attenuated. Moreover, the reciprocity arguments tie such obligations to something other than the occurrent rights and interests of our contemporaries. That something is the behavior of our predecessors in creating and sustaining things for the benefit of their successors. And finally, these arguments give guidance on the scope and content of our obligations to posterity.

General Justification

Much of the good we receive is produced by people with whom we cannot have direct exchanges. Perhaps we cannot discover their identities. Perhaps we know who they are but cannot produce anything they value, or reach them with anything we produce. But the version of reciprocity justified in Chapter Three does not always require direct, mutual exchanges. We can make anonymous gifts to charities, for example, in exchange for the benefits we receive from their anonymous donors. And sometimes the appropriate reciprocal response is like the Kula exchange, in which gifts are passed on, as it were, rather than traded. (Think of the donations people make to blood banks.)

The important point is that the obligation to reciprocate – the one that arises from the reciprocity cluster of virtues – does not evaporate whenever direct, mutual exchanges are impossible. On the contrary, the obligation arises whenever we have received a good for which some sort of fitting and proportional return is possible, and it is often perfectly fitting to make our returns to people other than those who have benefited us. The blood bank is again a good example.

Predecessors and Posterity

THESIS: Some obligations to future generations have their source in the good we have received from past generations.

ARGUMENT: 1) Much of the good we receive in our lives was produced by past generations. Some of it was the unintended byproduct of self-interested activity on the part of our predecessors. (E.g., private diaries, meant to be destroyed.) Some was the byproduct of purely intragenerational concerns. (E.g., the desire to astound and please contemporaries.) But some of it was in part intended for the future – not for us in particular, but for whomever might exist. 2) The indefiniteness of such an intention is analogous to the indefiniteness of our intention in giving blood: we intend that the gift benefit someone, but we do not *specify* a recipient. 3) The appropriateness of our making a reciprocal return for the goods we have received from past generations is analogous to the appropriateness of our making a return for the goods we have received from anonymous contemporaries with indefinite intentions. In each case, the awareness of the receipt of the good generates, in anyone who has the reciprocity virtue, a justifiable inclination to reciprocate as a matter of retrospective obligation. 4) We ought to have the disposition to reciprocate. That is, our having it is justifiable, all-things-considered. 5) If the disposition is justifiable, then so are the acts it disposes us to do (*ceteris paribus*). 6) We are therefore justified in reciprocating, as a matter of retrospective obligation, for the good we receive from past generations. 7) In this case, we obviously cannot reciprocate directly to the people who have benefited us. But we can 'pass on' the benefits: we can ourselves produce goods for the future – with the same sort of indefinite intentions our predecessors had. 8) Such production of goods for posterity can in principle satisfy the moral requirements of reciprocity. It can be a fitting and proportional return of good for good received.

Notice that the ontological problem that vexes other theories of obligations to future generations does not arise here. The reciprocity arguments do not ground these obligations in the 'rights' or 'interests' of 'members' of future generations. Thus there is no need to give an account of how non-existent 'people' can have rights or interests. Likewise, there is no need (for present purposes) for argument about whether the utility schedules of possible persons must enter into our calculations, or whether we must imagine that future generations are among the parties to a hypothetical social contract. Those are all important questions for moral theory as such, but the reciprocity arguments bypass them.

OBJECTION: Step 3 won't do. It says gifts from predecessors are 'analogous' to gifts from contemporaries. In some respects that is so, but not in a way that will make the argument work. Here is the point: Reciprocity is justified in terms of its importance for sustaining and enhancing productive social relationships. Each of the maxims was argued for on that ground. But nothing in that sort of argument supports the idea that we must make returns for things done by our predecessors. That will not help sustain our relationships with *contemporaries*. Why should contemporaries care what we do about gifts from the past as long as we take care of our business with *them*? Why shouldn't the maxims of reciprocity simply include the proviso that we have *no* debts to dead predecessors? After all, when a contemporary dies, we can no longer repay what we owe. We sometimes then *regret* our inability to reciprocate, and perhaps even blame ourselves for failing to do so in time. ('We have left undone those things that we ought to have done . . .') But surely it would be inappropriate for us to continue a futile effort to make a return in these cases. These debts are unpayable, as it were, and in that sense effectively extinguished. Our debts to the past are similarly unpayable. It cannot be a part of virtue to fail to recognize that fact – by supposing that we are obligated to invent some bogus method of 'repayment' (i.e., to the future). The appropriate response is just to recognize, with gratitude, the good we have received, along with the impossibility of reciprocating for it, and then get on with our lives.

REPLY: Ordinary monetary debts are not extinguished by a creditor's death. They are payable to the estate. Similarly, people often feel an obligation to help the children of a deceased friend – and cite that friendship as the source of the obligation. So there is nothing bizarre about supposing that we *might* have a continuing debt to the past – one that creates an obligation to repay in some way.

OBJECTION: Bizarreness is not the issue. The issue is whether this supposition about debts to the past is correct. Can obligations to third parties (or to the future) ever be justified on the grounds of reciprocity? If we have been benefited by Carl, then we should make a return to Carl. Or, with Carl's assent, make a return to him *by way of* a gift to someone else. ('You can help me by helping your mother.') But, we should not suppose that we are doing anything other than making a return to Carl. And we should not suppose that after Carl's death we can make a return to him at all – either directly or indirectly. This argument about obligations to future generations is doubly absurd: It proposes a return to one class of non-existent people by way of a gift to another such class.

REPLY: This objection is based on a correlativity principle that is inapplicable to these reciprocity arguments. The idea behind the objection is that if one person has an obligation, then there must be some identifiable beneficiary of that obligation – someone, or some group, for example, with a right to receive the benefit. But the reciprocity arguments imply nothing of the sort. The obligations of reciprocity are not grounded in the rights or interests of others (except as those things enter into the justifiability of the disposition to reciprocate). The obligations of reciprocity arise instead from the justifiability of the *virtue* of reciprocity – the justifiability of being disposed to make a return, as a matter of retrospective obligation, for all the good we receive. The returns we are obligated to make must be fitting and proportional. In some cases (e.g., filial obligations) that means making returns to the very people who have benefited us, but in other cases that is not so at all. If the benefit was not given *to* us, but rather was given with an indefinite intention, our return may be similarly indefinite. It need not be to the person who benefited us. Indeed, it need not be *to* any identifiable individual at all. What is justifiable is the disposition to reciprocate, and the obligations it generates. That disposition, together with the fact that our predecessors have produced, *for* the indefinite future, much of the good we now enjoy, generates the obligation for us to do something comparable in response. The something comparable is the production of goods for the indefinite future.

OBJECTION: That begs the question. The question is why reciprocity should be defined so broadly. Why should returns have to be made for goods given by our predecessors? How will that help us sustain things with our *contemporaries*? Why isn't it just sufficient, for the purposes of reciprocity, to keep our eyes fastened on the balances in our *existing* relationships?

REPLY: It would greatly limit current social transactions if people were generally disposed not to be bound, by reciprocity, for the conduct of their predecessors. Imagine what social life would be like if we had no assurance from reciprocity that our good works would be honored by future generations, no assurance that after our deaths our families and friends would tie up the loose ends of our reciprocal relationships with them; no assurance that people would feel some obligation – *because* of the good work we have done – to carry on in the same fashion. If that were so, we would have lost a significant way of controlling the outcome of our conduct. We would have lost an essential element in our ordinary motives for working for the future, and for creating things of enduring value.

OBJECTION: This should not be overstated. Our successors may preserve what we do, and enhance it, and appreciate it just because it serves their ends to do so. And that may be motive enough to keep some of us working at these long range projects. For an altruist, after all, the chance to please and help others is enough. No reciprocal return is needed.

REPLY: How prudent would it be to rely exclusively on altruism here? How justifiable would it be, all things considered? That is partly an empirical question, but it seems safe to assume that such reliance would not be justifiable. Even in direct reciprocal exchanges, after all, the deontic element of reciprocity is warranted. Surely the case for it is even stronger here.

Human life would be improverished without things of enduring value, and without the goods we get from the long-range projects of other people. Reciprocity helps to engender and enhance such goods by giving us all a measure of control over the conduct of our successors. If they are disposed to make fitting and proportionate returns for the goods we produce for them, we will have some assurance that our efforts will not be in vain. That assurance is not sufficient to create a motive to work for the future. (We may still ask 'Why bother?') But *without* that assurance people are much less likely to have an adequate motive. There are good reasons, then, for holding that the maxim for reciprocal returns should apply across generations.

OBJECTION: There is still something deeply unconvincing here. Why bring predecessors into the picture at all? We cannot change what they did, one way or the other. We've gotten as much as we are going to get from them, and we cannot make a return to them. If our contemporaries need reassurance – if they will not save and produce things for the future without the belief that others will honor and conserve those things – then we can give them all the reassurance they want. We can promise them that we will honor and conserve *their* achievements, and teach our children to do the same. That kind of bargain does not involve *either* our predecessors *or* our successors. It is just a deal we make with our contemporaries – presumably for our own benefit, in case we outlast them. So again, there is no obligation to the future at work here, and nothing based on the conduct of our predecessors.

REPLY: *How* are we to reassure our contemporaries? How are we to convince them that their work will not just be consumed or wasted or ignored after they are gone? In the absence of a practice of such conservation – *conservation of our predecessors' achievements for the future* – giving the needed reassurance would be a tedious business at best. Each of us would have to be assured, by direct transactions, that the people who are likely to control these things after we die will in fact honor and conserve our work. If people were disposed, however, as a matter of moral obligation for benefits received, to pass such benefits on to their successors, then the existence of that form of reciprocity alone would give the needed reassurance.

OBJECTION: But at what cost? Where are the benefits to us from giving such elaborate reassurance to contemporaries?

REPLY: If it turns out that there are in fact no benefits, or none that offset the cost, then this form of reciprocity presumably would wither away. The argument here, however, assumes that there are great benefits involved – benefits that we realize because people generally believe that the goods they pass on will be honored and conserved. On that assumption, the aspect of reciprocity under discussion here is well justified.

Fittingness

OBJECTION: Suppose we do have an obligation to make a 'return' in response to the goods we receive from our predecessors. It still does not follow that the return must be 'to' *future* generations. Surely the fittingness requirement is not that restrictive. Take the blood bank example again: Suppose my life has been saved by a transfusion, and the blood came from the Red Cross. Suppose we grant that I have an obligation to reciprocate for this. Fittingness does not require seeking out the actual donor whose blood saved my life, nor does it necessarily require donating blood. If there is a surplus of my type, or I am unable to donate, then surely some other kind of contribution – money or service – will do. Why, then, can't I reciprocate for goods from the past by responding to the needs of the *present*? Why must my reciprocation be 'to' the future? No doubt it *can* be. But that is not the point. If it need not be, then these reciprocity arguments do not justify obligations to future generations. They merely justify obligations to reciprocate (either to the present or to the future) for the goods received from predecessors.

REPLY: This objection moves much too quickly from case to case. The fittingness requirement *is* stringent enough to specify returns of comparable indefiniteness. Reciprocity is justified, after all, by reference to its effectiveness in sustaining the sorts of exchanges that make a productive social life possible. To the extent that indirect returns, or returns to indefinitely specified persons, are required to sustain productive social life, then they will be the ones that are fitting. Blood banks cannot be sustained if no one donates blood to them. So the notion that I can make a fitting return (for the availability or use of blood from a blood bank) by doing something *other* than donating blood to the bank (if I am able) is not generalizable. That is, given the purpose of sustaining the blood bank, *by means* of reciprocity, the only fittingness principle that meets the generalization test is one that specifies a return that helps sustain the blood bank. Clearly that will not be just 'Do anything you choose.' It will rather be something specific to the blood bank. Something like 'Give blood in return if you are able and your blood is needed, otherwise give service or money.' The *direct* gift of blood to a needy person, while perhaps obligatory for *other* reasons, does not count as reciprocity for the benefits received *from the blood bank*. What is fitting is something that helps to sustain the practice or institution involved. In the case of the goods we have received from predecessors, the practice involved is that of the preservation and enhancement, for future generations, of human society and achievements. It is from that practice, as engaged in by our predecessors, that we received the benefits. Contributions to contemporaries do not count as contributions to that practice, and hence do not count as fitting reciprocation for the goods we receive from it. Only contributions made for future generations are fitting.

OBJECTION: But much of the good we receive from our predecessors was not *intended* by them for the good of future generations. It was rather intended solely for themselves or their contemporaries. Do we owe reciprocity for that?

REPLY: Not in the form of an intentional contribution to the good of future generations. Only, at most, in the form of comparable byproducts, produced by sustaining the practices and institutions (e.g., the arts) that produced goods as byproducts for us.

Stasis

OBJECTION: If that is the case, then our obligations to future generations are paltry. At best they are merely enough to preserve the *status quo* with all its defects. We owe to the future only as much as we were given, and we must make our 'returns' in the very way we were benefited (e.g., intentionally or unintentionally), and to the very institutions that benefited us. Won't that tend merely to perpetuate the past? Won't it tend to perpetuate unjust institutions, if those institutions do some good?

REPLY: Three things may be said in reply. First, reciprocity requires returns of good for good received. Passing along injustice (i.e., unjust institutions) is not a return of good for good; it conflicts with reciprocity. On the other hand, most human institutions are imperfect. Other things equal, there is nothing wrong with preserving an institution *insofar* as it is a good one. That is merely another way of saying two things: Good things may justifiably be preserved, *ceteris paribus*; and one measure of how worthwhile it is to preserve an institution is the extent to which it is a good one.

Second, whether reciprocity tends merely to preserve the *status quo* or not will depend on what sort of practice (on behalf of posterity) we find ourselves obligated to contribute to. If we inherit a 'conservative' one, reciprocity will tend to preserve it. If we inherit a 'progressive' one, reciprocity will tend to preserve that. But that is not surprising. Changes in the *status quo* come from many sources. The fact that one occasional source (reciprocity) is not always a source need not be distressing.

Finally, about the paltriness of our obligations. This too depends on what we inherit. If the inheritance is a poor one, then the obligations of reciprocity will be paltry. If the inheritance is a rich one, the obligations will be extensive. In either case, however, it is important to note that reciprocity may not be the *only* source of obligations to future generations. I have argued only that it is one source.

The Content of the Obligations: General Observations

The application of the reciprocity arguments to particular cases is often a difficult business even in face to face transactions. In the case of acting for future generations those problems are magnified, and some general comments on them may be worthwhile. I shall make my remarks here under four headings: Substitutions, Savings, Increase, and Temporal Horizons.

Substitutions

Any application of the reciprocity arguments – whether to the future or to the present – will face the question of whether adequate returns must be 'in kind'. They clearly cannot always be, because returns in kind are often physically impossible. And just as clearly, even when returns in kind are possible they are not always fitting. Think of people who trade favors along the lines of their expertise: gardening advice for recipes; help with auto repairs for help with plumbing. Returns in kind would defeat the purpose in such cases. So reciprocity often requires 'substitutions'. It requires the return of some fitting and proportional good of a kind quite different from the one received.

In general, substitutions are necessary when in-kind returns are either impossible or unjustifiable. The latter category is the more difficult to use. An in-kind return may be unfitting in terms of the needs and expectations of the recipient – and therefore fail to be proportional in value as well. An in-kind return can be disproportionate in terms of its cost to the giver, as well as in terms of its value to the recipient. And an in-kind return may fail to conform to the savings and increase considerations discussed below. It may be unjustifiable, then, for quite a variety of reasons.

All of these matters are typically more difficult to assess when we are acting for future generations than when we are dealing with contemporaries. The ordinary difficulties of estimating other people's needs and values are compounded by uncertainties about the future. If the twenty-second century brings a new ice age, what its inhabitants will value most as a legacy from us is likely to be very different from the legacies we treasure. And the 'we' here disguises another difficulty. People differ remarkably in what they value from the past, and those differences are linked statistically to factors such as socio-economic status and education. If radical shifts in such factors are likely, the difficulty of predicting what would be of value to future generations would be increased.

The Limits on Substitution

Reciprocity is justified by reference to its value for sustaining the exchanges necessary for a productive social life. Such exchanges typically occur as parts of well-defined activities. The disposition to reciprocate, *as it operates in the context of a given activity*, is justified by reference to its value for sustaining *that* activity. We ought to be disposed to reciprocate for the good we receive from X, if sustaining X is justifiable and reciprocation will help sustain it. That effectively limits our choices. The good we receive from an art, for example, should be returned in ways that sustain that art. That does not necessarily mean a return in kind. (A painting for a painting.) But it does mean a return that promotes a particular artistic enterprise. A consequence of this is that each enterprise is to be sustained by the people who profit from it. The result is something like a user tax.

When this result is generalized, the problem of substitution looks more tractable. The presumption will be that we are to do things calculated to sustain, for the future, the very things we have benefited from. The range of options that serve that purpose will presumably be manageable. Substitutions outside that range will require further argument.

Identification of the range is still a tricky question, of course. (If the source of our pleasure is the work of a particular painter rather than painters generally, then the appropriate range for reciprocity is perhaps restricted to preserving the work of that painter.) In order to make an identification, we need detailed information about the particular case. But we are faced with comparable problems very often in daily life. The reciprocity arguments give us a framework in which to tackle them. The fact that the application faces ordinary difficulties is no objection to the theory.

Savings

Obligations of reciprocity to contemporaries come from the transactions we have with them. Obligations to future generations come from what we have received from our predecessors. The relative extent of those obligations is given by the extent of good we receive, and the relative weight of the obligations is presumptively equal. That is, how much we owe to the present as opposed to how much we owe to the future depends on differences in how much we have received from contemporaries and from predecessors, respectively. And under the general conception of morality, unless there is some reasoned argument to the contrary, the two sorts of obligations must be given equal weight. (See Chapter Two.)

As a consequence, the reciprocity arguments face no special

problem about savings – at least none that is as complex as that faced by utility or social contract theory. Recall, for example, the problem of constructing a just savings principle as faced in Rawls' theory of justice: We must ask there how much rational contractors in the original position would be willing to sacrifice (save) for the future. Tinkering with the notion of the original position in order to get an answer – by drawing the veil of ignorance more tightly over everyone, for example – simply solves the problem by refusing to treat it as a problem about the *future*. All of the parties are simply made to act as if they might be acting in their own interests. From the standpoint of reciprocity, the amount owed to future generations is fixed by reference to what we have received from the past – as adjusted by our ability to reciprocate for it while still satisfying our other obligations. Conflicting obligations have no special weight merely because they come from, and are owed to, contemporaries. Obligations to the present start on an equal footing with obligations to the future. Further argument is needed to resolve such conflicts.

Of course, arguments based on needs and values will always come down on the side of our contemporaries. Our nonexistent predecessors and successors do not have needs and values; only existing beings have them. So in general, the consideration of needs and values will add weight to the contention that conflicts should be decided in favor of contemporaries.

Yet there is no reason to suppose that our obligations to future generations would be seriously eroded by these factors. Obligations, after all, have moral priority over needs and values. It is not an absolute priority. (See Chapter Two.) But it is certainly enough to force a significant burden of proof on anyone who insists that needs or values (in a given case) outweigh obligations. Not just any need will do, for example; it will have to be of a scale sufficient to override a moral requirement.

It is obvious that, all things considered, needs and values often do override obligations. (Survival needs outweigh the obligation to keep off a private dock.) But it is just as obvious that a careful consideration of the issue will show that there is often no necessary conflict between needs and obligations at all – that it is possible, for example, to survive without violating other people's rights. In the case of our obligations to the future, it may well turn out that we can both have an affluent life and do the saving required by reciprocity. Whether we can have exactly the life we happen (pretheoretically) to want is not the issue. If upon reflection we can find *some* equally good life that is compatible with the fulfillment of our moral obligations, then that is the one that will be recommended by moral theory under the general conception. (See the discussion of compossibility in Chapter Two.) So arguments on behalf of our contemporaries are not likely to make large inroads into our obligations to the future – as long as our options (for survival and flourishing) are plentiful and varied.

OBJECTION: On the contrary, the reciprocity arguments saddle us with overwhelming obligations. We bear the burden of making returns for the cumulative efforts of *all* past generations. Surely that is an impossible task. And if we did as much of it as we could do, it would be all-consuming.

REPLY: Our predecessors' efforts *are* cumulative, but so is the momentum of the social institutions in which they are embedded. Our obligation to preserve and to transmit (to keep things moving) is therefore not nearly as burdensome as an obligation to get things started. And it is again controlled for each of us by the benefits we actually receive. To the extent that our obligations to future generations are merely obligations to preserve and transmit, then, they are not overwhelming.

Increase

OBJECTION: Our predecessors not only preserved but also invented and improved things. On the face of it, a fitting and proportional return for that could be nothing less than our producing comparable inventions and improvements for the future. Yet that seems an absurd 'requirement'. Doing my share to preserve and transmit works of genius is one thing; producing such works is another. And I have benefited from genius in many fields. Am I to be a moral failure if I do not make original contributions to all those arts and sciences and technologies?

REPLY: It is tempting to try to answer that question by adopting some formula that 'socializes' the burden. Perhaps we should say that as long as our society as a whole is inventing and improving things at an acceptable rate, our obligations in this respect are fulfilled. Or perhaps we should adopt some version of a 'representative individual' theory – designed to limit our obligations to what the average or typical person among our predecessors has produced.

But such approaches conflict with reciprocity. The disposition to reciprocate, as defined in Chapter Three, is the disposition to assume *personal* responsibility for making returns for *all* the good one has received. It rejects the logic of freeriders. (That is, it rejects arguments of the form 'If other people will do it anyway, I can get what I want without making a contribution.') And it rejects the burden-spreading approach insofar as that route is an evasion of personal responsibility. (E.g., 'I know she always comes to my recitals, but she gets big crowds for her readings. She doesn't need one more.') These evasions damage the disposition to reciprocate, and so do attempts to 'socialize' the obligations of reciprocity – to detach them from our personal responsibility for making returns for the goods we have personally received.

[It should be recalled, however, that the arguments of Chapter Three contain a caveat about intentions. The good that I receive by accident, as it were, I need only return by accident, so to speak. I need not make an intentional effort to repay it. This point will become important in the replies to objections below. To the extent that the good we receive from our predecessors was not consciously produced by them for future generations, our obligations to reciprocate for it are reduced.]

In any event, the solution to the problem of increase is quite straightforward. It is given by two simple observations. One is that we cannot be under an obligation to do or be things that are impossible for us. (I might make a competent physicist, or medical scientist, or philosopher, but not all at once. And not an Einstein or a Jonas Salk or an Aristotle.) The other thing to remember is that geniuses do not work in isolation. People around them help to create the conditions in which they can be productive.

What this means is that the fitting and proportional return for the increase intentionally produced by our predecessors is whatever comparable increase we ourselves can help produce – either through tackling the task directly or by helping those who do. The fact that our society is producing new technology and science and art at an acceptable rate does not relieve us of the obligation to make a *personal* contribution to that production. But given our personal limitations, it will almost always mean that we can discharge our obligations by playing a supporting, rather than a leading role in the production. Even leading players have limited range; they too must contribute to most enterprises only indirectly.

OBJECTION: This still requires us to live at full stretch. None of us can hope to complete the task. There is too much from the past for which we must reciprocate, and we have obligations to contemporaries as well. Reciprocity as defined here would impose crippling burdens on us. We would have to make the maximum effort at every moment. Anything less would be less than we can possibly do.

REPLY: That objection is based on a contestable empirical assumption: that we owe so much in the way of efforts to *increase* good for the future that our lives would be consumed by such efforts. Recall that the obligations of reciprocity to *contemporaries* are not consuming, nor are the obligations to sustain *good* for future generations. So it is just the obligations to *increase* good which now pose the threat. Or perhaps, all of these obligations of reciprocity taken together.

Suppose, for a moment, that these obligations are so extensive that we have time for nothing else. (I do not myself think they are. Or rather, I do not usually think they are. But ignore the factual question for the moment.) In this hypothetical case, what can be said of the disposition to reciprocate? Would it be oppressive? I think not, for the following reasons.

Reciprocity would be, *in effect*, in this hypothetical case, the disposition to lead a *full* life – a life full of the effort to contribute to others something comparable to what we have received. But there is nothing crippling about that. After all, the disposition to reciprocate is not a disposition to undertake these things (prospectively) *as* matters of obligation. The deontic element is an aspect of retrospective assessment and adjustment. So reciprocity does not generate a life of self-conscious self-sacrifice. Further, the range of things from which we may choose is vast and varied. The full life could be a rich one as well. We have benefited from mystics and poets as well as scientists and engineers; ascetics as well as aesthetes; merchants and farmers. The list is as long as the list of good things human society has offered us. To be consumed by doing those things – as many or as few as we can – and supporting the rest is hardly to be crippled. It is to be fulfilled.

OBJECTION: Fulfilled? Or exhausted? Reciprocity as you describe it is nothing but work.

REPLY: Or play. If the playful side of life is a good, then it too is something that we ought to sustain and improve for future generations. So reciprocity can in principle be a mixture of play and work – or better, a mixture of activities that are all engaging and enlivening. In fact, to the extent that social structures make that sort of life impossible for us, and consequently compromise our ability to live a fully productive life, they damage reciprocity. *Ceteris paribus*, they are unjustifiable. Reciprocity does not deaden our lives, but structures that force us into unwanted roles certainly can.

OBJECTION: Forcing is precisely the point. Reciprocity, as you define it, leaves us no time for our own pursuits. It forces us to spend our whole lives working off debts we can never hope to repay.

REPLY: The only forcing it does is to *dispose* us to make returns of good for good received. If (and I emphasize 'if') our lives are so filled with intentionally produced good received that we have no time for anything but reciprocation, then we are rich, indeed, and hardly to be pitied. And the choice of how we reciprocate is still largely our own.

OBJECTION: Still, there is something stifling about a theory in which everything we do is something we are in fact obligated to do for others. Where is generosity in this scheme? Where is delight and surprise in conduct that goes beyond what is required? Where is there a room of one's own?

REPLY: On the *assumption*, again, that life is that full of good received, then it is true that the disposition to reciprocate would (justifiably) make everything appear, in retrospect, as no more than what was owed. Generosity, then, would be something we would find in people's motives, and something we ourselves could be motivated by. It could still surprise and delight us. It would just not succeed in altering our retrospective assessment of the obligatoriness of what was done. But if the *assumption* is correct (about how much good we have received and how little of it we can repay) then surely the retrospective assessment generated by reciprocity is correct. Whether we are stifled by that assessment, or merely properly humbled by it, is a contingent issue about our psychology.

All of this is based on an assumption that I find dubious, however. That assumption is that our predecessors have produced so much good *explicitly for future generations* that we can never fully reciprocate for it. (Recall again that we do not owe intentional reciprocity for the goods they produced for *themselves*, but which benefit us by accident, as it were.) I think it more likely that the self-concern of our predecessors was as extensive as our own, and has consequently left us a good deal of room for non-obligatory conduct.

Temporal Horizons

I turn now to another vexing problem for the theory of obligations to future generations. It is the problem of fixing the time-frame for the obligations. Should we set our sights a hundred years ahead? Five hundred? A thousand? Or is the task to preserve things 'for all time?' The choice of a temporal horizon is obviously central to the task of fixing allowable rates of use – for both renewable and non-renewable resources. It is equally central to the choices we must make about methods of preservation and transmission. If we will exhaust our fossil fuels in two hundred years at the current rate of consumption, then it is obviously crucial to know whether our obligations extend to generations beyond that. If one method of toxic waste storage is safe for two hundred years while another is safe for five hundred, and if the latter method is much more difficult and expensive to use, then again we need to find the temporal horizon of our obligations before we can make the choice. The reciprocity arguments give the following guidance on the issues.

The Intentions of the Authors

In some cases it is possible to determine who produced a good we now enjoy, and with what intentions about its longevity. What counts as a fitting and proportional return in such cases will depend, in part, on the author's intentions. They will help establish presumptive standards for choices about rate of use and method of preservation. Take an example.

Suppose a sculptor creates a work for an outdoor setting, but some generations later people consider whether it is their obligation, on behalf of future generations, to move the sculpture indoors in order to prevent its deterioration. (Perhaps they will put a copy in its place outside and display the original in a museum. Think of Michelangelo's *David*.) Assume, for the moment, that they have the moral *right* to do this. The question is whether they have an obligation, of reciprocity, to do it.

The sculptor's intentions are pertinent, here – just as they are in the process of deciding whether we have any obligation of reciprocity at all. If the sculpture was meant to be ephemeral, and was preserved only through some unforeseen set of accidental circumstances, then the reciprocity arguments do not justify an obligation to preserve it at all. (Some other line of argument might do it, but not reciprocity.) Similarly, if the sculptor fully intended for the work to remain outdoors, and to be gradually ruined by weathering, then on the face of it, the reciprocity arguments do not justify an obligation to protect the sculpture from the elements. There is at least a presumption in favor of the proposition that we have satisfied our *obligation* to future generations by leaving the work in place. Whether we should do more than what we are obligated to do remains an open question.

Three things should be noted about this presumption, however. First, it is rebuttable. Changed circumstances, for one thing, may make straightforward preservation of the author's intentions impossible. Michelangelo would have foreseen the effects of 'normal' weathering, but he would not have foreseen the corrosive effects of automobile exhaust fumes. Consulting his intentions is not likely to be much help, then. At least, the answer arrived at by that route may have to be adjusted as circumstances change. More importantly, perhaps, the answer may have to be adjusted in response to evidence about the intentions of predecessors other than the 'author'. (See below.) Second, the presumption here only concerns obligations. We might well be justified in doing more than what we are obligated to do. And third, the presumption here is only about the obligations of reciprocity. We may have obligations to the future from other sources. Still, the guidance given by considering the author's intentions is considerable.

The Intentions of Others

In most cases, the good we receive from our predecessors comes from many people. Some of them may have been involved in the original production of the good but many more of them (typically) will have been involved only in its preservation. Insofar as the good we receive comes from all these people, the reciprocity we owe is *for* them all — that is, for all of their relevant activities. What counts as a fitting and proportional return, therefore, is what is fitting and proportional for it all. That has consequences for the problem of temporal horizons.

There are several possible situations. 1) The author's intentions may be unknown, whereas the intentions of others (call them the conservators) may be known. In that case the conservators' intentions create the same sort of presumption that an author's intentions do when they are known. The presumption is that we must make a return, for the future, that is comparable in its temporal horizons to what was envisioned by the conservators.

2) The author's intentions may not have been the sort that generated obligations of reciprocity at all — not because the author specifically intended to keep the product from us, but simply because the author did not specifically intend the product for the future at all. Yet the conservators intervened. Here again the conservators' intentions are the ones that control the presumption about temporal horizons.

3) There may, however, be a conflict between the author's and conservators' intentions. The author may intend a longer or a shorter life for the product than do the conservators. And the conservators may disagree among themselves. Yet it is for all their efforts that we are to reciprocate — since all of them were in part causally responsible for our receipt of the good. To resolve such conflicts, one must 'weigh' the competing views. In moral theory under the general conception of morality, one begins with the presumption of equality: everyone's values for a thing are presumptively of equal weight. At that point the weight of the evidence

favors the views of the simple majority. Then one introduces any justifiable 'weights' one can find for the various 'votes'. It seems plausible here, for example, to weight people's views by the level of their causal contribution to the good we have received. Sometimes conservators contribute relatively little – little more, perhaps, than the forbearance it requires to keep a maintenance-free monument intact. In other cases, conservators contribute much more. Once various people's views have been given their special weights (if any), one adopts the presumption consistent with the weighted majority 'vote'. Again, however, the presumption is rebuttable.

Res Ipsa Loquitur

The presumptions we can justify by considering the intentions of the authors and others are all subject to adjustment by the following consideration: The nature of the good we receive, given the context in which we receive it and the expectations we have about how it will be received in the future, will also play a central role in fixing temporal horizons. (Let the thing speak for itself, as the lawyers say.) Things our predecessors thought very little of, we may come to value very highly. (The work of a neglected artist. Certain antiquities.) Conversely, of course, things they prized may come to be regarded as worth very little – or perhaps as great evils. We are bound by reciprocity not to pass on what we judge to be evil. And our own estimates of the value of what we receive are to enter into the determination of a fitting and proportional return. All of this is part of reciprocity in every case, not just for future generations.

The special bearing this has on the problem of temporal horizons is this: We must try to estimate the value of the goods we have received *as* they will be received by future generations. If they will, in our judgment, be evils in a few generations (given predictable social changes), but until then be goods, our horizons must be set accordingly. On the other hand, if we judge that something now of slight importance will one day long hence become and remain something of fundamental value, that too should be considered. Such considerations defeat any presumption to the contrary (e.g., drawn from the author's intentions). They do so because they are definitive of reciprocity itself; to ignore them would be to fail to reciprocate.

The Weight of the Obligations

The obligations of reciprocity are in general ordered by social distance. That is, people who have the reciprocity cluster of virtues tend, as a consequence of those virtues, to resolve conflicts in favor of those closest to them. Families are put before friends, friends before acquaintances, and so forth. Insofar as reciprocity, generosity, empathy and conviviality are justifiable character traits (virtues), the priority-orderings they dispose us to make are also justifiable, presumptively. (See the arguments of Chapter Six.) Of course people vary considerably in terms of whom they feel close to, and the general presumption that conflicts ought to be resolved along the lines of social distance is often defeated by a showing that its results in a particular case would be unjustifiable.

Rebuttable or not, however, the priorities built into the reciprocity virtues have a significant impact on moral life. The speed and frequency with which we must make decisions about priorities means that we will often (justifiably) not even consider possible objections to our dispositions on these matters. Further, the level of uncertainty that attends moral reasoning about priorities will often (justifiably) tip the balance in favor of our virtuous inclinations. The result is an important place in moral life for priorities ordered by social distance.

Obligations to future generations are affected by the same priorities. Our predecessors, in whom we find the source of the obligations, do not any longer exist. Our successors, for whom we carry out the obligations, do not yet exist. The social distance in both cases is presumably infinite – in the sense that we cannot have genuine social relationships with these people. Reciprocity, empathy, generosity and conviviality, therefore, by default if nothing else, all dispose us to favor the living – people with whom we do have social relationships, no matter how indirect. Conflicts will therefore tend to get resolved in favor of contemporaries.

Several things temper this result, however. First, there is the fact that we often have time to reflect critically on the consequences of our preferences for the present. Some obligations to the future are postponable for long periods, and some mistakes in these matters are reparable. (Green space can be restored.) Further, in cases where a mistake would be *ir*reparable – such as the extinction of a whole species of animals – we may have a good deal of lead time. When we do have the time to consider, or reconsider, the consequences, we cannot justify acting unreflectively in these matters. And reflection can in principle defeat the presumptive priority we give to our obligations to contemporaries.

Second, reflection sometimes reveals that the supposed conflict is not a genuine one – that we can meet both our obligations to each other and to future generations. Buildings can sometimes be preserved for *use*, not mere display. New technology reduces costs. Upon reflection, people's values change.

Finally, there is the fact that people can cultivate a sensibility about the past or future that alters the priorities given by the reciprocity virtues. Biographers, for example, may develop a subtle and extensive sense of what their subjects were like, and powerful feelings may result – feelings 'toward' the person so imagined. People, as we say, can live in the past, or live for the future. If they do, their priorities tend to change – not because these people no longer have the reciprocity virtues, but precisely because they have those virtues and act in terms of them toward vividly imagined people of the past or future. Insofar as this is a justifiable way of life, the changed priorities are also justifiable.

CHAPTER 8

Law

Three questions are addressed in this chapter: When is obedience to law required by reciprocity? When is *dis*obedience to law required by it? What sort of restitution does reciprocity require criminals to make to their victims? The reciprocity arguments are relevant to many other issues in the philosophy of law, but a discussion of these three promises not only to be of interest to political and legal theory, but to serve to round out the development of the reciprocity arguments.

The obedience question, for example, raises the difficult issue of governmental authority – as distinct from coercive power – and the warrant for a 'general' obligation to obey the law. The disobedience question raises the issues of civil disobedience and rebellion. And the criminal justice question raises, in a particularly pointed way, the issue of restitution. Previous chapters have developed some of the necessary preliminaries for a discussion of these issues, but the reciprocity arguments have much more to contribute to them than those scattered remarks suggest.

Reciprocity and Obedience

In Plato's dialogue the *Crito*, Socrates proposes the germ of a reciprocity argument: The Laws have helped to make him what he is. They made possible the marriage of his parents, provided for his education, and sustained the society in which he flourished. Surely it would damage them if he disobeyed. Surely he must not damage things that have given him so much that is good. He owes obedience, he implies, much as he would owe obedience to a parent; he has a duty of gratitude. That line of argument is not given much development in the *Crito*, but it is well worth developing. I propose to do so here.

Recall the discussion of parental authority in Chapter Six. There it was argued that a filial obligation to reciprocate for benefits received, together with a justifiable parental power to restrict that reciprocation to acts of obedience, could create a filial obligation to obey. Both elements were held to be necessary for parental authority derived from reciprocity: Without receipt of the requisite benefits, children would have no obligation to reciprocate at all, let alone to reciprocate by obeying parental commands. And without a justifiable power in the parents to restrict their children's acts of reciprocation to acts of obedience, filial obligations of reciprocity could in principle be satisfied in many ways other than by obeying parental commands.

The same is true of legal authority. Two elements are needed: One is people's receipt, from 'the law', of the sort of benefits that generate obligations to reciprocate. The other is a justifiable power, in the government, to restrict those acts of reciprocation to acts of obedience. Without the benefits, people would have no obligation to reciprocate at all, let alone by way of obeying the law. Without the requisite legal powers in the government, people could in principle fulfill their obligations of reciprocity in ways other than obedience.

I shall not discuss the general issue of legal powers here. Reciprocity does not appear to have a theoretically interesting connection to it, and in any case the warrant for some minimal level of coercive legal power to protect life, liberty, and property, and to coordinate people's conduct, is derivable from every plausible sort of political theory. There are deep difficulties about what counts as a *legitimate* government (i.e., about who, among the claimants to such coercive power, justifiably has it), as well as about the proper scope of such power. And the reciprocity arguments developed here may make some indirect contribution to these issues. But the problem reciprocity addresses most directly is the problem of legal *authority*, where that is construed as the question of whether even a legitimate government, exercising its just coercive powers to create and enforce laws, can create in its subjects a moral obligation to obey those laws. On that topic the reciprocity arguments do have some interesting consequences.

In what follows, then, I will *assume* that the question of legitimacy has been settled to the extent that we can identify some governments as the possessors of justifiable legal power – the justifiable power, however limited in scope it may be, to make and enforce laws. I will *argue* that we have obligations to reciprocate for the good we receive from other people's obedience to such laws, and that obedience to law is often one fitting and proportionate return we can make for that good. I will *assume* that governments make an implicit general effort to see to it that their subjects' acts of reciprocation at least include obedience to law – that is, that governments try, in general, to restrict their subjects to modes of reciprocation that include obedience. And then I will *argue* that that restrictive effort on the part of governments is sometimes compatible with reciprocity (i.e., helps to create and sustain the virtue), and at other times is not. When it is, our obligation to reciprocate becomes an obligation to obey. Under those conditions, governmental power becomes governmental authority – the power to create moral obligations of obedience. But when a government's restrictive effort is not compatible with reciprocity (i.e., when the conduct it requires is contrary to what is required by the maxims of the virtue, and would tend to damage the virtue), then governmental power does not amount to authority, and we have no obligation of reciprocity to obey. In fact, as I will argue in the section below titled 'Reciprocity and Disobedience', we sometimes have an obligation of reciprocity to *dis*obey the law.

> The night Carla was killed she was with friends. They surprised her – let themselves in with Jacob's key and surprised her in the shower. They were dazed with wine and sun. Carla too. She had been with them all afternoon at the beach. They crowded into the hall outside her open bathroom door and called to her. There was Jacob, her lover, and his sister Marilia; Marilia's friends Tomo and Katherine and Paul. Carla shut off the water and looked around the edge of the curtain. Her short, black hair was slick against her head. She was, they thought, very happy to see them again so soon.
> 'Make some spaghetti,' she said. 'I'll be right out.'
> 'Others may make spaghetti if they wish,' said Jacob. (He always spoke formally, the more so if he were joking.) 'As for me,' he said, 'I shall be right in.'
> His sister said he would not. She and Carla laughed behind their faces, looking in each other's eyes. They all thought – everyone there thought – it was a peculiar moment.

'Don't misunderstand this,' Carla said to all of them, and she raised her arms as high as she could reach, and stepped out before them.

'Oh,' said Jacob, 'oh, that is clear enough even for me.' (Carla was known to think Jacob ponderous.)

The music was too loud, the kitchen was too crowded, the candles gave too little light, but the fragrance of the food was something to be cherished.

'A pity to eat,' said Jacob. He had one arm around Carla's waist, from behind, and his chin on her shoulder.

She touched his face with her hand. Her fingers smelled of garlic and lemon. She had said nothing so far – nothing at all since stepping out of the shower to get dressed. She had turned the music up so loud her friends had to shout to each other to be heard, but Carla herself was silent.

The police threw her from a helicopter into the bay. From a thousand feet. Her body washed ashore.

The Good that Comes from Law

Sometimes we profit from other people's obedience to law; at other times we suffer from it. We profit, for example, when legal rules are enforced to our direct benefit – as when we get help from the government for a particular problem we have. And we profit from the safety and predictability produced by general adherence to legal rules. We suffer, on the other hand, when those rules are enforced against us, in ways that do us some net damage. And we suffer from the inertia and limitations placed on us by general adherence to the law.

Those banal remarks suggest a number of things of considerable importance to reciprocity arguments. As follows:

The Good Comes from People's Obedience

For one thing, it is important to remember that at bottom reciprocity concerns transactions between individuals. For the moment, the arguments here will be concerned with the good we receive not from 'the law' as an entity, but simply from the efforts of other people to comply with legal rules. Reciprocity will generate a transaction with *them*, no matter how indirect or impersonal it might be. (It will not, presumably, generate the same transaction with people who do not follow the law.) Further, since the good we thus receive comes from other people's *obedience* to the law, our obedience in return seems, on the face of it, to be a fitting and proportional return.

Private vs Public Goods

Notice, however, that there are two quite distinct types of goods (and evils) that we get from other people's obedience. One type is 'private' – benefits that come to us but not necessarily to anyone else; benefits that come in discrete amounts or at particular times; benefits that are, as the economists say, partitionable. These may be called private goods. Examples include special licenses, tax exemptions, grants, and court degrees in cases where we are parties to the action. The returns we owe for such goods are presumably equally 'private'. They are our own, but not necessarily anyone else's; and they will be directed to the specific aspect of the law from which we have benefited.

The other type of good we receive is not partitionable. It is 'public' in the sense that if it is available to us, it is necessarily available to at least some others as well. The safety and predictability afforded to us by general adherence to the law is an example. We benefit from such things but so (necessarily) do others. The returns we owe are our own, but are also necessarily owed by others as well. And the returns will apparently be directed to the law in general – that is, to the maintenance of the sort of legal system that can provide public goods of the sorts we have received.

Mismatched Goods

There is no *a priori* guarantee, however, that the quantity of *public* good we have received from the law will be matched by (or even be directly proportionate to) the quantity of *private* good we have received. Socrates' position illustrates the point. He had benefited greatly from the public goods the laws of Athens provided, but he was also subjected to a private injustice. Reciprocity disposes us to return good for good – but not good for evil. And it disposes us to resist evil. So Socrates had a complex problem: How would it be possible to make an appropriate return for the public good received, while at the same time resisting the private evil?

Socrates' answer was that he could not justifiably resist the evil of unjust conviction by disobeying the execution order. It is clear, however, that the reciprocity arguments do not support his conclusion in any straightforward way. It simply does not follow, from the fact that we owe a return for the *public* good we have received, that we must obey *every* law. It only follows that we must make the sort of return that sustains or enhances the general obedience to law that produced the public benefits. In principle, making that kind of return might even require *dis*obedience in a particular case. (See the discussion of fittingness below.)

More to the point here, the reciprocity arguments would generate two obligations for Socrates: one to sustain the general practice of obedience to law; the other to resist the particular evil inflicted on him. Perhaps his obedience and martyrdom served both purposes. Perhaps, that is, it both reduced the incidence of injustice and strengthened the rule of law. But then again, it might not have done this. It might instead have promoted more unjust executions and brought the law generally into disrepute. The calculation of consequences here is largely an empirical matter.

Now it is of course true that if everyone always disobeyed the law when it hurt or hindered them, we could not have an effective system of law at all. So if we have an obligation of reciprocity to sustain the general practice of obedience to law, we cannot fulfill it with the maxim: Disobey whenever you suffer from the law. That maxim is not generalizable. But there are many less sweeping possibilities for a 'disobedience maxim' – ones that *are* coherently generalizable. The point here is just that we may often face a mismatch in the amount of public and private good we receive. When we do, the possibility arises that reciprocity may require a complex mixture of obedience and disobedience.

Negative Balances

No doubt every functioning legal system produces some good for everyone who lives under it. But the balance of goods and evils received from the law varies from person to person. As a consequence, so do the obligations of reciprocity. People from whom the benefits of the legal order are suppressed may owe no return at all, on balance. Reciprocity contains the seeds of revolution as well as conformity.

The Fittingness of Obedience

It does not follow, then, from the bare fact that we owe a return (to the people whose obedience to law has benefited us) that we owe *obedience* to law in return. What we owe is a return that helps to sustain the enterprise that benefited us. Since in this case that enterprise is obedience to law, our obedience in return will likely help sustain this enterprise. But not necessarily. In principle, *dis*obedience can be a more fitting return than obedience. Notice, however, that reciprocity requires acts that are *undertaken* as a fitting and proportionate return. The good that a malicious act just happens to produce by accident will not satisfy the requirement. (More precisely stated: People ought to be disposed to make reciprocal returns, as a matter of retrospective obligation. People who do not do so are not, *ceteris paribus*, acting as they ought – no matter how much good they produce unintentionally.) So while Robin Hood may qualify for the medal of reciprocity, Bonnie and Clyde certainly do not – no matter how much good they may have done unintentionally. Some arguments about the types of cases in which disobedience seems fitting will be given in the next section.

The point at stake now, however, is the fittingness of obedience. In general, it is appropriate whenever it is a proportionate way of sustaining or enhancing the practice of obedience from which we have profited. Obedience is *required* by reciprocity, other things equal, when it is the only way we can make a proportionate return.

The Disposition to Obey

The reciprocity arguments support a general disposition to obey the law. That is, there are good reasons for holding that people ought to be disposed to obey the law, *out of reciprocity*, in the absence of a sound argument to the contrary. The reasons are as follows.

First, note the qualification italicized above. A disposition to obey the law, *period*, is not what is at issue here. We are only concerned with cases in which people have received some good from others' obedience to law – good for which they owe a return.

Reciprocity disposes us to make a return, and the obedience disposition argued for here is simply that in such cases (i.e., when a return is owed) it ought, *presumptively*, to be given in the form of obedience.

[Whether we should also be disposed to obey the law when no good has come from it is a separate issue. Turning the other cheek is not reciprocity, and in fact a case can be made for thinking that such behavior damages the reciprocity disposition. See the arguments of Chapter Three.]

Second, note that the obedience disposition proposed here is meant to be open to countervailing argument. It may be, in a particular case, that obedience would entail a disproportionate sacrifice. (See below under the heading 'The Proportionality of Obedience'.) Or it may be, again in a particular case, that obedience would damage the very practice we ought to reinforce. The disposition argued for here allows for those situations. It simply produces a rebuttable presumption that unless we have good reasons to the contrary, we ought to make the return we owe in the form of obedience.

The issue, then, is whether that modest sort of presumption, and the disposition that produces it, is justifiable. It seems clear that it is. For one thing, the typical case is surely one in which obedience is at least *appropriate*. It will be what law abiding people will typically want in return for their own obedience. That is an empirical claim, but it seems safe enough. So obedience will typically be fitting from the standpoint of the recipients. And it certainly has the sort of symmetry, in principle, that is the defining characteristic of reciprocity: a return of good for good received, aimed at sustaining or enhancing the very practices from which we have benefited.

Further, even in those cases where *dis*obedience can be defended, it will not always be morally required. Civil disobedience, for example, may be a permissible method of working for law reform in particular cases without being morally required; in those cases various obedient methods may also be defensible. Similarly, though it may be permissible to stretch or ignore legal rules in order to avoid particular injustices, it may be equally permissible either to rewrite the rules or to follow them first and then protect vulnerable people from the potential injustice. Moral argument is often inconclusive about the details of our methods.

In short, it seems safe to say that obedience to law, out of reciprocity for the benefits we have received from others' obedience, is typically a fitting return. Economy alone suggests that we operate with the presumption that obedience is fitting, unless we have reason to think otherwise. Further, given the purpose of sustaining the practice of obedience, the opposite presumption (embodied in the maxim '*Dis*obey, unless you have reasons to the contrary') is quite probably incoherent – incoherent in the sense that it cannot pass the generalization test. If we all disobeyed unless we had evidence that obedience was fitting, it is unlikely that the legal practices from which we have profited could be sustained. The obedience presumption, however, embodied in the maxim 'Obey, unless you have reasons to the contrary,' clearly is generalizable.

The final step in justifying a disposition to obey the law (out of reciprocity) is simply to point to the frequency and velocity with which these obedience-decisions confront us. We thus have good reasons for concluding that people ought to *internalize* the obedience maxim – that is, that they ought to be *disposed* to obey, unless they have reasons to the contrary. (See the arguments of the 'Acting in Character' section of Chapter Two.)

The Proportionality of Obedience

It might still be objected that, for some people at least, obedience to law is typically a disproportionate response to the good they have received from other people's obedience. If so, then the conclusion about the justifiability of a disposition to obey will have to be modified.

Notice, however, that the 'obedience disposition' is explicitly tied to reciprocity. It does not dispose the victims of injustice to obey their oppressors. Reciprocity forbids a return of evil for evil, and requires resistance to it. Whether resistance ought to take the form of disobedience is considered below. But in any case it is clear that the reciprocity arguments do not support obedience to law where no benefit has been received from others' obedience to it. More to the point here, the arguments do not support obedience if it is disproportionate to the benefits received. That should be enough to counter the suspicion that the obedience disposition would produce slavish adherence to the law no matter what the cost.

But a disposition to obey is in effect a presumption that obedience is a proportionate, as well as a fitting, response. The question here is whether such a presumption is justifiable. I hold that it is, on the condition that the law in general scale people's legal obligations in accord with the principles of proportionate return. To explain:

Reciprocity requires me to return good for good – up to the level of good I have received, or to the level of my benefactor's sacrifice, whichever is the lesser. (See Chapter Three.) To the extent that the law – in general – fixes the level of people's legal obligations roughly in accord with those principles, it is reasonable to assume that obedience to law will be a proportionate response – for the legal obligations we have will already (in general) be scaled to benefits and sacrifice.

More concretely: Suppose that the criminal justice system contains a diminished responsibility defense that takes into account the wrongdoer's ability to obey the law, and scales punishments accordingly. Suppose further that tax obligations are in general scaled roughly to ability to pay, that less stringent standards apply to children than to adults, that conscription for military service is sensitive to the extraordinary burdens it might place on some people, that bankruptcy laws protect people against confiscatory court judgments, and so on. If such attempts to scale legal obligations to benefits and sacrifices are pervasive and generally successful in a given legal system, then it is reasonable for its citizens to presume (until they have evidence to the contrary) that their obedience to law will be a proportionate response for the benefits received from others' obedience. Further, to the extent that these citizens can reasonably expect to remain under such a system of law, it is reasonable for them to cultivate a disposition to obey. Indeed, they ought to have that disposition, for the reasons outlined in the previous section.

The justification for this conclusion, however, is tied to the nature of the legal system we can expect to live under for extended periods of time. Under a system that *ignores* the relevant matters of scale, it is not reasonable to presume that obedience will in general be proportionate. A disposition to obey, in those circumstances, is not justifiable.

These things are, of course, matters of degree, and not necessarily uniform across an entire legal system. Our property taxes, for example, are not well scaled to ability to pay, while our income taxes are considerably better in that regard. Penalties for traffic offenses are not scaled, but licensing requirements presumably ensure that drivers are equally capable of following the regulations under normal circumstances, and provisions are made for some exceptions (e.g., for emergencies, for the disabled). Standards of care are sensitive to some distinctions in ability to care (e.g., expertise, economic factors), and the reasonability standard allows some room for adjustment on a case by case basis. On the other hand, strict liability statutes and so-called objective standards are insensitive to some morally significant distinctions. In short, our legal system is not uniformly successful in scaling people's legal obligations to their benefits and sacrifices.

The obedience disposition can justifiably reflect that lack of uniformity. And in fact, people's attitudes toward the law *are* typically uneven – such that some sorts of disobedience are regarded as intolerable, others as tolerable or virtuous. Many people, as a matter of habit, evade taxes, disobey traffic laws, and ignore the 'spirit' of government regulations – while thinking of themselves as basically law-abiding, and certainly decent, citizens. So the idea of a complex obedience disposition – strong in some areas and weak or absent in others – is not at all novel.

The difference here is in the principle that controls *where* the disposition to obey is to be weak and where it is to be strong. In common conversation, the principle is usually a mixture of fairness and consequences. (People may say 'I don't think fiddling my tax returns is really cheating anybody, because everybody else does it, and it's unfair to expect me to stick to the letter of the law if they don't. The laws are unfair anyway. The rich don't pay any taxes, and the poor don't either. And besides, we're not talking about rape or murder. Nobody even notices or cares. If I get caught, I'll just pay the money. So?') The controlling principle entailed by reciprocity, however, is that the strength of the obedience disposition should match the strength of reasonable expectations that, in cases where we receive good from other people's obedience to law, our own obedience will be both a fitting and proportionate return.

Restitution

The argument so far has concerned the return of good for good as it applies to obedience. But reciprocity also requires that we make restitution for the damage we have done, and clearly some of the law is addressed just to that. (E.g., much of tort and contract law.) The disposition to obey those aspects of the law comes directly from the restitution element of reciprocity.

Again, however, there are some conditions: People ought to be disposed to obey in restitution cases only to the extent that it is justifiable to operate with a presumption that their obedience will be (or will be a part of) a fitting and proportional act of restitution. The arguments for attaching those conditions is essentially the same as the one given above for similar conditions on the good-for-good element of the disposition to obey. There is no need to repeat that argument here.

Resistance to Evil

A similarly abbreviated account may now be given of another important source (from reciprocity) of the obedience disposition. Reciprocity disposes us to resist evil. Institutions and practices that do so reinforce that element of reciprocity, and impose obligations on us thereby. To the extent that obedience to law constitutes resistance to evil, we ought to be disposed to obey it.

(Of course, this same element of reciprocity is a prime source of justifiable *dis*obedience to law. If obedience constitutes participation in, or acceptance of, evil, we ought to be disposed *not* to obey. See the arguments in the 'Reciprocity and Disobedience' section below.)

Punishment

These three aspects of reciprocity – returning good for good, making restitution, and resistance to evil – have consequences for the moral theory of punishment. As follows:

Some punishments are intended to be genuine goods for the ones who are punished. (Think of disciplining children to reinforce their good safety habits.) Other punishments enforce restitution, and still others are addressed to the task of resisting evil. In the latter case we may include attempts to control crime by purely custodial imprisonment. Presumably, attempts to control crime by reforming the wrongdoers are mixtures – of an attempt to give the wrongdoer a benefit and an attempt to prevent further evil. In all these cases, obedience to law, *out of reciprocity*, is controlled by the three elements of reciprocity just discussed.

But punishment may also be inflicted for purposes that reciprocity does not support. For example, it may be imposed for purely retributive purposes – where the object is simply to make wrongdoers suffer for the harm they have done. It is important to notice that reciprocity does not support submission to such punishment. On the contrary, that sort of submission conflicts with reciprocity, because to be disposed to reciprocate is to be disposed to *resist* evil, *but not to return it*. The retributive infliction of pain – if it has no purpose other than to 'get even' – is thus expressly forbidden by reciprocity. As a consequence, obedience to laws that inflict purely retributive punishment cannot be justified by appeal to reciprocity. In fact, if anything, reciprocity justifies resistance to such laws.

The situation is more complicated in the case of punishments imposed to promote public welfare – without any attempt to address specific evils or goods in a given case. Strict liability statutes in criminal law are an example. The question of fault is there waived aside in favor of a rule that presumably acts more effectively as a general deterrent. Example: If bartenders know that they will be punished, no matter how innocent their intent, if they in fact sell liquor to minors, then perhaps . . .

The complication introduced by such laws is this. We may well derive some public good from others' obedience to such laws, and therefore owe them some good (in the form of obedience) in return. Further, the enforcement of such laws may well be part of an effort to resist evil, and that is certainly something reciprocity disposes us to support. On the other hand, the faultless people who are punished by such laws may receive a 'private' evil that outweighs any public good they have gotten or will get from the enforcement of the relevant law. And while reciprocity disposes them to support resistance to the 'public evil' addressed by that law (e.g., the general laxness that makes it easy for minors to buy liquor), it also disposes them to resist the private evil they suffer. In such cases we cannot expect people to be disposed, out of reciprocity, to submit to punishment.

And in fact the situation is comparably complex anytime the punishments we impose on people are 1) neither good for them nor restitutive, *and* 2) inflict private evils that outweigh the public goods the punished derive from other people's obedience to that law. Capital punishment is a paradigm case – at least when the criminal wants to live. We cannot expect people to be disposed to obey such an order out of reciprocity.

In short, reciprocity only disposes us to return good, resist evil, and to make restitution for the damage we do. When punishment is imposed for one of those purposes, but is not fitting or proportionate, reciprocity disposes us to resist it. When punishment is imposed for purposes other than those, reciprocity either does not dispose us to accept it, or disposes us to resist it – depending on the effect obedience would be likely to have on the disposition to reciprocate.

Reciprocity and Other Considerations

Reciprocity is not the only source for an obedience disposition. Prudence, for example, disposes people to obey the law whenever disobedience would involve a significant and 'unnecessary' personal risk. Fidelity disposes us to honor contracts; honesty disposes us to make truthful declarations; generosity, conviviality and empathy dispose us to cooperate with others' projects; and so on. These virtues are at the bottom of an array of distinct arguments for a disposition to obey the law.

It does not take an elaborate argument to show that these distinct lines of argument will justify distinctly *different* obedience dispositions. For one thing, the various virtues tend to be occupied with different areas of the law (e.g., prudence with areas in which the law is efficiently enforced with significant sanctions; fidelity with contracts; and so forth). For another thing, the regulative principles used by the various virtues differ enough to produce different results for the same areas of the law. Prudence operates with something akin to risk-benefit analysis, filtered by a rather cautious decision-making strategy. (By contrast, the regulative principles of reciprocity are fittingness and proportionality.) Prudence thus has nothing to say against breaches of contract that are 'safe', and probably nothing to say in favor of them either. On the other hand, a disposition to maximize personal utility might well recommend ignoring such contracts, while a concern for social utility might reach the opposite conclusion. Arguments based on fidelity and honesty would certainly recommend honoring the contracts, regardless of how safe it might be to break them.

All of this stands as a caution against precipitous use of the results reached by way of the reciprocity arguments. Moral theory under the general conception of morality must in principle consider all those lines of argument. No doubt they will often support obedience to law in cases where reciprocity supports it, and recommend resistance in cases where reciprocity recommends that. And no doubt each of these lines of argument fills in some gaps left by the others. But the potential for conflicts is too high to be ignored.

In theory, conflicting arguments are to be weighed, balanced, and a decision reached all-things-considered. In practice, however, there are good reasons for operating with a rebuttable presumption that we ought to do what reciprocity recommends with respect to obedience to law. The reasons are these:

For one thing the reciprocity arguments are directly applicable to every question of obedience to law. This is not true of some of the other sources of argument. Fidelity, for example, is directly applicable to contractual and quasi-contractual situations, but not to other areas. If we are to treat one source of argument as presumptively controlling, it should surely be one that is applicable to the full range of issues at stake. Reciprocity meets that requirement.

A closely related point is this. Law is concerned with a very wide range of *social* transactions. If we are to rely, even presumptively, on one line of argument about obedience, it makes good sense to pick one that is itself concerned primarily with social transactions, and with a very broad range of them. Prudence, in these respects, is first too broad and then too narrow. It is not confined to social transactions, and yet it speaks only to those that involve some significant risk. Reciprocity is essentially tied to social transactions, and in fact applies to all of the fundamental sorts that laws typically address: the promotion of social welfare, the elimination or prevention of evil, the reparation of damage done, and the maintenance of stable, predictable and productive exchanges. That is a second good reason for thinking reciprocity is a good candidate for a presumptively controlling line of argument.

Third, the problem of obedience to law raises a double concern. One is the frequent need to subordinate the interests of a given individual to the interests of others. The other concern is for the protection of the individual against the tyranny of the group. Again, if we are to select a presumptively controlling line of argument, it seems sensible to pick one that explicitly embodies and attempts to reconcile those two concerns. Reciprocity does this. People owe, out of reciprocity, a return for all the good they receive – but only for the good, and only in proportion to its quantity. Each person's obligations from reciprocity are thus controlled by the conduct and interests of others – but are also limited. No one is expected to make sacrifices for nothing, or to be sacrificed for the good of the group. Reciprocity is, then, in this further sense a good candidate for the presumptively controlling argument. It is better, for example, at addressing our double concern about obedience to law than is utility theory, which always threatens to overwhelm an individual's interests on behalf of social welfare.

Fourth, and finally, there is the connection between reciprocity and justice. Suppose 'justice' refers to certain sorts of procedures (eg. for conflict resolution), certain sorts of institutional structures and regulative principles (e.g., for distributing benefits and burdens), and certain sorts of results in particular cases (e.g., equal shares; compensation for damages). Suppose further that we think the law should be aimed at achieving justice in all these senses. If so, then perhaps we should simply adopt justice as the presumptively controlling principle: Obey the law if it is just; do not obey it if it is unjust.

There are two problems with that approach. One arises from using 'justice' in a very broad schematic sense – to refer to whatever we may decide is right conduct in the areas of procedure, distribution, and rectification. 'Justice' is then glossed as 'what is right, in those areas,' and that tends to get equated to 'what can be justified, morally'. The problem is that that route abandons the notion of a presumptively controlling line of argument short of a full scale moral inquiry. Thus, if we are to have such a shortcut at all, it cannot be justice in this broad, schematic sense.

If we take, instead, a *substantive* conception of justice (i.e., a particular set of procedural, distributional and rectificational principles) then we have what appears to be a genuine alternative to the reciprocity arguments on obedience to law. For example, something along the lines of the form of argument used in Chapters Three and Five would go this way: Justice is X, Y and Z. People ought to be disposed to act in those ways, *ceteris paribus*. Insofar as obedience to law reinforces that disposition, people ought to be disposed to obey. But insofar as obedience damages the disposition, people ought to be disposed to disobey. The problem is that when we start to fill out the elements of the justice disposition, we quickly run into the notions of fairness, fair play and proportionality. Those notions are either embedded in, or are used to justify, substantive principles of justice. And when the notions of fairness and fair play are explicated, their similarity to elements of the reciprocity disposition is unmistakable. Reciprocity thus appears to be a more fundamental moral notion than justice – one in terms of which our concept of justice is in part constructed. If so, then that is one more good reason for adopting it as the presumptively controlling line of argument.

So if we are to have a presumptively controlling line of argument at all about obedience to law reciprocity appears to be a good source for it. The question now is whether we ought to adopt such a presumption.

Under the general conception of morality, the only justification for such a presumption is that it is better than full scale moral inquiry at helping us to do and be what we ought, all-things-considered, to do and be. There is not much doubt that we need some sort of presumption about obedience to law. Given the complexity of full scale moral inquiry, the frequency with which it would be required (if we were to try to use it to decide every question), and the likely repetitiveness of it as applied to recurring events in daily life, insisting on it in every case is out of the question. So we need to adopt some sort of presumption merely as a means of expediting decision-making. Reciprocity, as I argued in Chapter Four, is a *fundamental* virtue – underlying conceptions of justice and regulating all sorts of social transactions. The fundamental virtues are very powerful, theoretically, in shaping justifiable social institutions, due to their deontic character and necessity for primary goods. It is plausible to conclude, therefore, that the tendencies toward obedience and disobedience that reciprocity yields are not likely to stray too far, too often, from the conclusions that full scale moral inquiry would reach in any case. For those reasons, I conclude that we ought to treat the reciprocity arguments as presumptively sound with respect to obedience to law. Absent a sound argument to the contrary, we should obey when obedience is required by or is compatible with reciprocity, and disobey when obedience is incompatible.

What've we got?

'We got twenty seconds of a police inspector saying the old guy hasn't broken any law.'

It takes him twenty seconds to say that?

'You should see it. He's beautiful. Big rose-tinted shades. Designer. He's standing in front of the house, so we can use some of it.'

We can't use twenty seconds of it. The whole thing is only going to be forty-five.

'We got a neighbor saying the old man told her he was doing it so the sun wouldn't burn up his trees. Which is strange, because he doesn't have any trees. He just puts the water on his grass. And we got a shot of him chasing a fat cop back into the street.'

Doing what?

'Say again? You're breaking up.'

What was the cop doing?

'Telling the old guy that the water company was there to shut him down. The utilities people were out in the street where the meter is. They put some kind of governor on it. We got a shot of that too. The old guy is going to get 300 gallons a day now. Not a drop more. He *was* using *20,000* gallons a day if you believe it. Three hundred dollars a month for water, and he always paid his bill. We've got a supervisor from the water department saying that, but Sammy can do it quicker in the voice-over. We've got some shots of the alleged mess, but they're not too good. The thing is, the old guy's lawn looks fine. All that water and his lawn looks fine. He's been watering night and day for six months. The neighbors on both sides say they're swamped, but it's hard to show it. They do have strips of marshy grass along the boundary lines, and we've got a shot of Sammy stepping in the ooze, but we couldn't get anything that looks like a health hazard. The

injunction is a crock, if you want the truth. The neighbors
claim they have water in their basements sometimes, but they
won't talk on camera and won't show us. They just want the
old guy to quit watering. They don't like the *idea* of it. Keep
talking about the waste.'

What does the old guy say?

'Just shouts from his porch. Says it's nobody's business how
much he waters.'

So what's the story?

'Say what?'

What kind of *story* do we have here?

'What we have here is not a story. What we have here is a
situation. It'll play like Believe It or Not. We've got a shot of
a guy down the block scooping up pails of the runoff from the
gutter in front of his house and dumping them on his own
lawn. Big toothy grin. We can close with that. A work of art.
And Channel 4 isn't here.'

Reciprocity and Disobedience

Obedience to law is often a burden, but that in itself is no ground
for concluding, from the reciprocity arguments, that we ought *not*
to obey. Reciprocity does not dispose us to avoid burdens *just
because* they are burdens, any more than it disposes us to seek
them out for their own sake. What is at stake is simply making
the required return or restitution. The level of personal sacrifice
involved helps to determine what counts as a proportional return
in the first place, of course, but once that issue has been decided,
the unpleasantness or inconvenience or sacrifice involved in
obeying the law is largely beside the point. If we can find a painless
or pleasant way to make the return or restitution, then so much
the better.

Reciprocity does give grounds for disobedience, however – not
from the burdensomeness of being law-abiding, but rather from
the fact that obedience sometimes conflicts with the obligations of
reciprocity. There are two general types of cases: 1) Sometimes the
returns or restitution required by reciprocity cannot be made within
the law. 2) Sometimes evil cannot be resisted within the law.

Returns, Restitution and Disobedience
Ignoring the Law

Suppose the laws are as good as we can make them. Suppose further that they are quite generally obeyed by others – from which obedience we derive enormous benefits. Even under those idyllic circumstances, it does not take much imagination to think of cases in which our own obedience would *not* be a way of returning the benefit. Consider:

Rules are general. They apply to *types* of cases, to classes of people. People are classified, cases are typed, and rules are drawn for certain purposes, as means to ends. But whether the rules serve their ends well, or even serve them at all, depends on many things beyond the ken or control of the rule-makers. The ends may be exemplary, and the rules may be the best foreseeable means to those ends. Then the unforeseeable happens, and a rule designed to promote some good now does just the opposite in some range of cases. Examples abound. Perhaps a minimum wage law is passed to give people some measure of protection against the vagaries of the market. Then suppose it has the consequence of eliminating some part-time jobs typically held by teenagers, so it is rewritten to exempt teenagers. But then some employers see a way to cut costs by replacing full-time adult employees with part-time teenage workers. The scenario is familiar: A law aimed at a perfectly legitimate end has unfortunate side-effects, and every attempt to suppress those side-effects produces others.

People often ignore the law in such cases – not because they think the law is in general a bad one, but because they want to avoid its consequences in a particular case. Reciprocity supports such disobedience, under the following conditions.

First, the disobedience must be a good for *others*, not merely for the one who is disobedient. Reciprocity disposes us to do things for others, not for ourselves. Selfish motives and goods are not excluded, but they are at best accidental by-products of acts of reciprocation.

Second, the disobedience must be a good for some relevant class of people – i.e., for people to whom reciprocation is owed. Reciprocity does not justify speculative proffers of disobedience. ('Here. I'll cut some corners for you. You'll like it.') The circumstances at issue here are ones in which a return or an act of restitution is required, and disobedience will fulfill the requirement.

The people benefited by this form of disobedience must be ones whose own conduct has benefited the actor.

Third, the disobedience must be better, *as an act of reciprocation*, than any obedient method of making the required return or restitution. Ties go to obedience, because there is a presumption in favor of it. The task here is *not* to make a full-scale moral inquiry into the matter of whether disobedience is justified all-things-considered. The task is rather to find out whether disobedience is justified *as an act of reciprocity*. It can be that only if it is better than obedience for the purposes of reciprocation.

And fourth, the disobedience must be compatible with all of our obligations of reciprocity – not only with all the obligations to those on whose behalf the disobedience is carried out, but with all of the obligations to all who would be affected by the disobedience. This just follows from the compossibility requirement of *a priori* moral theory. See Chapter Two.

In sum, the law can justifiably be ignored, out of reciprocity, only in a fairly narrow range of circumstances: Such disobedience must in fact be a fitting and proportional return or restitution, and must be forced by the fact that there is no equally good obedient way of reciprocating.

A paradigm case, here, is that of the decent citizen caught unaware (through no fault of his own) by bureaucratic regulations. Reciprocity would dispose those in charge of enforcing the regulations to help him avoid the unjust consequences. Surely that is a fitting response on their part for the benefits they derive from his characteristic obedience to their regulations. Now suppose there is no possibility of getting a 'regular' exemption made. And suppose further that disobedience to law in this case would be the best way of fulfilling the obligations of reciprocity. If that were so, then reciprocity would dispose the enforcers to ignore the law.

OBJECTION: But surely that 'justifies' too much. *Anytime* this ideal citizen suffers from the law, the law-enforcers are apparently going to have to let him off the hook. Lots of laws require sacrifice. Getting exceptions for all the decent citizens who are thus 'hurt' by the law would not be possible. Yet by definition, they cannot avoid the hurt unless they ignore the law. This argument just licenses sweeping disobedience on behalf of the good guys.

REPLY: The argument does nothing of the sort. If helping someone avoid the law would do *harm* to others – others to whom we also owe a return of good – then the reciprocity arguments clearly do not justify it. The cases that fit into the argument offered here are only those in which the person's obedience to law is not going to produce the good intended by the law-makers, and in fact will produce unintended evil. In any reasonably just legal order, that is a fairly narrow range of cases to begin with. Add the condition that the disobedience must be *forced* (by lack of obedient options of equal or greater worth for reciprocity) and the range is narrower still. The final condition is that the disobedience must be compatible with all of our obligations of reciprocity. It seems obvious, then, that this argument for ignoring the law will not have sweeping consequences.

OBJECTION: Well, but now the argument is so hedged with restrictions that it looks as though it might have no consequences at all. Surely my obedience will always benefit a few people. So how can you ever be justified in ignoring the law on my behalf – and thus denying benefits to others?

REPLY: The issue is not benefits *per se*. The issue is rather benefits *of the sort* the particular law in question was intended to provide. If your obedience would not provide those anyway, then they are not being denied to anyone by your disobedience. And if you and I are under no obligation of reciprocity to generate other benefits by way of obedience to that particular law (i.e., if disobedience of it is compatible with all other obligations of reciprocity), then what is the problem? Disobedience might very well be justified.

OBJECTION: Point to a *case*. What you describe seems likely to be an empty class.

REPLY: Think of a young man who is in an accident a few months before his eighteenth birthday. He is left paralyzed from the neck down. He spends two years in various hospitals. On his twentieth birthday it suddenly occurs to someone that he did not register for the draft when he was eighteen. Suppose he is subject to a criminal penalty for the failure; for it fits no existing exception to the rule. Being law-abiding (and not without a sharp sense of the absurd), he calls the draft board to set the record straight. What should the draft board do? Prosecute him?

OBJECTION: There are circumstances under which it probably should prosecute. In order to get the rule changed, if nothing else. Or as a way of affirming the rule of law generally. The sentence can always be suspended.

REPLY: And the idea of prosecution can always be dropped to begin with. The law can be ignored. I submit that to do otherwise – in circumstances where decent citizens run afoul of provisions that were never intended to produce that trouble – makes a mockery of the law. In those cases it is blind obedience that damages the law. Disobedience strengthens it.

OBJECTION: There is a troubling emphasis here on the 'decent' citizen. Do you mean it? Is the law to have this flexibility only for people who have good conduct medals?

REPLY: The argument here concerns what is owed to people as a return of good for good, or as restitution. The reference to 'decent' citizens was simply a way of indicating that. Perhaps the indication was imprecise. We can owe restitution to villains, too. But the point is instructive. Reciprocity effectively disposes us to ignore the pleas of people who intend us no good. We are not disposed, out of reciprocity, to do them any harm; we are just not disposed to do them any good. So when such people are caught by the law – in some unintended and unforeseeable way – it naturally follows that we will not be disposed to ignore the law in order to help them. The crook who runs afoul of some esoteric provision of the IRS code will not get much sympathy.

Civil Disobedience

There are, however, people whose disobedience to law can dispose us, out of reciprocity, to disobey the law ourselves. They are the people whose disobedience benefits us, in ways that make our own disobedience a fitting and proportionate return. I will focus on certain cases of civil disobedience as examples of this – not because I think they are the only examples, but because they seem to be the clearest ones.

Suppose someone's 'original' act of civil disobedience is justified. (Perhaps out of reciprocity. See the 'Resistance to Evil' section below.) Suppose further that we benefit from this civil disobedience: It brings a significant injustice into sharp focus, improves chances for law reform, and so on. Out of reciprocity, we owe something in return. The point here is simply that we may owe disobedience in return, under the following conditions.

First, the original act of disobedience (i.e., the one that prompts our own) must have been a justifiable act when it was done. We do not owe a return of good for evil acts, or a deliberate return of good for morally neutral acts that just happen to have good consequences.

Second, the original act of disobedience must have been done with the specific intent to produce the *sort* of good it did in fact produce. Again, we do not owe returns for happy accidents.

Third, our own disobedience in return must help sustain or enhance the sort of good produced by the original disobedience. This is simply a restatement of part of the fittingness condition, but it has two consequences of importance for cases of civil disobedience. One is obvious: An original act of disobedience on behalf of conscientious objectors is not repayable by acts directed toward *unrelated* social problems. (E.g., It will not do to say 'Don't talk to me about sexism. I'm involved in other things, and I do my part for other people in those areas. I donate blood to the Red Cross, for example. Do you?') What counts as a related issue is of course often an arguable matter. If the struggle for civil rights for blacks is part of a global liberation movement, then anti-colonial activity may well be a fitting return for the good we get from civil rights activists. The details must be argued case by case, but the general point is clear: Here, as in any other area where reciprocity is due, we owe returns that are *relevant* to the task of sustaining or enhancing the sort of goods we have received.

The other consequence of this third condition (the fittingness condition) is more directly connected to civil disobedience. The consequence is that, frequently, *opposition* to the original disobedience, rather than disobedience in support of it, is required by reciprocity. This consequence comes from the fact that the impact of an act of civil disobedience often depends on the attention it gets, and the attention it gets is often a function of how dangerous and unusual the disobedience is. If the original act is followed by amnesty (from public officials sympathetic to it) and a wave of similar acts in return (also ignored by the authorities), the impact of the original act can be diluted. The point here, for the person who owes a return, is to pick an act that sustains or enhances the good produced by the original disobedience. Sometimes that will be joining in the disobedience, but at other times it will be quite the opposite.

Fourth, the disobedience in return must have some justification beyond its simply being a fitting and proportional response, in a particular case, for good received. This is so because there is a general presumption, from reciprocity, in favor of *obedience* to law. The argument for disobedience must defeat that presumption case by case. The burden is always on the advocate of disobedience to establish that it – and not some other fitting and proportional return – is the one that should be made, all things considered.

Fifth, and finally, is the familiar compossibility requirement. The act of disobedience must be compatible with the fulfillment of all of our obligations.

Acts of civil disobedience can, then, place us under an obligation to reciprocate in kind. There are significant restrictions on this result, imposed by the four conditions mentioned above. But the general point is nonetheless instructive: We can owe disobedience as a return for goods received from others' disobedience – as well as for good received from their obedience.

Restitution

We may in principle also owe disobedience as restitution. Suppose an official has made a damaging error – one that cannot be corrected through regular channels, but can be corrected by breaking a law. Suppose, for example, that certain government documents are patently in error, and those errors could lead to a citizen's indictment or loss of security clearance. If the documents are processed in the usual way, it is possible that the error will be revealed, and the potential harm avoided. But in the process there will be significant additional harm done to the innocent citizen. We may imagine that she has been suspended from her post pending resolution of the issue, has suffered significantly from anxiety, and so on, but that the matter has not yet been made public. The standard process would do that, and subject the innocent citizen to baseless suspicion and abuse. If the documents are illegally destroyed, however, the additional harm can be prevented, and most of the existing damage can be undone. In principle, reciprocity can dispose us to take such action *as a means of making restitution* – under some obvious conditions.

First, the disobedience must be undertaken as a means of making amends for some damage for which we are personally culpable. The disposition to make restitution is distinct from the disposition to resist evil, or help someone who is in distress. Restitution is an obligation of reciprocity that attaches only to wrongdoers. As a result, while innocent bystanders may also have an obligation to disobey (e.g., as a way of resisting evil) its source is not the restitution requirement. In the example sketched above, then, it is only the officials responsible for creating or processing the erroneous documents who might have a duty to make restitution by destroying them.

Second, it is obvious that the disobedience must be a fitting and proportional act of restitution. But what is often far from obvious, in particular cases, is whether it can be. In the documents case, for example, secret destruction of the records might do more harm than good. The source of the error might go unchecked, and later produce even worse damage to the same citizen. And if the illegal destruction of the records were discovered, it would be hard to prove that the documents had been erroneous, and the consequences for the innocent citizen might again be worse than those of routine processing.

Third and fourth, respectively, are the 'presumption' and 'compossibility' conditions. The disobedience must have some justification beyond its being an adequate method of making restitution. That justification must be strong enough to defeat the presumption in favor of obedience to law. And the act of disobedience must be compatible with all of our obligations.

Disobedience and Resistance to Evil

Many of the wrongs we suffer have nothing to do with the law, of course. People lie to us, or break promises, or do us other injuries that are beneath legal notice. But sometimes it is specifically other people's obedience to law that does the damage. (Think of officials who conscientiously impose and enforce unjust sentences.) And at other times, even more evidently, it is people's *dis*obedience that harms us. (Murder, theft, negligence, and so forth.) The evil we suffer from other people's obedience might provide a ground for civil disobedience or general rebellion. The evil we suffer from disobedience, on the other hand, might provide a ground for extra-legal law enforcement measures. I will explore each of those possibilities in turn.

Civil Disobedience

We have already considered civil disobedience as a means of making a fitting and proportional return to others for the good they have produced for us. But there is another source – one that produces a justification for what I have called 'original' acts of disobedience. It is this.

Reciprocity disposes us to resist evil. Some such evil comes from other people's obedience to unjust laws; still more comes from their unjust behavior in obedience to just laws (e.g., the imposition of unjustly harsh sentences). Suppose there is no effective way *within* the law to resist such injustice. We remain disposed to resist it, yet we are also disposed, out of reciprocity, to presume that obedience to law is the correct course. The conflict can in principle be resolved by choosing a course of disobedience designed to improve the law – and thereby strengthen the justification for a general disposition to obey – by resisting particular injustices. That is properly called civil disobedience.

Such civil disobedience can be justified by reciprocity under the following conditions. First, the disobedience must be likely to be an effective means of resistance to the evils we have suffered, or are likely to suffer. A variety of things count as resistance to evil: avoiding the harm; repulsing it; ameliorating it; putting it to some good use. What they have in common is a refusal merely to 'take' the harm. Disobedience that increases the damage, or leaves it unchanged, is therefore not effective resistance. We may not know in advance whether a given act of disobedience will in fact be effective. But we can know whether it is *likely* to be.

Second, the act of disobedience must be aimed, at least in part, at correcting the injustice at issue or preventing its recurrence – else the act would not count as civil disobedience. Third, the disobedience must be compatible with our other obligations. This is the standard compossibility requirement.

And fourth, there must be some additional justification for the disobedience – something beyond the fact that it is an effective piece of resistance, aimed at reform, and compatible with our other obligations. There must be some argument, in other words, that defeats the presumption in favor of obedience. In this case, it is provided by a showing that the proposed act of disobedience is likely to contribute to making the law more just, and is thereby likely to strengthen the argument for holding that there ought to be a presumption in favor of obeying the law. The presumption is thus defeated in a particular case, but strengthened overall.

Rebellion

Isolated injustice can be dealt with case by case, and insofar as various segments of the legal system are isolable, the injustice of whole segments can be addressed one by one. In these cases it is possible to resist evil laws (by civil disobedience) without attacking the entire legal system. But there are times when a piecemeal approach is either impossible, inappropriate or ineffective – times when the injustice at stake is so deeply rooted in the overall structure of the law, or so pervasive, that effective resistance by disobedience would amount to rebellion against the system as a whole. Reciprocity justifies such rebellion under the following conditions.

First, the legal system must generate a net balance of evil for the rebels. Unless it does so, an attack on the system as a whole will not be justified, out of reciprocity, because the net balance of good will justify an obligation to make returns that sustain or enhance the system as a whole. Note, however, that various groups of people within a given legal order may show very different net balances. Each person's obligations of reciprocity will reflect that person's particular balance. Everyone who has the virtue of reciprocity will be disposed both to return good for good and to resist evil received. Empathy and generosity, moreover, will dispose each person to help others. But the fortunate ones will have an obligation of reciprocity to sustain the system as a whole. Only the ones who suffer a net balance of evil from it will be disposed to rebel.

This sets up a persistent tension between social classes – a conflict of virtue, so to speak. Those who profit from general obedience to the system will be disposed (virtuously, out of reciprocity) to act to sustain that system. Those who suffer from general obedience will be disposed, out of the same virtue, to rebel against the system. But notice that even in the worst imaginable case reciprocity tends to eliminate such conflict. As follows.

Consider a system that permits slavery. Suppose the slaveholders profit greatly from general obedience to the system, and only the slaves suffer net evil. Suppose further that the reciprocity arguments are the *only* relevant lines for each party to take in deciding what to do, morally. (That is a wholly implausible assumption, but the point here is to consider the worst possible case of conflict.) Thus each person ought to do exactly what reciprocity requires: The slaves ought to rebel, and the slaveholders ought to try to preserve the system. It looks as though the conflict will be perpetual unless the slaves are totally successful in overthrowing their masters, or unless the masters can wholly suppress the rebellion. But that is not quite right. The obedience of the slaves, after all, is (likely to be?) a necessary condition of the slaveholders' profit from the system. To the extent that the slaves can rebel effectively at all, then, they can diminish the slaveholders' profit. That changes the slaveholders' net balance, and once their net goes over into the evil column, reciprocity requires them to resist the evil. And resisting the evil might well mean working to eliminate slavery itself, as the most effective means of eliminating the evils of the rebellion. The sort of exploitative injustice represented by slavery can therefore be self-eliminating, under reciprocity, even in this wholly implausible worst case. The initial rebellion will come from those who are exploited. But once it does, the suffering will extend to the exploiters. If that suffering is severe enough, the conflict will be self-eliminating.

The obvious objection, of course, is that there are two ways to make the conflict self-eliminating. One way (effective rebellion) frees the slaves. But the other way is the suppression, by the slaveholders, of effective rebellion. That eliminates the conflict also, and it entrenches the system. Given the typical imbalance of power in favor of the masters, it looks as though that resolution of the conflict would be more likely. And it would be generated by the 'virtue' of reciprocity.

Further thought defeats that objection, however. The obligations of reciprocity govern personal interactions, and while it is possible to imagine isolated reciprocal exchanges between master and slave, it is *not* possible to entertain seriously the idea that those reciprocal exchanges could be compatible with the measures necessary to eliminate the slave's power to rebel. The appalling history of slavery teaches us what those measures have to be, and it takes no argument to establish that they are incompatible with reciprocity.

What that leaves, as possible outcomes, is either perpetual, inconclusive strife (in cases where neither the rebellion nor the suppression of it can be fully effective) or a self-eliminating conflict resolved in favor of the rebels. Even without appealing to notions of justice, then, or to other ordinary human virtues, the reciprocity arguments have considerable power with respect to the worst-case conflicts. And it takes very little imagination to see that a full-scale moral inquiry (including, for example, appeals to social welfare, efficiency, prudence and so forth) is going to push things in the direction of conflict resolution. Perpetual conflicts, of the sort we are considering, are not likely to be justifiable all-things-considered.

What holds for the worst-case conflicts should also hold for lesser ones, *mutatis mutandis*. Under this first condition on justifiable rebellion, only those for whom the net balance is evil may rebel. The more fortunate people will be disposed to sustain the system, and the problem will then be one of conflict resolution. And here there will be a constant pressure to find alternatives that eliminate the suffering of the less fortunate. That pressure will come, in part, from the fact that *until* a net balance of good is established for everyone, the conflict will be perpetual. (The unfortunate ones will continue to rebel, out of reciprocity, and the fortunate ones will continue to prop up the system.) Perpetual conflict is not likely to be justifiable, all things considered, so there will be pressure to resolve it. And resolutions that preserve injustice are quite likely to conflict with reciprocity, and unlikely to be justifiable all-things-considered.

The remaining conditions on justifiable rebellion are either predictable or familiar, so I will not linger over them. The second one is that the acts of rebellion be done *in order* to resist evil. Reciprocity does not justify malicious or aimless disobedience, even for the oppressed. Third, the rebellion must be of a sort that could be effective in eliminating or mitigating the evil produced by the legal system. Reciprocity aims at the source of the evil at issue, and is not well served by acts that have the effect of sustaining it, or adding to it. Fourth, the rebellion must be compatible with our other obligations. And fifth and finally, the rebellion must have a justification that is strong enough to defeat the presumption in favor of obedience. Showing that the system generates a net balance of evil for the rebel is a large part of the task. But in addition, we will have to establish that there is no effective and obedient way of resisting the evil.

Under those five conditions, rebellion against the legal system as a whole is justifiable by way of the reciprocity arguments. These arguments not only provide support for civil disobedience, then, but also (depending on social conditions) for revolution.

Fighting Fire with Fire

Here is a familiar story-line: The forces of good are locked in mortal combat with the forces of evil. The two sides are more or less equal in physical power, courage and resolve, but the forces of good are at a disadvantage. They fight fair, while the evil ones will use any methods, violate any agreements, take any advantage. In the opening stages of the conflict, evil wins. The situation for the forces of good becomes desperate. They face a cruel choice: whether to abide by their sense of honor, follow their virtuous instincts, stick to their principles – or to join battle on the terms set by their evil adversaries. And here the story-line falters. Some myths, some parables, some allegories and stories teach fidelity to virtue. (What doth it profit a man if he gain the world but lose his immortal soul?) Others teach the necessity of victory. (What virtue is this that is powerless before evil?) Tragedy and triumph are possible in either scenario, as are nobility and knavery, absurdity and high purpose. Neither scenario seems quite right, and there is no morally satisfying middle ground. Aesthetic satisfaction is one thing. It may come, as it often does in the endings of these stories, from a stroke of luck, or magic, or the intervention of the gods. But such devices do not address the moral problem here, and we lack a controlling cultural myth that can guide our intuitions on the matter.

Reciprocity is not much help. In fact, it *exhibits* the problem rather than resolves it. On the one hand, we owe good in return for good, and nothing in return for evil except resistance to it. We have obligations of reciprocity to those who benefit us, but none to those who harm us. That much suggests that we can play as rough as we like with our enemies – as long as doing so does not damage the virtues or prevent us from fulfilling our obligations. On the other hand, however, reciprocity disposes us not to return evil for evil, and it is clear that some weapons we might use *would* damage that part of the virtue and prevent us from fulfilling those obligations.

The crux of the matter for reciprocity is what counts as doing evil in return for evil. And that is precisely the original problem faced by the story-line described above: Is it wrong to resist evil with its own methods? Are those devices, in that context, 'really' evil? Reciprocity gives us *some* purchase on this general problem. It clearly entails, for example, that we may not do harm to our benefactors, no matter how effective a tactic that might be. So that part of Machiavellian politics is ruled out. We cannot be ruthless toward our friends in order to defeat our enemies. The same principle rules out weapons of mass destruction, such as nuclear arms, that cannot be used in a way that picks out enemies. That is a significant result, but it still leaves a great deal unresolved. How ruthless may we be with our enemies on *behalf* of our friends, for example?

It helps a bit to confine the discussion to the context of obedience to law. Here the question becomes whether it is ever justifiable, out of reciprocity, to disobey the law in order to resist evil. The answer is yes, under the following now familiar conditions.

First, the disobedience must be compatible with *all* of our obligations – not just with our obligation to resist evil. We profit from some people's obedience to law, and owe them obedience in return. Thus we are obliged to choose methods of resistance that allow us to fulfill our obligations to return good for good. Second, the disobedience must be *intended* as resistance to evil. (Happy accidents do not count.) Third, the disobedience must be *fitting*. That is, it must count as resistance to the particular sort of evil that prompts it. And fourth, there must be some warrant for the disobedience – some justification over and above its being permissible and fitting – that will defeat the presumption in favor of obedience. Under these conditions, then, extralegal methods of resistance to evil are justifiable.

OBJECTION: This will not stand up to scrutiny. Reciprocity will drive us into the same kind of balancing operation that bedevils every other moral theory. We have obligations to save our benefactors from harm, and to resist evil. But the two are often incompatible. Sometimes the only choice we have involves doing harm to some of our benefactors in order to resist evil.

REPLY: The only thing we can do in such conflicts is to weigh the competing obligations.

OBJECTION: Exactly. And then weapons of mass destruction will come in again through the logic of those balancing operations, as will ruthlessness, 'for a good cause' arguments, scapegoating, and (as in Robert Nozick's illustration) killing the innocent person being used as a gunman's shield. In short, reciprocity puts us right back into the series of balancing conflicts that embarrass other moral theories. Take the infamous trolleycar problem developed in recent discussions of the principle of double effect – e.g., by Philippa Foot and Judith Jarvis Thomson. Five innocent people are in the path of a runaway trolley and will be killed if the driver does nothing. The only option available to the driver, however, is to switch the car onto a siding where it will kill another person. Your reciprocity principle gives a commonsense answer to the question of what to do in such a case. Assuming the driver must resist the evil of innocent deaths, he must kill the one and save the five. His obligations to the five outweigh his obligation to the one. But the balancing principle used here leads to notorious problems. It forces us to sacrifice innocent people *whenever* doing so would prevent greater evil – greater than would follow from our doing anything else. And that makes a complete mockery of human rights. After all, to take the infamous parallel to the trolleycar case, it might be that a transplant surgeon could save five terminally ill patients by cutting up one healthy donor. Would killing an unwilling donor in that way be justified out of reciprocity?

REPLY: No. Reciprocity concerns social transactions. It disposes us to resist 'moral' evil, but is silent on the subject of 'natural' evils (i.e., accidents, diseases, natural disasters, etc.). So any purchase the reciprocity arguments may have on these deeply perplexing cases will have to come from the other side of the disposition – from the obligation to return good for good, in a way that is fitting and proportional to the good received. In the stated case (about the organ transplants) we surely cannot be obliged to return the good we owe by means of the deliberate, lethal use of the victim-donor. And it is instructive to see just how bizarre the circumstances would have to be before such an act would even approach being an act of reciprocity. In order for such a murder to be a fitting and proportionate return, the people whose lives we save by means of it would themselves have to have saved *our* lives by murdering someone! (More exactly, they would have to have done so by an illegal act equal in gravity to that of murder.) In addition, our violation of law here would have to be compatible with our other obligations of reciprocity, and would have to have some warrant – over and above its appropriateness as reciprocity – that defeats the general presumption in favor of obedience to law. So the transplant candidate *is* safe from the knife, except in an almost unimaginably bizarre set of circumstances.

OBJECTION: Yes, but now the people threatened by the trolleycar are not safe. Not, that is, unless they have done something comparable to save the *driver's* life! What an absurd result!

REPLY: The absurdity is in trying to squeeze an answer to every moral question out of the reciprocity arguments *alone*. Reciprocity is not the only virtue; not the only source of arguments about what we ought to do; not the only source of obligations. It should be no surprise if it fails to decide some cases – or even fails to apply to them entirely. In the trolleycar case, the application is very indirect. Presumably all six potential victims have benefited us by their general good will and participation in the effort to sustain and enhance the conditions of productive social exchange. We owe them all something comparable in return. That certainly means lack of malice, and probably an active part in efforts to reduce human suffering. And that points toward saving the five. But reciprocity is not decisive in this case. Nor need it be.

OBJECTION: But why, then, think it is decisive in any case?

REPLY: It may not be decisive all-things-considered. But it certainly has a more direct purchase on some situations than others – for example by the structure of priorities it imposes on some choices.

OBJECTION: You mean that if the gunman's innocent shield is a personal enemy we can shoot through him with impunity?

REPLY: No. Reciprocity does not dispose us to inflict injuries on our enemies. But it does dispose us to give priority to our friends. So in a case where other considerations (utility, for example) might recommend ruthlessness for the greater good (killing the innocent shield to save a greater number of other innocent people), reciprocity might dispose us not to do so. It would do so if, for example, the innocent shield were a relative or a friend. What is objectionable about that? These matters of priority were considered in Chapter Six.

OBJECTION: What is objectionable is the way these arguments teeter on contingencies. Kill the innocent shield – unless, of course, he is your father. Save the five on the trolley tracks – unless, of course, you owe your life to the wretch on the siding. And if you are a transplant surgeon, hold your knife – except, of course, in bizarre circumstances.

REPLY: Arguments that do not teeter on contingencies are not full-fledged moral arguments under the general conception.

Stoner's Meadow is a broad, treeless valley, spread out like a grassy bay from the south side of Stoner's Pass, and hidden by the shoulders of six worn mountains in the Blue Ridge. The meadow is neglected now. Most traffic takes the Interstate through the mountains twenty miles to the north.

The one road into the meadow – a spur of the old highway through the pass – dead ends in the town of Stoner's Furnace. The railroad, built through the pass in the eighteen eighties, runs along one edge of town, over a high trestle across Stoner's Gap and down the flank of Jesse's Mountain. But the trains go straight through.

The last of Jesse Stoner's great-great grandchildren pulled out of Stoner's Furnace in 1900. People say there were over six hundred children in that generation of the family. It was good blood.

The family still comes back for reunions. At least a hundred of them come, once every three years, on the first Saturday in August. Most of them seem to live in Indiana now, though some are as far away as California. Very few carry the Stoner name.

They stay in motels thirty or forty miles away and come up to the meadow for a picnic together. The reunion lasts four hours. There are speeches from the oldest member of each of the seven branches of the family, a memorial service for members who have died since the previous reunion; singing, picture taking, talk. Old men who are writing family histories want to look at old town records. Some of them come back for a second look the next day, but that's all.

That's the way the reunions are now, and the three hundred twenty-seven people left in Stoner's Furnace do not have much to do with them, other than putting up a big tent on the softball field, for shade, and in case of rain. The Stoners pay for that, and clean up after themselves. The townspeople are not invited.

It used to be different. Everything was different. Beginning with the first reunion, in 1889, as many as two hundred Stoners would come. They would stay with relatives, or friends, or friends of friends. The town was crowded for four days, and a reunion was a civic event. It attracted revivalists, for example, and a good-sized traveling circus. That many people in festive spirits meant good business. The Stoners paid for a free day at the circus, and everyone in town was invited to everything.

The last time there was a circus was in eighteen ninety-eight. It was also the last time there was a big reunion. People don't use names, they just say a man got killed. Here, they say. These are the pictures. Here is what happened.

What happened was an elephant got loose. People ran. They shouted for each other, shouted for their children. Circus animals panicked. Children screamed and screamed. Somebody started shooting and the elephant charged. It knocked over a sideshow tent and trampled a man who was trapped underneath. Then it got tangled in the tent, and some circus people calmed it down. Children ran home to tell their mothers.

This was in the middle of the afternoon of a very hot day,

everybody says. The wind was whipping up the red clay dust. People couldn't see.

The dead man was a Stoner. People covered him again with part of the tent so his wife wouldn't have to see his body. People say she didn't want to see it, that she didn't even ask. Most women, when they tell this story, say they wouldn't be that way. Most men say, What's the point?

What everybody says is this. A sideshow cameraman made these pictures for postcards, and one of them got in the Richmond papers. Washington, even. See this one? That's the elephant, tangled in the ropes. That's where the dead man is.

Some of the Stoner men started arguing with the circus people. There were a lot of Stoners, and some of them were pretty mean. A lot of townspeople were on their side, and some of those men were armed. Riffraff, people say, but no names are mentioned, even though there are pictures of grinning men with rifles posing for the camera.

All of the circus people and a few of the Stoner men moved off from the main crowd into the big tent. People heard a grown man screaming once. They couldn't understand his words, and it sounded like rage, but maybe not. People think it was one of the handlers – one of the ones that took care of the elephants.

The elephant was chained up behind the big tent, away from everything. Most people couldn't even see it. Here's a picture of it, maybe, but it might not be the same one. See?

The picture's a little strange, because you can't see any chains. And the shadows aren't quite right for the time of day. That sideshow man was trash. Making money on a thing like that.

Here. This is what they did to that poor thing. They cut its hamstrings so it couldn't run. They drove it clear down to the Gap and out onto the trestle. Then they fixed chains around its neck. They hung it. See? With one of those cranes the railroad uses. Here's the picture. It's the one that was in the papers.

A lot of these postcards got sold. That sideshow man made a fortune because he had it so you couldn't buy just the one. You had to buy the whole set or none.

Restitution and Criminal Law

Reciprocity disposes us to repair the harm we do, and to expect reparations from people who have harmed us. A system of criminal law, if it is potent, should reflect this requirement. Otherwise, it will tend to undermine reciprocity. What that means, evidently, is that criminal sanctions should be designed to require criminals to make restitution to their victims and that the restitution should be controlled by the criteria of fittingness and proportionality. Implicit in those requirements are some consequences about the list of things that ought to be criminalized, and the way in which intention and motive ought to figure into the task of setting sanctions. Following the maxims of reciprocity in these respects would mean making significant changes in existing criminal law systems.

In the scholium to this chapter I cite some studies of recent efforts to bring restitution into the criminal law. Many states now have statutes that either permit or require restitution. Sometimes it is an alternative to standard penal sanctions, elected or not by the offender. Sometimes it is imposed as a condition on probation or parole, or taken from the prisoner's earnings while in prison, or assessed against the prisoner's estate. And of course the return of stolen property, if it is available, is a standard part of criminal law. In addition, there are two related devices. One is the so-called 'civil compromise' – a judicially administered settlement between victim and offender that can replace standard criminal procedures in some cases. The other is the state-funded victim compensation scheme, now in place in many states for victims of violent crime. The former is clearly part of an effort to bring restitution into the criminal law. The latter is not, unless it also requires offenders to contribute to the fund. In short, there has been a remarkable amount of recent legislative and judicial activity aimed at developing restitutive sanctions.

Nonetheless, it is clear that the reciprocity arguments would recommend significant changes in existing systems. Recent moves in the direction of restitution have not been controlled by reciprocity arguments in any explicit way. Rather, they appear to be controlled by the idea that some effort toward restitution is important both for rehabilitative purposes and for reducing the sense of alienation and dissatisfaction felt by victims. The thought seems to be that restitution is an important symbolic device, even if in most cases it demands very little from the offenders and yields very little for the victims. (The symbolic element is underlined in California where a 'victims' bill of rights' permits victims or next of kin to testify at sentencing and parole hearings.) In any case, restitution as it now exists in various jurisdictions is clearly an ancillary thing, not explicitly derived from either reciprocity theory or virtue theory generally.

For that reason, and also because there is such diversity in existing statutes on restitution, I shall take a clean slate approach. I shall simply ask what changes reciprocity would recommend in a public law system of criminal law that had *no* restitutive element. The consequences for systems that have some such element can then be worked out case by case. Preliminary consideration suggests that those consequences are likely to be considerable in every case.

The changes recommended by reciprocity do not reach every aspect of criminal law, however. In fact, they do not even approach some of the central questions of criminal law theory – e.g., definitions of criminal harm and criminal responsibility. Since it is important to understand both what the reciprocity arguments do and what they do not do, I shall go over some of the fundamental topics in criminal law theory briefly, noting where reciprocity gives guidance and where it does not.

Social Harm and Public Law

In modern, developed legal systems, criminal law is part of public law – in the sense that in most cases the state controls the initiative for, and the process of, prosecution, and the state exacts the sanctions for its own purposes. In torts, by contrast, the individuals who have been threatened or wronged control the prosecution and the sanctions are ordinarily meant to benefit them, rather than the public at large. Even punitive damages, assessed for non-restitutive purposes, go to the individuals who have been harmed.

The standard rationale for the public character of criminal law is that crimes produce social harm, and that the public at large, through the state, thus has a justification for taking over the prosecution and making sure the sanctions are addressed to the social harm involved. No one denies the harm done to the direct victims of crime, and no one denies that torts, breaches of contract, and other 'private' wrongs have social consequences, but standard criminal law theory asserts that, at least for central cases like murder, the wrongs are sufficiently 'social' to justify a public law response.

There are deeply vexing problems with this line of thought. It is, for example, difficult to give an account of the type or quantity of social harm that would justify a public law response to embezzlement but not to deliberate breach of contract. The two acts can be equally malicious, equally damaging to the immediate victims, and equally disruptive of public order. Or at least so it appears. One of the tasks of criminal law theory is to give an account of social harms that answers the question of why they warrant a public law response.

The reciprocity arguments do not address that question. They merely hold that *if* there are such harms, then whatever else the criminal law does about them, it ought also to guarantee restitution to those who have been harmed – restitution from the wrongdoer. Otherwise, the structure of criminal justice will tend to undermine two aspects of reciprocity: the disposition about restitution and the disposition about proxies. What that means, in general terms, is that the offender must make restitution both for the social costs of the crime (the harm to the public at large) and for the harm done to immediate victims. And it means that victim compensation schemes that rely only on public funds are not an adequate substitute. They may be a needed supplement, for reasons other than reciprocity, but if they *replace* restitution they are contrary to the maxims of reciprocity.

That is a wholly conditional judgment, however, based on the assumption that criminal wrongs will get a public law response. The prior question about *whether* criminal law should be public, or instead be a part of private law like torts, is a separate issue.

OBJECTION: In our system, most crimes are also torts. Victims can in principle sue for compensation. So the system of law *as a whole* is restitutive, even if its criminal law portion is not. The fact that most criminals are judgment-proof is tough luck, but no different in principle from the problem we have in getting compensation for other, equally damaging but non-criminal, wrongs. (You can be just as badly injured by a negligent driver as by a gunman. Uninsured, impoverished drivers are also judgment-proof.)

REPLY: The current system is not well designed to encourage restitution – either for social or private harm. Offenders do not 'pay their debts' *to society* by being incarcerated at public expense. And most victims do not seek restitution through the tort system. There are procedural obstacles; the effort is widely regarded as futile; some victims fear reprisals for taking the prosecutorial initiative; and most importantly, the non-restitutive criminal sanctions we employ typically guarantee that criminals will not be *able* to make restitution. In the abstract, just in terms of reciprocity, there is nothing wrong with a mixed system (public prosecution for public harms; private prosecution for private harms). But in practice, those systems do not conform to the maxims of reciprocity. More below.

Other Basic Premises of Criminal Law

Our criminal law (in theory) does not punish mere intent, nor 'mere' bad character. There must be an overt act, or a culpable omission. Moreover, the act must be more than mere preparation to commit a crime; it must be at least an attempt. There are exceptions to this so-called *actus reus* rule. Some jurisdictions have status offenses (e.g., vagrancy) and possession offenses (e.g., for narcotics) that do not fit the rule. And there are notorious conceptual problems as well: What counts as an act? Under what conditions is an omission culpable? How is the line to be drawn between preparation and attempt? The reciprocity arguments are not addressed to such issues and (as far as I can tell) do not give any implicit guidance to the effort to establish the legitimacy or illegitimacy of the *actus reus* rule.

Reciprocity is a bit more helpful with regard to *mens rea*. In theory, our criminal law defines as criminal only those acts, of 'responsible' moral agents, that are in some sense intentional. People may be held accountable for unintended consequences, for negligence, and for mistakes, but not, generally, for things done in ignorance of the 'nature and quality of their acts'. Reciprocity concerns social transactions – ones in which the parties are aware, in general terms, of the nature and quality of their acts. So the reciprocity arguments at least implicitly support the outlines of the *mens rea* rule. They do not, however, make any special contribution to solving the very difficult conceptual questions here about the nature of responsible agency.

Nor do the reciprocity arguments contribute to the justification of the 'legality' requirement – i.e., the prohibition of *ex post facto* criminal legislation, judicial or otherwise. That rule is certainly compatible with the maxims of reciprocity, but it gets its justification from other considerations.

The basic premises about harm and causation are more directly connected to the maxims of reciprocity, however, at least in the following sense: The obligations of reciprocity imply something like a 'no harm, no foul' rule. If no actual harm has been done, then there is nothing to make restitution for. So it seems plausible to insist that the substantive criminal law define as crimes only those things that cause identifiable harm. Similarly, it is plausible to insist that there be a relatively direct causal relation between the offender's conduct and the harm that occurs. Reciprocity requires restitution from specific individuals only for the harms they have done. Vicarious liability (insofar as it forces some sort of restitution) is therefore incompatible with the maxims of reciprocity, as is enterprise liability. That is a significant result, but it should not be overstated. Criminal sanctions can be justified for purposes other than restitution. (See below.) If it is clear that vicarious or enterprise liability does serve such purposes, and if it can be separated from the practice of restitution, then it will not conflict with reciprocity.

Criminal Sanctions

It appears, then, that reciprocity arguments are of slight theoretical importance for large areas of criminal law theory. The possibility of applying them profitably to the procedural side of criminal law also seems remote. But in one important area, reciprocity has a direct and dramatic bearing. That is the area of criminal sanctions. Reciprocity prohibits retaliation, directs that sanctions satisfy the restitution requirement, and provides criteria for grading offenses in that respect. My object here is to consider the case for restitutive sanctions, but it may be useful just to mention some other matters first. Criminal sanctions have had a variety of purposes, historically. Some of them are compatible with reciprocity; others are not.

NO RETALIATION Part of having the virtue of reciprocity is to be disposed to resist evil but not to retaliate for it. We are obligated not to return evil for evil. Retribution, then, in the 'pure' sense in which the only aim is to punish wrong-doers in proportion to their offenses, is contrary to the maxims of reciprocity.

PUBLIC SAFETY In principle, it is fully consistent with reciprocity to have some criminal sanctions (e.g., incarceration) that are specifically designed to prevent harm. In fact, it would be contrary to the resistance to evil maxim if we did not respond to 'clear and present dangers' by trying to prevent the threatened evil. Recall, however, that that maxim does not require us to go looking for evils to prevent. Prudence or benevolence might require some of this, but reciprocity does not. Reciprocity only requires resistance to the evil we actually confront.

REHABILITATION Here the reciprocity arguments – and the virtue-theoretic arguments generally – have a direct and unequivocal general recommendation. Criminal sanctions ought not to damage people's virtues; they ought, rather, to engender and enhance them. This applies to the effect they have on people who observe or administer the sanctions as well as on the ones who suffer them. Of course any individualistic moral theory, such as one generated from the general conception of morality, will place severe restrictions on the extent to which a structure can permissibly be designed to violate the boundaries and change the values of the people who are forced into it. Such restrictions will come, for example, from principles of justice, equality, and respect for person. And the more coercive and 'total' an institution is, the more suspect will be its program of moral education. So methods of 'active' rehabilitation will be limited, and it is arguable that criminal sanctions should not, in justice, be designed to inculcate virtue actively at all. But it certainly does not follow from even that strong position that sanctions may permissibly *damage* the virtues. Yet we have a fairly solid body of empirical evidence that our prisons do just that for significant numbers of inmates and employees. Insofar as they do, they are unjustifiable.

OBJECTION: An observation like that is empty and even insulting in the absence of some concrete suggestions for change. We all *know* it's unjustifiable, not to mention stupid, to have prisons that embitter prisoners and teach them how to be better criminals. The problem is to find a way to change prisons that will change that.

REPLY: I am not convinced that we lack the knowledge to design better prisons. What we lack is a conception of criminal sanctions that permits us to make the changes we know will have at least some good effects. As long as retribution is one of our goals, for instance, we are bound to be hostile to any form of rehabilitation that is 'pleasant' for the criminal. That will seem like rewarding the undeserving. In fact, an advocate of retribution will have to be hesitant about any genuinely effective rehabilitation programs. They are, after all, a genuine good for the wrongdoer. If they are also given at public expense – including the expense of the victim – they will seem even more perverse. So it is not surprising that we have been unable to make effective use of what we know about changing people's behavior. We doubtless need to know more, and to have good technical recommendations. But before we can put them in place, we will need to change our conception of the purpose of criminal sanctions. The reciprocity arguments contribute to that by giving grounds for ruling out retribution and supporting rehabilitation.

GENERAL DETERRENCE This aim for criminal sanctions, like that of public safety, is weakly constrained by the maxims of reciprocity, but within these constraints, is consistent with the virtue. Reciprocity disposes us to return good for good, and punishing the innocent, for example, is not likely to be consistent with that maxim (not to mention the maxims of justice). And in general, the sort of 'example' we make of criminals will have to be consistent with the restitution requirement, to which I now turn.

Restitution

The idea of restitution is fundamental to the private law portions of legal systems. In torts, contracts, administrative law, and even domestic relations law, when one party has been wrongfully injured by another, legal sanctions are typically aimed, in part, at repairing the damage. There are other goals as well (social policies, punitive aims, prevention), but 'making the victim whole' is one of the general justifying aims of legal intervention. Never mind that some victims cannot be compensated (e.g., those who are killed outright in an accident). Never mind that many defendants are judgment-proof, that fixing the proper type and amount of restitution is a difficult and messy business, and that the court becomes, in effect, a collection agency at public expense for the successful plaintiff. We recognize that there are inequalities built into the system. Defendants can, in effect, buy their way out of trouble. The system favors those who have the knowledge, initiative, resolution, and resources to hire lawyers to fight for them. All of that is cause for concern, and for proposals for reform, and for attempts to ameliorate ill-effects. But none of it shakes our conviction that the law *should* aim at restitution in these cases – our conviction that, wherever possible, victims *should* be made whole. In that respect, the civil side of our law, and systems of private law generally, are consistent with the maxims of reciprocity. Whether this part of the law actually works to sustain and enhance the virtue depends on how effective it is in securing restitution, and in persuading people that its efforts to do so are justifiable. But at least legal theory here is in accord with what reciprocity requires.

Not so for most developed systems of criminal law. They are addressed primarily to settling the issues between criminals and the public at large – not the issues between criminals and their immediate victims. Even where they do address the issue of restitution they do so only as an ancillary measure, and not for the reasons reciprocity gives. Reciprocity has been pushed into the background; its maxims are not explicitly included in the criminal law.

Of course not including the maxims is not equivalent to being inconsistent with them. (The rules of chess do not include them either.) Different enterprises have different rules, and as noted earlier, we might be able to salvage restitution here through an effective system of private law sanctions, leaving criminal law unchanged. The fact that tort law is currently ineffective in this respect may indicate we need to change *something*, but it does not necessarily point to making changes in the criminal law.

What does point to criminal law is the fact, previously mentioned, that its primary sanctions work directly *against* the restitutive aims of tort law. (A good analogy here is debtor's prison, which effectively denied most prisoners the means to pay their debts.) So if restitution is going to be as effective for crimes as it is for other wrongs, the criminal law will have to be changed in any case. Whether the restitution is administered through the tort system or not, criminal sanctions will have to be structured so as to make it possible for otherwise able convicts to make restitution, and to make it possible to enforce restitutive sanctions legally. What that means, I think, is that it would be best all-things-considered for the criminal law itself to include the restitutive sanctions. The reasons are as follows.

If restitutive sanctions are imposed, by any agency of the law, we will want the standard sorts of criminal sanctions to be sensitive to the difference that makes. If restitution by itself, for example, would be sufficient to produce the desired level of general deterrence, public safety, or rehabilitation, then adding further sanctions to it (for those purposes) would presumably be unjustifiable. And in general, if restitution in a given case were to reduce the need for the usual criminal sanctions, they would presumably have to be adjusted to reflect that fact – just as they are now adjusted to reflect individual differences in the dangerousness of convicts. Yet if the amount and type of restitution is to be set in a separate civil proceeding, in no way under the control of the criminal court, it would be very difficult to make the necessary adjustments – to coordinate restitution with the sanctions imposed by the criminal law. That and a number of other factors yield the conclusion that if we are to have effective restitution for crimes, the restitutive sanctions should be built into the *criminal* law. (The other factors include avoiding duplicative legal proceedings, dealing with the reluctance victims often have to initiate private actions against their attackers, and minimizing disparities in sentencing.)

How should a non-restitutive system of criminal law be changed to reflect the restitution requirement? A full answer to that question raises intricate issues in the theory of criminal law and in criminal justice administration that I cannot deal with adequately. (And of course it might turn out that, all things considered, reciprocity should be sacrificed in this area.) All I can do here is assemble some reasons for thinking that the needed changes are not, on the face of it, out of the question. It is worth remembering, in this connection, that persistent conflicts between fundamental virtues and potent social structures should not be taken lightly. If other considerations finally require us to leave such a conflict in place, they will have to be very powerful considerations indeed. What follows is meant to make a *prima facie* case for the proposition that we are not likely to find sufficient reason to permit this conflict to continue.

Whose costs?

Private law that is addressed to restitution restricts the class of individuals who have standing to sue. In general, the attempt is to limit standing to those who can make a *prima facie* case that they themselves have been directly and substantially wronged. The rules are complex and far from fully determinate, but they have evolved in a constant and sophisticated interplay between practice and theory. Moreover, private law deals with many of the wrongs covered by the criminal law. It seems plausible, as a first step, simply to import the relevant rules of standing into criminal law as a device for deciding whose (private) costs ought to be considered for restitution, and to permit private litigation in torts to handle the problem of refining the rules. New rules of standing could then be incorporated into the criminal law as they evolve from private litigation. The point is simply that while the question of who counts as a victim for purposes of restitution has its difficulties, we need not suppose that we have to start with it from scratch. We already have sophisticated and well-tested rules for dealing with its analog in private law, and it is the private law aim of restitution that we are proposing to import into criminal law. It seems only natural to import the relevant procedural devices as well, if they will fit with the other elements of criminal law.

The other 'party' whose costs must be considered is of course the public at large. The rationale for making criminal law part of public law, after all, is the contention that criminal acts produce 'social' harm. Reciprocity disposes us to make restitution obligatory for that as well. Just how that should be addressed is a problem. (See below.) But that it *should* be addressed is clear.

Calculations

The calculation of direct economic costs, both to the individual victims and to the public, goes as follows. Victims may have had medical expenses, opportunity costs, and losses of property. The public has had to bear the costs of apprehending the criminal, prosecuting the case, and administering the sanctions. There are also, for some crimes, public opportunity costs in the form of inconvenience (e.g., security checks at airports), changed patterns of life (e.g., reluctance to walk the streets alone after dark), and so forth. The calculation of such costs is a familiar matter to economists, and should pose no special problems for restitutive sanctions in the criminal law. Losses that are more difficult to economize are consequently more difficult to fit into a restitution scheme. In torts, it is now common to award damages for 'pain and suffering'. Even though such calculations are necessarily much less precise than those for direct economic losses, we are willing to make and enforce them (in a private law restitution scheme) on the basis of rough estimates derived from shared understandings about what kinds of anguish various sorts of injuries ordinarily produce. In crimes, of course, victims suffer in the same ways, and often much more severely (e.g., in cases where they are deliberately terrorized and humiliated by their attackers). And there can be analogous social harm associated with a crime – general fear or apprehension, for example. It is hard to see any reason, in principle, for excluding such harms from a restitution scheme. No one denies that they are *genuine* harms, after all, and reciprocity disposes us to make restitution obligatory for all the harm we do. If we are confident enough of our ability to put a price on these harms in tort law, it is hard to see why we should be any less confident of that ability in criminal law.

Assessments: Individual Victims

Making restitution, like making returns for good received, should be governed by considerations of fittingness and proportionality. Fittingness presents no special theoretical problems here. If the nature of the damage is clear, then the sorts of things that will repair it are clear. If it cannot be repaired, then some form of compensation acceptable to the victim is in order. But how much is enough? The proportionality rule here takes an interesting turn.

Full restitution is of course the first goal. That is analogous to the proportionality rule for returns of good for good: first try for a full return – i.e., an equal benefit return. The problem arises when it is either flatly impossible for the wrongdoer to make full restitution, or when his doing so would involve some sort of disproportionate sacrifice. I say 'some sort' of disproportion because it is hard to state the idea here precisely. The concern behind it is clear enough. We may think of the relative sacrifices in this way: Suppose there is no restitution scheme at all, and victims must recover through their own efforts. The marginal cost of those efforts is the level of sacrifice imposed on them by the criminal. On the other hand, the marginal cost of making restitution is the level of sacrifice imposed on the criminal by a restitution scheme. It is clear that these levels might be very different – and in fact, will almost certainly be very different if other sorts of criminal sanctions (e.g., incarceration) are imposed for purposes of public safety, general deterrence, or rehabilitation. The problem, then, is to say how much sacrifice from the criminal, relative to the victim's, would be a 'proportionate' one.

Here it helps to recall the purpose that reciprocity is meant to serve. It is meant to engender and enhance productive social exchanges by keeping them balanced. In cases where one person has injured another, that purpose requires restitution – a restoration of the initial 'balance'. So efforts at restitution must produce genuine goods for the victim, and be perceived by the victim as restitutive. But it is likely (and this is an empirical matter) that victims will make a distinction between mere token gestures toward restitution and genuine contributions toward it. And it is also likely (but this is also an empirical matter) that they will think that they have not received more than a token gesture if they have to make a *greater* sacrifice toward their own recovery than their attackers make toward restitution. Victims might *accept* less, just on the principle that something is better than nothing. But a sacrifice less than their own is likely to *add*, rather than subtract, from their sense of injury. It would be as if the criminal had said, 'Here, I've just hurt you. This will help. I didn't make as much effort on your behalf as you'll have to make to recover, but . . .'

So the criminal's sacrifice will likely have to be equal to or greater than the victim's if it is to make a contribution toward restoring the basis for productive social relationships. We needn't suppose that there was any good basis for them before the crime, or that the criminal act completely destroyed that basis. We need only suppose that the crime lowered whatever baseline there was. The restitution element of reciprocity is meant to restore that baseline. It can only make a contribution to that if the victim is able to perceive the effort as effectively restitutive. And in practice that seems to require (though again this is an empirical matter) that the wrongdoer make a *greater* sacrifice than the victim. It is as if we wanted the criminal to say, 'Here, I've harmed you. I can't fully repair the damage, but since I'm responsible for it, it is only fair that I work harder at your recovery than I've forced you to do.'

Now the question is, how *much* harder? That is a baffling question. We cannot let the parties settle it between themselves. If they could do that, without either party being coerced or duped, that would be ideal for the purposes of reciprocity, but by hypothesis, that solution is not open to us. Aside from its utopian character, we are assuming here that the law of crimes will remain a part of public law, and that the state will therefore have to control sentencing. So we will have to formulate some criterion for what counts as a proportional sacrifice – a more determinative criterion than is given in the preceding paragraphs. We will want the criterion to move the level of restitutive sacrifice up and down in direct relation to the seriousness of the damage done to the victim. But we will also want to make sure that restitutive sanctions are relatively determinate, non-arbitrary and uniform. That is a large order.

In that respect, however, restitutive sanctions are in no worse (and no better) a position than criminal sanctions generally. With respect to criminal sanctions generally we have not solved the problem of how determinate and uniform the sentences should be, nor the problem of who should impose them (jury or judge), nor how thoroughly the sentencing procedure should be isolated for the 'guilt' phase of the trial, nor what factors should initiate the sentences dictated by criteria written into the law. What we have in all these cases are more or less sensible, underdeterminative criteria, a procedure for applying them, and a further procedure for dealing with inequitable results. Here is a proposal for determining a proportionate level of restitutive sacrifice:

PROPOSED RULE: Set wrongdoers' sacrifices equal to what their victims would have to make to recover from their injuries by themselves (i.e., without the assistance of a legally enforced restitution scheme).

This has several things to recommend it. First, it is relatively determinate. The damage done by the crime can first be represented in money terms, and then relative sacrifices can be assessed in terms of relative earning power. If the criminal has done damage that it would take the victim two hours of labor to repair, then an equal amount of labor from the criminal (directed toward restitution) seems fair.

Second, this notion of equal sacrifice makes the proportionality principle for restitution symmetrical with the one for returns of good for good. (That is no doubt partly why it seems fair, at least as a second-best solution.) Recall the discussion of proportionate returns. There are two senses in which people can be said to have made a full return of good for good: 1) if they return the benefit fully, and 2) if they return the sacrifice fully. For returns, I argued, reciprocity should dispose us to try for equal benefits first, but if that imposes a greater relative sacrifice on the returner, to settle for an equal sacrifice. Similarly, we might think that there are two senses in which we can make restitution 'fully': 1) by repairing the damage fully, and 2) by making an effort toward that end that is fully the equal of what the victim would have to expend in order to recover. Reciprocity should dispose us to try for full reparation first, for reasons already mentioned. But in cases where we cannot get it, we will have to settle. Equal sacrifice seems a good settlement. It is analogous to the equal sacrifice rule for returns; it conforms to a well established and hence intuitively plausible idea of what a second-best solution might be like; and it is designed to reflect both part of the victim's demand ('Nothing less than what I would have to do to recover by myself') and what the criminal is most likely to think fair ('Nothing more than what it would cost the victim').

Finally, it should be noted that this proposal would mean that victims would ultimately make *less* sacrifice, in principle, toward their own recovery than the criminals make toward restitution. This is so because the criminal, in making an effort toward restitution that equals what the victim would have had to make, will reduce the effort the victim actually has to make. That is also responsive to the general notion that the transaction is certainly not balanced if I first do you harm and then do not work any harder than you do to set it right.

OBJECTION: There is a much more plausible second-best rule — one that is much less labored and much more in line with what the victim would want. (And that, after all, should be the primary consideration.) The better rule is simply this: If you can't make full restitution, then make as much as you can.

REPLY: That is either preposterously extensive or impossibly vague. If it means that restitution must be the one task that criminals devote themselves to for the rest of their lives, then it is preposterous. There is zero likelihood that that kind of general rule about restitution could be justified all-things-considered. We might admire, in the way that we admire a saint, a person who lives out a life of restitution for a monumental wrong. And we might well demand such a sacrifice for heinous crimes. But not on the *general* rule, surely, that every other task must be held in abeyance until 'as much restitution as possible' has been made. People have too many other obligations, and there are too many other competing goods and virtues, to make such a proposal even faintly plausible. Yet once we admit that 'as much as possible' means less than total commitment, we are faced with the question that leads to the equal sacrifice rule: How much is enough?

OBJECTION: But the equal sacrifice rule is full of complications. It introduces bizarre inequities. Criminals who are efficient or talented will in effect be penalized more than those who have no skills, because skillful efforts will produce something closer to full restitution than unskillful ones. Victims will likewise be penalized for having the misfortune to have been attacked by inept or stupid criminals. And victims who are themselves smart or efficient or talented or rich are going to get very little by way of effective restitution – at least from criminals who have no skills. Equal sacrifice from those criminals will produce next to nothing. In general, it will pay criminals to attack the rich and talented.

REPLY: Criminal sanctions as a whole ought to be designed so that crimes are never a paying proposition, no matter who the victim is. But it is true that under the equal sacrifice rule, and just in terms of the restitutive sanctions, it will pay criminals to attack the people whose marginal costs are the lowest. And if a choice has to be made, that is exactly the one we want. (Stealing the life savings of a poor and feeble victim is surely more despicable, and more damaging, than stealing the same amount from a vigorous and wealthy victim.)

OBJECTION: Where has the commitment to equal protection gone?

REPLY: There is no equal protection problem here in any formal sense. No one is *formally* singled out by the law for special protection. And if in practice it works out that the poor benefit from this rule, that surely will not offset the extent to which the rich in fact get (or can buy) better protection from the law than the poor. De facto inequalities like these are pervasive and uneliminable.

OBJECTION: That reply is too cavalier. We may not be able to eliminate *all* de facto inequalities but that is no reason to create new ones. Tying restitution to victims' marginal sacrifices does just that. In fact, restitution schemes of any sort do it. For example, under any restitution scheme the dispossessed will be more vulnerable to *lethal* attack, at least if there is no one around who would have standing to collect survivors' restitution. And in general, it will pay a criminal to kill rather than merely injure a victim in such cases.

REPLY: Not if the other criminal sanctions are properly designed. Again, restitution is just one of those sanctions. It is hardly surprising that the benefits of a restitutive scheme do not extend to people who are killed by a wrongdoer. That is true on the civil side as well. We do not recommend abandoning tort law because some victims are killed and have no one who can collect damages.

OBJECTION: That isn't the whole point. Another part of it is that the homeless, friendless, down-and-out of the earth will be especially vulnerable under this scheme. Their opportunity costs are low, and there is no one to make restitution to if they are killed.

REPLY: The dispossessed are no *more* vulnerable under a restitution scheme than they already are. Restitutive sanctions are to be *added* to standard ones, after all. It is true that some people will not benefit as much as others from the addition, but that is so for nearly any aspect of the law one can mention. In general, under this proposal, people will retain whatever level of protection is afforded by the standard sanctions.

OBJECTION: The problem of ineptness remains. People will just get relatively less restitution from unskilled or inept criminals. And it is no good to say that that is always true – that we always get less restitution from people who are effectively judgment-proof. This equal sacrifice rule magnifies the problem. If we just set some fixed amount of restitution, for example, in terms of a proportion of the victim's loss, then it would be the criminals who paid the price of their lack of skill. As it stands under the equal sacrifice rule, the victims pay.

REPLY: It is true of any reciprocal exchange between unequals that one of them will 'pay' – either in a shortage of goods received or in an overage of sacrifice made. There are good reasons, as I have noted, for opting for the shortage of goods received, by equating the sacrifices made.

OBJECTION: Here is another problem – from the other side, so to speak. In the context of the criminal law, the equal sacrifice rule looks suspiciously like *retribution* – in which the object is to make the criminal suffer as much as the victim did. Retribution is supposed to be ruled out by reciprocity.

REPLY: It is. But equal sacrifice isn't. The difference is in the aim, and that makes the whole process of restitution vastly different from retribution. In retribution the first and only aim is to equate the sacrifices. In restitution, the first aim is to make the victim whole. If the criminal can do that at little or no cost, sacrifice does not come into it. And even when sacrifice does come in, it is only a regulative principle, not the aim. The aim is still restitution.

OBJECTION: So then criminals can in effect buy their way out of trouble.

REPLY: Only out of restitution trouble. (And that would be true no matter what principle were used for fixing the amount.) But there are other sorts of criminal sanctions that are consistent with reciprocity: ones aimed at public safety, general deterrence, and rehabilitation. Making restitution need not buy off these sanctions.

OBJECTION: What about abuses? Victims may lie about the extent of their losses, especially about property losses. Courts may set outrageously high or low amounts of restitution. And if insurance companies are allowed standing as victims (once they have paid claims to insured victims) we can imagine the growth of a rather unsavory industry.

REPLY: Most of these are problems that are familiar to the law in other contexts, and for which it has procedural remedies. Both victims and offenders, for example, can be given the right to contest the amount of restitution set by the court. And we might, for social policy reasons, want to bar recovery by insurance companies unless they have been defrauded. (Think of arson cases.) But the matter of corporate victims does raise some special theoretical problems.

Assessments: Private Corporate Victims

The central problem here is how to apply the equal sacrifice rule. The calculation of losses to a business – from a theft, for example – is no more difficult than it is in the case of an individual victim. So what counts as full restitution is clear. But how are we going to match up the sacrifices to determine equal sacrifice?

In principle, the solution that is analogous to the one for individual victims appears to be this: Ask how much marginal effort it would require of employers and employees in the corporate victim to recover from the loss. That total (e.g., in hours of labor) is the marginal corporate sacrifice. Restitution then requires equal sacrifice from the offender. This solution is of course subject to many of the same objections leveled at the equal sacrifice rule above, but analogous replies can be constructed.

Assessments: Social Costs

Another important question about assessments, however, is what to do about the social costs of the crime. Here the proper analogy is to the notion of a fair share contribution to a joint enterprise. (See Chapter Three.) The joint enterprise in this case is the whole criminal justice system. Insofar as we obey the criminal law, pay taxes to support its operation, contribute services (e.g., jury duty) and so forth, we help to create and sustain the system. This is true of criminals as well as non-criminals. *Insofar* as they obey and so forth they contribute to the system. (And the evidence suggests that in stable, developed societies like our own there are very few thoroughgoing outlaws. 'Professional' criminals, in fact, rely on the general effectiveness of the criminal justice system, both for refuge and for providing the opportunity for crime. They contribute to the maintenance of the system by being law abiding in large areas of their lives. 'Occasional' or aberrational criminals contribute even more.) Now the type and size of system we construct – and therefore the type and size of a citizen's fair share contribution to it – will vary with the level of citizens' demands for benefits from the criminal law, and their expectations about what is needed to secure these benefits. The benefits at issue here are roughly in the areas of public order, public safety, and the protection of individual rights to life, liberty, safety, privacy, and property. But how extensive a system people want for those purposes, and what it will cost, varies widely. So far, this is exactly analogous to the cases of jointly produced public goods discussed in Chapter Three (e.g., blood banks).

Let us suppose that we have a justifiably extensive and cost effective criminal justice system, and that people generally contribute their fair shares toward sustaining it. And let us suppose that we would have that sort of criminal justice system (albeit a less extensive version of it) even if there were no significant crimes ever committed. We would have the system, in that case, for its general deterrent effect and for its help in coordinating people's efforts to protect public order, public safety, and individual rights. Now suppose someone breaks the law and the criminal law agencies take action to apprehend and sanction the criminal. The criminal has imposed a marginal cost on the system. Further, the criminal may have imposed marginal costs on other social institutions and practices. Those are the social harms, and social costs, for which the criminal ought, out of reciprocity, to make restitution.

But how much of this marginal cost should we obligate the criminal to pay? Full restitution would be the first choice, for familiar reasons, but that may be flatly impossible. Or it may be that full restitution would be as disproportionate here as in the case of the victim's costs. Here again it helps to remember the general justifying aim of reciprocity. Its aim is to engender and enhance productive social life. Restitution for harm done can only contribute to that if it is perceived by the recipients – the victims – as a fitting and proportionate attempt to make amends. The victims in this case are all the people who (in the absence of a restitution scheme) would have to bear the marginal increase in social costs caused by the crime. They would, presumably, have to bear only their *fair shares* of those costs. But for the reasons discussed above for victims' costs, they would want criminals to pay at least that much (i.e., at least what their fair shares would be), and more if possible. Both demands would in fact be satisfied if criminals contributed what would be their fair shares if there were no restitution scheme, leaving the remainder to be divided into now somewhat smaller fair shares for the public at large. (The criminal would then, presumably, pay one of those smaller fair shares as well. The increased tax burden, inconvenience, and so forth, would fall on the public at large, including the criminal.) All of that suggests the following rule:

Proposed assessment for social costs
Criminals ought to pay, in restitution, a fair share of the marginal social costs imposed by their crimes.

OBJECTION: But why only a 'fair' share of the marginal cost? What is 'fair' about anything less than the *full* marginal cost? The criminal is the one who has caused the harm. The rest of us shouldn't have to pay *anything*.

REPLY: The same can be said (and was said) about individual victims. It isn't fair for them to have to pay for their own recovery either. That is why we try for full restitution first. But we often have to settle for less. When we do, the equal sacrifice rule seems the best choice for compensating individuals, and for parallel reasons a fair share rule seems the second-best choice for social costs.

Collections

The remaining question is whether it is plausible to think that we could collect restitution from criminals – in significant amounts, and in a significant number of cases. It would be pointless (poignant?) to have shown a system of restitution to be plausible in other aspects but utterly hopeless when it comes to collections.

There is no doubt that adding restitution to the aims of the criminal law would create significant transitional problems for the criminal justice system. There would also be continuing administrative problems. But if restitution is scaled to sacrifice in the way I have outlined, it could in principle be collected in full from every criminal willing and able to work. Moreover, we would have a powerful incentive, under a restitution scheme, for structuring the prison, parole, and probation systems to maximize productive work opportunities for every willing convict, and to provide effective incentives for prisoners to elect to work.

(I distinguish incentives from threats. I assume that forced labor under threat of death or corporal punishment or starvation is no part of any morally justifiable restitution scheme. Work undertaken by prisoners in order to get special benefits is a different matter. The idea is to set the baseline at a morally justifiable level, for the purposes of other criminal sanctions, and then, without threatening to lower that baseline, to give convicts effective incentives to work. We know that while in prison, many convicts now elect to work to relieve boredom, earn money, acquire skills, increase their chances for early release, and enhance their social lives. A restitution scheme would presumably make good use of such incentives.)

There is a problem, of course, about timing. Victims need restitution immediately. Further, it may be that linking the criminals' payments too directly to victims could expose the victims to further harm. Both problems would be addressed by creating a fund, administered by the court, from which victims could recover the court-decided amount of restitution immediately, and into which criminals would pay at a rate that preserved their incentive to work. The state itself, of course, would be receiving some of the money for the social costs of the crimes, so some of the administrative machinery for a victims' fund would already be in place. While this sort of pay-out system would be out of place in private law, it seems perfectly in order in public law, where the state's other objectives (i.e., public safety, general deterrence, and rehabilitation) will often impose sanctions that delay restitution.

Summary

In short, the reciprocity arguments recommend the following with respect to criminal sanctions: 1) Eliminate retributive sanctions. 2)

Add a system of restitutive sanctions, both for social costs and victim costs, to those addressed to public safety, general deterrence, and rehabilitation. 3) Calculate the amount of restitution by reference to the fittingness and proportionality principles – where a proportionate return is either one that makes the victim whole or involves an equal sacrifice from the criminal. Methods of enforcement are beyond the scope of the reciprocity arguments, but in general it seems plausible to suppose that we can find reasonably effective and morally justifiable ones.

PART 3

SCHOLIUM

Introduction to Part 3

This part of the book is essentially an annotated bibliography to the arguments of parts one and two. It is arranged as a set of chapter-by-chapter notes. The notes are discursive, and in a few places argumentative. They also contain acknowledgments of the special help I received with specific arguments.

My reading on these topics has, I hope, been adequate to the task, though comprehensiveness was out of the question. The works I have cited are those that have made a direct contribution to my reflections. A few of them provided me with material I could simply shape to my purposes. Some suggested whole lines of argument; many provoked me into articulating counterarguments that I otherwise would not have developed. All of them encouraged me, over the years I worked on this project, to think that a book like this ought to be written.

Notes on Form

Philosophy has been written in many forms. Dialogues, treatises, literary essays, meditations, journals, handbooks, chains of aphorisms, novels, plays, and 'formal' proofs have all been tried, and there are successful examples of each. Plato, Hume, Camus, Descartes, Kierkegaard, Epictetus, Wittgenstein, Sartre and Spinoza give some idea of the range of possibilities. Each form has it shortcomings, brought out starkly by second rate attempts: dialogues that dilute the arguments; treatises that are boring and obscure; essays that lack precision; formal proofs that are procrustean projects. And so on.

The problem of form is a difficult one. On the one hand, we think the truth value of what we say is ultimately the only relevant test of our success as philosophers. If we can also write clearly, memorably, gracefully, or in a way that gives readers pleasure, so much the better, but that is secondary, and the desire to do it is too often connected with the desire for celebrity. On the other hand, we often think that if our work is unread or misunderstood because we fail to present it well, then we have also failed as philosophers. Philosophy is not merely a type of self-improvement. Communication counts, and therefore so does the choice and execution of the literary form.

Further, we often suspect that the kind of communication we want with readers cannot be achieved by a full frontal presentation. What we want readers to get, after all, is not merely a set of true beliefs. We want them to *understand* those beliefs – to learn their sources and warrants, to appreciate their subtleties, and to see their consequences. This can happen only if we write so that readers do philosophy as they read. The choice of literary form is therefore right at the center of the philosophical enterprise.

On the connection between moral theory and narrative forms, parables, and 'visions' of the good life, see the articles by R. W.

Hepburn and Iris Murdoch, 'Vision and Choice in Morality,' in Ian T. Ramsey (ed.) *Christian Ethics and Contemporary Philosophy* (New York, Macmillan, 1966), pp. 181–218 (reprinted from the supplementary volume for 1956 of *The Proceedings of the Aristotelian Society*).

A few of the essays in Berel Lang (ed.) *Philosophical Style* (Chicago, Nelson-Hall, 1980) are useful for exploring the issues about form raised here. See particularly the selections by R. G. Collingwood (pp. 94–112), Brand Blanshard (pp. 123–43), and Robert S. Brumbaugh (pp. 294–310).

F. C. T. Moore, *The Psychological Basis of Morality* (London, Macmillan, 1978) departs from 'accepted linearities' in philosophical argument by alternating sections of argument with what he calls 'annexes' – introductions to or comments upon the argument. He and I share a source of discontent (and he notes that many philosophers have had the same concern; see his p. 1), but our responses to it are very different.

I am also indebted to Martha Nussbaum, who allowed me to see her striking paper 'Flawed Crystals: James's *The Golden Bowl* and Literature as Moral Philosophy' while it was still in preparation. That paper has now been published in *New Literary History* 15 (Autumn, 1983):25–50. That whole issue of the journal is devoted to 'Literature and/as Moral Philosophy,' and contains rewarding discussions of Nussbaum's paper, and the general topic, by D. D. Raphael, Cora Diamond, Richard Wollheim, Hilary Putnam, and others.

Acknowledgments

What first prompted me to consider the use of narrative pieces in this book was a reading, in 1981, given at Hollins College by Robert Coover. It was a pleasure to renew an old acquaintance with him, and our conversation about philosophy and literary form was very valuable to me. Alice McDermott, when she was our writer in residence, was a tough but encouraging critic of a few of the early epigraphs, and the Faculty Writing Workshop at Hollins helped me with several others, as well as with the introductory material. Jeanne Larsen, in particular, made detailed and useful suggestions. Throughout, Charlotte Becker has been the most astute, and most encouraging, of my epigraph readers.

Readers of the entire manuscript have been about evenly divided on the question of whether the epigraphs are appropriate in this work. A more timid publisher might very well have insisted on a more conventional form. I am grateful to Routledge & Kegan Paul, their philosophy editor Stratford Caldecott, and their anonymous reader(s) for supporting my eccentric experiment.

General Conception of Morality

Practical Reasoning

The account of practical reasoning developed here is in the general category of the 'good reasons' approach. See, for example, Stephen Toulmin, *The Place of Reason in Ethics* (Cambridge, Cambridge University Press, 1948) and Kurt Baier, *The Moral Point of View* (Ithaca, Cornell University Press, 1958). In general, what it owes to these writers is the development of the idea that moral reasoning, like practical reasoning generally, has serviceable criteria of logical validity and soundness – which are to be understood in terms of the purposes of the activity one is reasoning about. My view differs, not only by standing upon the results these writers have achieved, but by framing the issues in terms of the notion of a well-defined activity. I thus recast considerably, for example, what Baier has to say about consideration-making beliefs. My account is meant to bring out more explicitly the connection of practical reasoning to the structure of the activity it guides.

This section also owes a great deal to the work of R. M. Hare and H. L. A. Hart. See Hare's *The Language of Morals* (Oxford, Clarendon Press, 1951) and *Practical Inferences* (London, Macmillan, 1971), and Hart's *The Concept of Law* (Oxford, Clarendon Press, 1961). Hare's work on the logic of imperatives, and Hart's analysis of 'secondary rules' (from which the notion of a rule of recognition is directly lifted, both in substance and in name) are what I have in mind. Joseph Raz (ed.), *Practical Reasoning* (Oxford, Oxford University Press, 1978) provides a useful anthology of recent work on practical reasoning, and a bibliography as well.

It should be noted that my insistence that the criteria of validity for practical inferences are 'standard' ones is not meant to imply that just any plausible translation of an argument into logical notation, or just any level of formal analysis one wants to choose (propositional, deontic, syllogistic, quantificational) will suffice. There are many subtleties here that require careful translation and careful choice of the appropriate formal analysis. I do not deny that the logic of imperatives differs in significant ways from the logic of obligations, for example. Nor do I mean to suggest that action-guiding statements can be manipulated (formally) in all of the ways ordinary indicative mood propositions can be. (The notorious inference pattern $p/\therefore p\vee q$, as applied to imperatives, for example, troubled writers for some time. Careful translation evidently solves that problem. But it is not necessary, for purposes of showing that there *are* validity criteria for practical inferences, to be able to show that such inferences have *all* of the properties of 'ordinary' ones. After all, ordinal scales of measurement do not have all of the properties of interval or ratio scales either. That does not mean that they constitute an improper or ill-defined use of numbers.) My insistence here is merely that the practical arguments we actually use to guide our conduct can all be given translations that are both accurate with regard to their original meanings in ordinary speech and testable by appropriate, well-established, logical techniques and criteria.

A good deal of the philosophical work on practical reasoning – perhaps most of the current work on the topic – addresses itself to the connection between reason and action. See, for example, Robert Audi, 'A Theory of Practical Reasoning,' *American Philosophical Quarterly* 19 (1982): 23–39. My project in this book is isolable from most of that work, but two recent books in the area should be mentioned here. One is Frederic Schick, *Having Reasons: An Essay on Rationality and Sociality* (Princeton, Princeton University Press, 1984), in which the project is to design a theory that accounts for a diversity of reasons for action – not only those of rational self-interest, but also those in which others' interests are direct motives for one's actions. The other is Stephen L. Darwall, *Impartial Reason* (Ithaca, Cornell University Press, 1983). Darwall's project is to show that practical reason is, at its base, *impartial* rather than self-centered. More specifically, [the book] argues that

> reasons to act are grounded in principles that it would be
> (relatively) rational to choose were a person to adopt a

perspective impartial between agents and to select principles for all to act on. This ties practical reason to principles of the right, conceived of as those that would be chosen in a Rawlsian original position. (p. 17)

The argument opens with a sustained critique of views that hold that in order for x to be a reason for a given agent to act, it must be in some sense 'based' in that agent's 'desires'. Darwall finds no adequate argument for such a view. Indeed, as he goes on to argue, 'intersubjective' values can be reasons for action, and are, under some circumstances, overriding reasons.

On a technical matter: Both Ronald Rogowski and Judith Thomson have expressed some dissatisfaction with the stringency of the conditions defined in the text for a completely defined game. Thomson, for example, observed that a 'game' under those conditions might be so rigidly defined – so empty of options for the players – that it would be difficult to call any move in it a good, bad, or indifferent move. (Think of a game in which the rules define exactly what each player must do on each move.) In that case we may wonder about the requirement that in a completely defined game 'Every move is, determinably, either a good, bad, or indifferent move for each player.' My reply is that this condition implicitly requires some minimal sort of teleological rule, and hence gives some sense to the value of any specified move. Thus, in a game for which the (implicit or explicit) teleological rule specifies that there is *no* 'point' and no 'winner', every rule-specified move that honors that condition would be a good one.

Moral Reasoning

My account here is most directly indebted to those who have argued that moral arguments are embedded in practices describable in terms of criteria, constitutive rules or institutional facts which are logically connected to particular action-guiding judgments, given relevant fact-situations. The relevant work here includes several papers by Philippa Foot: 'Moral Arguments,' *Mind* 67 (1958): 502–13, 'Moral Beliefs,' *Proceedings of the Aristotelian Society* 59 (1958–59): 83–104, and 'Morality as a System of Hypothetical Imperatives,' *The Philosophical Review* 81 (1972): 305–316. It also includes John Rawls', 'Two Concepts of Rules,' *The Philo-*

sophical Review 64 (1955): 3–32, G. E. M. Anscome, 'Brute Facts', *Analysis* 18 (1958): 69–72, and John Searle, 'How to Derive "Ought" from "Is",' *The Philosophical Review* 73 (1964): 43–58. See also Kurt Baier, 'Moral Reasons and Reasons to be Moral,' in A. I. Goldman and J. Kim (eds.), *Values and Morals* (Dordrecht, D. Reidel, 1978). In that essay Baier gives an especially clear presentation of his argument that a certain special conception of morality is rationally defensible as overriding. I depart from all this work, in the main, by adopting what I call the general conception of morality – a notion developed from my article 'The Finality of Moral Judgments,' *The Philosophical Review* 82 (1973): 364–70. Chapter One of Alan Donagan's book, *The Theory of Morality* (Chicago, University of Chicago Press, 1977), implicitly links the general conception to a long tradition in moral theory.

Readers will certainly profit from a study of W. D. Falk's important paper, 'Morality, Self and Others,' in Hector-Neri Castaneda and George Nakhnikian (eds.), *Morality and the Language of Conduct* (Detroit, Wayne State University Press, 1965) pp. 25–67. Falk explores at length, in subtle and exacting fashion, the arguments for and against including 'personal oughts' (i.e., considerations of prudence, self-interest and the like) in the notion of morality. This is something like the question of whether to adopt the general conception versus a special one defined so as to exclude self-regarding considerations. Falk's conclusion is that this is:

> a semantic issue which it is far more important to understand
> than take sides on. . . . [The adoption of the 'social'
> conception of morality] is unexceptionable as long as its
> implications are faced. . . . [That is, if one adopts it, one]
> must grant that 'morality' on this level is demoted from its
> accustomed place of being the sole and final arbiter of right
> and wrong choice. (pp. 65–66)

But there are disadvantages, Falk thinks, to choosing the other conception of morality as well. He says:

> If both alternatives are repugnant, it is because both fall short
> of expectations. . . . The concept of morality itself bears the
> accumulated scars of conceptual evolution. Its multiple

associations are a bar to summing it up in any one way.
(p. 66)

Readers not already familiar with it will also profit from William
Frankena's paper 'Recent Conceptions of Morality,' pages 1–24 of
the Castaneda/Nakhnikian volume cited above.

In addition, the analysis of rationality in two recent sources may
be worthwhile: Harold J. Brown, 'On Being Rational,' *American
Philosophical Quarterly* 15 (1978): 241–8, and Richard B. Brandt,
A Theory of the Good and the Right (Oxford, Clarendon Press,
1979), pp. 10–16. Brown defines and defends a notion of rationality analogous to deliberation in the Aristotelian sense; it has
interesting affinities to reasoned argument under the general
conception of morality. Brandt defines an agent's action as rational,
'to a first approximation':

> . . . if and only if it is what he would have done if all the
> mechanisms determining action except for his desires and
> aversions . . . that is, the *cognitive inputs* influencing decision/
> action – had been optimal as far as possible. (We shall see
> later that this condition is met if and only if every item of
> *relevant available* information is present to awareness,
> vividly, at the focus of attention, or with an equal share of
> attention.) Second, I shall call a desire or aversion 'rational'
> if and only if it is what it would have been had the person
> undergone *cognitive psychotherapy* (a term which cannot be
> fully explained before Chapters 5 and 6). Finally, I shall say
> that an action is 'rational' in the sense of fully rational if and
> only if the desires and aversions which are involved in the
> action are rational, and if the condition is met for rationality
> to a first approximation. (p. 11)

The notion of relevance here is, as Brandt notes on page 12,
'essentially a causal notion'. It thus differs from the one I use. But
his notion of all available information 'is intended to capture the
idea of the best justified system of beliefs available at the time' (p.
13). This leads to an account of 'the best thing to do' (pp. 14–16)
in terms of the concept of rationality, and the proposal that morally
right conduct be defined as the conduct 'permitted by the moral
code which a fully rational person would most strongly tend to
support, for a society in which he expected to live a lifetime.' (p.

224). He argues for this notion in Chapter 10. Although Brandt's approach is very different from mine (he would condemn mine as 'intellectualist'), the close connection between rationality and morality in the two is similar. And note, for both of us, the essentially 'open' character of judgments about the best thing to do (and hence morality). Such judgments are made in terms of available evidence, and are subject to revision whenever new evidence arises. But whereas I simply *identify* moral judgments with the judgments that are justifiable all things considered, Brandt does not want a straightforward identification of 'the best thing to do' with 'the moral thing to do'. My account avoids many of the complexities of Brandt's line of argument. Whether that simplicity is gained only at the expense of inadequacy I leave for the reader to assess.

It follows from the general conception of morality that matters of style and taste are relevant to moral judgments. It does not follow, however, that style, taste, manners, 'bearing' and so on are by themselves 'moral qualities', or that they are by themselves a reliable index to moral character. The temptation to treat them as such is often very powerful, and sometimes even seems the most reliable course to take when we are bewildered by other evidence. The conduct of adversaries, in conflicts where the stakes are very high and the circumstances very ambiguous, often gets a moral 'reading' on these grounds. See, for example, Diana Trilling's account of Jean Harris' murder trial, *Mrs. Harris* (New York, Harcourt, Brace, Jovanovitch, 1981). The dangers are obvious.

See also two essays by Bernard Williams, 'Moral Luck' and 'Practical Necessity' in his book *Moral Luck* (Cambridge, Cambridge University Press, 1981). The first of the two explores the extent to which people who act morally can render their lives 'immune to luck' – i.e., immune to retrospective reevaluation of a sort that is accurate, justified, and over the outcome of which the actors have no control *as they act*. The second essay discusses the sort of practical necessity involved in judgments reached by all-things-considered deliberation.

It might be objected that the general conception is a peculiarly culture-bound notion. C.f. Alasdair MacIntyre's description of the heroic virtues in *After Virtue* (London, Duckworth, 1981).

The rules which govern both action and evaluated judgment in the *Iliad* resemble the rules and precepts of a game such as chess. It is a question of fact whether a man is a good chess player . . . whether a move is the right move to make in a particular situation. The game of chess presupposes, indeed is partially constituted by, agreement on how to play chess. Within the vocabulary of chess it makes no sense to say 'That was the one and only move which would achieve checkmate, but was it the right move to make?' And therefore someone who said this and understood what he was saying would have to be employing some notion of 'right' which received its definition from outside chess. . . . [The analogy is dangerous, however, because we] play games such as chess for a variety of purposes. But there is nothing to be made of the question: for what purposes do the characters in the *Iliad* observe the rules that they observe . . .? It is rather the case that it is only within their framework of rules and precepts that they are able to frame purposes at all. . . . All questions of choice arise within the framework; the framework itself cannot be chosen.

There is thus the sharpest of contrasts between the emotivist self of modernity and the self of the heroic age. The self of the heroic age lacks precisely that characteristic which . . . some modern moral philosophers take to be an essential characteristic of human selfhood: the capacity to detach oneself from any particular standpoint or point of view, to step backwards, as it were, and view and judge that standpoint or point of view from the outside. In heroic society there is no 'outside' except that of the stranger. A man who tried to withdraw himself from his given position in heroic society would be . . . trying to make himself disappear. (pp. 118–19)

Of course MacIntyre is quick to point out that the narrator of the *Iliad does* step back, and MacIntyre's reading can certainly be disputed. His inference (?) that because all questions of choice arise *within* the framework, the framework cannot itself be chosen is surely misleading. It cannot be chosen *whole*. But it can certainly be examined bit by bit and chosen (or rejected) bit by bit. In Otto Neurath's apt metaphor, it is possible to rebuild a raft while it is afloat. We should not conclude too quickly that the people of the heroic age, or of so-called traditional culture, lacked the power and ability to 'step back' – to make all-things-considered judgments. From the outside, and especially from the omniscient narrator's point of view, characters all tend to look trapped. But they may be no more trapped than we (or Homer).

The description of the actual process of moral reasoning offered here agrees fairly well with Chapter 2 of Thomas Perry's *Moral Reasoning and Truth* (Oxford, Clarendon Press, 1976), but it differs sharply from Perry in its adoption of the general conception of morality. This results in corresponding disagreement with his account of the 'point' of morality (his Chapter 3), and of moral truth (his Chapters 6 and 7). It results in similar disagreement with all advocates of a 'special' moral point of view. See, for example, G. J. Warnock, *The Object of Morality* (London, Methuen & Co., 1971).

R. M. Hare, *Moral Thinking* (Oxford, Clarendon Press, 1981) describes a two-level process of moral thinking. At the first level, the intuitionistic one, agents uncover the implications of their moral intuitions for conduct. This can be an intricate process because our intuitions are many, complex, and subtle, and because morally problematic situations can be described in various ways so as to variously engage those intuitions. But Hare is concerned to press the point that, however complex or subtle, moral theorizing that stays at the intuitionistic level cannot give us rational grounds for either 'selecting' intuitions (and dispositions and sentiments), or resolving genuine conflicts among them. For those tasks we need the second level of moral thinking, the critical one. There we proceed by applying the logic of moral discourse – not the substance of it but the form – in particular the principles of universalization and prescription, to reach practical judgments that are 'overriding'. I share Hare's rejection of the sort of intuitionism he describes, and his insistence that it be supplemented by critical thinking. (I do not, however, think his description adequately captures the positions of some of the philosophers he labels as intuitionistic – e.g., Rawls.). It might be thought that moral theory under the general conception is not purified of moral intuitions – that in particular, its substantive rules about participation, teleology, and deontology cannot be 'selected' or coordinated 'within' the general conception itself. If so, then we are in need of something like Hare's level of critical thinking. But the general conception itself, through its procedural, transformational and recognition rules, possesses the means for self-corrective criticism. I choose not to describe this in terms of different 'levels' of thinking because I want to emphasize the sense in which the moral enterprise is a coherent, well-defined activity.

Rules of Morality

A few elements of this section, considered separately, are reminiscent of things in my book *On Justifying Moral Judgments* (London and New York, Routledge & Kegan Paul and Humanities Press, 1973). With respect to the identification of purposiveness as a constitutive feature of rational agency, it parallels to some extent the work of my mentor Alan Gewirth, *Reason and Morality* (Chicago, University of Chicago Press, 1978).

It should be noted, however, that the teleological and deontological rules I argue for are not vulnerable to the charge, sometimes leveled at Toulmin, that under the guise of stating the constitutive rules of morality as such they actually state the rules of a particular moral theory or way of life. The rules I state do not, for example, exclude a self-destructive life. That sort of exclusion is a question for moral theory, not for the theory of morality.

Social choice theorists might add something like the following to the account of transitivity given here: There are three possible preference relations: greater than, less than, and equal to. The first two relations are asymmetrical. All three are transitive. And a preference ordering, to be rational, must be complete. That is, every object in it must have one of those preference relations to every other. See, for example, Robert Goodin, *The Politics of Rational Man* (London, John Wiley, 1976). The notion of asymmetry follows directly from non-contradiction, as does transitivity. Completeness follows from the mutually exclusive and supposed exhaustive character of the three relational possibilities (plus non-contradiction and excluded middle). I do not adopt the completeness condition here because I do not wish to rule out the possibility of genuine indeterminacy (with respect to these relations).

Acknowledgments

An earlier version of part of this chapter was given as an A. Cedric Evans Memorial Lecture at the University of Nebraska at Lincoln in May of 1983. I am grateful to the members of that audience, and in particular to Robert Audi, for helpful discussion on the arguments. In addition, Ronald Rogowski, Judith Thomson, Thomas Grey, Kurt Baier, Paul Brest and Richard Flathman made useful general criticisms. Carolyn Razauskas is the one who initially pressed me to develop the notion of a well-defined activity.

Moral Theory

The Social Self

The relevant empirical literature treats the sorts of things mentioned in this section as established beyond dispute. See any of the reputable textbooks on child development: e.g., John H. Flavell, *Cognitive Development* (Englewood Cliffs, N. J., Prentice-Hall, 1977). Flavell says, in passing,

> It is difficult to conceive how there could be any significant cognitive development at all if the amount and quality of the infant's social relations with other human beings fell below some unknown minimum. Human beings are intrinsically social beings, and human cognitive development requires human social relations.

The Priority Problem

Marshall Sahlins cautions against the notion that human needs (or wants) are necessarily as extensive and varied as we find them to be in developed societies. In particular, he argues against the view that the life of hunters and gatherers was an impoverished, miserable, exhausting one – one that barely managed to eke out a subsistence. He presents an impressive range of evidence in support of the contention that hunters and gatherers typically lead affluent lives (in terms of the needs they have), and have a good deal of leisure. See 'The Original Affluent Society' in Marshall Sahlins, *Stone Age Economics* (New York, Atherton, 1972).

Acting in Character

For a careful explanation of the notions of 'personal disposition' and 'common trait', see Gordon W. Allport, *Patterns and Growth in Personality* (New York, Holt, Rinehart & Winston, 1961) chapters 14 and 15. There Allport explains in detail the following definition:

> A personal disposition is a generalized neuropsychic structure (peculiar to the individual), with the capacity to render many stimuli functionally equivalent, and to initiate and guide consistent (equivalent) forms of adaptive and stylistic behavior. (p. 373)

And he notes the relation of dispositions to motives:

> ... it is impossible to consider personal dispositions as units of personality wholly apart from motivation. In some cases they are the leading motives in life, especially if they are mature, functionally autonomous systems of purpose. They are not merely ways of *reacting* to the environment but ways of *meeting* it. (p. 373)

My usage of 'disposition' follows Allport.

For a careful analysis of the notion of a trait of character, see Richard B. Brandt, 'Traits of Character: A Conceptual Analysis', *American Philosophical Quarterly* 7 (1970): 23–37.

Unfounded Preferences and Disturbance

Readers should consult Richard B. Brandt's account of 'irrational' desires and aversions in Chapter VI of his book *A Theory of the Good and the Right* (Oxford, Clarendon Press, 1979).

Virtue Theory

In *Nichomachean Ethics* 1097b–1098b, Aristotle presents the outline of a theory of the good, a theory from which an account of the virtues can be developed. This so-called *ergon* argument (argument concerning the 'work' or 'function' of a thing) is as follows. (The translation is by W. D. Ross.)

> ... to say that happiness is the chief good seems a platitude, and a clearer account of what it is is still desired. This might perhaps be given, if we could first ascertain the function of man. For just as for a flute-player, a sculptor, or any artist, and,

in general, for all things that have a function or activity, the good and the 'well' is thought to reside in the function, so it would seem to be for man, if he has a function. Have the carpenter, then, and the tanner certain functions or activities, and has man none? Is he born without a function? Or as eye, hand, foot, and in general each of the parts evidently has a function, may one lay it down that man similarly has a function quite apart from these? What then can this be? Life seems to be common even to plants, but we are seeking what is peculiar to man. Let us exclude, therefore, the life of nutrition and growth. Next there would be a life of perception, but it also seems to be common even to the horse, the ox, and every animal. There remains, then, an active life of the element that has a rational principle. . . . Now if the function of man is an activity of soul which follows or implies a rational principle, and if we say 'a so-and-so' and 'a good so-and-so' have a function which is the same in kind, e.g., a lyre-player and a good lyre-player, and so without qualification in all cases, eminence in respect of goodness being added to the name of the function (for the function of the lyre-player is to play the lyre, and that of a good lyre-player is to do so well): if this is the case, [and we state the function of man to be a certain kind of life, and this to be an activity or actions of the soul implying a rational principle, and the function of a good man to be the good and noble performance of these, and if any action is well performed when it is performed in accordance with the appropriate excellence; if this be the case,] human good turns out to be activity of soul in accordance with virtue, and if there are more than one virtue, in accordance with the best and most complete.

But we must add 'in a complete life . . . [f]or one day, or a short time, does not make a man blessed and happy.

Let this serve as an outline of the good; for we must first sketch it roughly, and then later fill in the details.

Quoted from volume IX of *The Works of Aristotle* (Oxford, Clarendon Press, 1925), *Ethica Nichomachea* I. 7.

For an amusing and irreverent catalogue of the ways in which Aristotle's *ergon* argument can be given a fallacious interpretation, or an interpretation which, while not fallacious, does not yield the results Aristotle wants, see Bernard Suits, 'Aristotle on the Function of Man: Fallacies, Heresies and Other Entertainments,' *Canadian Journal of Philosophy* 4 (1974): 23–40. (Compare a more recent criticism of virtue theory: Gilbert Harman, 'Human Flourishing, Ethics, and Liberty,' *Philosophy & Public Affairs* 12 (1983): 307–22.) Suits argues, among other things, that on the most plausible constructions, Aristotle's remarks do not lead to the conclusion that man *qua* man has a function which has significance for a theory of the virtues. The reason Suits gives for this is that human beings *qua* human beings are 'immensely versatile'. And 'the more versatile the thing, the more difficult – and pointless – it is to [assign it a "proper" or "essential" function]' (p. 38). As a type, Suits insists, we are not much like the specialized things Aristotle alludes to (bodily organs, flute players, etc.). 'Man should be likened not to a tanner or a carpenter but, as a start, to a lidded pot, or to a stick, or to anything which suggests a multiplicity of functions, all "proper" functions according to the only criteria which apply' (pp. 38–9). There is something in this, but not much. The general characteristics cited in Chapter One (purposiveness, boundary keeping), in the context of the general conception, yield important conclusions. I think that we cannot plausibly derive a function for humans as a type. But it does not follow that we cannot derive a useful type description.

The major point at which my outline differs from Aristotle's concerns the focus on (or perhaps interpretation of) 'an active life of the element that has a rational principle.' I take it that what characterizes moral agents as a type (for the purpose of constructing an account of the virtues) is not just 'the rational element' but the way that element is characteristically embodied, so to speak. Morality, under the general conception, is the enterprise of reasoning out what we ought to do and be, *given the full list of traits characteristic of us*. It does not follow – simply from the outline of that project alone – that the virtues will turn out to be traits that accord rational activity pride of place in the way of life we eventually justify under the general conception. Aristotle, by identifying rational activity as *the* characteristic 'function' (*ergon*) of human beings, tips moral theory toward an account of the virtues as traits that help us develop and live out 'the rational element' of our lives – at the expense, if necessary, of other elements. Under the general conception, it is conceivable that moral theory would recommend the cultivation of dispositions opposed to rational activity.

Readers will also note the difference, in the above regard, from Joseph Butler's position. See the first of the *Fifteen Sermons Preached at the Rolls Chapel*, London, 1724, reprinted in Joseph Butler, *Five Sermons* (New York, The Liberal Arts Press, 1950). Butler there argues for three fundamental elements of human nature as determinative of virtue: benevolence, self-love, and conscience (i.e., the rational faculty that approves and disapproves of things).

Peter Geach, in *The Virtues* (Cambridge, Cambridge University Press, 1977) assimilates what he calls Aristotle's 'doctrine of teleology' to a form of 'as if' reasoning that is intellectually respectable in modern science, at least for heuristic purposes. He says:

> Aristotle's doctrine of teleology is that if we speak as if Nature had aims or policies we may work out what happens in the world by constructing reasoning formally parallel to human practical deliberations. . . . [T]his teleological way of thinking, conducted on essentially Aristotelian principles but without his obsolete natural science, is intellectually respectable. And in that way of thinking it makes good sense to ask 'What are men for?' We may not be so ready with an answer, even a partial answer, as when we ask 'What are hearts for?' 'What are teeth for?'; but Aristotle is right to my mind in desiderating an answer – the success in bringing men's partial organs and activities under a teleological account should encourage us to think that some answer may be found. But not as quickly as Aristotle thought: it does not show straight off what men are for if we know that men and men only are capable of theoretical discourse. (pp. 12–13).

Lisa H. Newton, 'The Political Animal', in J. Roland Pennock and John W. Chapman (eds.) *Human Nature in Politics*, NOMOS XVII (New York, New York University Press, 1977) pp. 142–56 gives a clear, forthright defense of the view that human institutions can in principle 'be pronounced good, as tending to fulfill human nature, or bad, as tending to warp or injure it' (p. 154). She locates the points at which such arguments are fallacious, but argues that the form of an Aristotelian account of these matters is valid.

James D. Wallace, in his book *Virtues and Vices* (Ithaca, Cornell

University Press, 1978) characterizes the form of an Aristotelian account of human excellence as follows:

1) It belongs to the nature of some kinds of things that they do a certain 'work' (*ergon*); for example, an eye *sees*, a carpenter *makes things of wood*. 2) A good one of such a kind is one that does its work well; a good eye is one that sees well, etc. 3) An excellence of a thing is a condition of the thing that 'makes the work of that thing be done well.' (p. 36).

Wallace rejects, as Geach and I do as well, Aristotle's quick identification of the human *ergon* with the activity of our 'rational part'. Instead, Wallace proposes to

characterize the human *ergon* as a social life informed by convention. . . . Human excellences, including virtues, will be capacities or tendencies that suit an individual for human life *generally*. These traits are such that if they were lacking altogether in a group of people, these people would be incapable of having the life characteristic of human beings.

These virtues may be contrasted with excellences that suit an individual for just one specific kind of activity. Woodworking skill, for example, is a virtue of carpenters. Together with other qualities, this excellence would tend to make a carpenter a good carpenter. An individual with all of these qualities, who lived amidst the sort of material and institutional circumstances necessary for the craft, and also was healthy and fortunate in other ways, could have a successful career as a carpenter. One can grasp what it is to do well at a specific kind of activity, such as woodworking, by understanding the point (or points) of the activity and appreciating the problems and difficulties encountered by its practitioners. One can at the same time see what qualities of a carpenter would contribute to his doing well at his craft.

The notion of a human *ergon* provides a basis for a similar study of human life and human good. We study a creature that naturally lives a certain kind of social life structured by conventions. Regularly, we find language, politics, inquiry, commerce, and arts among other things. Human beings have certain physical and psychological characteristics, which determine certain needs and interests. Finally, these creatures

live in a certain kind of world. . . . By studying this sort of
life, by noting the various purposes and goals of activities that
make up human life and the problems encountered in
realizing these purposes, we can come to understand what it
is for a human being to live well and what characteristics of
a human being contribute to living well. (pp. 37–8)

My approach differs from Wallace's in the following way:
Instead of trying to define 'the' human *ergon*, I define the general
conception of morality – 'the activity of finding out what one ought
to do and be, all things considered, *and then actually doing or
being those things.*' That activity is well-defined; it has rules
defining aims, participation, procedures and so forth. It is therefore
possible to construct an account of what traits participants would
need to do well at that activity. Those traits are the virtues, 'under'
the general conception. In order to make headway with this task,
of course, we need to have, in addition to a general account of the
activity, a general account of the sort of creatures who engage in
it (i.e., moral agents) and their circumstances. But we do not need
to suppose that there is some one thing that can be called 'the'
human *ergon*. It is the nature of the activity of conducting ourselves
morally (together with facts about our nature and circumstances)
that generates a theory of the moral virtues.

John Rawls considers related matters in section 66 of *A Theory
of Justice* (Cambridge, Mass., Harvard University Press, 1971),
pp. 433–9. Rawls there discusses what he calls broad-based
properties – ones we think it rational for people to have for almost
all possible (just) social roles. He then considers the connection
between such properties and fundamental or basic virtues, which
he tends to identify with dispositions to act on the basic principles
of right. See pp. 435 ff.

The title essay of Philippa Foot's *Virtues and Vices* (Berkeley,
University of California Press, 1978) argues that the (moral) virtues
are distinct from other beneficial traits in at least the following
ways: 1) They are excellences of the will, rather than of the body
or mind. And 'a virtue is not, like a skill or an art, a mere capacity:
it must actually engage the will' (p. 8). I take it that this is consistent
with the notion of a disposition to act, as I use the term. 2) The
virtues are 'corrective, each one standing at a point at which there
is some temptation to be resisted or deficiency of motivation to be

made good' (p. 8). I feel less sure of this point, except as an accurate observation about the cases in which we are ordinarily moved to discuss the virtues. But I see no reason, in principle, to refuse the label to traits moral agents typically have no difficulty acquiring or expressing in their behavior – e.g., a disposition to be concerned about their own welfare. What would the life of an agent who lacked that disposition be like? 3) Foot also argues for the plausibility of thinking of the virtues as systematically connected with good actions in a way that they cannot be connected to bad actions – so that, for example, we may say that a villain's acts 'took' courage yet still failed to 'be' courageous. Her discussion of this point (pp. 14–18) is subtle, and makes sense of some seeming contradictions in ordinary talk about the virtues. Yet I think we might be better served, for present purposes, by a more straightforward account: not every courageous act is praise-worthy *all things considered*. A courageous theft, for example, might be such a case. Yet we can (and at a suitable distance often do) admire it *as* a courageous act – i.e., for its courageous aspect. Peter Geach, in *The Virtues* (Cambridge, Cambridge University Press, 1977) asserts that the conscientiousness of a Himmler – 'his triumph over his own feelings in order to do monstrous deeds' – makes him all the more detestable. I agree, but not because I think conscientiousness, *to be a virtue*, must serve good ends. My reason comes rather from revulsion at the *vices* Himmler had – vices whose effects were magnified by some of his virtues.

Philippa Foot, in her 1983 Presidential Address to the Pacific Division of the American Philosophical Association, 'Utilitarianism and the Virtues', in *Proceedings and Addresses of the American Philosophical Association* 57 (1983): 273–83 argues that the hold consequentialism has on us comes from the assumption that we can give a theory independent sense to the phrase 'good state of affairs'. That sense, combined with the principle that more good is better than less, draws us toward consequentialism. But she argues that consequentialists can only give a theory *dependent* sense to 'a good state of affairs'. (Virtue theorists can give one too.) So the supposed pull on us toward consequentialism, from 'outside' the theory, evaporates. My own view is that within the general conception of morality we can give a sense to 'good state of affairs' and 'good disposition' and that this is the root of both the consequentialist and virtue-theoretic aspects of moral theory.

For my reasons for thinking that virtue theory is a necessary part of moral theory, 'independent' of its teleological and deontological aspects, see my book *On Justifying Moral Judgments* (London, Routledge & Kegan Paul, 1973), and my paper 'The Neglect of Virtue', *Ethics* 85 (1975): 110–22. Three more recent articles apply a virtue-theoretic approach to topics not dealt with in this book: 'The Free-Rider Problem' in Harlan B. Miller and William H. Williams (eds.) *The Limits of Utilitarianism* (Minneapolis, University of Minnesota Press, 1982); 'The Priority of Human Interests' in Miller and Williams (eds.) *Ethics and Animals* (New York, Humanita Press, 1983); and 'Killing and Giving Up' in Natalie Abrams and Michael Buckner (eds.) *Medical Ethics: A Clinical Textbook and Reference for the Health Care Professions* (Cambridge, Mass., MIT Press, 1983).

In the article on the freerider problem cited above I argue that rational self-maximizers would choose to develop in themselves dispositions that would tend to defeat prisoners' dilemmas. In a more recent article, John Kilcullen has argued that utilitarians would cultivate (in themselves and others) dispositions that block explicitly utility-oriented conduct in certain circumstances. Kilcullen's argument is careful, detailed, and convincing. See John Kilcullen, 'Utilitarianism and Virtue', *Ethics* 93 (1983): 451–66. He concludes with the remark that although his argument

> is available to utilitarians and other consequentialists, it is not specifically consequentialist; it is available also to those who deny (as I do myself) that every action is to be valued only for its effects, as long as they acknowledge that some actions are to be valued at least in part for their effects and that those may include actions which develop and preserve useful dispositions. (p. 466)

I certainly concur, and avail myself of something like his argument at crucial points in the argument for the virtue of reciprocity (Chapter Three).

William K. Frankena has, in a number of essays, explored the possibility of, and the place in moral theory for, an ethic of virtue. See especially his 'Pritchard and the Ethics of Virtue', *Monist* 54 (1970): 1–17. *The Journal of Religious Ethics* published, in the early 1970s, a series of articles on virtue theory. The central problem addressed in those articles, mainly in conjunction with the work of William Frankena, is how to fit an account of the virtues into morality *per se*. Are notions of virtue derivative from deontic ones, or vice versa? See, for example, Frederick S. Carney, 'The Virtue-Obligation Controversy', *JRE* 1 (1973): 5–19; William K. Frankena, 'The Ethics of Love Conceived as an Ethics of Virtue', *JRE* 1 (1973): 21–36; Stanley Hauerwas, 'Obligation and Virtue Once More', *JRE* 3 (1975): 27–44; and William K. Frankena, 'Conversations with Carney and Hauerwas', *JRE* 3 (1975): 45–62.

R. B. Brandt, 'W. K. Frankena and Ethics of Virtue', *The Monist* 64 (1981): 271–92 argues that a complete normative theory must have elements of both deontological and virtue theory, but that the latter is more fundamental. His discussion of the concept of non-moral virtue, and the general characterization he gives of the place of virtue in an ethical theory are instructive. See, however, an argument against the view that the virtues are morally primary, in Kurt Baier, 'Virtue Ethics', *Annual Proceedings of the Center for Philosophic Exchange*, 3 (1982): 57–70. And Robert B. Louden, 'On Some Vices of Virtue Ethics', *American Philosophical Quarterly* 21 (1984): 227–36 surveys some problems faced by theories that give the concept of virtue a dominant role.

Edmund Pincoffs has done illuminating work in virtue theory. In particular, readers will profit from 'Quandary Ethics', *Mind* 80 (1971): 552–71, and 'Legal Responsibility and Moral Character', 19 *Wayne Law Review* 905 (1973): 905–23.

A quite different approach to virtue ethics, by way of the notion of a paradigmatic individual, has been explored by several writers, notably and recently by Harold Alderman, 'By Virtue of a Virtue', *The Review of Metaphysics* 36 (1982): 127–53.

Susan Wolf, 'Moral Saints', *Journal of Philosophy* 79 (1982): 419–39 makes an argument to the effect that morality (under what I would term a special conception of it) 'should not serve as a comprehensive guide to conduct' (p. 434). Forcing her argument into my terms, what she argues is that from an all-things-considered point of view, we have good grounds for disapproving of any form of saintliness that either commonsense moral thought or common moral theories will generate. Yet from *within* a given *special* conception of morality, we are apparently forced to approve of its conception of saintliness. Wolf argues for the recognition that:

The moral point of view, we might say, is the point of view

one takes up insofar as one takes the recognition of the fact that one is just one person among others equally real and deserving of the good things in life as a fact with practical consequences. . . . Competing moral theories offer alternative answers to the question of what the most correct or the best way to express that fact is . . .. But it seems that alternative interpretations of the moral point of view do not exhaust the ways in which our actions, characters, and their consequences can be comprehensively and objectively evaluated. Let us call the point of view from which we consider what kinds of lives are good lives, and what kinds of persons it would be good for ourselves and others to be, the *point of view of individual perfection*. . . . It may not be the case that the perfectionist point of view is like the moral point of view in being a point of view we are ever *obliged* to take up and express in our actions. Nonetheless, it provides us with reasons that are independent of moral reasons for wanting ourselves and others to develop our characters and live our lives in certain ways. When we take up this point of view and ask how much it would be good for an individual to act from the moral point of view, we do not find an obvious answer.

The considerations of this paper suggest, at any rate, that the answer is not 'as much as possible.' (pp. 436–7)

In my terms, what Wolf is recommending is conduct based on the general conception of morality, with special attention to the connection between virtue theory, broadly conceived, and the various special conceptions of morality.

For criticism of Wolf's article, see Robert Merrihew Adams, 'Saints', *Journal of Philosophy* 81 (July, 1984): 392–401. What Adams finds fault with, as do I, is the narrowness of Wolf's conception of devotion to morality. He calls attention to the fact that the people we ordinarily *call* saints are *not* unattractive or uninteresting in the way that worries Wolf. It is not clear, of course, that the religious figures we call saints actually *are* 'moral saints' in Wolf's sense. And it is a merit of Wolf's article that it brings out the way in which standard teleological and deontological theories seem to generate unacceptable conceptions of secular saintliness. But Adams' arguments remind us that the problem here lies with the conception of morality that we hold. Under the general conception,

I would insist, Wolf's problem does not arise. (I am indebted to M. A. Allen for calling Adams' article to my attention.)

Two impressive articles that deal with the problems of a consequentialist account of motives and traits of character are Robert M. Adams, 'Motive Utilitarianism', *Journal of Philosophy* 73 (1976): 467–81, and Peter Railton, 'Alienation, Consequentialism, and the Demands of Morality', *Philosophy & Public Affairs* 13 (1984): 134–71. Adams explores the ways in which a utilitarian theory of motives would be distinct from act-utilitarianism. Railton raises issues about priorities and alienation that I consider (in somewhat different terms) in Chapter Six. He also makes important remarks about the (occasional) moral importance of alienation.

Marcia Baron, 'The Alleged Moral Repugnance of Acting from Duty', *Journal of Philosophy* 81 (1984): 197–220 rejects the sort of criticism that Railton brings against deontological ethics by arguing that we should

> break from the idea that acting from duty primarily concerns
> isolated actions. . . . [And] once we break from [it] . . . we
> see the vital role of the sense of duty as a *secondary* motive.
> . . . To say that one should always act from duty is not to
> say that one should always act from duty as a primary motive.
> One's sense of duty will serve generally as a limiting condition
> and at the same time as an impetus to think about one's
> conduct, to appraise one's goals . . . (p. 209)

My account, in Chapter Three, of the retrospective nature of the obligation to reciprocate is compatible with many of Baron's remarks here – especially those about the timing of moral reflection (e.g., p. 208).

Alasdair MacIntyre's book *After Virtue* (London, Duckworth, 1981) gives a provocative assessment of the state of modern moral philosophy, and an intriguing development of the structure of a theory of the virtues. Those of us who have heretofore been merely nibbling around the edges of the topic are much in his debt – not only for the originality of his conception, but for his interpretation (albeit highly debatable) of the historic shifts in virtue theory from Homeric Greece to the present.

The account given here, however, differs at many crucial points from MacIntyre's. I agree, to use his words, that '[o]ne of the features of the concept of a virtue . . . is that it always requires for its application the acceptance of some prior account of certain features of social and moral life in terms of which it has to be defined and explained.' (p. 174) I agree that one of the initial tasks of virtue theory is to give an account of the 'core concept' of a virtue – the *topic* of inquiry that people who disagree about the list of virtues nonetheless may have in common when they construct their lists. Further, I agree that this 'core concept' of a virtue will itself be described in terms of certain very general features of human social life. But there the agreement ends. To wit:

In my view, the features of life in terms of which the notion of a virtue is to be understood are the generic features of human life mentioned in this chapter (e.g., purposiveness, boundary-keeping), operating in the context of moral deliberation and conduct as defined by the general conception of morality.

For MacIntyre, by contrast, the relevant features are the concept of a practice, the notion of the narrative order of a single human life, and the notion of a moral tradition (p. 174). In my judgment, those choices are unjustifiably restrictive. Take his notion of a practice: 'By "practice" I am going to mean any *coherent* and *complex* form of *socially established cooperative* activity through which goods *internal* to that form of activity are realized . . .' (p. 175, emphases added.) Virtues are then defined (in a first approximation) as traits that enable us to achieve the goods internal to practices – that is, the goods that come only from participation in the practice. Traits that only enable us to achieve 'external' goods are thus ruled out by fiat. This is an unjustifiable restriction on the notion of a virtue. The goods internal to practices are unquestionably central to human social life. And no doubt a life in which only 'external' goods were pursued would be as bleak as Hobbes's imaginary state of nature or the Ik's very real plight. (MacIntyre's examples on pp. 182–3.) But that is not the issue. The issue is whether there is any reason to introduce this *a priori* restriction on the core conception of a virtue, thereby excluding many candidates for virtues. I can find no such reason, either in MacIntyre's book or in my own reflections. Certainly, virtue theory under the general conception must be able to consider the possibility that the pursuit of *both* internal and external goods (through virtues appropriate to each) might be justifiable. We therefore must have a core conception that does not rule out that possibility *a priori*.

The restrictiveness of MacIntyre's core conception is compounded by his insistence that the virtues be the traits (from among those defined above) that sustain us in the sort of quest for good that gives narrative unity to the whole of an individual human life. (pp. 201–4) At least, if I understand MacIntyre's thesis correctly, he means to exclude from the category of virtues abilities that are not necessary for, or run counter to, pursuing a sort of unified, life-long quest. That again is unjustifiably restrictive with respect to describing a core conception of virtue. It would rule out *a priori*, traits that enable us to break up the unity of our lives – to 'forget' the past, live for the moment, and so forth. Those possibilities may well be ruled out by moral theory, but they should not be ruled out *before* moral theory.

MacIntyre may well reply that he is working in a tradition, trying to construct an account that fairly represents the common topic of writers on virtue in that tradition. And he may point out that he has given arguments to support the choice of that tradition as against, for example, the views represented by modern moralists and amoralists. My response would be to note that those writers have also talked about the virtues, and that we need a core conception of the notion of a virtue that includes their versions of virtue theory. That is what we can derive, I think, from what I have described as virtue theory under the general conception.

Generalization

My description of a technique for finding ungeneralizable action-guides relies on the development of the Kantian project given by O'Nora (O'Neill) Nell in *Acting on Principle* (New York, Columbia University Press, 1975). Her account is the clearest and most cogent I have read. It claims, however, much more for Kantian theory than I am prepared to accept. In general, the limits I argue for here are my own, not hers.

Most of the relevant work by Kant may be found conveniently, in English translation, in T. K. Abbott, *Kant's Critique of Practical Reason and Other Works on the Theory of Ethics* 6th edition (London, Longmans, Green and Co., 1927). Difficulties and differences in translation abound, however. For crucial passages, the reader may wish to compare Abbott's translation with others (such as those by H. J. Paton, Lewis White Beck, John Ladd, and M. J.

Gregor). The authoritative edition of the texts in German is Kant's *Gesammelte Schriften*, 24 volumes (Berlin, Preussischen Akademie der Wissenschaften, 1902–66).

All current work on this issue is heavily indebted to Marcus Singer's *Generalization in Ethics* (New York, Alfred A. Knopf, 1961), and to the extensive debate that followed, over the next six to eight years, in the journals. Singer explores what he calls the generalization argument – that is, inferences of the form: If everyone were to do that the consequences would be undesirable; therefore, no one should do that. His inquiry is therefore not limited to cases in which contradiction can be found in an agent's intentions. And his inquiry is not limited to the *a priori* use of the generalization argument. That form of argument (mediated by the formal principle that similar cases must be treated similarly) is central to moral theory in general.

Philosophical analyses of generalization in ethics often treat promising as a paradigm case. For intriguing empirical evidence that a stable, productive society can exist without any institution of promising (as we understand the term), see Fred Korn and Shulamit R. Decktor Korn, 'Where People Don't Promise.' *Ethics* 93 (1983): 445–50. The society described in that article is that of the Tonga islands of the South Pacific. Further, of course, discussions of generalization in ethics typically treat inconsistency as intolerable for theory. For a discussion of the coherence of systems that permit inconsistency, see Nicholas Rescher and Robert Brandon, *The Logic of Inconsistency* (Totowa, N. J., Rowman and Littlefield, 1979). See also Susan Haack, *Deviant Logic* (Cambridge, Cambridge University Press, 1974).

The Presumption of Equality

The line of argument developed here was suggested by some remarks by Carl Cohen in *Democracy* (Athens, University of Georgia Press, 1971), pp. 264–5. For criticism of other attempts at justification, see D. E. Browne, 'The Presumption of Equality', *Australasian Journal of Philosophy* 53 (1975): 46–53. More recently, the whole idea of equality (including the presumption of equality) has come under attack by Peter Westen, in his article 'The Empty Idea of Equality' 95 *Harvard Law Review* 537 (1982). I do not think his arguments damage the conclusions here.

In correspondence, G. A. Cohen has called my attention to an important assumption in my use of the presumption of equality. I sometimes use arguments of the following form: 1) There are some good reasons (sound lines of argument) in support of doing X, and 2) there are some, but fewer, good reasons for not doing X. 3) All these reasons (lines of argument) are presumptively of equal weight. 4) There is, in this case, no sound argument that rebuts the presumption of equality. 5) So the reasons (arguments) must be weighted equally. 6) More reasons (arguments), of a given weight, in favor of doing X, outweigh fewer, of the same weight, against doing X. 7) Therefore, doing X is justified. The assumption here – in step 6) – is that the 'weights' of reasons or lines of argument are *additive*. Suppose, instead, that the weight of an argument were analogous to the density of a liquid. (Two gallons of density 2 plus 2 gallons of density 2 give *four* gallons of density 2 – *not* four gallons of density 4.) The *volumes* are additive, but the densities are not. (As I recall, Cohen put this to me as the proposition that arguments, unlike bricks, cannot be stacked up on a scale.) But which analogy is appropriate here? Is it volume or density? I think volume is the appropriate one. The notion of an argument's having 'weight' is a metaphor for the extent to which it establishes its conclusion with certainty. Under the general conception of morality, we are to establish conclusions all things considered. Each logically effective consideration that we introduce thus 'adds' or 'subtracts' from the certainty of a given conclusion in the same sense that additional evidence for an empirical generalization increases the probability that we are correct in making the generalization. That is why it is natural to use a metaphor like weight. It points to the (admittedly problematic) way in which more evidence, a more complete survey, can increase the certainty of a given conclusion.

Ultimate Justification

The strategy for grounding moral judgments described here is taken from my book *On Justifying Moral Judgments* (London and New York, Routledge & Kegan Paul, 1973). For a recent article on the attempt to ground moral obligation in rational motivation, attitudes or commitments, see David Zimmerman, 'The Force of Hypothetical Commitment', *Ethics* 93 (1983): 467–83.

Teleological Tendency

It is worth reiterating that the result obtained in this section is not – nor does it purport to be – an *a priori* deduction of a teleological *principle*, utilitarian or otherwise. The result here is merely a *tendency* toward the improvement of aggregate welfare, produced by the principle (derived *a priori*) that for any proposed act, every relevant interest must be taken into account. But this, by itself, does not place anyone under an affirmative obligation to act. Hence, there is no requirement, *a priori*, that any agent take others' interests into account at all, let alone maximize social welfare.

Deontological Commitments

Alan Gewirth, in *Reason and Morality* (Chicago, University of Chicago Press, 1978), argues for *a priori* deontic commitments from the fact of an agent's purposiveness. I think that only a teleological tendency comes from that fact (*a priori*), and that the deontic commitments come from another feature of agency – self-consciousness. In outline, Gewirth's argument goes this way. 1) By definition, agents must regard their own purposes as goods. 2) Consequently, they must regard the things that are necessary for purposive action *per se* as necessary goods – that is, goods that they must have to carry out their purposes. (These goods are certain levels of freedom and well-being.) 3) Regarding something as a necessary good for oneself is, Gewirth says, equivalent to claiming 'I must have those levels of freedom and well-being.' 4) That claim, he continues, is tantamount to claiming rights (for oneself) to freedom and well-being. 5) The generalization principle then requires the extension of that right claim to all rational agents. My reservations about this argument (not uncommon among Gewirth's readers) concern the moves from 2) to 4). It appears to me that what is entailed by 'X is a necessary good for me' is simply that 'Others' letting me have X is also a necessary good for me.' I do not think it follows (psychologically or logically) that I must demand these goods as rights. That *often* happens, but it is not necessary. The necessary connection, I maintain, is between self-consciousness and the deontic claims of boundary-keeping activity.

Some philosophers have argued that an adequate moral theory will not necessarily include what I have called a compossibility rule. Many of these arguments depend on adopting a special conception (or part of a special conception) of morality. If one holds, flatly, that making a promise creates a moral obligation (and that one makes a promise, for example, by uttering a guarantee, in good faith, of one's intention to carry out an act), then one can clearly have conflicting obligations. One can, for example, forget a previous promise and utter another one that conflicts with it. But that route to moral dilemmas is impeded by the all-things-considered aspect of the general conception. We have recourse to a second level consideration. Granted that a rule that generates obligations (*ceteris paribus*) leads to two competing obligations, which of the two ought to be performed all-things-considered? Two problems remain: 1) What about uses in which, all-things-considered, the two obligations *remain* equally weighty? 2) Why is it that we regard it appropriate for people to feel guilt or remorse about doing the lesser of two evils, even though it is clearly the act that is best all-things-considered? If we are to retain the law of non-contradiction, 1) must be solved by saying that each of the conflicting putative obligations defines an act that is morally permissible (and that one or the other must be done). Question 2) causes no problems on a virtue-theoretic account of the moral sentiments, for we can recognize the appropriateness of dispositionally produced guilt even though, in a particular case, we did the best thing.

Recent debate about the role of a consistency requirement for ethical theories includes E. J. Lemmon, 'Moral Dilemmas', *Philosophical Review* 71 (1962): 139–58, Bernard Williams, *Problems of the Self* (Cambridge, Cambridge University Press, 1977) Chapters 11 and 12, Ruth Barcan Marcus, 'Moral Dilemmas and Consistency', *Journal of Philosophy* 77 (1980): 121–36, Earl Conee, 'Against Moral Dilemmas', *The Philosophical Review* 91 (1982): 87–97, Philippa Foot, 'Moral Realism and Moral Dilemmas', *Journal of Philosophy* 80 (1983): 379–98, and Alan Donagan, 'Consistency in Rationalist Moral Systems', *Journal of Philosophy* 81 (1984): 291–308. These essays focus on cases in which moral agents appear to have conflicting obligations and ask 1) whether we have reason to believe that at least some such apparent dilemmas are genuine ones, and 2) if so, whether that entails that the moral principles involved are defective. Lemmon, Williams and Marcus all argue that there are genuine moral dilemmas – i.e., conflicting moral obligations not resolvable 'without residue' by priority rules or doctrines of *prima facie* duty. Marcus argues that on a plausible interpretation of ethical consistency, the existence of such conflicts need not indicate inconsistency in an ethical theory. Foot argues that while first order moral oughts (e.g., those that state the promises we have made) may conflict without indicating theoretical inconsistency, second order oughts (that tell us what is the right thing to do in a given case) may not. Donagan argues that the case for the reality of such dilemmas has not been made.

Acknowledgments

I am grateful for many conversations, over the years, with Arthur Poskocil. He has helped me to understand some of the psychological literature on the concept of self, and both he and George Ledger gave me valuable bibliographic leads. Mardi Horowitz deserves some thanks here, for complicating things with clinical realities. Paul Brest pressed me to answer objections to the choice of moral agency as the proper 'type' for a theory of the virtues.

Reciprocity

The Grounds for Reciprocity

The empirical evidence for the existence of a social norm of reciprocity is overwhelming. The literature I have found most useful (arranged by date of original publication) is this: Bronislaw Malinowski, *Argonauts of the Western Pacific* [1922] (London, Routledge & Kegan Paul, 1950); Marcel Mauss, *The Gift* [1923–24] (Glencoe, IL., The Free Press, 1954); Raymond Firth, *Primitive Polynesian Economy* 2nd Ed. (London, Routledge & Kegan Paul, 1974); Ruth Benedict, *The Chrysanthemum and the Sword: Patterns of Japanese Culture* (New York, Houghton, Mifflin and Co., 1946); Alvin Gouldner, 'The Norm of Reciprocity', *American Sociological Review* 25 (1960): 161–78; George C. Homans, *Social Behavior: Its Elementary Forms* [1961] (Rev. Ed.: New York, Harcourt, Brace, Jovanovich, 1974); Peter M. Blau, *Exchange and Power in Social Life* (New York, John Wiley & Sons, 1964); Marshall Sahlins, *Stone Age Economics* (New York, Aldine, 1972); and Peter P. Ekeh, *Social Exchange Theory: The Two Traditions* (Cambridge, Harvard University Press, 1974). The bibliography in Sahlins' book, and the extensive appendices to the chapter 'On the Sociology of Primitive Exchange' are excellent.

For recent reviews and criticisms of the relevant work in social psychology, see Robert L. Burgess and Ted L. Huston (eds.), *Social Exchange in Developing Relationships* (New York, Academic Press, 1979), especially the chapter on equity theory; and Kenneth J. Gergen, Martin Greenberg and Richard H. Willis (eds.), *Social Exchange* (New York, Plenum, 1980), especially the chapter titled 'A Theory of Indebtedness'. J. K. Chadwick-Jones, *Social Exchange Theory: Its Structure and Influence in Social Psychology* (New York, Academic Press, 1976) is also useful for an overview of the criticisms that have been brought against exchange theory generally. Robert Axelrod, *The Evolution of Cooperation* (New York, Basic Books, 1984) presents the results of his important work on prisoner's dilemma games. The object of that work was to investigate the conditions under which cooperation 'will emerge in a world of egoists without central authority.' (p. 3.) His approach was to define a 'fundamental form' of the prisoner's dilemma, and then to test various strategies for acting in iterated dilemmas of that sort – where the actors are assumed to be egoists who a) recognize other players, b) remember the history of past interactions, but c) do not know how many times the game will be iterated, d) cannot make effective threats or commitments to other players, e) cannot effectively predict other players' moves, f) cannot eliminate other players or avoid playing, and g) cannot change the payoffs in the matrix. Cooperation can emerge in such a situation only if the game is iterated but players are uncertain how many iterations there will be. Features a)–c) of Axelrod's 'fundamental form', together with the assumption of self-interest and the payoff schedule of the prisoner's dilemma matrix, certainly represent accurately some aspects of deeply problematic and important real-life situations. The other simplifying assumptions (d through e above) are much harder to justify if one wants to extrapolate game theoretic results to concrete situations. Axelrod is certainly aware of this in principle, as his discussion in chapters 8 and 9 often shows. But I find his remarks on international affairs (e.g., cold war politics; see pp. 186–7) very disturbing. He appears there, at least, to have forgotten the drastic change that the real world of nuclear weapons introduces by altering assumptions f and g above.

Nonetheless, Axelrod's results are intriguing. He invited game theorists to submit strategies for play (in the form of computer programs). These strategies were then run against each other in round-robin tournaments. He reports that

> ... the winner was the simplest of all strategies submitted. This was TIT FOR TAT, the strategy which cooperates on the first move and then does whatever the other player did on the previous move. A second round of the tournament was conducted in which many more entries were submitted by amateurs and professionals alike, all of whom were aware of the results of the first round. The result was another victory for TIT FOR TAT! The analysis of data from these

tournaments reveals four properties which tend to make a decision rule successful: avoidance of unnecessary conflict by cooperating as long as the other player does, provocability in the face of an uncalled for defection by the other, forgiveness after responding to a provocation, and clarity of behavior so that the other player can adapt to your patterns of action. (p. 20)

Understandably, Axelrod speaks of the tit for tat strategy as reciprocity, but it is clear that a variety of strategies with the success properties he describes would warrant that title. Which one would be the 'winner' in real life situations is not clear. For example, it is not clear what the winning strategy would be if (in my terms) resistance to evil were distinguished from retaliation. (Axelrod speaks of each non-cooperative response to non-cooperation as retaliation, and for the context he is addressing that makes sense. But there are other contexts to consider.)

Even so, as circumscribed as Axelrod's experiments were, his analysis of them is very suggestive. In particular, what his results suggest about the evolution (cultural and genetic) of reciprocal behavior confirms and elaborates the account of 'reciprocal altruism' given by some evolutionary biologists. Tit for tat ('reciprocity') is a very robust strategy – i.e., it does well against a wide variety of other rules – and the strategies that exploit its 'weaknesses' do not themselves do very well overall. On the assumption that, over time, the strategies with poor overall results would tend to be abandoned, reciprocity would do better and better overall.

Chapter 3 of Axelrod's book is devoted to an analysis of the 'collective stability' of various strategies – where stability is defined as the ability of a group using a given rule to 'resist invasion' by individuals or groups using another rule. The question is whether, if tit for tat (or some other rule) were in general use among players, what would happen in confrontations with deviant rules – e.g., ones designed to exploit the general pattern of play. Here it is shown that though general adherence to either tit for tat or a totally non-cooperative strategy would be stable when challenged by isolated players, only so-called 'nice rules' (like tit for tat) can resist invasion by groups of players using a different rule. (A 'nice' rule is one that never engages in unprovoked non-cooperation.)

This result is a formal confirmation (under simplifying assumptions) of my arguments in this chapter about 'criminal' and 'free-rider' versions of the reciprocity disposition. Axelrod's Chapter 4, about the system of live and let live reciprocity that occurred for a time along some sections of the front line trenches in World War I, is a striking real world illustration of these matters. It shows reciprocity to be possible, and sustainable, under very adverse conditions. But it also shows that it can be broken down.

Axelrod's Chapter 5, written with biologist W. D. Hamilton, argues that the tit for tat cooperation strategy could get started at the genetic level (among organisms without 'foresight'), even from a circumstance in which complete non-cooperation were the general rule. This game-theoretic formulation is a lucid presentation of the material on evolutionary biology cited elsewhere in these notes.

Chapters 6 and 7 of Axelrod's book give an argument for practicing reciprocity in all sorts of non-zero sum situations. The elegance of the argument is possible only because the controlling assumptions of the analysis have ruled out some important distorting factors (e.g., deception; coercion). And I would argue that the flaw that Axelrod finds in the tit for tat strategy (the sometimes self-perpetuating effect of retaliation) might be somewhat mitigated by the distinction, in practice, between resistance to evil and retaliation for it. Moreover, as I said, I find the effects of the simplifying assumptions most disturbing in Axelrod's discussion of social structure (Chapter 8) and high stakes political behavior (e.g., his comments on retaliation in international affairs, Chapter 9). Still, this game-theoretic defense of reciprocity is extremely valuable. (It should also be said that the book is very clear and very readable.)

In general, theorists have found it much more difficult to give a causal explanation for the development of 'altruistic' behavior – defined as giving without the expectation of reciprocal return – than to give a comparable account of reciprocal behavior. See Lauren Wispé (ed.), *Altruism, Sympathy and Helping* (New York, Academic Press, 1978) for a collection of articles on the topic, approached from fields as diverse as evolutionary biology (E. O. Wilson) and law (John Kaplan).

Ronald Wintrobe, 'Taxing Altruism', *Economic Inquiry* 21 (1983): 255–70 first distinguishes altruism (giving to others that is not conditional upon the expectation of a return) from 'cooperative egoism' (giving in the expectation that the gift will be reciprocated). He then develops an economic model in which the social welfare, 'contagion', and 'survival' properties of the two forms of giving are shown to be quite different, and in which (under some conditions) 'when a community becomes more altruistic, the welfare of everyone in it declines.' (p. 255.) As with most such theories, the central controversy attaches to the assumptions in the model.

In normative ethics the importance of reciprocity has often been asserted – at least if one is willing to treat discussions of requital, proportional justice, duties of gratitude and duties of fair play as aspects of reciprocity. See below under the heading Relevant Philosophical Literature. An obvious connection to religious traditions should also be noted. The centrality of reciprocity to both Confucian and Rabbinic ethics is discussed briefly by Joseph P. Schultz, 'Reciprocity in Confucian and Rabbinic Ethics', *Journal of Religious Ethics* 2 (1974): 143–50. Readers are referred to the *Analects* V:11; XV:36 (in the translation by Legge) in which reciprocity is said to be the one word that may serve as a rule of practice for all of one's life, and to a comparable passage in the late Confucian classic *The Book of Rites*. In Rabbinic sources the norm of reciprocity appears as the notion of giving measure for measure.

There is a line of argument in social anthropology that cautions us to pay attention to the fact that:

> obligations to give, to receive and to return [are] not to be
> understood merely in terms of rational economic principles
> or material self-interest, but also fundamentally in terms of
> underlying cultural premises that provide objects with their
> contexts and significance, and form the basis for construing
> the implications of their passage from one person to another.

See Edward L. Schieffelin, 'Reciprocity and the Construction of Reality', *Man* 15 (1980): 502–17. This is indeed an important reminder, for without attending to it, it is impossible to make sense of the diversity of exchange practices – e.g., in what constitutes a fitting return, when exactly-balanced exchanges are socially desirable, and so forth. It does not follow, however, as Schieffelin suggests it might, that the particular 'structure of cultural thought' in which exchange is embedded is 'logically prior' to exchange. No doubt the particular forms of exchange found in a given culture – the etiquette of it, the substitution-of-goods rules and so forth – are derivative. But the propensity for *some* sort of reciprocal transactions must surely be as primitive as the propensity to develop some sort of self-concept.

James Scott, *The Moral Economy of the Peasant* (New Haven, Yale University Press, 1976), gives an instructive account of the workings of an equal exchange principle in his chapter 6, 'Implications for the Analysis of Exploitation: Reciprocity and Subsistence as Justice.'

It might be thought that the universality of the norm of reciprocity is compromised by evidence about societies that undergo prolonged and severe deprivations of food and effective means of production. Colin Turnbull's striking description of the *Iks* comes to mind: *The Mountain People* (New York, Simon and Schuster, 1972). A careful analysis, however, shows merely a shift in the type of reciprocal exchange in these societies – away, for example, from generalized exchange toward balanced, immediate direct *quid pro quo* transactions. The norm remains, but the forms change. See the study carried out among the *So* people of northeastern Uganda (a tribe living somewhat to the south of, and 'historically and linguistically related to' the *Iks*): Charles D. Laughlin, Jr., 'Deprivation and Reciprocity', *Man* new series 9 (1974): 380–96.

Evolutionary Biology

The material from evolutionary biology that is most relevant to the present study is the work on reciprocal altruism. See Robert L. Trivers, 'The Evolution of Reciprocal Altruism', *Quarterly Review of Biology* 46 (1971): 35–57. That article gives an account of the circumstances under which a genetic predisposition to self-sacrificial behavior would be 'adaptive' for individuals, where what is adaptive is defined as what maximizes inclusive fitness. Inclusive fitness, as that notion was developed by W. D. Hamilton, is a measure of an individual's success in perpetuating its own genes – both by its own reproductive success (Darwinian fitness) and the success of its genetic relatives. See W. D. Hamilton, 'The Genetical Evolution of Social Behaviour', I and II, *Journal of Theoretical Biology* 7 (1964): 1–52. A genetic disposition to maximize inclusive fitness is not equivalent to a disposition to reciprocate, however. There are other behavioral strategies that could express such a genotypic trait – e.g., certain systematic priorities for directly promoting the interests of kin. Of course the presence of behavior that has the effect of maximizing inclusive fitness does not by itself establish that the behavior has a genetic basis, and the problem is complicated further if one finds (as we seem to in the case of our own species) a variety of conflicting behavior patterns, each of which could in principle contribute to inclusive fitness, but none of which quite fits the theory. In human societies, for example, patterns of affiliation sometimes follow genetic lines, but not always. Patterns of reciprocal relationships sometimes conflict with kinship priorities, and so on. The answer from sociobiologists is fair enough: What they are proposing is a genotypic influence on behavior, not a genetic determination of it; we should expect to find only diluted versions of the predicted maximizing behavior, and many cases in which social learning and other environmental factors overwhelm genetic predispositions. That, of course, makes it difficult to distinguish evidence for the genetic influence from evidence against it, except in species (e.g., the social insects) with which scores of generations can be subjected to controlled experiments. Given the unsettled state of the science on this subject, I think it wise to ground my arguments for reciprocity on directly observable behavioral traits rather than inferred genetic ones.

In principle, however, sociobiology could have a significant bearing on moral theory – particularly on a theory of the virtues. If, for example, it can be shown that certain dispositions that we ordinarily call virtues (or vices) are 'hard-wired' into human genotypes, then that would have to enter into the account of what it will take for a being of that type to flourish. It will not by itself *decide* questions about what we ought to do and be (for one thing, genetic engineering is a possibility), but it will help define the considerations relevant to deciding those questions.

Richard D. Alexander, 'The Search for a General Theory of Behavior', *Behavioral Science* 20 (1975): 77–100 gives explicit attention to the connection between Marshall Sahlins's analysis of reciprocity and the concerns of evolutionary biology at pp. 91–5. Alexander also has some interesting suggestions about the selective advantage of not being aware, and not allowing others to become aware, of one's selfish or reciprocity-seeking motives. This, and the

evolutionary account of self-deception generally, have an interesting bearing on the maxim of reciprocity that limits prospective
attention to matters of reciprocation.

Roger D. Masters has explicitly addressed the connection
between evolutionary biology and political philosophy, arguing
that we probably have genetic predispositions suitable to the subtle
interplay of cooperation and competition in the small group interactions characteristic of our hominid ancestors. Cultural changes
– particularly the development of large scale societies – have put
those dispositions under considerable stress. He says:

> It is in this context that political philosophy can be understood
> as a response to the predicament facing human civilization.
> Precisely because the ambiguity of cooperation and
> competition is natural to humans, it is never completely clear
> how we should relate to each other. And because both
> selfishness and altruism have a natural root that has been
> transformed by cultural change, it is rare that political
> institutions are universally acceptable and stable.

Quoted from Roger D. Masters, 'Of Marmots and Men: Animal
Behavior and Human Altruism', in Lauren Wispé (ed.) *Altruism,
Sympathy and Helping* (New York, Academic Press, 1978),
pp. 59–78, at p. 72. Masters' discussion makes plain, however,
how speculative these matters are.

A more recent article by the same author is perhaps even more
appropriate for present purposes. See Roger D. Masters, 'Is
Sociobiology Reactionary? The Political Implications of Inclusive-
Fitness Theory', *Quarterly Review of Biology* 57 (1982): 275–92.
In that article, Masters rejects criticism to the effect that evolutionary biology, as applied to human social behavior, is inherently
biased toward 'conservative' political views. He points out that the
political implications of the theory itself must not be confused with
the political leanings of its advocates, and argues that whatever
political implications the theory has come from its kinship with
various varieties of individualist political theory – varieties he
describes as based on cost-benefit and social contract principles.
Such principles, he points out, have produced both radical and
conservative political theories. Critics who object to the conservative tendencies of individualistic theory are reminded of conservative versions of collectivist theory. Those critics are not likely to

be soothed by Masters' argument, however, since it operates at such a general level, and many of the criticisms and fears about the political implications of sociobiology have to do with its more particular implications with regard to racism, sexism, hierarchical social structure, and aggression.

Reciprocity and Self-Esteem

Emerson, in an essay titled 'Gifts', puts the connection to self-esteem as follows:

> The law of benefits is a difficult channel, which requires careful sailing, or rude boats. It is not the office of a man to receive gifts. How dare you give them? We wish to be self-sustained. We do not quite forgive a giver. The hand that feeds us is in some danger of being bitten. We can receive anything from love, for that is a way of receiving it from ourselves; but not from anyone who assumes to bestow. We sometime hate the meat which we eat, because there seems something of degrading dependence in living by it . . .

See *The Complete Works of Ralph Waldo Emerson*, Volume III (Boston and New York, Houghton, Mifflin and Co., 1903) p. 162. Emerson overstates the case, at least as a general rule, but it is clear enough that reciprocal returns help us avoid the sense of 'degrading dependence', and it is plausible to think that Emerson's remark about love in the quoted passage is also connected to reciprocity. How else could it be that receiving a gift from love 'is a way of receiving it from ourselves'? I am indebted to James Wallace, *Virtues and Vices* (Ithaca, NY., Cornell University Press, 1978) for calling this passage to my attention. Wallace takes it as pointing to the need for tact in one's acts of benevolence. (p. 154) I do not think that would be enough to obviate the difficulty mentioned by Emerson. But Wallace's analysis of the remark about gifts from love almost captures the point. He says we can receive anything from love because:

> the benefactor's concern for the good of the recipient underlines the worth and importance of the beneficiary to the benefactor. The recipient, feeling diminished by his dependence, is reassured by a demonstration of concern *for*

him, an affirmation that he matters. Such concern, of course, is an essential element in kindness, generosity and compassion. Unfortunately, even if a kind and generous person is tactful and makes his motives absolutely clear, a beneficiary may still resent and hate him. (p. 154)

Yes, I would say, exactly in those cases where the beneficiary cannot make an adequate return or cannot believe that the gift is itself, in effect, a proportionate return from the giver. Reciprocity speaks to the situation in a way that benevolence does not. Since I think that reciprocity is a virtue in part because it does sustain self-esteem in this way, I do not agree with Wallace when he continues the passage above by asserting that '[s]uch a response [resentment or hate] reflects poorly on the beneficiary ... and argues a defect in him' (p. 154). I say, not necessarily. It does not argue a defect, for example, if the giver has carelessly put the beneficiary in a position in which reciprocation is impossible.

Note, however, that the social psychological literature on self-esteem raises some complications for moral theory. It is by no means clear what the 'optimal level' of self-esteem is, in part because high self-esteem can inhibit the perception of 'negative information', to the detriment of the individual. The resulting self deception can be either functional or dysfunctional. But the link between lack of self-esteem and depression seems solid. See, for a review and references to the literature, Victor Gecas, 'The Self Concept' in Ralph H. Turner and James F. Short, Jr., *Annual Review of Sociology* 8 (1982): 1–33 at pp. 20–3.

Elements of the Disposition

Robert Axelrod, *The Evolution of Cooperation* (New York, Basic Books, 1984), on the basis of his experiments with and analyses of strategies for coping with iterated prisoners' dilemmas, proposes some maxims as guidance for people who confront analogous dilemmas in real life. (See my fuller comments above on his book.) The maxims he proposes are:
1   Don't be envious.
2   Don't be the first to defect.
3   Reciprocate both cooperation and defection.
4   Don't be too clever. (p. 110)

These maxims have an obvious similarity to some of the maxims of reciprocity, but it is notable, first, that Axelrod does not distinguish resistance to evil from retaliation, and does not give detailed discussion to matters of fittingness, proportionality, scope, and obligatoriness. This is not due to any failure of imagination on his part, but rather to the structure of prisoners' dilemmas. Reciprocity operates in a much broader range of circumstances.

One difficulty with the massive empirical literature on reciprocity is the lack of agreement about important elements of the disposition. Leaving aside discussions that concern 'reciprocals' (i.e., complements), one still finds disagreement about whether reciprocal transactions are those that are made 'in kind', are part of an agent's rational self-maximizing strategy, are exactly balanced *quid pro quo* exchanges, and so on. This has led at least one writer to suggest that anthropologists abandon the term, or at least use it with great restraint. See Geoffrey MacCormack, 'Reciprocity', *Man* 11 (1976): 89–103.

My argument is a normative one, in support of a particular version of the reciprocity disposition. Much of the descriptive work (especially the work in behavioral and social psychology) uses somewhat different definitions, but the following is nonetheless of interest if used carefully.

Laboratory experiments done by social psychologists suggest that behavior in accord with the norm of reciprocity is distinct from 'economic' or rational self-maximizing conduct. Reciprocation occurs in contexts where subjects have no rational expectation of gain, and it varies directly with the subjects' perception that the 'prior help' (for which reciprocation is to be made) was given voluntarily. See Richard E. Goranson and Leonard Berkowitz, 'Reciprocity and Responsibility Reactions to Prior Help', *Journal of Personality and Social Psychology* 3 (1966): 227–32, and Esther R. Greenglass, 'Effects of Prior Help and Hindrance on Willingness to Help Another', *Journal of Personality and Social Psychology* 11 (1969): 224–31.

Ervin Staub, *Positive Social Behavior and Morality*, Volume 1 (New York, Academic Press, 1978), Chapter 8 summarizes the social psychological evidence on reciprocal exchanges, and aptly notes the fact that most of the research he reports has concerned helping behavior in 'minimal relationships' (p. 335) – i.e., situations in which the interactions observed were brief exchanges, or the parties involved had only brief exposure to each other. He notes, by comparison, that studies of reciprocal behavior among friends show less concern for immediate, *quid pro quo* exchanges, and more attempts to initiate exchange in an effort to sustain reciprocal relationships (p. 369).

Studies of the cognitive, motor, and affective development of blind infants provide fascinating evidence of the importance of reciprocal exchanges. See, for example, Selma Fraiberg, *Insights from the Blind: Comparative Studies of Blind and Sighted Infants* (New York, Basic Books, 1977), especially Chapter VI. See also H. Als, E. Tronick, and T. B. Brazelton, 'Affective Reciprocity and the Development of Autonomy: The Study of a Blind Infant', *The Journal of Child Psychiatry* 19 (1980): 22–40 which describes the step by step development, through reciprocal exchanges with adults, of a blind infant. And an earlier, more striking paper by Lauren Adamson, together with Als, Tronick and Brazelton, describes the early development of a sighted infant born to blind parents: 'The Development of Social Reciprocity between a Sighted Infant and Her Blind Parents', *Journal of Child Psychiatry* 16 (1977): 194–207. In that case, the mother, who had been blind from birth, characteristically failed to orient her body (and especially her face) toward the infant during play, bathing and feeding activities. The infant, initially quite disturbed by this, soon 'reciprocated'. She imitated her mother's averted gaze and unusual body postures in *their* interactions, while remaining eager for face to face encounters with sighted adults.

'Following' a norm of reciprocity is one thing, but becoming aware of it as a norm is another. See Thomas J. Berndt, 'Lack of Acceptance of Reciprocity Norms in Preschool Children', *Developmental Psychology* 15 (1979): 662–3 for an indication of recent research.

As mentioned, one of the problems with the social psychological literature on reciprocity is that of definition. In one painstakingly conducted study of the development of friendships among children, for example, the notion of reciprocity was used to refer to immediate exchanges *in kind* – e.g., a joke for a joke, or piece of gossip for a piece of gossip, fantasy for fantasy. See John Mordechai Gottman, *How Children Become Friends* (Monograph published by the University of Chicago Press for the Society of Research in Child Development, 1983). There was some positive correlation to the success of friendship development, but it was not uniform across the dimensions of the interactions measured. The same author's study of marital relationships reports that dissatisfied couples showed higher levels of *both* 'negative affect' *and* 'positive affect' reciprocity than did satisfied couples. See J. M. Gottman, *Marital Interaction: Experimental Investigations* (New York, Academic Press, 1979). The author concludes that we should be very careful about assuming that well-functioning relationships are necessarily characterized by positive reciprocity. See pp. 28–9 of *How Children Become Friends*. Another study, which defined reciprocity in terms of adherence to a *quid pro quo* attitude ('exchange orientation') toward interactions in relationships found that such adherence was correlated positively with satisfaction levels among roommates, but negatively with satisfaction among married couples. See Bernard I. Murstein, Mary Cerreto, and Marcia G. MacDonald, 'A Theory and Investigation of the Effect of Exchange-Orientation on Marriage and Friendship', *Journal of Marriage and the Family* 39 (1977): 543–8. Such studies give empirical support for the contention in these pages that a return *in kind* is not a necessary feature of productive social exchanges. And the studies on family vs. friends give support to the point made about 'bookkeeping', or 'reciprocity accounting' developed in Chapter Six. Intuitively, they also support the notion that the reciprocity disposition should include only the notion of retrospective obligation. Unfortunately, however, they do not directly address the notion of reciprocity defined here – the return of good for good (not necessarily in kind), the refusal to return evil for evil, and so on.

In an interesting study by Israeli social psychologists, it was found that people's perception of a needy person's interest in helping others correlated significantly with their willingness to help that person, and that this sort of 'reciprocity arousal' dominated the variable of social status. (Previous studies had shown people to be more willing to help others as the others' perceived social status increased.) See Yoel Yinon, *et al.*, 'The Reciprocity-Arousing Potential of the Requester's Occupation and Helping Behavior', *Journal of Applied Social Psychology* 11 (1981): 252–8.

It has sometimes been suggested that studies purporting to confirm the norm of reciprocity may confound two notions: truly reciprocal exchanges, in which donors give because they have received prior help; and cases of aid-giving triggered simply by the donor's perception of the recipient's need. The latter sort of case suggests what might be called a norm of social responsibility. For a study designed to separate the two notions – and which confirmed the pervasiveness of reciprocity but not responsibility – see L. Krishnan and D. W. Carment, 'Reactions to Help: Reciprocity, Responsibility and Reactance', *European Journal of Social Psychology* 9 (1979): 435–9.

For a review of the literature in the area of social psychology called 'equity theory', see 'Equity and Social Justice' by Elaine Walster and G. William Walster in *The Journal of Social Issues* 31 (1975): 21–44. Equity, in that context, is roughly what is meant by reciprocity in these pages, though it seems to include retaliation. Note the Walsters' remarks about retaliation and self esteem (pp. 22–4). The effort to make and seek restitution is commonly observed in the studies surveyed (p. 23). But so, of course, are efforts to deny responsibility (pp. 23–4).

For an alarmed reaction to U.S. foreign trade proposals based on the notion of reciprocity (with protectionist trading patterns) see Keith A. J. Hay and B. Andrei Sulzenko, 'U.S. Trade Policy and "Reciprocity"', *Journal of World Trade Law* 16 (1982): 471–9. The alarm is based on the argument that such a policy (particularly if it includes retaliation) would throw existing world trade arrangements into disarray, to no one's advantage. But most of the problem would be caused, it seems, by elements explicitly excluded from the concept of reciprocity used here: An insistence on returns in kind, equated to benefits rather than sacrifices, and including retaliation.

On Proportionality and Retrospective Obligation

Consider this passage from Marshall Sahlins' essay 'On the Sociology of Primitive Exchange' in his *Stone Age Economics* (New York, Aldine, 1972), p. 223.

> The casual received view of reciprocity supposes some fairly direct one-for-one exchange, balanced reciprocity, or a near approximation of balance. [But] . . . in the main run of primitive societies . . . balanced reciprocity it not the prevalent form of exchange. A question might even be raised about the

> stability of balanced reciprocity. [It] . . . may tend toward self-liquidation. On one hand, a series of honorably balanced dealings between comparatively distant parties builds trust and confidence, in effect reduces social distance, and so increases the chance for more generalized future dealings. . . . On the other hand, a renege acts to sever relations . . . [and leads toward 'negative' reciprocity]. May we conclude that balanced reciprocity is inherently unstable? Or perhaps that it requires special conditions for continuity?

Criticism, to the effect that negative, balanced and generalized reciprocity can all characterize 'close' relationships – given suitably different cultural traditions – may be found in Sally Price, 'Reciprocity and Social Distance: A Reconsideration', *Ethnology* 17 (1980): 339–50. Gloria Wentowski, 'Reciprocity and the Coping Strategies of Older People', *The Gerontologist* 21 (1981): 600–9, describes a two year study of 50 people (mean age 71) in terms of the reciprocal exchanges that help them build and sustain networks of helpers. The author notes pointedly that *immediate*, exactly balanced exchanges are often used to keep people at arm's length, whereas deferred (balanced) exchange builds continuing relationships (p. 604).

For a review of experimental work on the substitutability of various sorts of resources used in reciprocal exchanges, see Edna B. Foa and Uriel G. Foa, 'Resource Theory: Interpersonal Behavior as Exchange', in Kenneth J. Gergen, Martin S. Greenberg and Richard H. Willis, eds., *Social Exchange* (New York, Plenum Press, 1980).

Relevant Philosophical Literature

Many philosophers have mentioned the importance of reciprocity, connecting it to notions of equity, requital, gratitude, fairness and justice. But few of these mentions amount to arguments of use here. Notable exceptions are the following:

Aristotle, in Books VIII and IX of the *Nichomachean Ethics*, discusses friendship in terms of mutual awareness of reciprocal good will, and reciprocal exchanges. He holds that stability in a friendship depends on the preservation of a sort of equal exchange. Among equals, in 'perfect' friendships, the exchanges are absolutely equal (see 1156 b). Among unequals, the exchange operates by a rule of proportionality. See 1162b–1163b. He also argues that in cases where friends disagree about what constitutes an adequate return, the first recipient should be the one to decide: 'For if the giver receives in exchange an amount equal to the advantage which has come to the recipient or the amount the recipient would have given for the pleasure, he will have the equivalent return from the recipient.' (1164b)

These two books of the *Nichomachean Ethics* are a rich source of observations about how social relations may be sustained. Many of the details (how people are likely to feel about this or that) are culture bound, but the fundamental aspects of the sorts of exchanges Aristotle discusses are of general applicability.

The connection between notions of fair play and gratitude, on the one hand, and obligations to reciprocate (particularly political obligations) should also be noted. Plato's *Crito* is, of course, the classic source. See the analysis, and accompanying translation by A. D. Woozley, *Law and Obedience* (Chapel Hill, N.C., University of North Carolina Press, 1979); Richard Flathman has a careful discussion of the issue in his book *Political Obligation* (New York, Atheneum, 1972). A more recent and extended consideration may be found in A. John Simmons, *Moral Principles and Political Obligation* (Princeton, N.J., Princeton University Press, 1979), Chapters V and VII. For a useful bibliographic essay on this topic, see Mario Morelli, 'The Fairness Principle', *Philosophy and Law Newsletter* (published by the American Philosophical Association), Spring, 1985, pp. 2–4.

The notion of fair play, or doing one's share, has been used to discuss the obligations people might have to contribute to joint enterprises from which they have benefited and in which they are in some sense participants. The notion of gratitude is used to discuss the obligations people might have to make returns (of appreciative affect and acts) to those who have intentionally benefited them. On fair play, see first H. L. A. Hart, 'Are There Any Natural Rights?' *The Philosophical Review* 64 (1955): 175–91; and John Rawls, 'Legal Obligation and the Duty of Fair Play', in Sidney Hook (ed.), *Law and Philosophy* (New York, New York University Press, 1964), pp. 3–18. Then for criticism, see Robert Nozick, *Anarchy, State and Utopia* (New York, Basic Books, 1974), Chapter V, and Simmons, *op. cit.*, Chapter V.

Richard Arneson, 'The Principle of Fairness and the Free-Rider Problem', *Ethics* 92 (1982): 616–33, gives a valuable criticism of Nozick on this topic, and argues for a 'revised' principle of fairness, as follows:

> . . . where a scheme of cooperation is established that supplies a collective benefit that is worth its cost to each recipient, where the burdens of cooperation are fairly divided, where it is unfeasible to attract voluntary compliance to the scheme via supplementary private benefits, and where the collective benefit is either voluntarily accepted or such that voluntary acceptance of it is impossible, those who contribute their assigned fair share of the costs of the scheme have a right, against the remaining beneficiaries, that they should also pay their fair share. (p. 623)

Arneson's contention is that a justification of Lockean property rights likely to be acceptable to Nozick will also justify the revised principle. He goes on to suggest that people who accept a more liberal account of Good Samaritan obligations than libertarian writers allow will also have reason to accept the revised principle.

On gratitude, one may profitably begin with Plato's *Crito*, and A. D. Woozley's commentary on it. Sidgwick has illuminating, but brief, discussions of gratitude, both in Book III (Intuitionism) and in Book IV (Utilitarianism) of *The Methods of Ethics* 7th Edition [1907] (Chicago, University of Chicago Press, 1962). By gratitude Sidgwick means 'requital' of unbought benefits – 'a settled disposition to repay the benefit in whatever way one can on a fitting opportunity' (p. 437) – typically accompanied by the 'special affection' called gratitude. He finds such a principle endorsed by both Common Sense and Utility. His views on the psychological complexity of the disposition (p. 438) are especially rewarding. He makes the point that we often give without clear expectation of return, but that this is not inconsistent with having a 'vague trust that requital will not be withheld.' Sidgwick's analysis of common intuitions about gratitude and requital is characteristically subtle and adept (pp. 260–1). He finds, however, 'no clear accepted principle' upon which the appropriate amount and form of the return can be decided (p. 261). That is, of course, one more reason for taking the task of moral theory to be more than explicative.

Simmons, *op. cit.*, Chapter VIII, gives further references on this topic.

Kant makes two remarks of interest on the topic of gratitude. (It must be admitted that they are interesting largely because it was Kant who made them.) They may be found in *The Metaphysics of Morals*, Part II, Sections 32–4 (Indianapolis, Bobbs-Merrill, 1964). One is to the effect that gratitude is a duty, not a maxim of prudence. The reasoning seems to be that the importance of gratitude comes from the fact that it promotes benevolence, but that to return a benefit for the purpose of getting even more from particular benefactors is to treat them as means, not ends in themselves. The other remark of interest is the observation that there is a sense in which an act of pure benevolence can never be fully requited, since the initiator of the exchange always deserves some extra (moral?) credit for being first. As a comment about people's psychological reactions to the receipt of benefits, the remark is shrewd. (The response to 'I love you' is always a little lame. I love you too?) But I can find no reasoned basis for saying that the initiator deserves more moral credit than the reciprocator. Both may act selfishly or altruistically, for example. And even the supposed psychological advantage largely disappears when the reciprocation is managed imaginatively. (Delayed, for example.)

But all of the above work on obligation is of mostly indirect relevance here. None of it – indeed, none that I know of – deals directly with the virtue-theoretic issues at stake in my arguments. Instead, it deals directly with obligatory acts. Its question is not 'Ought I be *disposed* to reciprocate?' but simply 'Am I obligated to reciprocate?' Those who argue in favor of the obligation typically mention the utility that acts of reciprocation have – e.g., in securing other people's continued benevolence (in the case of gratitude), and sustaining cooperative enterprises (in the case of fair play). Those who argue against the obligation typically do the following: They argue (via examples) that it is counterintuitive to suppose that benefactors can create obligations at will by forcing, or dumping, unasked for benefits on others. Restrictions can of course be put on the principles of fair play and gratitude so as to rule out these counterintuitive cases, but then it begins to look as though these principles either define supererogatory acts or collapse into principles about promising, consenting, accepting and so forth.

The sticking point of all of these arguments against reciprocity is the issue of having an obligation to reciprocate for benefits one has merely *received*, rather than accepted. It is my contention that the virtue-theoretic argument for reciprocity avoids the standard difficulties, and I have argued these points in the text. But it may be useful to put them in the context of some recent discussion. To wit:

In Chapter V of *Anarchy, State and Utopia*, Robert Nozick gives a series of counterexamples designed to embarrass the principle of fair play – i.e., the notion that one is obligated to do one's fair share in supporting practices and institutions from which one has received benefits. John Simmons, in Chapter V of *Moral Principles and Political Obligations* accepts the force of Nozick's examples as against the notion that people who merely 'receive' benefits are thereby obligated to reciprocate. He thinks it would be absurd to conclude that such obligations exist. (Cf. Arneson's arguments to the contrary, cited above.) Simmons argues, however, that there is a sense in which one can 'accept' a benefit which 1) is distinct from consenting to the practice or institution that produced it, and 2) generates an obligation, out of an elementary notion of fairness, to do one's part.

As should be evident from the arguments of this chapter, I disagree with Simmons about what Nozick's examples show. Those examples all involve what is taken to be an intuitively apprehended wrong involved in the demand that a person reciprocate for benefits merely received rather than actually accepted. I say 'intuitively apprehended' because the judgment that reciprocation is wrong is not shown to follow from some independently established principle, but rather is something we are supposed to concede simply from contemplating the facts of the cases. Those cases are of roughly the following sorts: 1) Dubious benefits are forced on unwilling participants. 2) Genuine benefits are forced on unwilling participants. 3) Genuine benefits (appreciated in retrospect) are thrust on people without their prior knowledge. 4) Genuine benefits are produced accidently by malicious conduct. 5) Genuine benefits are produced from which the recipient cannot be excluded – even though the benefactors would exclude the recipient if they could. (They are, perhaps, enemies who have produced a public good.) I have considered some of these sorts of cases explicitly, and the line of argument I would take against them all is clear. It is this: Assume, for the sake of argument, that reciprocity does dispose us to return these benefits. Then the next question will be one of fittingness and proportionality. That question is answered, in each case, by considering the sort of act(s) that produced the benefit, the value of the benefit, the level of sacrifice various returns would entail, and so forth. Returns are then to be matched to the type and size of the benefit. But it is clear that reciprocity will itself prohibit us from making some of these fitting and proportional returns. It will, for example, prohibit us from retaliating for malicious acts which (accidentally) benefit us. And it will give no support for returning good for dubious goods received. Further, moral theory under the general conception requires that our acts of reciprocation be generalizable. It may well be that a *fitting* response in some of these cases (e.g., forcing benefits, in return, on unwilling people) is not generalizable *given the aims of reciprocity*. I would argue – indeed have argued – that most of the supposed counterexamples disappear under this sort of scrutiny.

The ones that remain (e.g., the supposed unfairness of an obligation to reciprocate for benefits one is merely 'born into') are handled by virtue-theoretic arguments. How *should* we be disposed to respond to such benefits, if not by reciprocity? I suggest that moral argument will answer that the reciprocity disposition in these cases is fully justifiable.

There is a valuable article by Allan Gibbard, 'Human Evolution and the Sense of Justice' in Peter A. French, Theodore E. Uehling, Jr., and Howard K. Wettstein (eds.) *Midwest Studies in Philosophy*, Volume VII (Minneapolis, University of Minnesota Press, 1982) pp. 31–46. In that essay, Gibbard considers what sort of 'sense of justice', if any, it is plausible to suppose might have evolved through the mechanisms of kin-selection and/or individual selection as those notions are currently understood. He regards such accounts as highly speculative, but argues that the most plausible one would be based on the connection between individual selection and reciprocity, rather than kin-selection and benevolence. The sense of justice so evolved would, he thinks, be a 'flexible' one 'subject to the formation of consensus' about what specific sorts of outcomes are 'fair' or 'just'. (p. 42) That is, what is likely to have evolved is the disposition to develop, and resolve bargaining conflicts in terms of, shared standards or concepts of justice. The 'sense' of justice, then, would be the disposition (with concomitant sentiments) to find such resolution (in terms of shared standards) satisfying or acceptable. Given a heterogeneous, complex, large, and swiftly changing society, however, there might now be relatively little purchase for such a vague 'sense' of justice, taken alone. Nonetheless,

> It will not do simply to give up the concept of justice. Shared standards of justice, if they exist, can stabilize the outcomes of bargaining situations in complex societies, as they can in small, homogeneous societies – to the mutual benefit of all. Once we realize that, it seems to me, the reasonable course is to try to resolve our uncertainties and disagreements as to what justice demands by looking to our reasons, apart from a concern with justice, for wanting to maintain shared standards of justice. Our sense of justice itself . . . will make a poor oracle. Knowing what benefits shared standards of justice can produce, however, we may enlist the human sense of justice in the service of our benevolent concerns. (p. 43)

Fred Berger, in his article 'Gratitude', *Ethics* 85 (1975): 298–309, asserts that

> . . . while some form of reciprocation [for benevolence] is requisite, this need not be, and often *ought not to be*, the giving of the same or an equivalent benefit to the grantor. Not only is this not always possible, but sometimes it would destroy the force of the original gift. . . . [I]t can be an insult to return it or to show that we feel obligated to make a like return. . . . It is one thing to show that we think we owe a sign of appreciation; it is quite another thing to show we think we owe a gift in return. (pp. 302–3)

In my view this sort of observation indicates the complexity of the *fittingness* problem, not the inappropriateness of reciprocity. It may be that the fitting return is comparable benevolence to third parties. In any case, reciprocity is not meant as a *substitute* for gratitude. (Nor, as Berger notes, can gratitude be an adequate substitute for reciprocity. See p. 303.)

In addition to the literature just discussed, readers may wish to explore some of the recent work on restitution. See especially Randy Barnett, 'Restitution: A New Paradigm of Criminal Justice,' *Ethics* 87 (1977): 279–301; and Margaret R. Holmgren, 'Punishment as Restitution: The Rights of the Community', *Criminal*

Justice Ethics 2 (1983): 36–49. And on another aspect of reciprocity, see Joseph Kupfer, 'Sexual Perversion and the Good', *The Personalist* (1978) 59: 70–7. Kupfer argues that '[v]arious patterns of sexual behavior and relationships are perverse because they generate tendencies which compete with and undermine good habits' (p. 72). The relevant good habits are responsivity, risk-taking and reciprocity (p. 72), but '[r]eciprocity is the central relation missing in paradigms of perversion' (p. 74). The test for whether a non-reciprocal activity such as masturbation is a perversion is the extent to which engaging in it undermines the capacity for entering into reciprocal relationships. That is an empirical matter, both in an individual case (It is perverting *him*.) and in general (It is perverse.) (p. 75). The general line of argument used by Kupfer is applicable to discussions of virtues and vices *per se*, and has interesting similarities to the one used here.

Donald Regan, in *Utilitarianism and Co-Operation* (Oxford, Clarendon Press, 1980) argues for a version of utilitarianism in which 'what each agent ought to do is to *co-operate, with whoever else is co-operating, in the production of the best consequences possible given the behavior of non-cooperators*' (p. 124). Regan's argument is that his is the most satisfactory version of utilitarian theory – and he consequently says very little in defense of utilitarianism as such. Still, his argument is not merely an interscholastic one. Non-utilitarians will profit from it. And there are some similarities to the maxims of reciprocity here. (Just to the maxims, however, Regan's approach is not virtue-theoretic.) Specifically, the similarity is in the notion of cooperating *with those who are doing likewise*. Regan says, in discussing practice, 'the proper question about which behaviour of other agents to take into account is not "When?" . . . The proper question is "Whose?".' (p. 206)

Derek Parfit, *Reasons and Persons* (Oxford, Oxford University Press, 1984), Chapter 1, discusses 'self-effacing' moral theories – ones that recommend that agents develop, as a means to achieving the aims of theory, beliefs or dispositions counter to the precepts of theory. He also considers ways in which theories may be indirectly self-defeating and still be coherent. These matters are a central concern of virtue theory, and Parfit's remarks on them, while terse, are helpful. His review of prisoners' dilemmas in Chapter 2 is also to the point. It confirms, I think, the point that virtue theoretic solutions to these dilemmas are possible.

Michael Ignatieff, *The Needs of Strangers* (New York, Viking, 1984) argues that if we focus on what humans *need* (in order to flourish), we will find much of the debate between liberals and socialists to be misplaced. His concerns are more properly described as being about mutual aid than about reciprocity, but they are relevant nonetheless.

Acknowledgments

A small portion of the material in this chapter was published in my article 'Reciprocity and Social Obligation', *Pacific Philosophical Quarterly* 64 (1980): 411–21. I thank the editors for permission to reprint those paragraphs.

The objections developed and answsered in this chapter owe a great deal to discussion with Richard Arneson, Charlotte Becker, Paul Brest, Richard Flathman, Joel Kidder and Murray Schwartz. In particular, Joel Kidder raised the issue of entrepreneurial 'gifts', and other members of the audience at the Syracuse University philosophy department colloquium, where I first tried out some of these arguments in 1978, pressed the issue of undeserving benefactors. Paul Brest and Richard Flathman raised questions about well-intentioned but clumsy or reluctant benefactors. Murray Schwartz pressed the point about the potential vacuousness of the non-retaliation rule. Richard Arneson raised the issue of preserving a place for 'pure gifts', and Charlotte Becker made criticisms of several versions of the sections on fittingness and proportionality. Those sections, together with the one on returning good for good received, were read at colloquia at the California Institute of Technology, Stanford University, the Virginia Philosophical Association, and the University of Pennsylvania. I am grateful to participants in those discussions for helpful suggestions.

On reciprocity generally, discussions with Ellen Messer have been particularly useful. In 1975, Robert Trivers pointed me in the direction of relevant work in evolutionary biology, and more recently Richard Wrangham pressed me to consider that work more carefully. Discussions on these topics with Marcus Feldman and Christopher Peacocke were very helpful. In 1977, my colleague William Nye gave me invaluable bibliographic advice. Frances Horowitz, Gloria Liederman and Robert Scott provided bibliography on reciprocity in infant and childhood behavior. Laurence

Thomas has, for several years, been generous with both bibliography and argument on moral psychology.

Related Virtues

The discussion in this chapter is merely a summary of some matters that follow more or less directly from the arguments of Chapter Three. I have not approached these topics through the work of others or attempted myself to bring each of these related virtues into the foreground for independent analysis. Doubtless that would have been illuminating for other purposes, but it would have been distracting here. One of the difficulties with discussions of the virtues is the nomenclature. If the focus is gratitude, elements of empathy and reciprocity tend to get packed into the same frame. If the focus is practical wisdom, matters of temperance and self-control tend to get included. Tracing out all these connections and trying to construct a coherent typology of the virtues in terms of which the work of Plato and Aristotle, Augustine and Aquinas, Butler and Hume, Mill and Sidgwick, Wallace and MacIntyre can all be profitably cross-referenced is a task for another time. (And for a mind that is more learned, patient and scholarly than mine.) I note here simply those works or passages thereof, beyond the ones noted for the relevant sections of Chapters Two and Three, that I found particularly useful for the limited task at hand.

First I acknowledge with gratitude my debt to L. A. Kosman, for an afternoon's conversation in which he steered me back once more to Aristotle's ethics, and (for the first time) to some of the best recent work on it. Some of that work, and references to much more, may be found in Amelie Oksenberg Rorty (ed), *Essays on Aristotle's Ethics* (Berkeley, University of California Press, 1980).

Second, there is the richly detailed and rewarding work on the Greek notion of temperance or self-control: Helen North, *Sophrosyne* (Ithaca, Cornell University Press, 1966).

Third, some of the reflections in this chapter were prompted – often into widely divergent paths – by the following: On practical intelligence, Aristotle, *Nichomachean Ethics*, Book VI, esp.

1140–5. Also the comment thereupon by Alasdair MacIntyre, *After Virtue* (London, Duckworth, 1981) pp. 143–5. Also from MacIntyre, *After Virtue*, the following passages:

> ... What we have to learn from heroic societies is twofold: first that all morality is always to some degree tied to the socially local and particular and that the aspirations of the morality of modernity to a universality freed from all particularity is an illusion; and secondly, there is no way to possess the virtues except as part of a tradition in which we inherit them and our understanding of them from a series of predecessors in which series heroic societies hold first place. (p. 119)
>
> I take it that the difference between the heroic account of the virtues and the Sophoclean amounts precisely to a difference over what narrative form captures best the central characteristics of human life and agency. This suggests an hypothesis: that generally to adopt a stance on the virtues will be to adopt a stance on the narrative character of human life. ... If a human life is understood as a progress through harms and dangers, moral and physical, which someone may encounter and overcome. ... the virtues will [be] those qualities the possession and exercise of which generally tend to success in this enterprise and the vices likewise as qualities which likewise tend to failure. Each human life will then embody a story whose shape and form will depend upon what is counted as a harm and danger and upon how success and failure, progress and its opposite, are understood and evaluated. (p. 135)

James D. Wallace, *Virtues and Vices* (Ithaca, N.Y., Cornell University Press, 1978) has a discussion of the virtues of conscientiousness (Chapter IV) that is instructive. He says 'Honesty, truthfulness, fairness, and being a person of one's word [by contrast] to kindness and generosity, are commitments to forms of behavior rather than concerns for the happiness, security and comfort of other people.' (p. 90) He calls those traits of character that focus in a certain way upon the observance of forms of behavior *conscientiousness.* (p. 90) And he goes on to show how such traits contribute to the resolution of n-person prisoners' dilemma situations (Hobbes situations). I expect that reciprocity, in Wallace's terms, would be a virtue of conscientiousness.

Wallace discusses generosity under the heading of benevolence (Chapter V), and his discussion of compassion under that same heading has some affinity to what I call empathy. He distinguishes a class of obligatory acts of giving from obligatory (reciprocal) exchanges, and provides a thoughtful account of why generosity is a virtue. The following remark, in particular, is illuminating:

> . . . the fact that a trait is generally useful and agreeable to the possessor and to others is not sufficient to make it a virtue.
> . . . In order for a trait to be a virtue, it must tend to foster good human life in fundamental ways. It must be the perfection of a tendency or capacity that connects and interlocks with a variety of human goods in such a way that its removal from our lives would endanger that whole structure. (p. 153)

On my own view, that is too restrictive a notion of virtue, but the argument I make for reciprocity and its related virtues certainly is to the effect that they are virtues in Wallace's stringent sense.

L. A. Kosman, 'Being Properly Affected: Virtues and Feelings in Aristotle's Ethics.' in Rorty, *op. cit.*, pp. 103–6 argues that for Aristotle, virtue is not only a set of dispositions to act in certain ways but a set of dispositions to feel certain emotions, in certain ways, to certain degrees. That seems correct, not only about Aristotle, but about any plausible account of the virtues. That is explicitly acknowledged in the present chapter, and (mostly by implication) in Chapter Three as well.

Nel Noddings, *Caring: A Feminine Approach to Ethics* (Berkeley, University of California Press, 1984) argues against an ethic of principle and in favor of an ethic developed from and controlled by the sentiment of caring. Her evocation of the importance of this sentiment stands as an implicit rebuke to any ethic that tries to proceed without giving feelings a central place in moral conduct. I would, however, assign sentiments to virtues, and treat caring as one among many important elements of moral theory.

Lawrence A. Blum, *Friendship, Altruism and Morality* (London, Routledge & Kegan Paul, 1980) is also intriguing. Blum's focus is on the 'altruistic emotions' of sympathy, compassion and human concern. His object is to counter what he calls the Kantian view of the moral status of these emotions, to discuss friendship as a context in which the altruistic emotions play a fundamental role, and to say something about the connection between those emotions and the virtues. Blum is reluctant to take a firmly virtue-theoretic approach in these matters because he senses in such an approach an inhibition to consider possibilities for changes in our attitudes and behavior (pp. 204–7). I disagree, in part because I think the emotions are themselves partly the products of learned dispositions. An adequate account of them will *have* to be virtue-theoretic, no matter what unfortunate inhibitions that raises. But since such an account will emphasize learning, it will not *necessarily* inhibit our consideration of possibilities for change. And it will certainly secure the point – one that Blum is concerned to make against the Kantian view of emotions – that these elements of moral life are *not* necessarily capricious, unpredictable, or unreliable. (Or rather, it will secure the point that when these elements of a given individual's emotional responses *are* capricious, they are 'insufficient' or 'inadequate'. See his Chapter II.) Virtue theory gives us a powerful way of articulating these important matters.

Lester H. Hunt, 'Generosity', *American Philosophical Quarterly* 12 (1975): 235–44, gives a useful exploration of the concept of generosity as it is reflected in ordinary speech.

Virtue, Social Structure, and Obligations

The issue that requires comment in this chapter is the connection between virtue theory and social structures, and there it is primarily the empirical hypotheses that need attention. I shall, accordingly, concentrate my systematic efforts in these notes on the empirical matters, and give only a scanty set of references to philosophical work in moral psychology.

Socialization Theory

Ervin Staub, *Positive Social Behavior and Morality*, volume 2: Socialization and Development (New York, Academic Press, 1979) provides an extensive and useful review of the research findings on the way children are socialized toward norms of sharing, helping, caring, and acting reciprocally. Most of the existing research has focused on the effects of parental discipline, direct instruction by way of precepts, role models, and role playing. Less work has been done on what Staub calls 'natural socialization' – the effect on agents of their own participation in social structures and the environment. Staub is convinced that this is the heart of the matter: 'Learning is primarily the result of the experience of, or participation in, an activity.' (p. 215) The roles people play in that activity (whether assigned or chosen), the rules of the activity (both implicit and explicit), and the successes people have are all important factors in the socialization process. (See pp. 215–16). Staub also gives a useful summary of the material on reciprocity. See Chapter 8 of volume 1 of this work.

David A. Goslin (ed.) *Handbook of Socialization Theory and Research* (Chicago, Rand McNally, 1969) provides a large and varied body of material against which to test the acceptability of the hypotheses in this chapter. There are over 600 pages on theoretical perspectives alone, ranging from an evolutionary approach, to social learning theory, to acculturation theories, to psychoanalytic theory, to a cognitive developmental approach. My hypotheses, while they have some of the flavor of social learning and acculturation theories (and no explicit trace of evolutionary, psychoanalytic or cognitive-development theories) are not meant to take a position on those fundamental theoretical issues. There is a great deal that is agreed upon among these theorists, after all, and my hypotheses are merely meant to capture some of that in a way that is useful for virtue-theoretic arguments. The articles in the theory section of the *Handbook* that I found especially pertinent to my purposes are Albert Bandura, 'Social Learning Theory of Identificatory Processes', pp. 213–62; Justin Aronfreed, 'The Concept of Internalization', pp. 263–324; and Lawrence Kohlberg, 'Stage and Sequence: The Cognitive-Developmental Approach to Socialization' pp. 347–480. The article by Robert A. Scott, 'The Socialization of Blind Children', pp. 1025–46 may be studied profitably in conjunction with the material on blind infants and reciprocity cited in the notes to Chapter Three. For a coherent overview of the field, see Edward Zigler and Irwin K. Child, 'Socialization' in Gardner Lindzey and Elliot Aronson (eds.) *Handbook of Social Psychology* 2nd Edition (Reading, Mass, Addison Wesley, 1969), volume 3, pp. 450–589.

A more recent review article, also useful for present purposes, is Jeylan T. Mortimer and Roberta G. Simmons, 'Adult Socialization', in Ralph H. Turner, James Coleman, and Renée C. Fox (eds.) *Annual Review of Sociology* 4 (1978): 421–54, especially at pp. 429–32, where theoretical perspectives on socialization are organized somewhat differently. Role theory (which stresses the adoption of norms and attitudes appropriate to the roles defined by the social setting), identification theory (which stresses the power of identification with a role model), and so-called generalization theory (which stresses the generalization of 'successful' strategies from one social setting to another) are all directly congruent with the hypotheses described in the present chapter. Two other approaches (symbolic interactionism and exchange theory) give a more central place to the intentions of the agent in a sort of self-socialization process. For a study that explicitly tested role theory with respect to the internalization of attitudes, see Seymour Lieberman, 'The Effects of Changes in Roles on the Attitudes of Role Occupants' in Harold Proshansky and Bernard Seidenberg (eds.),

Basic Studies in Social Psychology (New York, Holt, Rinehart & Winston, 1965) pp. 485–93.

For a polemical, but readable and well argued account of socio-logical theories about the process of becoming deviant, see David Matza, *Becoming Deviant* (Englewood Cliffs, N.J., Prentice Hall, 1969). Matza reviews the inadequacy of theories that try to explain deviance as the product of objective conditions (e.g., poverty) acting on a largely passive person, and argues instead for a more 'human' or 'subjective' or 'common sense' view. People become deviant, he argues, through their active affiliation with a social world that invites them to deviate and invests their behavior with a significance that promotes the idea (in themselves and others) that they 'are' deviants. His view is entirely consistent, I think, with the hypotheses stated in the text of this chapter.

Cognitive Development Theories

Jean Piaget, *The Moral Judgment of the Child* (New York, Harcourt, 1932) proposes a staged account of moral development in which both cognitive development and social experience play fundamental roles in the child's progress from 'heteronomous' moral judgment (in which judgments are based on conformity to received rules and anticipated consequences) to 'autonomous' moral judgments (in which judgments are based on responses to rules established in reciprocal social conduct that is sensitive to human needs). Lawrence Kohlberg, 'Stage and Sequence: The Cognitive-Developmental Approach to Socialization' in D. A. Goslin (ed.) *Handbook of Socialization Theory and Research* (Chicago, Rand McNally, 1969) proposes a six-stage theory, inter-actional in the way Piaget's is, that describes a step-wise progression in moral reasoning, ranging from pre-conventional, crudely egoistic thinking through appeals to authority and conven-tional rules to appeals to universalized, rationally grounded prin-ciples. Kohlberg's work, in particular, has spawned a voluminous literature. See *Ethics* 92 no. 3 (1982), Special Issue on Moral Development for references to this literature and a discussion of some of the issues. That issue of *Ethics* also has articles on the social learning theory approach to moral development. Much of what is controversial about developmental theories (e.g., their claims about the universality and invariance of the progression from stage to stage; their apparent endorsement of particular moral theories) need not concern us here. But one apparent divergence from the hypotheses described in this chapter does need to be addressed. Cognitive development theory holds that moral development occurs 'naturally', as it were, as individuals wrestle with the tasks of moral judgment and conduct. But that is only an apparent divergence. Nothing in the theories (as I read them) denies that people may acquire dispositions in the way described by the hypotheses here, nor that suitable social structures are necessary to sustain them. And nothing in the hypotheses (as I intend them) is meant to deny the connections – whatever they may be – between cognitive development and the sorts of moral reasoning people do in order to reach moral judgments.

Experimental Social Psychology

A convenient resource for relevant information from experimental social psychology is the series edited by Leonard Berkowitz, *Advances in Experimental Social Psychology* (New York, Academic Press). Volume 1 was published in 1964. The articles typically contain extensive references. I shall cite these volumes as Berkowitz, vol. xx (19xx).

The hypotheses in this chapter all concern what might be called the conformity of the individual to the group. That should certainly not be taken to indicate that I (or the scientists who have studied the matter) think that the causal connections are only one-way here. Individuals who remain participants in a structure often do not conform to significant elements of the structure, and others adjust the rules to accommodate themselves. See Serge Moscovici and Claude Faucheux, 'Social Influence, Conformity Bias, and the Study of Active Minorities', Berkowitz, vol. 6 (1972): 150–202. Furthermore, it would be a dismal doctrine that held that moral reflection could not bring about changes in one's attitudes, conduct, and hence dispositions. Happily, there is no evidence for that view, and there is evidence for its denial. See Abraham Tesser, 'Self-Generated Attitude Change', Berkowitz, vol 11 (1978): 289–338.

The 'compliance effect' described in hypothesis (I) has been confirmed in a wide variety of settings. The most striking experiments are perhaps those of M. Sherif, 'A Study of Some Social Factors in Perception,' *Archives of Psychology* 27 (1935), S. E.

Asch, 'Effects of Group Pressure upon the Modification and Distortion of Judgments', in H. Guetzkow (ed.) *Groups, Leadership and Men* (Pittsburgh, Carnegie Press, 1951), pp. 177–90, and Stanley Milgram's obedience experiments, *Obedience to Authority* (New York, Harper & Row, 1974). For a review of these matters see Vernon L. Allen, 'Situational Factors in Conformity', in Berkowitz, vol. 2 (1965): pp. 133–75. Many important papers on this topic (including the one by Asch noted above) may be found in Harold Proshansky and Bernard Seidenberg (ed.) *Basic Studies in Social Psychology* (New York, Holt, Rinehart & Winston, 1965).

On the 'multiplier effect' described in hypothesis II, most of the evidence I have found was gleaned from studies designed to test related hypotheses. See, for example, the discussion and references concerning the effects of actual participation on commitment to a belief in William J. McGuire, 'Inducing Resistance to Persuasion', Berkowitz, vol. 1 (1964): pp. 192–231. Richard L. Moreland and John M. Levine, 'Socialization in Small Groups: Temporal Changes in Individual-Group Relations', in Berkowitz, vol. 15 (1982): pp. 137–93 is also useful on the subjects of commitment and role transition.

On the 'potency effect' described in hypothesis III, the evidence again comes from a variety of lines of research. One concerns leadership and legitimacy. See Edwin P. Hollander and James W. Julian, 'Studies in Leader Legitimacy, Influence, and Innovation', Berkowitz, vol. 5 (1970): pp. 34–70. The work on the effects of exposure to media violence and pornography is also relevant. See two studies, Richard E. Goranson, 'Media Violence and Aggressive Behavior: A Review of Experimental Research', Berkowitz, vol. 5 (1970): pp. 2–33, and Ross D. Parke, *et. al.*, 'Some Effects of Violent and Non-violent Movies on the Behavior of Juvenile Delinquents', Berkowitz, vol. 10 (1977); pp. 136–73. On pornography and violence, see Neil M. Malmuth and Ed Donnerstein, 'The Effects of Aggressive-Pornographic Mass Media Stimuli', Berkowitz, vol. 15 (1982): pp. 104–36.

On the 'internalization effect' described in hypothesis IV, see the review article by Martin L. Hoffman, 'Moral Internalization: Current Theory and Research', Berkowitz, vol. 10 (1977): pp. 85–133. The article has extensive references. Most of the studies cited seem to assume that internalization occurs in some fashion consonant with hypothesis IV, and then test hypotheses about specific aspects of the process. Also of importance is the article by Thomas D. Cook and Brian R. Flay, 'The Persistence of Experimentally Induced Attitude Change', Berkowitz, vol. 11 (1978): pp. 2–59.

Some Recent Philosophical Work

John Rawls gives an account of moral development in *A Theory of Justice* (Cambridge, Harvard University Press, 1971). He says he draws upon the work of psychologists William McDougall, Jean Piaget, and Lawrence Kohlberg. Rawls' account makes reference to three 'stages', each governed by a psychological 'law' or tendency.

The first stage is the morality of authority, in which precepts are given by parents or other authority figures, take their legitimacy from the potency of the persons giving them, and are internalized in the process of the reciprocal, loving exchanges that characterize good dependency relationships. Rawls states the relevant psychological principle as follows:

> First Law: given that family institutions are just, and that the parents love the child and manifestly express their love by caring for his good, then the child, recognizing their evident love of him, comes to love them. (p. 490)

The workings of this morality of authority are stated in terms of a child's development in a family, but Rawls recognizes that the process is applicable to dependency relationships generally and that we never entirely shed such precepts and associated moral feelings. The second stage is called the morality of association, and is controlled by the following principle:

> Second law: given that a person's capacity for fellow feeling has been realized by acquiring attachments in accordance with the first law, and given that a social arrangement is just and publicly known by all to be just, then this person develops ties of friendly feeling and trust toward others in the association as they with evident intention comply with their duties and obligations, and live up to the ideals of their station. (p. 490)

The idea here is one of assuming a role in a social enterprise, and developing the cooperative virtues needed for it. This has an obvious affinity to the socialization process I describe for people whose participation in a potent social structure is successful and prolonged. My description is meant to be applicable, however, to the virtues necessary for all three of Rawls' stages.

Stage three is the morality of principles. It is the process of developing a conception of the principles that govern just social arrangements and becoming 'attached' to them directly, rather than merely indirectly and accidentally through attachment to people who live by them. The relevant psychological principle here is the following:

> Third law: given that a person's capacity for fellow feeling has been realized by his forming attachments in accordance with the first two laws, and given that a society's institutions are just and are publically known by all to be just, then this person acquires the corresponding sense of justice as he recognizes that he and those for whom he cares are the beneficiaries of these arrangements. (p. 491)

Rawls is aware that some people will object to his inclusion of the notion of justice in these principles. (See his remarks on pp. 491–3.) His answer is that psychological laws that 'do not mention the justice (or fairness) of the arrangement in question . . . are bound to be very limited in scope. . . . The justice or injustice of society's arrangements and men's beliefs about these questions profoundly influence the social feelings . . .' (p. 492). I agree with the observation, but think the reference to justice is too restrictive. People develop vices, after all, by participating in unjust institutions that are nonetheless potent for them (i.e., comprehensive, legitimating, and integral). Rawls comes close to acknowledging this when he speaks of the 'sense' of justice and what people 'believe' about the justice of an institution. But even that, in my view, is too restrictive. A 'life' of crime may be, through intricate psychological processes, 'legitimate' for a person precisely *because* it is believed by him to be *un*just. I think of Sartre's analysis of Jean Genet in this connection, Jean Paul Sartre, *Saint Genet: Actor and Martyr* (London, W. H. Allen & Co., 1964), translation by Bernard Frechtman.

One point Rawls makes about his principles of moral psychology, however, is so directly related to the concerns of this book that I want to quote it at length:

[Another] . . . observation is that the three laws [above] are not merely principles of association or reinforcement. While they have certain resemblances to those learning principles, they assert that the active sentiments of love and friendship, and even the sense of justice, arise from the manifest intention of other persons to act for our good. Because we recognize that they wish us well, we care for their well-being in return. Thus we acquire attachments to persons and institutions according to how we perceive our good to be affected by them. The basic idea is one of reciprocity, a tendency to answer in kind. Now this tendency is a deep psychological fact. Without it, our nature would be very different and fruitful social cooperation fragile if not impossible. For surely a rational person is not indifferent to things that significantly affect his good, and supposing that he develops some attitude toward them, he acquires either a new attachment or a new aversion. If we answered love with hate, or came to dislike those who acted fairly toward us, or were averse to activities that furthered our good, a community would soon dissolve. Beings with a different psychology either have never existed or must soon have disappeared in the course of evolution. A capacity for a sense of justice built up by responses in kind would appear to be a condition of human sociability. The most stable conceptions of justice are presumably those for which the corresponding sense of justice is most firmly based on these tendencies. (pp. 494–5)

That the sort of 'response in kind' principle Rawls mentions is in fact a principle of moral psychology seems beyond dispute. (It is not, of course, equivalent to the *virtue* of reciprocity.) And that this principle of moral psychology must be involved in any adequate account of moral development is also clear. I prefer, however, to state the relevant aspect of it more generally for the purposes of this chapter – in terms of 'successful' participation, however that might be defined by the agent.

For an account, on a grand scale, of the way in which comprehensive social structures might be aimed at developing and sustaining virtue – in particular, aristocratic, humanistic ideals – see Werner Jaeger, *Paideia: The Ideals of Greek Culture*, in three volumes, translated from the German by Gilbert Highet (Oxford, Basil Blackwell, 1946, 1947).

M. F. Burnyeat, 'Aristotle on Learning to Be Good', in Amelie Oksenberg Rorty (ed.) *Essays on Aristotle's Ethics* (Berkeley, University of California Press, 1980) pp. 69–92 provides a careful account of the way in which Aristotle's views on moral development – particularly his views about the role moral theory can play in moral development – are crucial to an understanding of the substantive arguments Aristotle gives. Burnyeat's comments on cognition and emotion are particularly rewarding, as is the discussion of the proper audience for various sorts of moral argument.

The problem of structural conformity may be discussed profitably in the context of the ethics of a profession. See, for example, David Luban (ed.) *The Good Lawyer* (Totowa, N. J., Rowman & Allenheld, 1984) for a recent collection of papers on this topic. Bernard Williams' contribution, 'Professional Morality and Its Dispositions', pp. 259–69 has an especially direct connection to the concerns of this chapter, but the papers by Richard Wasserstrom, Susan Wolf, and Virginia Held are also directly useful.

Acknowledgments

I am indebted to Kay Deaux and Robert Scott for bibliographic advice on some of these topics.

Families

Literature from Social Science

There is a vast social science literature on marriage and the family, and I do not pretend to have made a systematic study of it – beyond the point at which I discovered that, for the most part, it was not relevant to the arguments of this chapter. What I needed, for present purposes, was a grasp of the range of different familial structures and the range of plausible explanatory hypotheses about them. Much of the relevant, basic material from social science is cited in the notes to Chapters Three and Five. The citations here are essentially addenda to those earlier notes.

The analysis of profound relationships often seems superficial or wrongheaded, and social exchange concepts – including reciprocity – are particularly vulnerable to abuse. In particular, I have strong objections to attempts to construct a whole 'theory' of the family or of friendship in these terms. See T. Ivan Nye, *Family Relationships: Rewards and Costs* (Beverly Hills, Sage Publications, 1982) for an example of a sociological theory of this sort. As I emphasized in the text of this chapter, the reciprocity arguments do *not* yield a moral theory of familial relationships *per se*. Rather, they merely form the core of an account of familial obligations.

For an illuminating 'microsociological' proposal for understanding the role conventional marriage plays in people's lives (in our society), see Peter Berger and Hansfried Kellner, 'Marriage and the Construction of Reality', *Diogenes* 46 (1964): 1–24. The interaction in a marriage is there described as a continuous, verbal and nonverbal 'conversation' that has the effect of redefining the partners' social world and validating (to themselves) their places in it. If, as the authors suggest, people are largely unaware of the nature of this process, a good deal about their relationships would necessarily be obscure to them.

For an account of the connection between reciprocity and the maintenance of autonomy in 'balanced dependency' families (e.g., ones in which the males are completely dependent on the females for household management and the females are completely dependent on the males for economic support) see Takie Sugiyama Lebra, 'The Dilemma and Strategies of Aging Among Contemporary Japanese Women', *Ethnology* 18 (1979): 337–54. This paper focuses on the strategies adopted by aging women as they lose their ability to reciprocate in the ways that had formerly preserved their autonomy.

The empirical data on the relationship between forms of reciprocal exchange and degree of social distance is complex. Marshall Sahlins, 'On the Sociology of Primitive Exchange', in M. Banton (ed.) *The Relevance of Models for Social Anthropology* (New York, Praeger, 1965) hypothesizes that as social distance decreases, reciprocal transactions become 'generalized' – i.e., of a sort where exact accounts are not kept, and indeed no return at all may be explicitly expected. But there is a good deal of data that show that people in intimate relationships are *sometimes* less likely to be 'generous' than they are with strangers. Takie Sugiyama Lebra, in 'An Alternative Approach to Reciprocity', *American Anthropologist* 77 (1975): 550–65, considers this problem and argues that it is necessary to understand the purpose of reciprocal exchanges as they are embedded in social practices in order to make sense of the data. Intimates, for example, are often less courteous to each other than they are to strangers, and that can affect patterns of reciprocity. People can use gifts to humiliate others, and that too affects the pattern. In short, Lebra argues, there is not a tidy correlation between social distance and reciprocal transactions.

Readers who find the talk of resource distribution, depletion and development repulsive in the context of a discussion of profound relationships may wish (out of charity to this author) to remind themselves of the effect of reading other discursive analyses of marriage. See, for example, Clifford J. Sager and Bernice Hunt, *Intimate Partners: Hidden Patterns in Love Relationships* (New York, McGraw-Hill, 1979). I mention that book in particular because it is a sort of self-help marriage manual organized around the idea of 'rules of the game' – some hidden, some not.

Even more sobering is Gary S. Becker, *A Treatise on the Family*

(Cambridge, Mass., Harvard University Press, 1981), which gives a startling economic analysis of marriage and the family. Becker begins with some standard economic assumptions: that 'individuals maximize their utility from basic preferences that do not change rapidly over time', and that the behavior of individual utility maximizers is coordinated by equilibrium mechanisms in implicit or explicit markets for all sorts of material and non-material goods (p. ix). He then gives an analysis of the division of labor in marriages, cultural practices with regard to polygamy and monogamy, fertility rates, divorce rates, altruistic behavior in the family, and many other topics. Some of his conclusions are provocative. With respect to the division of labor, for example, he derives the following theorem: 'At most one member of an efficient household would invest in both market and household capital and would allocate time to both sectors' (p. 18). His analysis of forms of marriage shows that 'women tend to gain from polygyny' (p. 39), but predicts that as the demand for quantity of offspring is replaced by a demand for 'quality', the incidence of polygyny will decrease (p. 53). The details of his calculations are not much at issue. The controversy instead surrounds the assumptions that lie behind those calculations – assumptions about the applicability of economic analysis to these topics, and assumptions about the range of things an economic analysis of them should consider. On the latter issue, for example, it seems clear that the results concerning the division of labor would be quite different from Becker's if we imagined (as he does not) that both parties were to take into account the way in which the 'household specialist's' contributions to the marriage are likely to decrease as the children grow up. (I owe that point to informal discussion with Marianne Ferber.)

A simulation game (for familial interactions) called 'Reciprocity' has been developed by Marie Withers Osmond. It is described in her article 'Reciprocity: A Dynamic Model and a Method to Study Family Power', *Journal of Marriage and the Family* 40 (1978): 49–61.

The notion of a 'domestic cycle', as used by anthropologists, is closely related to what I have termed a developmental form of marriage. See the papers in Jack Goody (ed.) *The Developmental Cycle in Domestic Groups* (Cambridge, Cambridge University Press, 1958). In his introduction to the volume, Meyer Fortes constructs a 'paradigm distinguishing three main stages or phases in the developmental cycle of the domestic group' (p. 4). First is a stage of expansion, lasting from marriage until the birth of the spouses' last child. Next (perhaps overlapping) is the phase of fission, as the children establish their own families and to various extents 'hive off' from their parents. Finally, there is the phase of replacement, beginning with the children's preparations for taking over the parents' estate, and ending when, after the parents' deaths, they are 'replaced' by the families of their children. The ways in which that cycle is worked out are greatly varied. For example, in some societies, the newly married couple continues to live with, and under the control of, the bride's parents until their first child is born, then is expected to establish a separate household. In other societies, the couple will stay with the groom's parents, or be expected to establish a separate household immediately. In some societies the oldest son's family is expected to 'replace' the parents, in others it is the youngest child, male or female. Fortes says '*Mutatis mutandis*, this paradigm [expansion, fission, replacement of the domestic structures] can be applied to all social systems' (p. 5).

The November, 1982 issue of *The Annals of the American Academy of Political and Social Science* (Volume 464) is devoted to the topic of 'Middle and Late Life Transitions.' (The editor of that issue is Felix M. Berardo.) The articles are apparently intended to be general surveys of various problem areas. Some contain useful demographic information and bibliography.

Nancy Chodorow, *The Reproduction of Mothering* (Berkeley, University of California Press, 1978) makes a sustained and deeply interesting argument about the sexual division of labor in parenting. She begins with the observation that in virtually every society of record, it is women who have been the 'primary parents' through the child's early years – women who have done the 'mothering', as that verb is used to refer to caregiving as opposed to biological relationships. She reviews the arguments for a genetic or a physiological basis for this practice and finds them unconvincing. She notes that while this division of labor may have been a socio-economic necessity in certain kinds of prehistoric societies, it is no longer so. The problem, then, is to explain why this pattern of role assignments is so persistent. She concludes that standard socialization theories – specifically what she calls 'role-training' accounts – are inadequate to explain the persistence of the pattern. What

she proposes instead is a psychoanalytic account of the psychodynamics of women's mothering, an account that predicts that 1)
men mothered by women will grow away from their families and
need to participate in the public sphere; 2) women mothered by
women will have more generalized relational capacities and needs
than men; and 3) women and men who are the products of
women's mothering will want to create the kinds of interpersonal
relationships that make it likely that women will remain in the
domestic sphere – in the sphere of reproduction – and will in turn
mother the next generation (p. 38).

I quote from Chodorow's concluding summary:

> . . . because women mother, the early experience and
> preoedipal relationship differ for boys and girls. . . . The
> greater length and different nature of [girls'] preoedipal
> experience, and their continuing preoccupation with the
> issues of this period, mean that women's sense of self is
> continuous with others and that they retain capacities for
> primary identification. . . . In men, these qualities have been
> curtailed, both because they are early treated as an opposite by
> their mother and because their later attachment to her must
> be repressed. The relational basis for mothering is thus
> extended in women, and inhibited in men, who experience
> themselves as more separate and distinct from others. (p. 207)

In Chodorow's view the resultant perpetuation of a sexual division
of labor with respect to mothering is far from benign:

> The sexual division of labor and women's responsibility for
> child care are linked to and dominate male dominance.
> Psychologists have demonstrated unequivocally that the very
> fact of being mothered by a woman generates in men conflicts
> over masculinity, a psychology of male dominance, and a need
> to be superior to women. (p. 214)

If this is correct, nothing but a radical change in parenting practices
can break the cycle. The reciprocity arguments, moreover, support
breaking any cycle that compromises the possibility of genuinely
reciprocal social relationships. A sexual division of child rearing
labor, considered alone, does not imply such a compromise. But
if, given our psychology, the division of labor we do have will in
fact tend to reproduce (in both men and women) the psychology

of male dominance, then that is a different matter. The psychology of male dominance does compromise reciprocal relationships, and is opposed by the reciprocity arguments. I cannot assess the adequacy of Chodorow's re-interpretation of psychoanalytic theory, nor its cogency as an account of child development, but the possibility it raises is a striking reminder of how intricate and deep the connection may be between social structure and character traits. A 'static' assessment of people's resources and contributions to a relationship will not suffice. We must understand how particular patterns affect life-prospects, and reproduce themselves in succeeding generations.

Two books that antedate Chodorow's should also be mentioned in this context. Dorothy Dinnerstein, *The Mermaid and the Minotaur* (New York, Harper & Row, 1976) uses an evocative style to present the view that the psychology of male dominance is the result of the fact that women are the primary parents. She too appeals, in part, to a psychoanalytic account of psychodynamics. Juliet Mitchell, *Psychoanalysis and Feminism* (New York, Pantheon Books, 1974) is a general attempt to defend Freud against some feminist criticism.

Evolutionary biology, particularly the hypothesis that individuals are genetically disposed to maximize their inclusive fitness, obviously also has something to add to a discussion of 'deep' connections between human traits and social structure. See the notes to Chapter Three on this topic.

For other material on socialization, see the overview and references in Reuben Hill and Joan Aldous, 'Socialization for Marriage and Parenthood', in David A. Goslin (ed.) *Handbook of Socialization Theory and Research* (Chicago, Rand McNally, 1969), pp. 885–950.

A great deal of theorizing about the family has been based on assumptions about sex and gender role differences. For overviews of recent psychological research on this topic, see Kay Deaux, 'From Individual Differences to Social Categories: Analysis of a Decade's Research on Gender', *American Psychologist* 39 (1984): 105–16. A more extensive analysis, by Deaux, of sex and gender research will be included in the *Annual Review of Psychology* for 1985, and there will be an authoritative chapter on the subject by Spence, Deaux and Helmreich in the third edition of the *Handbook of Social Psychology*.

Until quite recently, empirical studies of parent–infant interactions had focused on the effects of parental behavior on the infant, and most had focused only on maternal behavior. There is now, however, a slowly growing literature on the effects of infant behavior on the parent (again, mostly, the mother). The evidence of reciprocal effects is striking. See Michael Lewis and Leonard A. Rosenblum (eds.), *The Effect of the Infant on Its Caregiver* (New York, John Wiley & Sons, 1974).

For a readable and concise introduction to ethnographic findings on marriage, see Lucy Mair, *Marriage* (Penguin Books, 1971), and for a brisk overview of ethnographic data on the varieties of family structures, see William N. Stephens, *The Family in Cross-Cultural Perspective* (New York, Holt, Rinehart & Winston, 1963). The survey was drawn from reports on '250 representative human societies'.

William J. Goode, *World Revolution and Family Patterns* (New York, The Free Press, 1970) is instructive for the range of evidence there assembled to support the contention that family patterns world-wide have been moving in roughly the same direction during this century – away from 'traditional' families characterized by strong and extended kinship bonds toward some type of 'conjugal' or 'nuclear' family. Goode carefully avoids, however, the simplistic economic explanation that attributes such change to industrialization. He insists that, in addition, the history of the family in each locale must be studied, and the observed changes put in that context. See pp. 1–6, and 366–80. The relevance of Goode's study for present purposes lies mainly in its power to bring to mind the complexity and subtlety of the ways in which family structure is interlocked with other fundamental social structures. Even if moral theory can generate principles of universal applicability, their local application all-things-considered is an enormously difficult task.

I have profited from a number of histories of the family which address the remarkable changes in Western European and American family life and intimate relationships. These studies, together with ethnographic data, prompt (and enrich) a much needed restraint on the rather cavalier generalizations often found in theories about the family. Charles E. Rosenberg (ed.) *The Family in History* (Philadelphia, University of Pennsylvania Press, 1975) contains an instructive and disparate set of six articles on the social history of the domestic sphere, ranging from essays on early modern England, traditional China, and nineteenth century Genoa (by Lawrence Stone, Wolfram Eberhard and Diane Hughes, respectively) to an essay on family continuity in two European banking houses. The introductory essay by Rosenberg gives a concise summary of the trends in, and difficulties of, this 'new social history'. Edward Shorter, *The Making of the Modern Family* (New York, Basic Books, 1975) pieces together an account of changes in the family life of 'everyday' people in Western Europe during the last three centuries. For the description of the family in the eighteenth and nineteenth centuries he relies on the 'medical topographies' prepared by provincial doctors, the administrative reports and crude statistical descriptions of low level bureaucrats, and the writings of amateur 'antiquarians' and folklorists. Most of the evidence comes from France and Germany. Shorter is careful to point out the limitations of such evidence, but argues for its superiority over the traditional sources for such social history – that is, the writings of upper/middle and upper-class people and a few autobiographical documents from working-class people whose representativeness is questionable. And his evidence convinces him that what he calls a surge of sentiment – in courtship, in mother–child relationships, and in the emotional lives of family members generally – characterized a deep change in family relationships during the eighteenth and nineteenth centuries. On his reading, prior to the nineteenth century, what was remarkable about the 'typical' lower-class family was its lack of what I would call profound relationships and its lack of privacy – both with respect to relationships between its members and with respect to their relationships to 'outsiders'. His account stands as a caution against moral theorizing based on unexamined assumptions about 'the' nature of familial relationships.

Lawrence Stone, whose pioneering work on this topic began many years before his massive book was published, develops some of the same themes with respect to English life in *The Family, Sex and Marriage in England 1500–1800* (New York, Harper & Row, 1977). He says, 'The critical change under consideration [in this book] is that from distance, deference and patriarchy to what I have chosen to call Affective Individualism. I believe this to have been perhaps the most important change in *mentalité* to have occurred in the Early Modern period . . .' (p. 4). Stone's book is richly detailed and richly rewarding.

Peter Gay, *The Victorians*, volume I, *The Education of the Senses* (Oxford, Oxford University Press, 1984), assumes the validity of the broad outlines of psychoanalytic theory, and then assembles and interprets a vast body of material of and about the period between 1820 and 1914. Unlike Shorter and Stone, he assumes that fundamental social changes occur only in the forms in which people are allowed to express or are forced to repress the same underlying psychic needs and drives. In this respect, the premises of his book are comparable to Nancy Chodorow's work on the reproduction of mothering, and (in form only) to those of evolutionary sociobiology.

Reflections on profound relationships – at least my reflections on them – may too often focus on the good, or at least ambiguous and controlled, cases. There is also horror and chaos. The literature on child abuse, battered wives, and the legal machinery of domestic relations law is an antidote to idealization. See, for example, William Aiken and Hugh LaFollette (eds.) *Whose Child? Children's Rights, Parental Authority and State Power* (Totowa, N.J., Rowman and Littlefield, 1980) and Laurence Houlgate, *The Child and the State* (Baltimore, Johns Hopkins University Press, 1980) for material on children, and the literature on the sexual abuse of women cited in Alison Jaggar, *Feminist Politics and Human Nature* (Totowa, N.J., Rowman & Allanheld, 1983). For clinical and demographic material on child abuse, Joanne Valiant Cook and Roy Tyler Bowles (eds.), *Child Abuse: Commission and Omission* (Toronto, Butterworths, 1980), has a valuable collection of reprinted papers on the forms, frequency and consequences of child abuse. I note especially Richard J. Gelles, 'Violence Toward Children in the United States', pp. 35–49; C. Henry Kempe, *et. al.*, 'The Battered Child Syndrome', pp. 49–63; Bertram S. Koel, 'Failure to Thrive and Fatal Injury as a Continuum', pp. 73–6; C. Henry Kempe, 'Sexual Abuse: Another Hidden Pediatric Problem', pp. 97–109; Stephen J. Pfohl, 'The "Discovery" of Child Abuse', pp. 323–40; and Richard J. Gelles, 'The Social Construction of Child Abuse', pp. 341–50. Some of the articles in the book are oft-cited pioneering work – e.g., Kempe, *et. al.* on the battered child syndrome, which was first published in the *Journal of the American Medical Association* 181, 1 (1962): 17–24. The level of philosophical analysis throughout the book, on the concept of child abuse and normative judgments concerning it, leaves much to be desired, and the section on the 'sources' of child abuse is predictably unsatisfying, but the descriptive papers – both the anecdotal and statistical ones – provide the sort of information and references that sound moral theory on these matters must begin with. This dark side of profound relationships reinforces the importance of reciprocity.

Philosophical Theory

Jeffrey Blustein, *Parents and Children: The Ethics of the Family* (Oxford, Oxford University Press, 1982) prefaces an account of family structures, parental and filial duties with an informative survey of what some major figures in Western philosophy – from Plato to Russell – have had to say about the family. (He notes that while historians of philosophy have generally neglected the topic, moral philosophers themselves have not.) I will not recapitulate that historical material here, except to point out the following: 1) Philosophers have long been divided about whether or not familial relationships are subversive of other social structures, especially those in the 'public' sphere. The basic source of concern is the priority people typically give to familial matters – a priority that can result in withdrawal from public life, disobedience to civil authority, the creation and perpetuation of unjust property arrangements, and deeply entrenched, self-perpetuating inequality of opportunity. Plato gives an early indication of such concerns in *The Republic*, and egalitarians are suspicious of family structures for such reasons. Blustein has these concerns, but argues that human welfare generally is strongly enough tied to good familial relationships that we do not have sufficient reason for accepting a thoroughgoing egalitarian revision of them. See his Chapter Four: Equal Opportunity and the Family. The reciprocity arguments also cut against egalitarian concerns in this regard. 2) Philosophers have also differed sharply about the sources and extent of parental authority. Many of their arguments on the matter mirror ones on political authority (natural authority, divine right, consent of the governed, physical necessity, personal and social welfare). The reciprocity arguments about parental authority also have analogs in reciprocity arguments for political authority. See my Chapter Eight. 3) Useful discussion of the reciprocal aspects of filial obligations can be found in Aristotle, *Nichomachean Ethics*, Books VIII and

IX. Blustein also cites as helpful Cicero, *On Moral Obligation*, Seneca, *On Benefits*, and Aquinas, *Summa Theologica*, Questions 31 and 106. He found more to admire there than I did, and I profited from his discussion.

Blustein's own account, like mine, focuses mainly on deontological matters but is insistent that they do not exhaust moral concerns about family life. His account takes matters of reciprocity very seriously, but he does not think reciprocity plays as big a role in familial obligations as I think it does. My views on the matter, however, come from a virtue-theoretic approach. His do not. We agree, nonetheless, that reciprocity arguments cannot give a complete account of either parental authority or marital, parental, and filial duties.

I am a bit unclear about some central issues in Blustein's account, but in outline it appears to be this: For a variety of reasons related to the development and welfare of individuals, extensive parental duties of care are justified. Initially, these duties attach to social roles, and biological parents may assign their roles to others who are willing, able, and likely to care adequately for the child. (But biological parents apparently may not refuse parental duties of care if there is no one else to take over.) As children grow, reciprocal parent–child relationships create additional duties of justice, gratitude, and friendship. Parental authority and filial duties are justified, initially, as means to the parents' fulfillment of their parental duties. Here Blustein appeals to, but does not discuss, a startling (and, I think, false) 'general moral principle', which I quote in full:

> (1) If A has a duty to B to do x for B, then B has a right against A to x; (2) If B has a right against A to x, then B may be able to give it up and thereby release A from his duty to do x; (3) If B does not or cannot give up his right against A to x, then B has a duty to facilitate or at least not prevent A's discharging his duty to do x. (p. 171)

The consequence is that in cases where young children are incapable of releasing their parents from parental duties (because the correlative rights are 'inalienable', for example), the children have a duty to allow their parents to care for them effectively. (Those filial duties evaporate, however, if the parents neglect or abuse the child.) As children grow older, parental and filial duties of care get attenuated, and may be replaced with intimate reciprocal relationships. Blustein's account is, in sum, a sustained and thoughtful defense of the deontological aspects of the parent–child relationships now common among well-educated, not-particularly-religious, urban families in our society. The reciprocity arguments give quite a different cast to these issues.

Onora O'Neill and William Ruddick (eds.) *Having Children: Philosophical and Legal Reflections on Parenthood* (New York, Oxford University Press, 1979) is a useful collection of recent articles and court cases on parent–child relationships. It also includes short selections from Rousseau, Locke, and Mill. Two articles in that book are especially pertinent to the present chapter: 1) Michael Slote, 'Obedience and Illusions', pp. 319–26, emphasizes the ways in which the notions of parental and divine authority are embedded in the illusions we need (or feel a need for) in potent childhood experience. The general tenor of his remarks is dismissive of reciprocity arguments as a source of parental authority or filial duty. He suspects such arguments are rationalizations designed to shore up sentiments we acquire, as children, in the profound relationships we have with our parents, and which we would do better to shed as adults. For obvious reasons I differ with him about the cogency of the reciprocity arguments. But I have no stake in defending a particular account of the psychogenesis of the arguments. It may well be that they occur to us initially because we wish to preserve some childish illusion, and I am grateful for Slote's reminder that particularly in these obscure and powerful child–parent relationships, quick arguments that 'seem' or 'feel' right are suspect. None of that is evidence against the reciprocity arguments, of course. It is instead a proper caution. 2) Jane English, 'What Do Grown Children Owe Their Parents?' pp. 351–6, deploys a series of examples designed to show that while there are many things grown children *ought* to do for their parents, there is nothing that they 'owe' for the parents' sacrifices on their children's behalf. The examples depend on a distinction between love (the correct ground for these filial duties, in English's view) and debt for favors. I do not accept that distinction in the way English wields it. Friendships and love relationships, in my view, are full of debts that come from the gifts we receive. Whether we should think of them that way, as we act, is a separate question. It is not an objection to the reciprocity arguments to show that it is inappropriate for us to 'act out of a sense of debt' in a given case.

A. John Simmons, *Moral Principles and Political Obligations* (Princeton, Princeton University Press, 1979) has argued at length against the notion that the mere receipt of benefits creates a ground for moral obligations, and he extends his account to political obligation. I have commented on parts of his argument in the notes to Chapter Three. Other elements of his argument, however, developed in his book and also in his essay 'The Obligations of Citizens and the Justification of Conscription', Working Paper, Center for Philosophy and Public Policy, University of Maryland, 1983, are more directly connected to the concerns of both this chapter and Chapter Eight. For example: Simmons argues (in the paper cited, at pp. 10–12) that children do not have extensive filial obligations of reciprocity because so much of what parents do for their children is simply the fulfillment of parental duty. *Sometimes* we are obligated to reciprocate in some way for dutiful acts, but not always. (Simmons makes the point more carefully in his book, on pp. 179–81.) And Simmons thinks that the fulfillment of parental duties typically does *not* generate reciprocal obligations. I think his conclusion is based on an insufficient range of cases. What he has in mind are cases in which we 'ought' to feel gratitude for the dutiful performance. But consider: The reciprocity arguments as I have explicated them insist that we ought to be disposed, as a matter of moral obligation, to make a return for all the good we receive. It is true, of course, that if people *owe* me x, and x is all I get from them, our account is settled. But their giving x to me – their dutiful behavior – often carries with it more than just the value of x itself. Some people do their duty grudgingly, after all, or in a way that makes recipients feel cheap, or uneasy, or threatened. Other people do their duty in a way that helps to create an atmosphere of trust, or makes recipients feel worthy, confident, and secure. Those goods may be over and above what was owed, and reciprocity disposes us to make a fitting and proportionate return for them, as a matter of moral obligation. Just how we should do this is not the issue here. (We might do it by making sure we contribute to others' sense of worth or confidence or trust.) The issue here is rather the fact that dutiful parental behavior may generate obligations of reciprocity. Whether those obligations are typically extensive or not is an empirical question. I suspect that they are; but even if not, filial obligations of reciprocity will arise from all the supererogatory things parents do for their children – and that class of parental acts, in loving parent–child relationships, is usually very extensive indeed. Simmons has difficulty with reciprocity arguments here in part because he is caught up in this sort of analogy:

> Parents not only have a duty to care for their children but are (normally) morally responsible for the necessity of caring for them. It is as if, instead of just pulling you from the water, I had first pushed you in (accidentally or intentionally) making me responsible for your need. In such a case, it is far less convincing to claim that anything is owed me as benefactor; and by analogy it is unconvincing to insist that filial obligations arise from parental benefaction. ('The Obligations of Citizens . . .' p. 11.)

The more apt (but still not quite right) analogy is the case in which I resuscitate you, thus creating an opportunity for you to live, and since the situation into which I have brought you is temporarily a perilous one (let's say we are stranded on an island), I take care of you until you are strong enough to fend for yourself. Obligations of reciprocity are perfectly intelligible in such a case, and also in the case of parent–child relationships. Furthermore, the reciprocity arguments point to the circumstances in which such 'benefaction' would not generate reciprocal obligations – namely, in cases where my 'help' is not a good at all.

Simmons also discusses parental authority. ('The Obligations of Citizens . . .' pp. 7–8.) He argues that parents often rightly demand obedience, and that it would in those cases be wrong for the children to disobey. But in general, he says, children have no moral obligation to fulfill their parents' demands 'simply on the grounds that their parents have made them' (*Ibid.*, p. 8). The reciprocity arguments yield the same result.

Ferdinand Schoeman, 'Rights of Children, Rights of Parents, and the Moral Basis of the Family', *Ethics* 91 (1980): 6–19 argues that parents have a right against the state to raise their children 'in an intimate setting', for reasons quite independent of considerations of child welfare, efficiency, or 'property rights'. The reasons have to do, he thinks, with the importance in human life of intimate relationships, and the degraded quality of life (for adults) that extensive state interference in family matters would produce. This is a difficult and risky argument, which must give an account of how the intimacy needs of the abusive parent, or the smothering parent, or the neglectful parent are to be treated. I think virtue-theoretic arguments would be a more appropriate route to take here than the one Schoeman has pursued, but he is surely right in thinking that the usual basis for parental authority (the child's welfare) is inadequate as a ground for much of the moral and legal autonomy we currently grant to the family.

For an analysis of Hobbes' views on filial obligation, and references to other relevant work on Hobbes, see Gilbert Meilaender, '"A Little Monarchy": Hobbes on the Family', *Thought* 53 (1978): 401–15.

Robert Baker and Frederick Elliston (eds.) *Philosophy and Sex* (Buffalo, Prometheus Books, 1975) assemble some essays by contemporary Anglo-American philosophers on the following topics: the 'semantics of sex', sex and morality, marriage, sexual deviance, and abortion. The book includes these frequently cited papers: Sara Ruddick, 'Better Sex', Carl Cohen, 'Sex, Birth Control and Human Life' (prefaced by the text of *Humanae Vitae*, which Cohen attacks), Richard Wasserstrom, 'Is Adultery Immoral?', Thomas Nagel, 'Sexual Perversion', Robert Solomon, 'Sex and Perversion', and Judith Jarvis Thomson, 'A Defense of Abortion.' There is also a sixteen page bibliography.

Feminist Political Theory

Until the mid-nineteenth century, Western political philosophers were nearly unanimous that public, political life was properly a male preserve. Women in general were thought suited only for a supporting role in domestic or private life. Evidence to the contrary was either ignored or waved aside. Moreover, the domestic sphere has typically been sharply separated from the public, and the moral principles and virtues appropriate to private life defined very differently from those appropriate to public life. These dichotomies have had profound, self-perpetuating consequences, the extent of which we are still slowly exploring. For a review of some of these matters in the history of political theory see Jean Bethke Elshtain (ed.) *The Family in Political Thought* (Amherst, University of Massachusetts Press, 1982).

Susan Moller Okin, *Women in Western Political Thought* (Princeton, Princeton University Press, 1979) gives an illuminating analysis of the political theories of Plato, Aristotle, Rousseau, and Mill. A particular merit of her analysis for present purposes is its showing that 'functionalist' theories of the good – like Aristotle's – have been at the bottom of so much slipshod moral argument on the question of sex roles. Theorists who are very sensitive to the dangers of such argument when they are discussing the political consequences of differences among men, time after time seem incapable of the same sophistication when it comes to the political consequences of observed differences between men and women.

Elizabeth H. Wolgast, *Equality and the Rights of Women* (Ithaca, Cornell University Press, 1980) argues that egalitarian reasoning is not an adequate basis for an account of women's rights. I remain unconvinced by her argument because I think the characteristic differences between men and women can best be handled, for the purposes of rights theory and moral theory generally, by adopting a presumption of equality that puts the burden of proof on anyone who wishes to claim that those characteristic differences justify different rights and obligations. Operating without that presumption, at least in the human societies I know something about, promotes a familiar list of abuses. Perhaps in a different world – one in which there had been no history of systematic injustice to women and various minorities – we could proceed as Wolgast recommends. We could then consider each potentially significant difference separately, without needing any overarching procedural safeguard against injustice. (We would still need closure devices, however, and my arguments for the presumption of equality on that score would still stand. See Chapter Two.) But that is an option for some 'possible' world, not for this one. Wolgast's arguments, it seems to me, entirely miss the importance of the procedural device of the presumption of equality.

For a detailed (and witty) argument that social arrangements that encourage or enforce the economic dependence of wives on their husbands unjustifiably compromise the wives' self-esteem, see B. C. Postow, 'Economic Dependence and Self-Respect', *The Philosophical Forum* 10 (1978–79): 181–205.

Alison M. Jaggar, *Feminist Politics and Human Nature* (Totowa, N. J., Rowman & Allanheld, 1983) gives a detailed examination of four forms of feminist theory about human nature and politics:

liberal, traditional Marxist, radical, and socialist-feminist. The book is replete with bibliographic references to recent feminist writing. Her consistent contention is that socialist feminism shows the most promise, but I suspect that that is because it is (relative to the others) rather unformed. Were it better formed, and were Jaggar inclined to be as critical there as she is with other versions of feminist theory, she would likely reach quite a different result. For obvious reasons, I find her treatment of liberal feminism most disturbing, and this is an appropriate place to develop some remarks about it.

It is true, as Jaggar says, that liberalism in general is individualistic and egalitarian – in the sense that it measures the justifiability of social and political structures by how well they satisfy the interests and needs of all the people who inhabit them. And it is true, as she says, that liberals are characteristically committed to operating with the thinnest possible conception of the good. But it is not true, as she seems to suppose, that liberal political theory as such must stand or fall with the defects of some of its versions. It is not tied to a simplistic atomistic conception of the self, or a 'rational essence' view of human nature. Liberal theory as such can work with as sophisticated and as 'full' an account of human nature as science and metaphysics can provide. Its commitment to liberty is not, in principle, just to negative liberty; its commitment to equal consideration of the full range of human wants, needs, preferences, and satisfactions does not preclude an account of false consciousness, unfounded preferences, errors of judgment, impaired judgment, and the like. And its commitment to the thinnest *possible* conception of the good does not, in principle, preclude its being driven toward a thick conception by cogent argument. What distinguishes liberal political theory as such from other sorts of political theory is not where it stops, but rather where it starts, where it puts the burden of proof, and what sort of arguments it will accept for the justification of social and political arrangements. It starts with the presumption that *actual* human needs, desires, preferences, and projects – as they are felt and expressed by identifiable individuals – are the 'stuff' that must be addressed by theory; that the aim of theory is to design social structures that fulfill such actual needs, satisfy such actual desires, reflect such actual preferences, and promote such actual projects; and that every moral agent's needs, desires, preferences, and projects are presumptively of equal moral weight. Liberal theory puts the burden of proof on anyone who wishes to make 'hypothetical' or reconstructed needs, etc. the 'stuff' of theory, or to give unequal weight to various elements of the stuff. And it insists that the justificatory test for any social or political structure is just how well actual people fare with it. In practice these theoretical presumptions and commitments have meant that most liberals have defended social structures whose rules are (or are meant to be) neutral with respect to a wide (but not unbounded) number of competing conceptions of the good; have defended an extensive egalitarian system of 'negative' rights; and have found the justification of 'positive' rights to be more problematic. Such conclusions depend crucially, as Jaggar argues, on the conception of human nature that a theorist holds. Liberals, as philosophers, are disposed to find and use the best conception of human nature reason can construct. Given the way scientific and philosophic views of human nature change, however, caution on these matters is advisable for a moral theorist. That, and not some fixation on a particularly 'liberal' conception of human nature, is the source of the commitment to the thinnest possible conception of the good. At least that is so for me.

Acknowledgments

The arguments about priorities and social distance were criticized by James Cargile several years ago. I profited from his remarks, and from subsequent discussion with Denise Bielby, Ramón Gutiérrez, and Ellen Messer. The structure of the argument about priorities (and Cargile's comments on it) were first presented in the context of human versus animal interests. See 'The Priority of Human Interests', in Harlan B. Miller and William H. Williams (eds.) *Ethics and Animals* (New York, Humana Press, 1983). I thank the editors and publishers for permission to reuse that material, in altered form, here.

Notes to 'Friends'

Non-chapters do not warrant bibliographic essays, but I cannot forbear mentioning that there is a good deal about friendship, either directly or by implication, in the material cited in the notes to chapters three and six. The following are also rewarding:

For a careful and illuminating discussion of Aristotle's views of friendship – a discussion that itself makes an important contribution to philosophical reflection on the topic, see John M. Cooper, 'Aristotle on Friendship' in Amelie Oksenberg Rorty (ed.) *Essays on Aristotle's Ethics* (Berkeley, University of California Press, 1980) pp. 301–40. Cooper concludes that:

> There are to be found in the Aristotelian corpus . . . two interesting and telling arguments to show that true friendship is an essential constituent of a flourishing human life. If my interpretations are correct, Aristotle argues, first, that to know the goodness of one's life, which he reasonably assumes to be a necessary condition of flourishing, one needs to have intimate friends whose lives are similarly good, since one is better able to reach a sound and secure estimate of the quality of a life when it is not one's own. Second, he argues that the fundamental moral and intellectual activities that go to make up a flourishing life cannot be continuously engaged in with pleasure and interest, as they must be if the life is to be a flourishing one, unless they are engaged in as parts of shared activities rather than pursued merely in private; and given the nature of the activities that are in question, this sharing is possible only with intimate friends who are themselves morally good persons. (pp. 330–1)

Cooper also points out (p. 334, n2) that '. . . [some] family relationships are in fact the original and, in some ways, the central cases of [friendship].'

Gilbert Meilaender, *Friendship: A Study in Theological Ethics* (Notre Dame, University of Notre Dame Press, 1981) explores several tensions between friendship (philia) and the ideal form of love (agape) spoken of in Christian theology. Friendship is preferential while agape is universal; friendship is reciprocal while agape is selfless; friendship is loyalty to a person while agape is fidelity to a higher law. Meilaender finds the philosophical problems raised by such tensions in Greek and Roman texts on friendship, as well as in Christian writings. There is also an interesting parallel here with problems raised by modern secular ethics. It is hard to square the universalistic, principled, and rational character of utilitarian and Kantian ethics, for example, with the preferential, reciprocal, and loyal character of friendship. Friendships based on principle are not very satisfying. Neither are acts of love done out of respect for the moral law.

David L. Norton and Mary F. Kille (eds.), *Philosophies of Love* (Totowa, N. J., Rowman & Allenheld, 1983) is a useful collection of excerpts – from Plato, Aristotle, and a range of 19th and 20th century writers – on the topics of romantic love, erotic aspirations toward an ideal, agape, 'Tristanism' and chivalric love, friendship, and fellow feeling.

Future Generations

Sustained philosophical inquiry into the topic of obligations to future generations seems to be a recent phenomenon. A careful combing of the classics in moral philosophy would probably uncover a good many remarks in passing on the subject, but I have found nothing that rises above the level of exhortation. In popular lore, if present practices are any indication, there appears to be an acceptance of some sort of reciprocity principle in these matters – e.g., in disapproval of the spendthrift heir. But that is hardly argument, and the recent philosophical work on the topic has for the most part either ignored reciprocity arguments or been dismissive of them. The following, however, have been instructive.

The hypothesis in evolutionary biology that individuals tend to maximize inclusive fitness (see the Notes to Chapter Three) suggests a genetic predisposition to favor close relatives over distant ones, and distance may be defined along the line of succeeding generations as well as among contemporaries. Hamilton says 'As regards selfish traits in general . . . [b]ehavior that involves taking too much from close relatives will not evolve.' W. D. Hamilton, 'The Genetical Evolution of Social Behavior', I, *Journal of Theoretical Biology* 7 (1964): 1–16, at page 16. Hamilton's analysis gives a precise definition of what, under his hypothesis, would count as 'taking too much'.

Richard Titmuss, *The Gift Relationship* (New York, Pantheon Books, 1971) gives a valuable analysis of the motives typical of blood donors in various types of blood banks, and makes a sustained argument for the medical, economic and moral superiority of non-commercial, 'community volunteer' systems. The statistical and technical information in the book is drawn from the 1960s, but the form of the argument is certainly not dated. Titmuss makes no claims about the origin of altruistic and reciprocal gift-giving motives, but he shows how they can be coordinated to sustain a complex, highly technical social practice. Moreover, a clear implication of his argument is that sustaining blood banks by means of coordinated altruistic and reciprocal acts has good consequences for other aspects of social life. For a useful criticism of Titmuss, see Kenneth J. Arrow, 'Gifts and Exchanges', *Philosophy & Public Affairs* 1 (1972): 343–62.

Annette Baier, 'The Rights of Past and Future Persons', in Ernest Partridge (ed.) *Responsibilities to Future Generations* (Buffalo, N.Y., Prometheus Books, 1981) explicitly connects obligations to future generations to the obligation to 'pass on' the benefits we have received from past generations. And, though she is skeptical about finding an adequate theoretical basis for the obligations, she cites (as salient for philosophical reflection on them) the interdependence of persons in the 'cross-temporal moral community' into which they are born. (pp. 178–9) These matters are also preliminaries for the reciprocity arguments. Partridge's book is a useful collection. It contains many of the standardly cited papers on the topic (e.g., the one by Golding discussed below).

Martin Golding, 'Obligations to Future Generations', *Monist* 56 (1972): 85–99 argues that obligations arise within moral communities – among beings who share a social ideal, a conception of a good life. We include as members of our moral community those for whom we can give content to the notion of the 'good *for* them'. We can have obligations, in principle, to beings whose 'claims' we are ready to recognize as entitlements to receive good from us. As a consequence, the notion of an obligation to very remote future generations makes little sense, since we have no clear conception of what the good for them will be. I am suspicious of this argument. Of course, since reciprocity requires us to transmit things that are genuine goods for future generations, it is true that if we have no clear conception of what will be good for them, then we will be baffled about how to act. But being baffled does not necessarily entail being relieved of our obligations. We are often baffled in this way, after all, in face to face transactions. ('Nothing I do for him seems to turn out right.') In those cases it is common to think that our obligation to produce a good for the recipients is discharged by producing something that will *probably* be good for them, given our best evidence about what is *likely* to be good for them. We know enough about the probable course of events on this planet to be able to make some predictions of that sort even for the remote future.

John Rawls, *A Theory of Justice* (Cambridge, MA, Belnap Press of Harvard University Press, 1971), section 44, works out the general outline of his theory's implications for justice between generations. The hypothetical parties to the social contract are not to know to which generation they belong. The problem they face is therefore one of establishing a 'just savings principle', based on their knowledge of the conditions they might actually face once the veil of ignorance is lifted. The parties to the contract know that they are contemporaries. Past generations have either saved or not. So the question is, why would the parties choose to save at all? Rawls says that they would choose to save if they 'are regarded as representing family lines, say, with ties of sentiment between successive generations. This [motivational assumption] seems natural enough . . .' (p. 292).

D. Clayton Hubin, in 'Justice and Future Generations', *Philosophy and Public Affairs* 6 (1976): 71–83 argues 1) that the notion of obligations to future generations – i.e., to non-existent persons – makes no sense, but that we may have obligations to our partners in the social contract to conserve so that future generations can have good lives. 2) He then argues that a Rawlsian ideal contract theory is a promising route for showing that some of those obligations are obligations of justice rather than 'benevolence'. But 3) he argues that the argument cannot be made in the way Rawls has tried to make it – i.e., by effectively representing future generations in the social contract by denying contractors the knowledge of which generations they belong to. 4) Hubin concludes that all the contractors need to know is that people generally treat their children's interests as in some sense their own, and would (if they had children) want some saving done for that generation. Given that, contractors would choose to adopt some sort of limited savings principle for the immediately succeeding generation(s) as a condition of justice.

R. I. Sikora and Brian Barry (eds.), *Obligations to Future Generations* (Philadelphia, Temple University Press, 1978), in Part I, contains a series of papers that grapple with the notion of the interests of potential or possible persons – especially in terms of whether utilitarian theory requires that we take such interests into account. Several of these articles also raise the question of optimum population size. The reciprocity arguments, as I noted in the text, skirt some of the metaphysical problems that plague standard theories. Full scale moral inquiry cannot skirt them, of course, but even so, the reciprocity arguments provide a necessary reminder: not every moral obligation need be an obligation to someone. Obligations, regarded as morally required acts whose requiredness originates in voluntary human acts, can bind us to act in ways that produce and benefit new generations.

Michael D. Bayles (ed.) *Ethics and Population* (Cambridge, MA, Schenkman Publishing Co., 1976) contains essays by Jan Narveson, Peter Singer and Derek Parfit that show the difficulties raised – for any moral theory that includes utilitarian concerns – by the question of how many people there ought to be in future generations. This issue, while in some respects very different from the questions raised in the present chapter, nonetheless has an indirect bearing on them – not on the reciprocity arguments themselves but on the all-things-considered moral reflection that includes them.

Derek Parfit, *Reasons and Persons* (Oxford, Clarendon Press, 1984) contends that the view we take of personal identity has important consequences for moral argument – especially moral argument about the priority we should (or should not) attach to our own interests over those of other people, our own present interests over our future ones, and the interests of our contemporaries over those of future generations. On what he calls 'Non-reductionist' views of personal identity, identity is an all-or-nothing thing – not admitting of degrees or indeterminacy. Such views are forced to give determinate answers to all of the familiar amnesia, transplant, fission, fusion, metamorphosis, and reconstitution problems that have bedeviled discussions of personal identity. And these determinate answers, he argues, will lead to some irrational, or improbable, or indefensible moral judgments. Adopting what he calls a 'Reductionist' view, on the other hand, will lead to different, more defensible, moral conclusions. A reductionist view of personal identity is one in which everything that can (truly) be said about who or what a person is can be expressed in a series of propositions about a series of particular physical and psychological facts, much as (Parfit's analogy) all the truths about the existence and nature of a nation can be expressed in propositions about the conduct, dispositions, beliefs, and so on of particular people. In neither case is there any 'deeper fact', any deeper unity, to the identity of the person or nation so described. When we come to believe this about ourselves, Parfit argues, we will draw very different conclusions about what matters, morally. Our own future happiness and survival, for example, will matter less, relative to our occurrent aims, and relative to the aims of others, than it does if we hold a non-reductionist view. And the reductionist view, he holds, will give a very different cast to our reflections on the distribution and quantity of good – both within and across generations. Parfit's argument is intricate and provocative. It is also long. This is no place to attempt an assessment of it. Suffice it to say that however important Parfit's argument may be for other aspects of moral theory, I do not think it affects the shape of the reciprocity virtue or the cogency of the reciprocity arguments.

Michael D. Bayles, *Morality and Population Policy* (University, Ala. University of Alabama Press, 1980), Chapter 2, outlines a duty of limited benevolence that requires us 'not to render it substantially unlikely that future generations can indefinitely sustain a minimum quality of life' (p. 20). On the assumption that we are in fact 'reasonable self-interested persons of limited benevolence' whose conduct is in fact guided by principles of self-interest and limited benevolence, then we have good reason, he says, to adopt the duty he describes. He argues that well established political-social values (e.g., freedom, equality, security, and welfare), together with standard conditions on moral principles (e.g., universalizability) provide the basis for the arguments for the duty. And he argues that such a duty could avoid some of the standard objections to proposed objections to obligations to future generations.

Brian Barry, 'Justice as Reciprocity' in Eugene Kamenka and Alice Erh-Soon Tay (eds.) *Justice* (New York, St. Martins Press, 1980) pp. 50–78 explores the 'universal idea that justice is (or is in part) reciprocity if considered as 1) 'requital' – returning good for good received, 2) fidelity to agreements voluntarily made, and 3) mutual aid: playing one's part in a practice of helping the needy. Barry finds a warrant in 'rational' behavior for all these things (i.e., a duty of reciprocity in them) but finds those duties unable to handle problems of intergenerational and international justice. Barry's skepticism here, however, is based on his doubt that any general principle of returns for benefits received can be justified, and his doubts that any very extensive practice of looking after the interests of future generations existed among our predecessors. If the latter surmise is correct, even a strong reciprocity principle would fail to yield extensive obligations to future generations.

A thoughtful essay by Norman Care, 'Future Generations, Public Policy, and the Motivation Problem', *Environmental Ethics* 4 (1982): 195–214 considers this question: 'What in people can we draw upon to *motivate* them to follow the policies that morality requires regarding our legacy for the world of the future?' (p. 197) His concern is that even if we conclude (when we are considering social policies about future generations) that a certain level of sacrifice is morally required, we still face the problem of overcoming our own and other people's resistance to sacrifice, and in the case of future generations, some standard motivational devices are unavailable to us. In particular, attitudes of love and concern that often develop out of our knowledge of and interest in particular individuals are not available. Neither, he thinks, is the sort of 'community bonding' that develops out of a sense of participation in a shared enterprise. (He calls this reciprocation.) But his reason for thinking that this sort of motivation is unavailable is that

> We (current people) and they (future people) are not . . . able
> to reciprocate with each other concerning the constituent
> ideas and controlling aims of any associations or enterprises
> which we jointly participate in or endure. (p. 209)

I agree with the premise but not with the conclusion, because I think the sort of community bonding produced by the disposition to reciprocate (as it is acted out in social life) can and often does generate a sense of continuity with the past and future, and a sense of obligation for the benefits received from predecessors. The motivation problem thus becomes, in part, the problem of creating and evoking the disposition to reciprocate, and connecting it to conduct undertaken on behalf of our successors.

Readers may also wish to examine an unusual book by Edward A. Wynne, *Social Security: A Reciprocity System Under Pressure* (Boulder, CO., Westview Press, 1980). Most of the book is an attempt to describe patterns of donee–donor relationships in terms of a norm of reciprocity. The author believes that the norm is somehow transmitted genetically, but he gives no argument for this, and nothing in his analysis seems to hang on it. There is no rigorous normative argument in the book, but there is a good deal of historical material of interest, and a good deal of commonsense observation. Chapter 3, titled 'The Great Exchange', concerns intergenerational reciprocity.

Law

Obedience and Authority

J. Roland Pennock and John D. Chapman (eds.) *Political and Legal Obligation*, Nomos XII (New York, Atherton Press, 1970) contains a number of good essays aimed at getting a clear understanding of problems of political obligation. The essays by Kurt Baier, Richard Flathman and Nannerl Henry were especially useful to me.

Several influential philosophical essays on obedience and authority are collected in Edward Kent (ed.), *Revolution and the Rule of Law* (Englewood Cliffs, N.J., Prentice-Hall, 1971). I am especially indebted to Robert Paul Wolff, 'On Violence', pp. 60–76, John Rawls, 'The Justification of Civil Disobedience', pp. 30–45 (but see, for a fuller account, the arguments on that topic in his *A Theory of Justice* (Cambridge, Harvard University Press, 1971)), and Virginia Held, 'Civil Disobedience and Public Policy', pp. 92–110. There is an intriguing line of criticism of the Rawlsian account in Daniel M. Farrell, 'Dealing with Injustice in a Reasonably Just Society: Some Observations on Rawls' Theory of Political Duty', in H. Gene Blocker and Elizabeth H. Smith (eds) *John Rawls' Theory of Social Justice* (Athens, Ohio, Ohio University Press, 1980), pp. 187–210.

For an excellent summary of the problems with, and plausible options for, consent theories of political obligation, see Hanna Pitkin, 'Obligation and Consent I', *The American Political Science Review* 59 (1965): 990–9. Part II of her essay is in the same *Review* 60 (1966): 39–52.

For a contractarian account of the obligations of citizenship, see Michael Walzer, *Obligations* (Cambridge, Harvard U. Press, 1970). Walzer says

> Obligation, then, begins with membership, but membership in the broadest sense, for there are a great variety of formal and

informal ways of living within a particular circle of action and commitment. Membership itself can begin with birth. Then the sense of obligation is acquired simply through socialization. ... One does not acquire any real obligations simply by being born or by submitting to socialization within a particular group. These come only when to the fact of membership there is added the fact of *willful* membership. (p. 7, emphasis added)

My argument denies the final sentence of that passage.

Richard E. Flathman, *Political Obligation* (New York, Atheneum, 1972) gives a subtle and detailed account of what he calls the practice of political obligation. Practices are similar to what I call well-defined activities, and Flathman argues for the justifiability of political obligations, within our practice of them, in a way that suggests an all-things-considered approach. See his chapters 7 and 8. Socrates' arguments in Plato's *Crito* are Flathman's models. He insists that none of the separate arguments there (consent, utility, gratitude) can be inflated into an adequate justificatory account. All are relevant. I find that approach (and Flathman's arguments for it) persuasive, and while I give more weight to reciprocity arguments than he does, I certainly do not think they are sufficient, by themselves, to give a full account of the general topic of justifying political obligations. On pp. 278–90 of his book, Flathman gives a lucid account of the connection that gratitude for benefits received may have to the obligation to obey the law. His conclusion is that benefits are a relevant but not sufficient condition for such an obligation, and that the argument cuts both ways: i.e., people systematically deprived of benefits have some reason to disobey. In a more recent book, *The Practice of Political Authority* (Chicago, University of Chicago Press, 1980) Flathman sets an analysis of the notions of *an* authority, *in* authority, authoritativeness, power and authority, and autonomous agency and authority in the context of a critique of recent political theory. His discussion of what he calls the 'formal-procedural' approach to these matters was especially useful to me.

For a careful assessment of the nature and merits of Socrates' arguments in Plato's *Crito* – together with a translation of the dialogue – see A. D. Woozley, *Law and Obedience: The Arguments of Plato's Crito* (Chapel Hill, University of North Carolina Press,

1979). Woozley remarks, as evidence of how much our thinking has changed on these matters, that 'The idea that the duty [to obey the law] might flow from a relationship between subject and fellow subjects never seems to have occurred to [Socrates].' (p. 135) Questions of fairness and reciprocity to other subjects were not under discussion in the *Crito*. Instead, the topic was whether, and if so how, the duty to obey might flow 'from a relationship between subject and ruler (the ruler being, not the government of the day, but that whose authority a legitimate government carried – specified in the *Crito* variously as the city, the state, and the laws themselves).' (p. 135)

M. B. E. Smith, 'Is There a *Prima Facie* Obligation to Obey the Law' *Yale Law Journal* 82 (1973): 950–76 argues against a *prima facie* obligation to obey. Obligations of gratitude and fair play are considered in Section I of the paper (pp. 953–60). John Simmons gives the same matters a fuller discussion in his *Moral Principles and Political Obligations*, cited below. Since in outline Smith's and Simmons' arguments are similar, I shall let my remarks on the latter serve for both, except to point out, as against Smith, that my argument for a presumption in favor of obedience is not equivalent to an argument for a *prima facie* obligation. What I am concerned with is the justification of a *disposition* to obey, absent evidence against it. Such a disposition is obviously not justifiable *a priori*; its justification depends on the general character of one's experience with the law. But if one's experience is on balance good, and the other conditions are right, the 'presumptive' disposition to obey can be justified.

A. John Simmons, *Moral Principles and Political Obligations* (Princeton, Princeton University Press, 1979) gives a careful, subtle and clear account of some arguments for and against treating obligations of reciprocation as a basis for political obligation. I am very much in debt to his work, even though I disagree with his generally negative conclusions. For one thing, of course, he does not approach these matters by way of virtue theory. I think that explains some of the inadequacy he finds (often rightly) in the reciprocity arguments he considers. But that aside, I am unconvinced by his central negative arguments. Simmons first divides the obligations of reciprocity into obligations of fair play and obligations of gratitude. The former are analyzed in terms of *accepting*, as opposed to merely receiving, benefits. They are then found inadequate to give a general account of political obligation. Obligations of gratitude, in Simmons' view, can only arise under the following conditions. (He regards these as necessary conditions, but is 'not at all sure they are jointly sufficient.' (p. 179))

1   The benefit must be granted by means of some special effort or sacrifice.
2   The benefit must not be granted unintentionally, involuntarily, or for disqualifying reasons. [E.g., self-interest.]
3   The benefit must not be forced (unjustifiably) on the beneficiary against his will.
4   The beneficiary must want the benefit, or, 4a, it must be the case that the beneficiary would want the benefit if certain impairing conditions were corrected. [Example of an impairing condition: an addiction that prevents me from seeing the benefit in a friend's efforts to cure me.]
5   The beneficiary must not want the benefit not to be provided by the benefactor, or, 5a, it must be the case that the beneficiary would not want the benefit to be provided by the benefactor if certain impairing conditions were corrected. (pp. 178–9. Material in brackets is mine.)

It is not clear to me what Simmons' justification is for these conditions. They are clearly designed to avoid some common objections to obligations of gratitude, and to explicate common ideas about the topic. But the conditions are not, as far as I can tell, *conceptually* necessary, so one wants to have some theoretical framework that entails them. The virtue theoretic account of reciprocity given in Chapter Three is meant to provide a framework for necessary conditions of this sort, and some of the ones I give do correspond to elements in Simmons' list. But my account also diverges from his at significant points (perhaps because my topic is reciprocity *per se*, not gratitude), so I am unwilling to concede conclusions that depend on conditions not found in my account, and for which I cannot find a justification.

That aside, however, I am not convinced by Simmons' central arguments against gratitude as a ground of political obligations. Those arguments are the following: 1) Gratitude only obligates us to make 'some sort' of fitting return. That is not a specific enough requirement to ground an obligation to obey. I have dealt with this in the text of this chapter. It is true that it does not follow *simply* from the fact that I owe a return that the return must be in the form of obedience, but other factors, together with that fact, can establish the obligation to obey. 2) Simmons also argues that he doubts we can ever owe debts of gratitude to institutions, or to the office holders in them who provide us with benefits in the line of duty. But of course my arguments ground the obligation to obey in our debts to fellow citizens whose obedience to law benefits us. And 3) the same response undercuts Simmons' final argument – that the benefits we receive from government cannot satisfy his conditions 1 and 2. The benefits we receive from other people's obedience, however, certainly can.

In a more recent paper, Simmons speaks more directly about reciprocity, and gives similar arguments. See A. John Simmons, 'The Obligations of Citizens and the Justification of Conscription', Working Paper, Center for Philosophy and Public Policy, University of Maryland, 1982. There he argues that whatever political obligations of reciprocity we may have do not include an obligation to submit to conscription for military service. He says:

> . . . we need to remember what the content of an obligation of reciprocation is normally taken to be like. What we owe a benefactor is almost never determined with any precision by the context, but varies with our capabilities, the benefactor's needs, and the value of and sacrifice involved in providing the benefit. What we certainly do not owe a benefactor is whatever he demands as repayment. We must, of course, take the benefactor's needs into account in a special way, and our reciprocation should be at least as responsive to his needs as the benefit he provided was to ours. But this does not mean that he is empowered to specify which of his needs we will consider or to what extent we will satisfy it. There is considerable latitude in discharging such an obligation, and the best guide is only a very vague sense of what constitutes a 'fitting' return. Put in another way, obligations of reciprocity are not 'content-specific' in the way that, for example, a contractual obligation is.

But these facts, by themselves, seem sufficient to sink any attempt to defend a 'reciprocation account' of the obligation

to serve in the military (or, more generally, a reciprocation account of political obligation). Even if we are obligated to reciprocate for the benefits we receive from government, we are not obligated to reciprocate in all (or perhaps any) of the ways governments demand. We are not morally required to serve in the military, to obey every law, or to pay precisely the amount of tax imposed on us simply because we are told to do so. The government, as benefactor, has no special claim to dictate the content of our obligation or to pass final judgment on what constitutes a fitting return. . . .
(pp. 12–13)

What Simmons' argument misses, I think, is the extent to which the fittingness requirement is 'content-specific'. It requires us to make a return to the very enterprise from which we received the benefits. There will always be conceptual difficulties in determining the precise scope of the enterprise – the defense effort *per se* as opposed to the military, for example. But it is not difficult to decide that the reciprocation we owe for national defense is different from what we owe for public health. Insofar as the benefits we receive are distinguishable, so are the returns we should make. As to who has the 'final' say in deciding what counts as fitting, that is settled by a second-level inquiry into justifiable procedural rules. If there are good reasons for centralizing that decision-making power (e.g., in the hands of the government), and it can be done in such a way that the obligations imposed are properly scaled (to benefits received and ability to repay), then we can justify obedience to law.

Simmons is surely correct, however, to point to the way in which the reciprocity arguments tie obligations to the facts of particular cases – to the actual benefits given and received, and the actual abilities and needs of the parties. And Sara Ruddick, 'Drafting Women: Pieces of a Puzzle', Working Paper, Center for Philosophy and Public Policy, University of Maryland, 1982, pp. 8–9, suggests that 'participant-beneficiary' arguments are likely to yield somewhat different citizenship obligations for women than for men. She thinks that 'underlines a general weakness of the theory' (p. 8). On the contrary, I think it is a strength of reciprocity theory that it refuses to require obedience from the oppressed, and that, in general, it scales obligations to benefits and abilities. Doubtless this complicates the account of political obligation, but that is not an objection unless the complexity misrepresents the nature of moral and political life.

Iredell Jenkins, *Social Order and the Limits of Law* (Princeton, Princeton University Press, 1980) argues that:

> Our recognition that we are obligated to obey the law – the 'ought' that we here feel and acknowledge – is not derived from more basic premises and proved by some process of logical deduction. Rather, it exists as an experienced occasion – a fact – inherent in certain existential situations. This fact functions as a value (an 'ought') – as do love, compassion, courage, loyalty and a horde of other fact-values – when we recognize its worth and accept its demands. But the acknowledgement that we are obligated is not something that permits or eludes logical proof. It is empirically existent, so we can explain when and why people do feel obligated, and we can even understand and control to a large extent the conditions under which they do and do not, will and will not, feel obligated. But we cannot muster a logical argument to prove to the doubtful that they *ought* to feel obligated; we can only put them in situations where as a matter of fact they *will* feel obligated. (p. 195)

He then goes on to elaborate the conditions of the 'lived relation-ships' that 'just do' generate the sense of obligation. These turn out to be quite similar to the conditions under which Hart and Rawls maintain that a duty of fair play arises. As might be expected, I reject the idea that the sense of obligation that arises in lived relationships cannot be given a reasoned moral justification or disjustification. Aside from the fact that I have offered one which I think is cogent, Jenkins gives no reason for thinking that this sense of obligation is in fact a moral primitive, and I suggest we should be suspicious of doctrines that introduce such primitives precisely at points where there are longstanding, well-developed arguments and controversy about them. That smacks too much of an *ad hoc* adjustment designed to reach predetermined conclusions, and the cogency of the adjustment is not improved by the circu-larity introduced in the third sentence of the quoted passage above. Nonetheless, Jenkins' description of the way in which our experience of these moral bonds is tied to our social lives is provocative. He says (italics his)

> The attitudes and behavior of men toward one another are governed by the sentiment and conviction that relationships that have been mutually established are not to be unilaterally ruptured or altered. (pp. 196–7)

As a general proposition (and that is how he advances it; as a 'sheer fact about human nature') that proposition is surely false. Nothing prevents us from developing relationships whose transformation rules give unilateral powers to participants. And we in fact do this frequently in friendships. But Jenkins' way of putting these matters is a nice reminder that we should look to the transformation rules of a particular activity when we are trying to get an account of why participants do in fact feel bound by its deontological rules. And we can, in my view, go on to ask whether those transformation rules are morally justifiable.

E. D. Watt, *Authority* (London, Croom Helm, 1982) provides an illuminating exploration of various senses of 'authority' – e.g., de facto, intellectual, moral, religious, rightful, and civil authority. His discussion is particularly valuable for the pithy way in which it describes persistent popular errors, such as identifying authority with its abuse, and conflating various typologies of modes of behavior with respect to authority (e.g., Weber's categories of charismatic, traditional, and rational-legal leadership) with modes of legitimation for authority. Watt argues that any claim for the legitimacy of authority will necessarily have to rely on the notion that there is some reason that justifies it. Leadership behavior may *be* charismatic, but if followers or leaders, when asked to *legitimate* such authority, think there is no *reason* for obeying it, they cannot be said to have a conception of its legitimacy. He says

> It is by reference to some activity that every instance of authority may be understood, and . . . justified. The limits of any authority are likewise understood by reference to the activity within which it operates. . . . If the instructions of parents or of firemen ought to be obeyed, it is in matters to do with child-rearing or putting out fires, and for reasons having to do with the importance of those activities. Reasons of some kind are associated with authority of every kind . . . (p. 105.)

My contention here is that reasons drawn from the reciprocity arguments are relevant to questions of parental and civil authority – indeed, to authority in any social setting that either is or ought to be characterized by reciprocal social transactions.

Mortimer R. Kadish and Sanford H. Kadish, in their book *Discretion to Disobey: A Study of Lawful Departures from Legal Rules* (Stanford, Stanford University Press, 1973), examine in detail the topic of whether, and if so when, officials and private citizens, in their roles as such, may lawfully depart from the 'mandatory' legal rules. On a conventional rule-of-law view of the duties of citizens, it may at first appear that neither has a lawful discretion to disobey. But the authors argue for the existence of a category of acts of 'legitimated interposition' (for officials) and 'legitimated disobedience' (for citizens). Their justification of departures from the law is thus given in terms of arguments internal to the legal system – specifically in terms of what is necessary to fulfill legally defined roles. Their inquiry is thus very different from mine, and it is unusual in addressing directly the very many forms of ordinary (justified) disobedience not reached by discussions of civil disobedience and rebellion.

Restitution

Call to mind the passions, suffering and circumstances that surround and fill the actual operation of the criminal justice system: rage, guilt, hopelessness, self-righteousness, vanity, shame, fear, arrogance, disorientation, intransigence, pride, cynicism, pettiness, contempt, cunning. . . . Or read an account of a trial from the point of view of the victim or the accused – an account that makes clear how little the law could ever do, in some cases, to satisfy the principals that justice was being done. A good recent article for that purpose is Dominick Dunne's description of the trial of his daughter's killer: 'Justice', *Vanity Fair* 47 (March, 1984): 86–106. Part of the shock there is due to the slick magazine presentation, and the particular magazine involved. And some of the shock is even due to Dunne's occasional lapses into film script forms. But at the core of his account is the sort of suppressed rage that colored his perception of every detail of the trial, and his sense of being shoved to the periphery of a process in which he and his family should have been central. California, where the trial took place, has a 'victim's bill of rights' which gives victims and next of kin the right to make statements during sentencing and parole hearings. And in principle California law awards compensation to victims of violent crime. In this case, however, those aspects of the process seem to have been wholly ineffective – perhaps even counterproductive – gestures. But the point of this paragraph is *not* simply to point to the disheartening effect of putting an essay in criminal law theory up against the intractable elements of the reality it is supposed to help us handle. The point is also to make the comment that we should not let the intractable part of the reality obscure the fact that we still need to make the structure of the criminal justice system as good and as effective as we can. We will not be able to do that if we are driven away from theory in despair. Readers who want their despair to flourish may read Joe McGinness, *Fatal Vision* (New York, G. P. Putnam & Sons, 1983).

Alan T. Harland, 'Monetary Remedies for the Victims of Crime: Assessing the Role of the Criminal Courts', *UCLA Law Review* 30 (1982): 52–128 provides a detailed survey of the status of criminal restitution statutes in the United States as of 1982, with references to some of the theoretical literature on the topic and allusions to similar developments in England and Europe. The following material in Harland's article is particularly useful in setting the context for my arguments about restitution.

First, matters of nomenclature. I tend to use 'reparation' and 'restitution' interchangeably, and so, apparently, does a good deal of legal writing on the subject. Harland points out, however, that there have been various jurisprudential attempts to distinguish restitution from restoration (e.g., return of the exact items stolen), and from reparation in compensation (i.e., repayment of part of the value of the loss). The typical strategy in law now, according to Harland, is to reserve 'restoration' for returns of stolen goods and to define 'restitution' as either full or partial payment of damages in lieu of restoration. See Harland, pp. 60–4.

On recent legal history Harland says, in part:

> . . . the systematic rise of restitution sanctions in the United States may be linked to the appearance of suspended sentence and probation laws. . . . [s]pecific mention of restitution or reparation was noted in [the probation statutes of] eleven states and federal law by the late 1930's. In the absence of

statutory provisions, criminal courts apparently have no power to require restitution. A power to grant restitution, however, has been read into statutory provisions permitting suspended sentence and probation conditions, even though the statutes do not explicitly mention restitution.

In the last two decades, the inclusion of restitution in criminal legislation and adjudication has received considerable impetus from three sources. First, various prestige authorities have endorsed the use of restitution. The influence of these authorities is exemplified by the outright adoption in several jurisdictions of the Model Penal Code's restitution provisions. A second influential factor has been the remarkable growth of interest in the field of victimology and the search [for ways] to provide victims with some form of compensation for their losses. Finally, the federal government has pursued an active role in the use of restitution by making federal funds available to support restitution programs throughout the country. (Harland, pp. 57–8. Footnotes omitted.)

At present

... although explicit criminal code provisions for some form of restitution are not quite universal, legislation authorizing or requiring its use does exist in almost every jurisdiction in the United States. In particular, in the last few years several states have passed broad-ranging criminal legislation which advocates legislation, whenever feasible, as a formally declared state policy.

Legislative and judicial interest in pursuing restitution through the criminal process has been paralleled in this decade by a rapid growth in the number of restitution programs, operated by every type of agency in the system, from police to parole authorities. (Harland, pp. 55–6. Footnotes omitted.)

Harland devotes only seven pages of his seventy-six page article to a consideration of 'rationales' for restitution. He says:

As the foregoing presentation of the substantive and procedural parameters of restitution clearly demonstrates, the question of *how* the sanction should be administered has been the subject of extensive, if often unreflective, discussion. In contrast, the question of why restitution should be enforced through the criminal process has remained largely unaddressed. . . . Rather than being based on any profound reconsideration of the fundamental purposes of civil versus criminal courts or tort-crime differences, the current swing towards endowing criminal courts with greater restitutive responsibilities appears inescapably grounded on considerations of practicality and convenience. (Harland, pp. 119–20. Footnotes omitted.)

In pages 64–77 of his article Harland reviews the various stages in the criminal process at which current statutes either permit or require restitution. He says that 'Statutory authorization of restitution is far more commonly linked to conditions of probation than to any other dispositional alternative in the criminal justice system.' (p. 69.) But there are civil compromise statutes that permit a judicially supervised settlement between victim, prosecutor and offender. There is 'pretrial restitution', in which prosecution is withheld, or a criminal record is expunged, in exchange for restitution from the offender. And there is a growing effort to combine restitution with incarceration. (See pp. 75–7.)

On some procedural matters there is apparently a good deal of vagueness. In particular, the list of eligible recipients is often not well defined, and there is a 'major ambiguity' about the eligibility of insurers and other 'third parties'. Other uncertainties attend decisions about the range of crimes for which restitution may be ordered and the sorts of losses to be covered. Questions of calculating costs, adjusting them with respect to competing sanctions, and enforcing restitution have also been faced. See Harland, pages 77–119 for these matters. It is noteworthy that an 'ability to pay' rule is typically used in calculating the amount the offender must pay.

A useful source of information on restitution schemes worldwide (prior to 1970) is Stephen Schafer, *Compensation and Restitution to Victims of Crime* 2nd Edition (Montclair, N.J., Patterson Smith, 1970). It contains brief country-by-country overviews, based on official and/or academicians' responses to the author's questionnaire. Coverage is spotty, and in some cases not representative. For South America, for example, only Argentina is included, and the section on Africa only includes the Union of South Africa.

China is not included either. An appendix to the book contains the texts of some relevant statutes from jurisdictions in the United States.

C. Howard, 'Compensation in French Criminal Procedure', *Modern Law Review* 21 (1958): 387–400 reviews the development of restitution and compensation procedures in French criminal law in the first half of the 20th century. As the article shows, incorporating elements of private law into the criminal law is a tricky business. But I have not argued for restitution on this ground. My views are quite consistent with a solidly public law character for criminal law.

John F. Klein, 'Revitalizing Restitution: Flogging a Horse that may have been Killed for Just Cause', *Criminal Law Quarterly* 20 (1978): 383–408 presents a vigorous attack on the notion of bringing restitution back into the criminal law. His objections are in part procedural and practical (how to assess; how to collect), in part based on concerns about fairness (e.g., from malicious prosecution). But he also wants to show that adding restitution would mean making a fundamental change in a legal system that separates private and public actions. He notes the history of injustice that led to the separation, and doubts that there is much to be gained from a fundamental change in the public law character of criminal law. He does not consider the matter from the standpoint of virtue theory.

For papers concerned with some of the practical aspects of implementing and developing a system of restitution in criminal law, see the two volumes of conference proceedings edited by Joe Hudson and Burt Galaway, *Restitution in Criminal Justice* (Lexington, MA, D. C. Heath, 1977) and *Offender Restitution in Theory and Action* (Lexington, MA, D. C. Heath, 1978).

Randy E. Barnett, 'Restitution: A New Paradigm of Criminal Justice', *Ethics* 87 (1976–77): 279–301 argues vigorously for a shift in the 'paradigm' in terms of which we view criminal law – away from the 'response to social harm' view to one in which the leading concern is justice to the victim. Justice, here, means making wrongdoers repair damage they have done to their victims. The amount of restitution to be made would be controlled entirely by the amount of damage done (including social costs), adjusted to ability to pay only as a practical matter of insuring that victims get as much as possible up to full restitution. Barnett envisions the growth of a large victim-insurance industry, work colonies in which restitutive work would be done, and various private settlement arrangements. The object would not be (directly) to suppress crime. His approach to the question is entirely in terms of rights-theory, moderated by concern for administrative practicalities. It leaves out of account virtue-theoretic arguments and (at least direct) concern for social welfare. Not surprisingly, he reaches conclusions incompatible with the reciprocity arguments.

On the grounds for assessing restitutive sanctions for social costs, see Margaret R. Holmgren, 'Punishment as Restitution: the Rights of the Community', *Criminal Justice Ethics* 2 (1983): 36–49.

Acknowledgments

For helpful, if discouraging, discussion on the section on restitution I am indebted to Lynn Henderson, Murray Schwartz and Paul Brest. Lynn Henderson, in particular, provided useful bibliographic leads. Correspondence from Margaret Holmgren renewed my interest in the topic.

Index of Names

Index of Subjects